Beyond Barbie and Mortal Kombat

Beyond Barbie and Mortal Kombat

New Perspectives on Gender and Gaming

edited by Yasmin B. Kafai, Carrie Heeter, Jill Denner,
and Jennifer Y. Sun

The MIT Press   Cambridge, Massachusetts   London, England

First MIT Press paperback edition, 2011

© 2008 Massachusetts Institute of Technology

For information about special quantity discounts, please e-mail special_sales@mitpress.mit.edu.

This book was set in Adobe Garamond Pro and Rotis Sans by Graphic Composition, Inc.

Printed and bound in the United States of America.

Library of Congress Cataloging-in-Publication Data

Beyond Barbie and Mortal Kombat : new perspectives on gender and gaming/edited by Yasmin B. Kafai . . . [et al.].
    p.   cm.
  Includes bibliographical references and index.
  ISBN 978-0-262-11319-9 (hardcover : alk. paper)—978-0-262-51606-8 (pb.)
  1. Video games for women. 2. Video games—Social aspects. 3. Video games industry—Social aspects. I. Kafai, Yasmin B.
GV1469.16.W66B49 2008
794.8—dc22

2007041509

Barbie Fashion Designer™ is a registered trademark of Mattel, Inc.
Hula Hoop® is a registered trademark of WHAM-O, Inc.
Lara Croft™ and Tomb Raider™ are registered trademarks of Eidos Interactive Limited.
Adobe, Flash, and Macromedia are registered trademarks of Adobe Systems Incorporated in the U.S. and/or other countries.
Myst® is a registered trademark of Cyan, Inc. and Cyan Worlds, Inc under license to Ubisoft Entertainment.
Quake™ is a registered trademark of Id Software, Inc. in the U.S. Patent and Trademark Office and/or some other countries.
The Sims™ is a registered trademark of Electronic Arts, Inc.
Pokémon is a registered trademark of Nintendo, Inc.

10 9 8 7 6 5 4 3

Contents

Acknowledgments

The Beyond Barbie and Mortal Kombat project—the workshop, conference, and then the book—began at the DiGRA conference where Yasmin Kafai, Carrie Heeter, and Jill Denner met in June 2005. Although that conference brought together a vibrant international community of game researchers, players, and designers, the few conference sessions that touched on issues of gender and games were given and attended predominantly by women. So we wondered—has nothing changed?! Thus, the idea was born to create a follow-up to the book *From Barbie to Mortal Kombat* in which a decade ago Justine Cassell and Henry Jenkins so eloquently presented the field and its issues. A few weeks later, after a visit to the National Science Foundation, a proposal was written and we brought on board Jennifer Sun, an industry representative, to complement our perspectives of game researchers, educators, and designers.

Our first thanks go to Ruta Sevo, the then-director of the NSF program Gender in Science and Engineering, whose foresight and vision led to speedy funding that made all this possible. Without her, the workshop, conference, and book might have remained just mere ideas. She also encouraged us to include young researchers to set the stage for the next generation, and to invite an international community. Jolene Jesse took over after Ruta's retirement and joined us as an observer at the workshop and conference meetings.

The international workshop took place on May 8, 2006, at the University of California, Los Angeles, with a full day of discussions about the past, present, and future of gender and computer games. More than twenty-seven participants from academia and industry joined us that day, including doctoral students from three continents. The workshop turned out to be an energetic, poignant exchange among industry professionals, academics who helped launch the domain a decade earlier and continue to lead research efforts, faculty who have more recently begun studying gender and games or designing games for girls, and graduate students preparing to launch their careers. Many of the ideas from the workshop discussions have found their way into the chapters included in this volume. In addition to the authors, we also would like to thank the following participants for their insightful comments: Daniel James, the CEO of Three Rings, Inc.; Joost Raessens, an associate professor from Utrecht University in the Netherlands; and Elizabeth Sweedyk, a professor from Harvey Mudd College. Our graduate student participants came from three continents to join the discussions: Pippin Barr, Jody Clark, Rebecca Hains, Elisabet Nilsson, Coe Leta Stafford, Evan Straub, and Hanna Wirman.

The workshop closed on May 9, 2006, with the well-attended conference Girls 'n' Games that presented in lively discussion the issues to the larger public. Many thanks to Victoria Vesna, chair of the UCLA Department of Design | Media Arts, for hosting this event.

Finally, we want to thank the Entertainment Software Association, who generously provided free exhibit passes to all workshop participants for the Electronic Entertainment Expo trade show. Our ivory-tower discussions were complemented with views on the game industry from the exhibit floors. As we learned at the time of writing this introduction, this exhibit was the last of its kind and as such marks the end of an era.

We hope that the ideas and issues discussed in this book will advance both products and research about gender and computer games in new directions. Ten years from now, the situation certainly will be different and, one hopes, for the better. Perhaps there will be no need for a *Far Beyond Barbie and Mortal Kombat* to be written. But this will be for the next group to decide, perhaps while meeting at a conference somewhere and wondering . . .

Preface: Pink, Purple, Casual, or Mainstream Games: Moving Beyond the Gender Divide

Yasmin B. Kafai, Carrie Heeter, Jill Denner, and Jennifer Y. Sun

Ten years have passed since the publication of *From Barbie to Mortal Kombat,* a groundbreaking volume edited by Justine Cassell and Henry Jenkins. The title of that book refers to two cultural icons that illustrated the key issues surrounding gender and digital games in the 1990s.[1] Mortal Kombat served as a vivid example of the violent video games believed to be preferred by boys, while Barbie was associated with the princess image that is stereotypically feminine. The themes discussed in the Cassell and Jenkins book include how most games featured narrow gender stereotypes, how few games on the commercial market were of interest to girls and women, how female players wanted different gaming experiences, and how women were not a visible part of game production. In addition, gaming was seen as part of a broader pathway into technology, and girls were missing out. However, in 1996, when *Barbie Fashion Designer* became the most successful game of the year, it proved that there was a viable market for girls.

Today, women and girls are playing digital games in increasing numbers. Foundation and industry reports (ESA 2006; Pew/Internet 2005) have documented considerable growth in the female gamer segment in the past ten years. According to the Entertainment Software Association, 38 percent of game players are female, although the percent of females rises to 42 percent for online games. In particular, females are believed to be the dominant presence in casual games. A study by Macrovision Corporation of their own casual game site found that 71 percent of their game players were female, and the most popular games were puzzle games, followed by card games.[2] Females are an equal or dominant presence in some massively multiplayer online (MMO) games (Krotoski 2005), though still a minority in most. This increase in numbers has led to the assumption that gender equity has been achieved. If more

Yasmin B. Kafai, Carrie Heeter, Jill Denner, and Jennifer Y. Sun

girls and women are playing, then what is left to discuss? On some levels, it appears as though discussions about gender and games could be put to rest.

The most visible proponent of this position has been Gee (2003), who cast aside gender as an issue that is only of relevance to academics.[3] He suggests that feminist researchers or those interested in gender would be well served to pay more attention to the cultural aspects of gaming. His take on the gender issue is that there is "no doubt that videogames, like most other popular cultural forms, overstress young, buxom, and beautiful women in their content. Furthermore, with several major exceptions, these women are often not the main characters in the games. However, as more girls and women play these games, this will change" (p. 11).

The chapters in this volume provide evidence that it is still critical to consider gender in order to understand and improve on the design, production, and play of games. The authors continue the discussion started with *From Barbie to Mortal Kombat,* and revisit gender and games with new perspectives on who plays, how, where, why, what, and with whom, and what role gender has in these distinctions. We have brought together essays and interviews from some of the original contributors, but also included new media theorists, game designers, educators, psychologists, and industry professionals. The authors in this book show that addressing the role of gender in gaming requires far more than simply increasing the number of female players. Although the presence of women and girls in a range of game worlds is encouraging, most games continue to replicate and perpetuate the gender stereotypes and inequities found in our society. A brief excursion into the game industry illustrates why.

Some Things Haven't Changed: The Gaming Industry

In its pursuit of greater profits, the gaming industry has made some gestures to limit the aspects of a gaming culture that turn off so many potential female gamers. In January 2006, the organizers of the Electronic Entertainment Expo (E3) proclaimed the dismissal of the "booth babes"—those young, nubile, scantily clad women who frequently promoted the hot new games. The Entertainment Software Association (ESA), the producers behind E3, a gathering for a 7.3-billion-dollar-a-year industry, signaled that things were about to change when it announced that exhibitors attending that year's meeting would be slapped with a hefty fine if they promoted their products using women in bikinis, or anything else that favored showing skin over substance. This press release generated considerable buzz and goodwill in the media. Some women began to wonder whether their presence was finally being taken seriously. However, a visit to the expo a few months later proved otherwise: there were still plenty of booth babes around.[4] It is unclear how serious the organizers were about imposing their fines beyond paying lip service to a growing female gamer population. But the game companies clearly saw their male customer base as the more important one.

Game design and production is another area in which women's participation is still not taken seriously. The Game Developers Conference (GDC) is the flagship meeting for this industry group. For many years at this conference there has been a popular event called the Game Design Challenge, known for being zany and provocative. Three award-winning male game designers are invited to compete. They are given two months to develop a design, and ten minutes to present their ideas to the audience. In the past, the game design task has involved ideas that will force contestants to break the mold of typical game genres, such as Emily Dickinson poems and world peace. Not coincidentally, the challenges often focus on topics that are usually associated with women. The task for the Game Design Challenge for GDC 2007 was to design a game that could be played with fabric, thread, and a needle. At the end of the panel, one female audience member asked the question "Considering that sewing has been the domain of females for hundreds of years, I'm curious as to why you didn't invite any women to participate in this panel?" The panel organizer responded that this was not an issue in setting up the challenge. The debate continued online, and there were conflicting views on the importance and appropriateness of including a woman in the competition.[5] For the first time ever, in 2008, the GDC Game Design Challenge included a female designer (Brenda Brathwaite, interviewed in chapter 23).

In bringing this book to print, the editors have been challenged to explain why there is still a need to talk about gender and gaming. Our reasons include women's experiences like the ones just described, statistics from the male-dominated business of game development, as well as a desire to help keep the dialogue in both industry and academia from resorting to simplistic female-versus-male comparisons when talking about play style and interest. To talk about games and gaming communities requires a consciousness about who plays and who designs, as well as a clear description of who does not and why. In the following parts we situate the issue of girls' and women's interest and participation—or the lack thereof—in the context of broader historical, technological, and theoretical developments. We recognize that any discussion of girls' and women's participation in game play cannot take place without considering the girl game movement, what preceded it, and its implications for the kinds of gaming worlds that are available today.

The Girl Game Movement: Then and Now

Gaming in the 1990s was centered on Nintendo and Sega consoles at home and in arcades, with girls and women greatly outnumbered. Study after study reaffirmed that girls and women were not interested in technology, and by extension, in games. There were many reasons listed, which included the pervasive presence of violence found in many games, the need for spatial abilities to perform well in these games, the depiction of females as sexual objects, and the lack of general experience with technology. Many argued that game production was biased because most game designers were men who designed for players like themselves. One of the reasons that the lack of girls' and women's participation in gaming is considered problematic beyond its entertainment scope is that gaming is considered a gateway into computer science and information technology careers (AAUW 2000; Margolis and Fisher 2002).

In recognition of this untapped market, the industry responded in the mid-1990s with games developed specifically for white, North American girls. These were primarily games that could be played on a home computer or a game console. The success of some of these girl-specific games proved that there was in fact a market for them. However, many of the smaller companies met the same fate as other technology start-ups during the general downturn of the technology industry a few years later, and were either bought out by large corporations or simply disappeared. But the industry learned an important lesson: interest in computers and games is not limited by gender, and commercially successful games can be designed for girls.

The girl game movement of the 1990s featured very different conceptions of how to design games for girls. Some of this has been laid out in the introductory chapter to *From Barbie to Mortal Kombat* by Cassell and Jenkins (1998), and by de Castell and Bryson (1998), who describe the different ways that industry approached gender differences and applications to game design. But here we take a look at which of these approaches has had a lasting impact on the types of games that are still popular.

The most visible part of the girl games movement included so-called pink games for girls with traditional values of femininity. Games in this genre were predicated on strongly gender-typed toy preferences, and spurred research on female and male differences in interests, activities, preferences, and uses of games and toys (e.g., Brunner this volume; Joiner 1998; Klawe et al. 2002). For example, *Barbie Fashion Designer,* the most successful title of the series, allowed girls to design their own clothes, print them out on fabriclike paper, and then dress their actual Barbie for play—all activities that played on girls' apparent interest in their appearance and clothing. A later analysis explained how the Barbie software leveraged with great success girls' existing play patterns (Greenfield and Subramahayan 1998). There is still a market for highly feminine girl games today. For example, games around the successful franchises My Little Pony and Powerpuff Girls are very popular.

A second direction within the girl game movement provided a counterpoint to the original pink games, but still aimed to build on girls' expressed interests. Games in this genre might be called "purple" games in a tribute to Brenda Laurel's flagship company, Purple Moon, founded in 1995. These games featured activities that built on girls' real-life interests in sharing secrets and building friendships. At about the same time, the company Her Interactive started a series of *Nancy Drew* games, building on the vast popularity of the book series. Many similar companies were created by women aiming to make a difference by tapping into the girl game market and promoting game characters and play options that were not widely available. In one of the games developed in the *Friendship* series by Purple Moon, players can assume the role of a girl named Rockett who is new in school and trying to negotiate her way through a series of social challenges with classmates in order to gain friends.

Purple games dominate the market for girls today and have expanded their reach into an adult audience; for example, *Nancy Drew* games have been joined by *Animal Crossing* and *Diner Dash*. These games target a primarily female demographic, with less emphasis on ultra-feminine aspects of young girlhood than pink games have, and with increased focus on real-life issues of interest to girls and women.

Yasmin B. Kafai, Carrie Heeter, Jill Denner, and Jennifer Y. Sun

Both pink and purple games, which used girls rather than boys as a starting point for their designs, created considerable concern among feminist researchers (Cassell 2002). It was feared that their promotion of traditional values about what it means to be a girl, their limited choices of identification with femininity, and their creation of separate, girls-only spaces would lead to a ghettoization of girls (Seiter 1993). Clearly, limiting the available games to only those girls say they want will prevent them from learning new skills and being exposed to new ideas. For example, Hayes (this volume) expresses disappointment that Nancy Drew does not include tools for modding (modifying the game). If the industry believes girls aren't interested in programming, then modding tools will not appear in girl-focused games, preventing girls who play Nancy Drew from getting interested in programming. In addition, as Pelletier (this volume) points out, what girls and boys say they like about games may be a strategy for asserting their gender identity (rather than as a result of being either male or female).

But one of the most problematic aspects for many was the essentialization of girls and boys—the assumption that all girls share the same likes and dislikes and the same for boys. Focusing only on what is different about girls and boys ignores what they do have in common. Lazzaro (this volume) eloquently lambasts this approach. Focusing on male-female differences also ignores the substantial differences that exist within gender. A recent meta-analysis pointed out that most of the observed differences between men and women in psychological studies are rather small, with the exception of motor performances and views on aggression (Hyde 2005). Many researchers now focus on contextual factors and their impact on situating gender. For instance, a follow-up study of Kafai (1998) revealed that most of the gender differences in children's video game designs disappeared once the design context for the games changed.

Today, in 2007, there has been a noticeable shift from pink or purple games to a more complex approach to gender as situated, constructed, and flexible. These views are apparent in both the games that are available, and the research that is being done on gaming. For example, recent research builds on the concept of gender as a socially constructed identity (de Castell and Bryson 1998). Theorists like Butler (1990) have introduced the notion of "gender play," meaning that both girls and boys, and men and women, experiment with gendered expressions. Butler conceptualizes gender from a human feminist perspective as "an attribute of a person, who is characterized essentially as a pregendered substance, or 'core,' called the person . . . " (p. 14). Much of the research has focused on where and how society places constraints on gender performances and thus impacts a gendered-identity formation.

The recent surge in user-driven gaming environments has brought these theoretical perspectives into practice. The Internet (Turkle 1995) and, more recently, massively multiplayer online communities (MMOs) allow players to choose avatars of any sex, permitting experimentation with gender identity. Yee (2007) estimates that half the female avatars in World of Warcraft are played by men. Both Lin and Yee (this volume) report that women and men who play female avatars are subjected to constant attempts to discover the player's "real" sex. Along with game worlds that permit exploration of alternate gender identities, some games challenge existing gender stereotypes and provide room for exploration. One example is the game Sissyfight 2000, developed by Zimmerman (2003) to illustrate how one can challenge norms about social interactions by asking players to engage in cruelty as they role-play being a young girl at the playground. Lara Croft is the most notorious, if not the first, game to cast a female as the very violent main character who dismantles her enemies without losing her overexaggerated feminine physique. This game has had wide appeal for both men and women. Lazzaro (this volume) points out the limitations of making games for niche markets based on demographics. Doing so limits market size and does not maximize fun. She argues that there are greater similarities in what female and male players find fun about games than there are differences.

Another recent development is that girl games are no longer games that are only played by girls; it also includes games made by girls. Although Kafai (1995) pioneered this approach in the early 1990s, the availability of game development software that did not require extensive programming has led to additional girl-made games (Denner and Campe this volume; Pelletier this volume; Kafai 2006). One striking feature of these new approaches is their focus on modding features (Seif El-Nasr and Smith 2006), which allows players to customize aspects of game avatars, levels, and activities. In the early 1990s such modding features were not part of commercial game packages; only hackers were able to change games. As production values increase, commercial games are increasingly expensive to create. Companies have recognized the benefit of leveraging players' energy and involvement with the game by releasing tools for

Yasmin B. Kafai, Carrie Heeter, Jill Denner, and Jennifer Y. Sun

user-generated content such as modding, construction and commerce of objects, and tools for recording movies of game scenes (machinima). The recent successes of player-generated content such as Second Life by Linden Lab and Whyville by Numedeon seem to suggest that players, girls and boys alike, are drawn to these participatory features. Hayes (this volume) observes that use of these participatory features provides a gateway to technological expertise, and that far more male than female players create game content in these ways.

This history of the girl game movement shows how conceptions of gender differences have changed over time and can create very distinct outcomes for game mechanics, character design, and context setting. It is our contention that the dialogue about gaming is limited when gender is seen as a fixed entity and focused just on avatar design. We contend that these are not the only possible ways to address gender differences in game design and research. As the chapters in this book illustrate, there is a much broader landscape of gaming and gamers to consider.

Beyond Barbie and Mortal Kombat: New Opportunities and Challenges

With this edition, we intend to move the discussion about gender and games beyond the debate of Barbie versus Mortal Kombat and look at how gender intersects with the broader contexts of gaming and game production available today. While the number of girls and women players has significantly increased, it remains unclear how extensive gender differences are in what players want, whether girls and women are finding gaming experiences that appeal to them, and whether balanced gender roles are being represented. The fact that girls and women now play games in increasing numbers is not an indication that the conversation about gender should end. Instead, more information is needed on which games they play, why, and with whom they play them, and whether they take advantage of in-game opportunities to generate, not just consume, game experiences. We need more information on how girls and women are entering gaming and why they are not. And we need to take note of the ways in which gender is both performed and constrained. This information, instead of equal play time, has become the new standard for equitable participation in this technological gateway. The chapters in this book present perspectives from research, design, education, and industry and situate the opportunities and challenges of talking about gender and games in three contexts: gaming, game industry and design, and serious games.

Gaming

Initially, games were stand-alone, almost exclusively single-player experiences at home or in the arcade. Gradually games migrated to the Internet where a new genre called massively multiplayer online (MMOs or MMORPGs) role-playing games opened new venues for gamer participation, and new console games also allow for multiplayer games. Perhaps the most important development was a shift in game production to allow players to edit their avatars and become more involved in the active creation of their game worlds and play experiences—all aspects that are impacted by players' perceptions and enactments of gender.[6] As one example, *The Sims* demonstrated a multiplayer online game play that appealed to a general gaming community, including girls and women who joined in large numbers to populate their domestic worlds with characters and guide them through life. Another currently popular online game community is *World of Warcraft,* with more than six million paying members, approximately 16 percent of them women (Yee 2007).

The emergence of gaming communities has opened new avenues for research on girls and women as players, and some of the findings are described in this volume. For example, T. L. Taylor describes how women negotiate their entry into professional gaming communities, and the interview with Morgan Romine provides an account of her experience as a professional woman gamer. Holin Lin examines more closely how locations such as dormitories, Internet cafés, and homes in Taiwan facilitate or hinder women's participation in gaming, whereas Mizuko Ito looks at how the media mixes in Japan create crossover potential between boy and girl games. Nick Yee reports his survey of more than thirty thousand gamers about their purposes and partners for gaming. Communities like Whyville attract a large number of teen girls and boys to play games, interact with friends, and test out identities, as investigated by Yasmin Kafai.

Much of the early research in the girl game movement focused on teens and their interest in games, while today there is a significant population of women gamers. We hope that future studies will outline possible trajectories of how people move from being girl to woman gamers. The interviews with industry professionals included in this volume point to a range of different pathways into gaming, none alike. Older women (who grew up before the advent of digital games) are the primary players of casual games, which include puzzles and solitaire. T. L. Taylor observes that puzzles and stories are genres deeply rooted in conventions outside the digital realm. Recent research challenges a popular belief that the appeal of casual games to women is that they can be played in short periods of time, between other off-line tasks. According to Macrovision's study of their own game site, two-thirds of the people said their casual game sessions last for at least an hour, and another third said their sessions last more than two hours. It may be that this form of game appeals to women because it is possible to play in short chunks of time. However, a majority of players end up playing for long periods. Several chapters in this volume discuss gateways to gaming—situations or invitations to play that initially draw players into a game or game genre. Once there, players may expand their gaming and play-style repertoire.

In the same vein, we also need to study gaming customs in different cultures without essentializing nationalities. The chapters by Holin Lin, Mizuko Ito, and T. L. Taylor present careful ethnographic studies that illustrate ways in which gender is performed in various local contexts. The takeaway message is that we need to move from the juxtaposition of girls versus boys and focus our attention on whether males and females really do play differently and have different interests. As Butler (1990) makes clear, "if one 'is' a woman, that is not all one is" (p. 4). Gaming activities are not neutral or isolated acts, but involve a person's becoming and acting in the world as part of the construction of a complex identity.

Game Design and Industry

As we illustrate earlier in this preface, conversations about gender and gaming must be situated within the context of the gaming industry. The industry continues to be dominated by men, and overall has been resistant to acknowledging the importance of gender. This resistance is particularly clear when one examines the working conditions in which games are designed and produced. In her chapter, Mia Consalvo describes how women in the industry struggle to combine their passion for games with the realities of the production process. According to a recent survey, women make up only 10 percent of all employed programmers and designers in game companies. The sweatshoplike atmosphere when moving a game into production in some companies has implications for who persists in those environments. Similarly, in her interview, Brenda Brathwaite talks about the need to balance work and family life. In response to these challenges, Tracy Fullerton, Janine Fron, and Celia Pearce describe strategies for not only creating a more diverse workforce but also for making games that are less stratified by gender. In many previous discussions, the lack of women in the industry, especially among game designers, has been held responsible for the stereotypical representations of women. It was said that game designers created games for players like them. With a more differentiated gamer population, there is a need for different perspectives in the design of games. Game design is about player choice and the design of these choices is impacted by conscious and unconscious designer values, as Mary Flanagan and Helen Nissenbaum argue. They suggest Value-AddedDesign, a design approach that helps discover, integrate, and validate the values designers intend to bring to the games they create.

Serious Games

Within the serious games movement, which includes games for learning, health, and social change, a major focus is on educational and training games. Serious games appropriate the medium of games, used initially to entertain, as a way to educate, persuade, or change behavior. For example, Kristin Hughes created a mixed-reality mystery game to increase girls' technological self-efficacy and to interest girls in science. Flanagan's *RAPUNSEL* teaches programming through a game where players can program their characters' dance moves. As digital games have moved from the margins to the mainstream of entertainment media, there has been a renewed interest in using games to teach in schools, informal learning settings, and the home. Gee (2003) argued that digital games present a naturally suited learning environment because they involve a wide range of important skills, from problem solving and teamwork to comprehension of the nature of narrative and rules and states underpinning game worlds. Some teachers use commercial games such as *Civilization* in their classroom, adding pre- and postgame instruction to facilitate learning. Simulation games already have a long-standing history of successful classroom use and learning, with and without computers.

Little attention, if any, has been paid to gender issues in the context of serious games.[7] In their chapter, Carrie Heeter and Brian Winn look at gender as it intersects with educational games in a classroom context. They anticipate that the setting, combined with the gaming medium, will activate players' cultural expectations for the performance of gender. They conclude that designing for diverse play styles and selecting reward mechanics that further learning can make educational games better for all players.

One of the reasons why the connection between game playing and learning has received much more attention by researchers of gender than by other researchers is because many have identified playing games as one possible pathway into technology. Elisabeth Hayes examines in her chapter to what extent game play is associated with other technology experience and expertise. History has shown that simply getting more girls into games (and computers) does not increase women's participation in college engineering and computer science professions. In fact, the numbers have been stagnant for the past ten years. The approach of making games for learning has often been seen as a way to get girls more interested in computers and technology. The approach suggested by several authors in this edition promotes a promising alternative—making games for learning (Kafai 1995, 2006). Rather than just playing commercial games, giving players the skills and tools to design and program their own games and stories allows them to learn about academic content and to develop skills in a new way. For example, Caitlin Kelleher describes her work on Storytelling Alice, a 3D programming environment optimized for storytelling, and demonstrates how it is possible to design tools that get girls into programming by leveraging their interest in creating characters and stories. And Jill Denner and Shannon Campe describe the games created by girls in an after-school program designed to increase their fluency and confidence with information technology.

The ideas and findings presented in this edition are intended to broaden and enrich the discussion about digital games and design possibilities. Serious games, casual games, and pink and purple games are thought of as "not real games" by many in the industry. These "edge" forms of gaming violate mainstream expectations of what a game is supposed to be. They are also one of the frontiers for new approaches to girl games; they involve a larger proportion of women, including many authors of this volume. Our hope is to see not only the continued evolution of games but also the evolution of social spaces in which games are created and discussed, so that they no longer oppress or objectify girls and women. These aspects have gained heightened relevance now that the discussion about the value and importance of digital games has been moved into the forefront in educational circles. The concern about the lack of diversity in game designs and participation is not shared only by gender researchers. Now that the production of games demand multimillion-dollar production budgets, many feel the need for smaller independent productions that allow for a wider variety of game genres, mechanics, and play. We, like others, want more games that provide motivating, challenging, and enriching contexts for play—and we want these games to be created by and available to a range of players. In the spirit of the Olympic games, which started a hundred years ago as an exclusive male domain but now include women in all but two sports, we say *"Let the games begin!"*

Notes

1. We will refer throughout this introduction to different types of games as digital games. We are aware of the distinctions between video and computer games, which in the nineties were based on platform differences (console versus personal computer) and often targeted younger versus older players. As games have moved to the Internet, these differences have become less important. There is also debate on whether software such as Barbie Fashion Designer is actually a game in the traditional sense, but, again, with the arrival of new genres such as alternative reality games and casual games, definitions of what makes a game are in constant flux.

2. This report was published as a news release on the Macrovision Web site and can be retrieved at http://www.macrovision.com/company/news/releases/newsdetail.jsp?id=Wed%20Jun%2028%2014:30:07%20PDT%202006.

3. Gee (2007) is aware of the criticism he has received for this statement about gender and games, which he wrote in an introduction for *Gaming Lives in the Twenty-First Century* edited by C. L. Selfe and G. E. Hawisher (pp. ix–xiii), New York: Palgrave Macmillan.

4. The ESA published the exhibit guidelines in their E3 handbook; a discussion in the news about the E3 booth babes can be found at news.com.com/2100-1043_3-6071057.html. Yasmin Kafai also wrote an op-ed piece that was published in Gamasutra's Soapbox on June 9, 2006, and can be retrieved at www.gamasutra.com/features/20060609/kafai_01.shtml. In chapter 1, Henry Jenkins and Justine Cassell quote a response by one of the Gamasutra readers to the Soapbox op-ed piece.

5. For the full description of the event and responses from the community, please check out "An Excellent Panel with a Serious Flaw" and accompanying comments on lucida .typepad.com.

6. While we present these features as new game designs, it is also possible that game companies implemented these changes for the simple economic reason that player participation

Yasmin B. Kafai, Carrie Heeter, Jill Denner, and Jennifer Y. Sun

in content generation prolongs the playability of their games and thus gives game studios more time to produce the next version.

7. Research in the 1980s documented gender differences in interest (Malone 1981) for certain game features and spatial reasoning involved in game playing (Loftus and Loftus 1983). Research in the 1990s looked at preferences, computer use, and problem solving (Joiner 1998; Joiner et al. 1998; Klawe et al. 2000).

References

AAUW (2000). Tech-Savvy: Educating Girls in the Computer Age. Washington, D.C.: Educational Foundation of the American Association of University Women.

Butler, J. (1990). *Gender Trouble.* New York: Routledge.

Cassell, J. (2002). Genderizing HCI. In J. Jacko and A. Sears (eds.), *The Handbook of Human-Computer Interaction* (pp. 402–411). Mahwah, N.J.: Lawrence Erlbaum.

Cassell, J., and H. Jenkins (1998) (eds.). *From Barbie to Mortal Kombat: Gender and Computer Games.* Cambridge, Mass.: The MIT Press.

Cassell, J., and H. Jenkins (1998). Chess for girls? Feminism and computer games. In J. Cassell and H. Jenkins (eds.), *From Barbie to Mortal Kombat: Gender and Computer Games* (pp. 2–45). Cambridge, Mass.: The MIT Press.

de Castell, S., and M. Bryson (1998). Dystopia. In J. Cassell and H. Jenkins (eds.), *From Barbie to Mortal Kombat: Gender and Computer Games* (pp. 2–45). Cambridge, Mass.: The MIT Press.

Entertainment Software Association (2006). 2006 Essential Facts about the Computer and Video Game Industry. Washington, D.C.: ESA. http://www.theesa.com/archives/2006/05/2006_essential.php.

Gee, J. (2003). *What Videogames Have to Teach Us about Learning and Literacy.* New York: Palgrave.

Greenfield, P., and K. Subraramahyan, (1998). Computer games for girls: What makes them play? In J. Cassell and H. Jenkins (eds.), *From Barbie to Mortal Kombat: Gender and Computer Games* (pp. 46–71). Cambridge, Mass.: The MIT Press.

Hyde, J. S. (2005). The gender similarities hypothesis. *American Psychologist, 60*(6), 581–592.

Joiner, R. W. (1998). The effect of gender on children's software preferences. *Journal of Computer-Assisted Learning, 14*(3), 195–198.

Joiner, R., D. Messer, K. Littleton, and P. Light (2002). Gender, computer experience and computer-based problem solving. *Computers and Education, 26*(1/2), 179–187.

Kafai, Y. B. (2006). Playing and making games for learning: Instructionist and constructionist perspectives for game studies. *Games and Culture, 1*(1), 34–40.

Kafai, Y. B. (1998). Video game designs by children: Consistency and variability of gender differences. In J. Cassell and H. Jenkins (eds.), *From Barbie to Mortal Kombat: Gender and Computer Games* (pp. 90–114). Cambridge, Mass.: MIT Press.

Kafai, Y. (1995). *Minds in Play. Computer Game Design as a Context for Children's Learning.* Norwood: Lawrence Erlbaum Associates.

Klawe, M., K. Inkpen, E. Philipps, R. Upitis, and A. Rubin (2002). E-GEMS: A project on computer games, mathematics, and gender. In N. Yelland and A. Rubin (eds.), *Ghosts in the Machine: Women's Voices in Research with Technology* (pp. 209–227). New York: Peter Lang Publishing.

Krotoski, A. (2005). Socialising, subversion, and the self: Why women flock to massively multiplayer online role-playing games. In N. Garrelts (ed.), *Digital Gameplay: Essays on the Nexus of Game and Gamer* (pp. 174–188). Jefferson, N.C.: McFarland Press.

Loftus, G. R., and E. F. Loftus (1983). *Minds at Play.* New York: Basic Books.

Malone, T. W., and M. R. Lepper (1987). Making learning fun: A taxonomy of intrinsic motivations for learning. In R. E. Snow and M. J. Farr (eds.). *Aptitude, Learning and Instruction. Volume 3: Conative and Affective Process Analyses* (pp. 223–253). Hillsdale, N.J.: Erlbaum.

Margolis, J., and A. Fisher (2002). *Unlocking the Computer Clubhouse: Women in Computing.* Cambridge, Mass.: The MIT Press.

Pew/Internet (2005). *How Women and Men Use the Internet.* Report published December 28, 2005. Washington, D.C.: Pew Internet & American Life Project. http://www.pewinternet.org/pdfs/PIP_Women_and_Men_online.pdf.

Seif El-Nasr and B. Smith (2006). Learning through game modding. *Computers in Entertainment, 4*(1). http://portal.acm.org/citation.cfm?id=1111293.1111301.

Seiter, E. (1993). *Sold Separately: Children and Parents in Consumer Culture.* New York: Rutgers University Press.

Turkle, S. (1995). *Life on the Screen: Identity in the Age of the Internet.* New York: Simon and Schuster.

Yee, N. (2007). The Deadelus Project. http://www.nickyee.com/daedalus/archives/001365.php.

Zimmerman, E. (2003). *Play as Research: The Iterative Design Process.* Unpublished Paper. http://www.ericzimmerman.com/texts/Iterative_Design.htm.

Part I Reflections on a Decade of Gender and Gaming

The 1998 edition *From Barbie to Mortal Kombat* was anchored by the sales of more than half a million copies of Barbie and Purple Moon software. For the first time in the history of digital games, there was a clear economic demonstration of a game market for girls. A then very small group of academics, designers, and entrepreneurs debated possible explanations for the success and further developments of the girl game movement. Ten years later, the edition *Beyond Barbie and Mortal Kombat* is situated in a very different context: the game industry is one of the major forces in mainstream entertainment media, and game studies is establishing its own academic field with journals and conferences. It is rare that we collect accounts of those who have participated in these developments to place them in a historical context. The chapters in this part provide observations and personal accounts to build a bridge between the two editions.

This part starts with the chapter "From *Quake Grrls* to *Desperate Housewives*," by Henry Jenkins and Justine Cassell, reviewing the historical context that set the stage for the conference and the first edition. The book was conceived and written amid conflicting discussions about gender and computer games in academia and industry. On one hand, there was considerable debate on whether feminists should be concerned about participation of girls in computer games; on the other hand, a small number of female-run start-up companies served this new market hoping to reach out to female consumers. The authors discuss political, economical, technological, entrepreneurial, and aesthetic aspects that led to the girl game movement. Today, casual games, advergaming, and serious games present new directions, but to what extent the industry is willing to acknowledge the increased presence of girl and women gamers is still unclear.

But ten years ago *Barbie Fashion Designer*™ wasn't the only game in town. In fact, a close second was the *Friendship* series created and distributed by designer and entrepreneur Brenda Laurel. She established Purple Moon with the explicit goal of designing products that reflected her sociological and ethnographic research into young girls and their play patterns. The chapter presents excerpts from her book *Utopian Entrepreneur* (2003) covering the start-up, development, and closure of Purple Moon, much of which had been chronicled in the news media, but here it is presented from a more personal perspective. Today, many game design companies are traded at the stock market or as part of larger media conglomerates, so the feminist entrepreneurship that characterized this time period is rather rare. The software she produced is no longer on the market but she gathered experiences first with research at Interval and then with productions at Purple Moon. She also generated a rich set of principles on how to think about research as design, which are still valid today in the industry.

Finally, we asked Cornelia Brunner, part of a research team with Margaret Honey and Dorothy Bennett at the Center for Children and Technology in New York, to reflect on a decade of their research about gender and games, and what she refers to as "technological desire." In her chapter, "Games and Technological Desire," she describes how the existence of sophisticated new simulations, worlds, and game kits for kids to play with necessitates careful thinking of how the kinds of metaphors underlying both entertainment and educational games privilege and scaffold ways of thinking and learning that invite students, particularly girls, who are not drawn to the epic drama genre. She discusses other kinds of situations, environments, and activities in these game worlds that provide them with a guided set of learning experiences, allowing them to take advantage of the freedom to imagine and invent and the relative comprehensibility of the underlying logic structure such worlds can offer. Brunner draws upon queer culture to clarify that *masculine* and *male* do not mean the same thing, neither do *feminine* and *female*. She proposes the "*butch-femme* continuum" for analyzing gendered experiences. While some might have issues with this import, it offers one possible way out of the dichotomy that has dominated so much of research and industry to describe players and define game mechanics.

As much as these chapters highlight trends from the past ten years, they also point toward present consistencies in business and academia. Industry has an uncanny way of repeating itself: ten years ago *Barbie Fashion Designer* represented the girl game market while today the popular television series *Desperate Housewives* developed into a game that tried to become an anchor for the new market segment of women gamers. As long as industry focuses in their game designs on gender differences it might be hard to promote recent findings that gender similarities outweigh gender differences in much of psychological research. The later chapters continue the discussion started ten years ago with the hope of broadening our perspectives.

1 From *Quake Grrls* to *Desperate Housewives:* A Decade of Gender and Computer Games

Henry Jenkins and Justine Cassell

A decade ago, the two of us organized a conference called From Barbie to Mortal Kombat: Gender and Computer Games as a part of a series of events sponsored by the MIT Women's Studies Program around the theme of gender and cyberspace. At the time, there was a widespread concern that so many of the early settlers of the electronic frontier had been, well, cowboys, and that women were lagging behind in their colonizing of a set of technologies and technological practices that everyone knew were going to be central to the future world of work, education, citizenship, and recreation. The conference was situated squarely within the MIT Women's Studies Program's efforts to encourage discussion on the obstacles and opportunities that were shaping women's access to cyberspace.

Today, few worry about women's access to cyberspace—the gap between the sexes in online participation has largely closed; a whole variety of political, economic, social, and cultural practices have reshaped the Web so that we scarcely think of it as a male-dominated space. Yet two of the issues that inspired our original conference remain pressing: (1) the debate about whether girls do and can and should play computer games, and (2) the concern that women are still vastly underrepresented in the fields that design digital technology.

Ten years ago, the idea of a feminist conference about computers and video games was itself controversial. One of the members of the women's studies faculty expressed her concern that there were not enough "critical voices" in the conference (by which she meant, people who were critical of video games, not people who wanted to end discriminatory practices within the game industry). For her, games were industrial products—not sites of cultural production—and there was some skepticism that getting girls to spend time playing games was any kind of step forward for the women's movement. And yet, for feminists within the game industry, games were seen as a site to right all kinds of wrongs—in how many women are entrepreneurs, in girls' relationship to technology, in the very definition of technology. The conference, happily, was a platform for all these perspectives. And in the audience, listening intently, were as many industry representatives as academics.

The excitement generated by the conference was enough to convince the two of us—and the MIT Press—to publish a volume from the proceedings. Our book captured a snapshot of an important moment in the evolution of video games, one where feminist interventions seemed on the verge of transforming both who played games and what kinds of games they played. The book *From Barbie to Mortal Kombat: Gender and Computer Games* (1998) has remained a solid seller ever since: one of the standard books on the shelves of many game industry executives and a textbook regularly assigned to students taking game studies classes at colleges and universities around the world.

Now a decade later, Yasmin Kafai, Carrie Heeter, Jill Denner, and Jennifer Sun have hosted a workshop and a conference at the University of California, Los Angeles, exploring what has changed and what has remained the same in the relationship between gender and computer games since our event. Whereas we had difficulty identifying feminists who were researching games as we were putting together the first conference, more than thirty women and men participated at the UCLA event (and indeed, most of us knew at least as many more who were also doing work in this area who didn't attend). Many of those who attended the UCLA event were elementary and high-school students at the time of the first event: many shared personal narratives of how they became interested in games—narratives that reflected one or another aspect of the girl games movement of the mid-1990s.

At the time of the original MIT event, we were both untenured faculty members and now we are being asked to play the (uncomfortable) role of senior statespeople passing the torch to the next generation. As we do so, we return with a heightened awareness of how little has changed, how much has changed, and how much needs to be done if more meaningful changes are going to occur. In what follows, we go into more depth concerning the era in which the first conference took place in order to uncover the conditions that led to what we might half-ironically call "first-wave game feminism."

From Barbie to Mortal Kombat: Gender and Computer Games—the conference and later the book—was undertaken in the midst of an era of limited but very real optimism about the ability of female-run start-up companies to transform the game market and create new kinds of games that might appeal to a broader range of female consumers. In the mid-1990s, a couple of Barbie video games were released by small companies without any success whatsoever. Nevertheless, *Barbie Fashion Designer*™ was a top seller in the 1996 Christmas season, and continued throughout the year to outsell industry standards, such as those set by *Quake*™ or *Myst*®, establishing that there was potentially a rather large market for female-centered software titles. At the same time, Brenda Laurel, one of the most respected women in the computer industry, established Purple Moon games with the explicit goal of designing products that built on her sociological and ethnographic research into young girls' play patterns, and her belief that computer games themselves would change for the better all around if girls' interests were taken into account. A number of other companies were also producing girl-targeted titles; independent artists, such as Theresa Duncan (*Chop Suey*), were designing playful interactive works with a distinctly feminine sensibility; the major games companies were being forced to reconsider their marketing and design decisions to factor in female consumers more fully; and the introduction of *Lara Croft: Tomb Raider*™ represented a significant new era for the female action hero in games. Taken as a whole, these trends became known as the girl games movement.

However, as should be clear even from the list above, the girl games movement took shape around a series of competing goals and expectations:

1. **Economic** By the mid-1990s, the platform game market (production of games to be played on proprietary platforms such as Nintendo or PlayStation) had entered an age of heightened competition and an oversaturated market: 90 percent of American boys already were playing computer games. To survive, these game companies understood that they would need to expand their market. Thus, then as now, three major targets were identified: casual gamers, older gamers, and women gamers. Any product that could succeed in attracting one or more of those prized demographics might hold the key for the company's long-term viability.

2. **Political** The gender gap in technological fields was growing rather than shrinking, despite decades of feminist intervention, and the computer was increasingly coded as a "masculine" technology within the culture. Some

felt that computer games might hold a key to getting girls engaged with computers at an earlier age, a sort of head-start program for technological literacy. If, so the theory went, girls could be interested in computer games, and thereby in computers, then they might be more willing to stay engaged with science and engineering as they grew older.

3. **Technological**   The introduction of the CD-ROM as a staple of the home computer opened a new opportunity for female-centered games to find their market. Before the CD-ROM, consumers were required to buy the platform systems to play games and this set the bar too high for female consumers, for whom there was not yet a critical mass of interesting products available. Once the home computer became the locus of game play—either through CD-ROM games or Web-based games—then people who had bought the computer for other purposes could take a chance on buying software for girls or playing an online game. Moreover, while three major companies (Sega, Nintendo, and Sony) determined what products would be available for their platforms, the CD-ROM and Web game markets were open to competition. Technological changes had lowered the barriers of entry into the marketplace.

4. **Entrepreneurial**   A growing number of women had tried working within the mainstream game industry and had enjoyed some degree of success, but they wanted to develop independence so they could create products that more fully reflected their perspectives and experiences. The girl games movement caught the rising tide of female entrepreneurship in American culture when women were starting new businesses at a rate significantly higher than men, and in doing so, were introducing new kinds of products, opening new kinds of markets, developing new forms of business management, and creating new kinds of customer relationships.

5. **Aesthetic**   The girl games movement promised new kinds of content, new models of play and interactivity, new visual aesthetics, and new approaches to the sound track. The girl games movement set a goal of making games radically different from those on the market, so that they could attract new kinds of consumers. This made the girl games movement a hotbed for innovation and experimentation of all sorts, with a strong push toward more psychologically nuanced characters, softer color palettes; more richly layered sound tracks, new interface designs (including *Barbie Fashion De-*

signer™, which helped bridge the gap between computer and real-world play), and more complex stories.

These five factors shaped the girl games movement. We were interested in the ways that the girl games movement brought together feminist academics and female CEOs in an effort to transform the current state and the future direction of a sector of the entertainment industry.

We accepted as a given that companies would come to make games for girls but we wanted to know what kinds of games for what kinds of girls, with what kinds of goals in mind. In the original edition, we included chapters by cultural scholars, educational theorists, developmental psychologists, academic technologists, computer game industry representatives, and female game players. Some chapters suggested that girls should be encouraged to play existing computer games with an eye toward their future benefits. Some suggested, instead, that girls should be lured into playing computer games through the design of games that cleverly imitated girls' current pursuits. Some spoke of how girls could appropriate computer games by leaving the rules the same but setting up all-female clubs designed to beat boys at their own game (so to speak). Winding through the chapters was the issue of whether games should be designed to reflect girls' existing tastes and interests or to transform them, and whether this question represented a contradiction within feminist entrepreneurship. Feminism has always sought to critique and reinvent gender roles, whereas entrepreneurship has had to start where the market is. An anonymous poster on a newsgroup on educational equity (called "edequity online") in 1997 summed up the core question:

> I have a survey up on the web about girls' interests and I've gotten nearly 1,000 responses from teenage girls, a large portion of which yearn for computer games about makeovers, shopping, and cheerleading. It's what the girls *WANT*, although this desire is clearly guided by the media and the parents. . . . Is it worth while to use the pink and lavender, girl-stereotype marketing, to sell computer games for girls that get them to be more tech-savvy and comfortable with computing? Perhaps it is worth making pastel legos to get more girls thinking spatially and building and constructing instead of only playing with dolls. As I design

computer games for girls, I ask myself this question on a daily basis. My take is, the girls who aren't stuck in the "hairspray and nail polish" rut don't need me to turn them on to technology. The ones who need the additional skills are precisely the ones who would be attracted by pink and lavender.

Of course, designers and critics alike have continued to find it difficult to avoid essentializing gender as designers seek to identify what types of games girls want to play and reformers seek to promote the kinds of games they think girls should be playing. Often, both sides have lost track of the fact that gender is a continuum rather than a set of binary oppositions: one is never going to design games that adequately reflect the tastes, interests, and needs of all girls. At the 2006 workshop, Cornelia Brunner offered a provocative way out of this essentialist trap, suggesting that we replace *male-female* with the *butch-femme continuum* that has repeatedly surfaced in queer theory and politics. Brunner's suggestion may ultimately lead to replacing one set of problematic distinctions with another, but it does highlight the fact that gender identity is complex, contradictory, fluid, and socially constructed. Designing games as if the category of girl is biological and ahistorical is bound to get us into trouble.

Today, there is no pink aisle at most local game stores. The female-run start-up companies were by and large bought up by existing games companies—many of them by Mattel, which was eager to protect Barbie from any significant rivals. Brenda Laurel has left the game industry to take up the challenges of training "utopian entrepreneurs" and socially committed designers. And if you mention girls' games to many in the game industry, you are apt to get sneering looks and dismissive comments—as if the whole thing had been a bad dream they want to wish away.

From the start, it was clear that a large segment of the men who worked inside the game industry, not to mention the guys who played the games, had no interest in thinking seriously about gender and no interest in broadening and diversifying game content. Our book was reviewed everywhere from *Ms.* to *Playboy* (which labeled the review "A Battle-Ax to Grind"). Much of the popular press response drew a wall around "real gamers": one could be a feminist or a gamer but not both. For example, over at Amazon.com, many readers focused on factual details at the expense of engaging with the book's larger arguments—how dare we not mention Sonia Blade from *Mortal Kombat*? How come we didn't discuss *InfoCom*'s early female character? What about Chun-Li from *Street Fighter II*? Never mind that women are being excluded from full participation within the digital realm—that's not *Mortal Kombat* on the cover! One British newspaper critic never got beyond the acknowledgments section, attacking Jenkins for being too gushy in acknowledging his wife and his coeditor. So many of the young males who responded to the book seemed worried that some maternal presence might force them to tuck in their shirttails or that the companies would stop making games to their tastes once women became gamers.

We hoped this response would fade, as gamers realized the benefits to be reaped from a diversity of game designers, and a diversity of game players. But, in a striking parallel to responses to our book ten years ago, one of the first responses to Yasmin Kafai's piece for Gamasutra about the conference was from a gentleman who accused Kafai of not having her facts right and not being a real gamer:

> Every year, some headcase with a list of "facts about" comes out of the closet, when in reality there is no comprehensive fact-list, but rather a theory that caters to agenda-bending. Then they write a feel-good article and forget to balance "fact/truth" and being objective. Those who do so deliberately are viewed abjectly or worse. . . . Women are not scarce in our industry because they are scorned or put upon- I have known over 20 in my career, and all but a few were awesome on every level. They are scarce because they are less attracted and inclined to our industry on a historical, cultural, and personal level. Just for an example, how many women do you know would be willing to crunch away on a 120 hour work week for 2 months on something they may not love? My own wife said "screw that &*@#!." 5 women out of those 20 I mentioned quit for that very same reason. Of over 100 men I have known in my industry, only 5 of them quit for that reason. This is a difference on a psychosomatic AND phisiological level. Just one example, but valid.

From such responses, it would be easy to conclude that very little has changed—at least not for the better—in terms of women and games over the past decade. But such a pessimistic response would not reflect the enthusiasm and excitement about games as a medium displayed by so many young feminists at the UCLA conference. There weren't many girls' games but there were millions of girl gamers.

Looking back, Will Wright's game *The Sims*™ may have represented a significant turning point in the relations between gender and computer games. By some estimates, more than half the people who purchased the game were female and this female fan base was what made *The Sims* the top-selling games franchise of all time. And today Maxis, which has a high number of female designers and executives, contrasts sharply to the kind of situation described by Kafai's interlocutor.

In the original book, we discussed what would happen when the first wave of girls' games started to influence the mainstream of the game industry, wondering whether it was possible or desirable to develop gender-neutral games that supported multiple play patterns and sustained diverse consumer interests. As Jenkins suggested elsewhere, *The Sims* "shares many of the traits associated with the girl's game movement without calling attention to them as such"(Jenkins 2003), resulting in a game that attracted a large number of female consumers. Working through a features-of-girl-games checklist that Brenda Laurel proposed, Jenkins found that the leading characters were "everyday people that girls can easily relate to," that the game supported exploration and variable outcomes rather than fixed goals and hierarchical scoring, that the game emphasized characters and stories over speed and action, that the settings were everyday and not larger than life, and that success came through social networking rather than through combat and competition. All of this was to focus on the formal and thematic elements of the game—that is, to read *The Sims* through the lens of the girl games movement.

Yet what was transformative about *The Sims* in the end had very little to do with its design features or content. It came through the policies that Will Wright and his team at Maxis developed around user-generated content. From the start, *The Sims* inspired a vigorous fan culture: fans designed their own characters, furniture, wallpaper, and rugs and inserted them into the game, and they used the game play to generate images they could use to illustrate their own fan fiction. Here we were seeing a games culture that looked more like traditional fan cultures (which historically were dominated by female participants) where the appropriation and reworking of media content is second nature.

Very little time was spent at the 2006 UCLA conference discussing game content or the efforts of the mainstream game industry to reach female consumers. Rather, the focus had shifted onto participatory culture, onto the social dynamics that emerged as players created their own identities and communities within massively multiplayer online games, onto the ways that players were modifying existing games to serve alternative purposes, onto workshops that were teaching young people game design skills, and onto research initiatives that resulted in the production of games for use in the classroom. Today's gamers grew up in an era of consumer-produced content all around—Web pages, blogs, and music sampling and mashing. If the game industry would not produce the kinds of games women wanted to play, women would simply make their own.

As much as we value amateur and grassroots media production, though, we could not help but think something was missing from this scenario, especially if the result was that feminists were no longer struggling to ensure that the commercial sector was more responsive to their concerns, or that game content might be more diversified. The debate about gender and games has always operated at multiple levels: it was first a debate about how to ensure that young girls had access to the technologies that would shape their futures; it was also a debate about how more women could participate in the emerging digital industries; and it was a debate about representation (about what kinds of stories and play experiences were going to circulate broadly in our culture).

We should measure success differently across these fronts: there is a marked increase over the past decade in the number of women playing games; some recent surveys have suggested that the majority of women have at least played games at some point, though they start playing games later, tend to play games to spend time with a boyfriend, tend to play a less diverse range of games, and play games for a shorter period of time per session. But there has been almost no increase in the number of women working within the game industry and, as several writers in this book suggest, work conditions remain overtly hostile to female employees. This issue concerns us not simply because we want to see women have greater opportunities in the workplace, but also because incorporating women alongside men in design meetings would seem to be the most effective way to assure the diversification of game content.

While computer games were slated to get girls into computer science and other technology fields, the number of girls and women in computer science has gone *down* over the past ten years. Contrary to what we might have expected—certainly to what we had hoped—the girl games movement failed to dislodge the sense among both boys and girls that computers were "boys' toys" and that true girls didn't play with computers, while true computers were just for boys. In fact, recent rhetoric has even marked computer use as dangerous for girls who may, so the story goes, expose themselves to predators by their creation of online personae (Cassell and Cramer 2007). As in so many domains, the marketplace has a hard time changing gender stereotypes on its own. Without a more general cultural sense of the diversity of gendered experience, girl games are just another tool with which to construct a gender divide.

While the past decade has seen enormous technological shifts in terms of what the game-play experience looks like (3D graphics have become the industry norm; open-ended game structures are becoming more common; game peripherals are enabling new forms of interactions with the medium; improvements in artificial intelligence are allowing for more sophisticated game characters and for emergent behaviors), there have been surprisingly limited shifts in the genres that dominate the game marketplace or the range of fantasies being represented by game characters. The game industry is still designing games primarily for men, with women seen as—at best—a secondary market and more often as an afterthought. If a mainstream game attracts women, it is viewed by most game industry executives as a happy accident.

The exceptions are on the fringes—or on what the hard-core gamer market sees as the fringes: casual games, serious and educational games, and advergaming. Each of these has represented a space that for its own reasons has welcomed women as participants.

Casual Games   The leading producers and distributors of casual games report that women constitute between 70 and 80 percent of their market, with the greatest concentration among women in their thirties or above. Speaking at the recent conference, Daniel James, the CEO of Three Rings, Inc., cited the power of the social networks that women were forming around casual games, suggesting that female gamers were very effective viral marketers and could make or break the release of a new title in this space.

Serious and Educational Games   The past decade has seen the emergence of a strong, committed, and highly visible movement around serious games (i.e., games that serve a variety of functions other than entertainment—education, corporate and military training, policy making, political and social activism, medicine and mental health, etc.). In each of these cases, game designers must factor in women as potential players in a much more overt way if they wish to serve their various prosocial ends. As we described ten years ago, when a group of educators with software design experience was asked to design software specifically for boys or for girls, they designed different kinds of games. When they were asked to design software for generic students, they again designed the type of software that they had designed for boys. The results of this "gender-blind" design are nefarious. When children were asked to solve a reasoning problem in the form of an adventure game involving kings, pirates, and mechanical forms of transport such as ships and planes, the boys did substantially better than the girls. However, when the characters in the game were honey bears and the transport included a pony and a balloon, the gender difference totally disappeared. The boys did slightly worse, but the girls' performance improved almost twofold and they did a little better than the boys (cited in Gurer and Camp 1998). It would be a big mistake to introduce games into the classroom if the results had the effect of further disadvantaging girls. As a consequence, a great deal of the research found in this new collection centers on the challenge of designing gender-neutral or female-friendly games for pedagogical purposes.

Advergaming   It has been predicted that advergaming, or product placements in games, will become an eight-hundred-million-dollar business by 2009. Right now, the primary drive toward game-focused advertising has come from companies that are worried by dramatic declines in the amount of time men in their teens and twenties spend watching television. To reach this desired demographic, they are moving to where the boys are—games. Yet, as the role of games as an advertising medium expands, signs of a counterpressure are already showing. Many of the top brands advertised in television produce consumer goods that target girls and women, and these advertisers will be pushing for more games that will attract female consumers.

Significantly, these three sectors represent the only places in the current game industry that are being driven by entrepreneurial impulses. Over the past decade, there has been enormous consolidation in the game industry as a small number of publishers have bought up and now control smaller game companies. In some cases, as in Maxis's relationship to Electronic Arts, these companies maintain some autonomy within their mother companies and still create distinctive products. Yet, in many cases, these smaller game companies have been harnessed to major game franchises, producing endless expansion packs (a fate that Maxis itself hasn't been able to escape) for their most successful titles. Newer and smaller companies are being forced to work from the fringes, entering spaces that are not yet dominated by the giant game publishers and seeking out new consumers. If the push for girl games in the 1990s came from female-run start-ups and established companies looking for new and untapped markets, the push in the twenty-first century for more female-friendly content seems to be coming from companies that are seeking consumers that are not already owned and controlled by Electronic Arts or Activision.

Yet, if these smaller companies are showing some interest in wooing women as part of an alternative market strategy, in the absence of some sort of feminist enterprise, there is nothing to prevent them from falling back on the same gender stereotypes that have plagued the girl games movement from the beginning. A case in point is the new *Desperate Housewives* game, which debuted at the 2006 Electronic Entertainment Expo (E3), the game industry's major trade show, the same week as the UCLA conference. The game is loosely modeled on *The Sims* in that it involves the simulation of domestic life within a suburban community (the world of Wisteria Lane as depicted on the television series). The players adopt the role of a previously unknown housewife who awakes one day with amnesia and seeks to find out more about who she is and how she fits in with the community. *USA Today* (Slatzman 2006) quotes Mary Schuyler, the producer of the game: "As fans of the show would expect, the game is loaded with gossip, betrayal, murder and sex—you know, all the things women like." Once again, in a striking parallel from a decade ago, the industry claims it is designing to the tastes of its female consumers: "each company's extensive focus-group testing shows, as Philips Media Home president Sarina Simon puts it, 'this is what girls want'" (Tanaka 1996). The

Desperate Housewives game reflects, for better or for worse, some of the trends that we have been describing, yet it also suggests, as we tried to do ten years ago, the limits of applying market forces to reshape the construction of gender in popular culture.

The television series *Desperate Housewives* has proven enormously popular with female viewers—but the game may have difficulty achieving the complex balance of melodrama and comedy that has been the hallmark of the series. Indeed, the series itself had difficulty preserving its quirky and somewhat ironic tone as it moved into the second season. Creating a game based on the series, however, represents the kind of transmedia strategy that has been successful in generating female interest elsewhere in the world. Mizuko Ito (this volume), a University of Southern California anthropologist who does work on game culture in Japan, argues that a key factor in closing the gender gap among gamers in Japan had to do with the integration of game content into larger "media mixes," such as the transmedia strategies that have emerged around hot anime and manga properties. She suggests that girls in Japan embraced games as another source of content that interested them as it flowed organically from one medium to the next. Scott Sanford Tobis, a *Desperate Housewives* television series writer, described the game as an "additional episode," offering new insights into the characters and introducing new situations into the story.

Given the appeal of casual games for women, the game company based the title heavily on a series of mini-games including the integration of cooking challenges and card games as core activities within a larger framework. The *Desperate Housewives* title hopes to bridge casual games and longer play experiences. For some time, observers of the game industry have questioned whether the current models for content will serve the interests of even the core gamer market for much longer. The average gamer is older each year simply because people are continuing to play games later in life than anyone would have imagined. The generation that grew up playing *Super Mario Bros.* is now entering young adulthood. They now need to manage their game-play time alongside expectations from partners and offspring. Women often complain that the units of time demanded by most games are impossible to negotiate given the expectations they face within their families. All this points toward the desirability of developing games that allow shorter units of play time. The

Desperate Housewives game that shipped therefore included a series of short episodes, structured like a season of the series, and playable in about ten hours total. And to further appeal to casual gamers, the game sold for $19.95, well below the price for most hard-core gaming titles.

Moreover, the game reflects the pressure to open up games as a site for advertising. A partnership with the advertising company Massive Incorporated resulted in an unprecedented amount of in-game advertising and product placement. IGN Entertainment said about this aspect of the game: "Most of the products in the house will be real-world name brands. Thanks to a deal with Sears, washers, dryers, and vacuum cleaners will all have familiar logos on them. When your character walks out to the mailbox, coupons will arrive from time to time. Thanks to a print option, you can take these coupons to their respective store (in the real world) and use them towards a purchase" (IGN 2006). In short, the domestic setting is motivated by—and helps to motivate—product placements for the kinds of consumer goods that most aggressively target women. In turn, this focus on branded goods probably contributes to a focus on cooking, cleaning, and other household activities that do not necessarily play a central role on the television series itself.

That said, the women who attended the recent Beyond Barbie conference had pretty strong responses to the idea that cooking games and gossip were "all the things women like." They saw this push toward stereotypically feminine content as a return to some of the pink box thinking that doomed previous generations of experiments at creating "girl games." This gets at the Scylla and Charybdis of designing games for girls, which is to tread lightly between designing for "the girl" (as if there is only one sort) and designing for no girls at all. When the game was released in late 2006, the response was mixed. The game press tended to respond negatively, singling out many of the elements identified here as breaking with the expectations of their hard-core readership (as summarized on Metacritic.com):

> This game has got it all: a contrived plot, bad voice acting, terrible dialogue, and loads of technical bugs. And let's not forget about the slew of obvious advertisements, which gives the impression that this should have been a "free-to-play" sponsored game, especially since it downloads real product coupons to your computer as you play. (GameDaily)

Not even the most jaded gamers are this desperate. (*Computer Games* magazine)

Desperate Housewives: The Game is cheapened, slightly, by rampant product placement. Every time your character washes her hands or throws a dark load into the washer, you're exposed to the name of some corporate sponsor. (G4TV)

The title was reviewed more sympathetically by those who saw it less as a traditional game and more as an extension of the television series:

With heavy representation from four basic soap-opera food groups (murder, sex, jealousy, and amnesia), the game is a pleasant surprise for those of us who were expecting something more, well, Wisteria Lame. (*Entertainment Weekly*)

The episode-style campaign is an absolute pleasure and will no doubt please fans of the show. (GameZone)

The game set no sales records but was regarded within the game industry as a modest success. It remains to be seen whether it will spawn any further efforts to design games for housewives (desperate or otherwise).

So the debate continues. Our book sought to ask readers to question their assumptions about what kind of games should be designed for girls. Today, we might rephrase that question to ask how gaming culture has and will change as a result of women's more active presence. Either way, we are caught in a discussion that brings together market pressures and political agendas and tries to negotiate the complex relationship between gender and technology.

References

Cassell, J., and M. Cramer (2007). Hi tech or high risk? Moral panics about girls online. In T. McPherson (ed.) *Digital Youth, Innovation, and the Unexpected (MacArthur Foundation Series on Digital Media and Learning)*. Cambridge, Mass.: The MIT Press.

Cassell, J., and H. Jenkins (eds.) (1998). *From Barbie to Mortal Kombat: Gender and Computer Games*. Cambridge, Mass.: The MIT Press.

Gurer D., and T. Camp (1998). *Investigating the Incredible Shrinking Pipeline for Women in Computer Science, Final Report—NSF Project.*

IGN Entertainment (2006). *E3 2006: Desperate Housewives: The Game Preview.* http://pc .ign.com/articles/707/707757p1.html.

Jenkins, H. (2003). Further reflections on *From Barbie to Mortal Kombat.* In A. Everett and J. T. Caldwell (eds.), *New Media: Theories and Practices of Digitextuality* (pp. 243–253). New York: Routledge. http://www.metacritic.com/games/platforms/pc/ desperatehousewives?q=Desperate%20Housewives.

Metacritic.com. Reviews of *Desperate Housewives: The Game.* http://www.metacritic.com/ games/platforms/pc/desperatehousewives

Slatzman, M. (2006). "Housewives" sets up shop in computer game. *USA TODAY,* March 23. http://www.usatoday.com/life/television/news/2006-03-23-housewives-game_x.htm.

Tanaka, J. (1996). No boys allowed. *Newsweek,* October 28.

2 Notes from the Utopian Entrepreneur

Brenda Laurel

At the reunion conference celebrating the anniversary of From Barbie to Mortal Kombat, *I was asked to review the history of the girl games movement. I invited the audience to return with me to the days of pinball—a culture that most in the audience didn't remember because it happened before they were born. Women and girls played pinball with a vengeance in my college days, and the pinball arcade scene—although often filled with smoke and boys—was an environment where females felt comfortable and competitive. Not so the early computer arcades or the male-centric aisles of consumer electronics stores where computer games first appeared. But women stormed the testosterone clubhouse to play* Pac-Man *and* Pole Position, *and they have been perpetually at the wheel of driving games in arcades for twenty-five years.*

The emergence of the girl games movement was a response to a culturally situated moment, and its demise was the result of a corporate power grab that left both the girl game industry and its acquiring predator, the game division of Mattel, in smoking ruins. The good news is that girls and women now have a righteous presence in the world of games. The provocative news is that games that engage the social, cultural, and narrative proclivities of girls and women are still few and far between. The new game controllers introduced by Nintendo at the 2006 E3 show are the most visible sign that the game industry is about to blow wide open the audience for games and accept—after thirty years of denial—that the audience includes the whole magnificent diversity of human culture. I'd like to think that the girl games movement planted some of the seeds of change that are now beginning to bloom.

Thus far in my career, I've been at the front of four major paradigm shifts. In 1977, I got involved in the embryonic personal computer business, designing interactive fairy tales for the Cybervision system—a personal computer with

2K of usable RAM. At Atari in the early 1980s, I was part of the first big boom of the computer game industry. In the late 1980s, I cofounded a company devoted to the budding field of virtual reality. Through Interval and Purple Moon, I participated in the evolution of the Web economy in the 1990s. Along the way, I've learned that our steps always falter in the wake of a great new idea, especially one that captures the collective imagination.

Throughout my two decades in the computer game business, I ached for a chance to create alternatives to the chasing, shooting, fighting, exploding, hyper-male world of games. Why weren't there any computer games for girls? And why did I end up losing my job every time I suggested it? It couldn't be just a sexist conspiracy. The boys' game business generated billions of dollars; surely even the most virulent sexist in Silicon Valley would be perfectly happy to reap the corresponding billions from girls if he could figure out how to do it. Nor was the male culture of computer games simply an artifact of the history of the industry. Something more complex and subtle was going on, and I knew it had to do with the construction of gender embedded in every aspect of our lives—in play, identity, work, technology, and business.

I had worked for some of the most powerful companies in the game business, but until 1992, games for girls weren't even a twinkle in anyone's eye. Traditional marketing wisdom in the industry held that girls weren't a viable segment. In fact, they wouldn't even constitute a niche market. Everyone knew girls simply didn't like computer games and wouldn't play them. Examples would be trotted out as proof. My favorite was *Barbie,* published in 1985 by Epyx for the Commodore-64. Barbie was at the mall, shopping for the right outfit to wear on her date with Ken. Now, "everyone knows" that girls aren't good at shooting games, so the designers reasoned that the game should make it easier for them. The brilliant solution: make projectiles that move slowly. And so it was decided that the action component of the game would consist of throwing marshmallows. "You see," the game execs would say, "they did everything right, but sales were dismal." Therefore you can't sell computer games to girls. Post hoc, ergo propter hoc.

Our first goal at Interval was to articulate the research question. It seemed too narrow and trivial to ask simply, "Why hasn't anyone made successful computer games for little girls?" This question has some ready-made answers. Computer games as we know them were invented by young men around the time of the invention of graphical displays. They were enjoyed by young men, and young men soon made a very profitable business of them, dovetailing with the existing pinball business. Arcade computer games were sold into male-gendered spaces, and when home computer game consoles were invented, they were sold through male-oriented consumer electronics channels to more young men. The whole industry consolidated very quickly around a young male demographic—all the way from the game-play design to the arcade environment to the retail world—and it made no sense for a company to swim against the tide in all three of these areas at once. And that's just the obvious stuff. Given all these barriers, who knew if girls and women would play computer games or not? Were there intrinsic gender differences that caused females to be repelled by computer games? How should we understand the exceptions—games that attracted a higher than usual percentage of female players, like *Mario Bros., Tetris,* and *Myst*? What would it take to design a computer game that a large number of girls really liked?

Even though the occasional computer game like *Pac-Man* was a hit with girls and women, scoring sometimes as many as 25 percent female players, conventional wisdom remained fundamentally unchallenged. Whenever a girl title was attempted, it was launched all alone onto the shelf without adequate marketing or retail support, and the inevitable failure became another proof that girls would not play computer games. As late as 1994, Sega decided to steer clear of the potential girls' market because they feared being seen as doing things for girls would alienate their male audiences. By the way, our research showed that—initially at least—their fears were indeed well founded.

We spent several months consolidating our findings and then transforming them into design principles to use in developing products for preteen girls. I hired veteran Apple interface designer and fine artist Kristee Rosendahl to help us apply what we had learned to the design of merchandise and Web development. Teen-magazine maven Pamela Dell, who introduced herself to me via e-mail, eventually joined up as lead writer and invented Rockett and her friends. After a stage of advance development inside of Interval, we formed a company and launched three interconnected businesses—interactive CD-ROMs, the Purple-Moon.com Web site, and an array of Purple Moon collectibles. We were emphatic about defining the company not by its products but rather by the people it was meant to serve. Purple Moon was a girls' company.

The Purple Moon Experience

We launched our first products—two CD-ROM games and the Web site—in 1997. Our first two Friendship Adventures, *Rockett's New School* and *Secret Paths in the Forest,* were both in PC Data's top-fifty entertainment titles during the holiday season (right up there with *John Madden Football*) with sales at approximately ten times our original forecast. From launch until February 1999, the Web site served more than 300 million pages, with about 240,000 registered users who visited us at least once a day and viewed an average of thirty-five pages per visit. These girls collected about five million virtual treasures and sent each other nearly ten million Web-based postcards. Over the life of the company, we launched seven more CD-ROM titles, including more Friendship Adventures, creativity products, and the first-ever line of sports games for girls. Throughout its life, Purple Moon maintained a strong, ongoing commitment to research.

Our crucial first Christmas sell-in exceeded our expectations, and the ample press coverage was 95 percent positive. Nevertheless, we received a crushing review from a middle-aged guy in the *New York Times* who asserted that he didn't need to let little girls play with him because he knew a bad game when he saw one. His piece got reprinted without a byline in Silicon Valley's most important paper, the *San Jose Mercury News,* with the headline "This Rockett's a Dud." Meanwhile, we were in the crosshairs of radical feminist Rebecca Eisenberg, who wore pink chiffon with combat boots and wrote for the *San Francisco Chronicle.* Eisenberg's strident accusations of gender crimes were eventually reprinted by *Ms.* magazine. Feminists were confused; is it good or bad to reflect the social realities of most girls' lives?

Although the vast majority of press was great, the negative reviews hurt because they often came from those we thought would be our allies. We were wrong, it was said, to bring up such issues as popularity. Girls shouldn't think about this, and so we shouldn't encourage them. After talking to thousands of girls and seeing survey results from thousands more, I say "Horsefeathers." Popularity is a pervasive concern for preadolescents. Emotional health is not about whether preteens think about popularity but how they think about it and what kinds of values they employ in deciding how to behave.

A utopian entrepreneur will likely encounter unexpected criticism—even denunciations—from those whom she might have assumed to be on her side. By trying to do anything socially positive at all, the utopian entrepreneur opens herself to the endless critique that she is in fact not doing enough. For example, those few feminists who vehemently attacked Purple Moon games raised no objection to other contemporary girl games that seemed much more heinous, like the appearance-obsessive *Cosmopolitan Makeover* or the remarkable bimbosity (to coin a word) of *Clueless*. I am reminded of the old saw: the one who attacks you is likely to be the one closest to you on the road.

Here's some dialogue from *Rockett's Secret Invitation,* a game about her struggle to decide whether to join a clique:

DARNETTA   [giving advice to Rockett] Because they think this thing about you is cool, they want to be your friend because of it. But if they find out the thing isn't exactly true, they won't be down with you?

ROCKETT   That's right. That's totally my problem. So what should I do?

DARNETTA   Rockett, you don't need friends like that.

I wondered, did anyone notice that this wasn't Barbie?—that Rockett struggled mightily to be ethical and self-defined? The answer is YES—girls noticed. And many of their parents did, too. After the company's demise we received hundreds of letters thanking us for our work. It seems that everyone I meet at conferences or public events knows a girl who still plays Purple Moon. Even my youngest daughter sometimes dusts off her copy of *Secret Paths to the Sea* and solves a puzzle for the hundredth time because she needs the wisdom and emotional balm of the story she knows she will find at the end of the path.

Our characters exhibited loyalty, honor, love, and courage. They also struggled with gossip, jealousy, cheating, lipstick, smoking, exclusion, racism, poverty, materialism, and broken homes. When we had to choose, we sacrificed political correctness in order to meet girls where they were, in the realities of their own lives. Girls' responses over the years have made me certain that it was the right thing to do.

In the Purple Moon Rockett series, we explored interactive uses for what writers call "backstory"—the facts and feelings that lie beneath the surface narrative. We arrived at the idea of placing backstory elements such as journals, notes, and artifacts in characters' lockers. Locker contents could change depending upon a player's choices and the passage of time. Our writers and artists also created backstory elements that could be found on the Whistling Pines Web site, in the school newspaper, and in the yearbook office. Players and fans were encouraged to create new backstory materials through activities on the Web site and in the context of individual games. Both kinds of affordances drew on the power of narrative construction as a play pattern. The click-and-reveal interaction in the original Living Books games embodied a more open-ended approach to the same play pattern.

Hypertexts and branching structures represent another approach to interactive fiction. Choose Your Own Adventure books use these techniques. Of course, computers offer us vastly more space than printed books for creating range and subtlety in branching narratives. Purple Moon's Rockett series represented branching alternatives as mood choices for characters as they encountered various situations. Although generations of games prove they can work well when they are well crafted, branching architectures have two inherent limitations. One is the combinatorial explosion that can result if the branching tree is not pruned. The other is that each branch must be authored—an extremely labor-intensive endeavor.

I consider our work to have been a cultural success in the sense that it touched the lives of millions of girls and offered them fresh views of girlhood and a new portal into the technology. But our business failed. It failed for reasons having to do with investors' expectations, market conditions, and some weakness in strategic planning. A few choices made differently would have made Purple Moon a financial success. I have learned a great deal, and I'm not dead yet.

When Purple Moon had its plug pulled by its investors—only six days after we had shipped our eighth CD-ROM title—we determined that we would need to close our Web site. Even though the hosting bills were paid through the end of the month, the intellectual property was in legal limbo, and more serious, with no operating company, there would be no one to watch the safety alerts and keep our promise to girls to make the site a safe place. So with much sadness and beating of breast, we scrambled to create the semblance of a graceful ending in the midst of our corporate catastrophe. We put together a farewell screen on which our characters told the girls it was time to say goodbye. There was a cartoon portrait of the Web team created in *Rockett's Adventure Maker,* and I posted a message to the girls about how things don't always go the way we want, but we have to learn from our mistakes and carry on with honor and keep a positive attitude, et cetera, et cetera, stiff upper lip.

I was bombarded with e-mails sent to my personal address, which would have required some Web-searching, from girls and parents dismayed at the closing of the company and the site. I found myself explaining *bank-rupt-cy* to ten-year-olds, trying to help girls get their hands on merchandise they needed to complete their collections, and struggling to comfort heartbroken girls who had lost their online friends when the site closed down. Most of them had followed the practice of not giving out personal information to people met online, so the only connection they had with Purple Moon postcard pals was on the site itself. All of us were devastated that there hadn't been time to warn girls so they could figure out another way to connect with friends they had made.

Somehow Nancy Deyo, Purple Moon's dauntless CEO, finagled the funds to reopen the site temporarily, to give girls a chance to reconnect with their friends. That's when we noticed the miracle. During the nine days that the site was down, it had acquired 274 new registered users. It turns out that the program was still running behind the farewell screen. Girls who had bookmarks inside the site could get in, and most of the girls who were using it didn't know that there was anything unusual going on. The only way new users could have registered would have been their friends helping them sign up from the inside, where we had cleverly installed a button labeled "Want to let a friend sign on? Click here." Once the site reopened, the number of new registered users quickly regained its preshutdown level of about four hundred girls per day. The interesting thing here is that this happened without a penny in marketing expenditures. It was as though the dead rose up and walked.

Here's one of the perversities of dot-com-capitalism: if Purple Moon had not actually produced any real products, I'd probably be "posteconomic" today. Just as the dot-com-economy started spinning straw into gold, Purple Moon was spending real money to make real products to go onto real shelves in real stores. In investment terms, that was a big mistake. Even though we had an extremely popular Web site, the embarrassing detail of real goods prevented us from passing for a dot-com-company in the venture community. And so, instead of the wild valuations that made some of our younger friends multimillionaires, the valuation of Purple Moon could never exceed some small multiple of our revenues—because we actually *had* revenues.

Because Purple Moon did not make it to the big IPO or a lavish acquisition, it would be understandable to conclude that the methods I'll advocate here don't work—no million-unit titles, just respectable sales in a new market segment that got crowded real fast. Our eight CD-ROMs and our Web site won all kinds of awards but didn't make us profitable in time to satisfy our investors. There are other measures of success, however, and I think things can be learned from our experience.

Research as Practice

The Purple Moon experience proved to me beyond any doubt that one must talk to people, not just to see if they like one's idea, but to find out what's going on with them, what their issues and tastes are, how they actually spend their time. I don't mean self-validating focus groups—I mean learning about people with one's eyes, ears, mind, and heart wide open. Such research does not necessarily require massive resources, but it does require a good deal of work and a concerted effort to keep one's assumptions in check.

I think one of the main reasons why the video-game business has been so horribly stunted in its growth is that it has been unwilling to look beyond itself to its audience. I can't count the number of times I've listened to middle-aged male executives hold forth on who boys are and what they want. These are guys who remember when Eisenhower was president. At best, they are living in the fifties; at worst, they are living in fifties-style denial of the fact that boys' lives today are radically different—and perhaps even more culturally impoverished—than their own boyhoods were. To be fair, I've heard women—Mattel executives and others—speak with equal confidence about what girls are like, based at best on their own experiences growing up in a different time, and at worst on the perennial gender stereotypes that are reinforced by the great machine of consumerism.

When I advocate research, I'm not talking about what we typically call market research. Market research, as it is usually practiced, is problematic for a couple of reasons. Asking people to choose their favorites from among all the things that already exist doesn't necessarily support innovation; it maps the territory but may not help you plot a new trajectory. On the other hand, most people are not very good at inventing new objects of desire. If we had asked someone in 1957 what new thing they would like to play with, chances are they would not have asked for a plastic hoop that they could rotate around their hips. Somebody had to invent the Hula Hoop®.

Well then, one says, the point is to find good, frisky inventors. Who needs a bunch of pencil-heads in white coats asking questions? Innovation is for the creative people. No one in one's right mind would suggest that research is a replacement for creativity. Research does no good if one doesn't empower creative people to invent novel, cool things. Doing research and paying attention to one's findings can simply better the odds of success by illuminating the space of possibility and focusing creative energies.

The team I managed at Interval was extremely fortunate to partner with Cheskin Research. I learned from Cheskin's methodology that it's not enough to understand people statistically—we need to find out what their lives are really like. Some of that is quantitative information—how much television they watch or how often they play video games. Some of it is qualitative—what makes them insecure or how they represent themselves to other people. Some of what we need to know may be scientific—how good they are at pattern-matching, and how do their vision and reflexes change with aging? Some things are better approached through personal conversations and stories—what are their favorite things to do? Or, what magical powers would they like to have? These sorts of questions aren't particularly useful if the answers are multiple choice—we can't learn much from "none of the above."

When I talk about Purple Moon research, people always want to know what we found out. It's pretty hard to summarize findings of such scope and variety. In terms of computer games, girls didn't mind violence as much as they disliked the lack of good stories and characters. Regarding computers themselves, girls were much more likely than boys to blame themselves rather than the machine when things went wrong. Did computer games discriminate against girls? The answer is probably yes. Science has produced provocative evidence that girls perform less well than boys at tasks involving mental rotation under time pressure, for example, and that they tend to prefer more body-centric navigational methods than boys, relying more on landmarks for cues. If these things are true, then featureless mazes and the left-to-right scrolling of traditional video games have privileged male players. And we haven't even touched on games' social content yet.

Social differences are more complex and difficult to quantify. Through a variety of methods, we satisfied ourselves that there are real differences in how American preteen boys and girls organize themselves socially. The status hierarchy for boys tends to be based on explicit factors such as strength, speed, and skill at some tasks. Competition among boys tends likewise to be fairly explicit. By contrast, a girl's social status among her peers is likely to be influenced more by her network of affiliations than by any explicit measure. Covert tools such as exclusion and secrets are prominent means of social competition. This is one of the "ugly" observations that so upset feminist critics of our work. But it seemed to us that acknowledging these tendencies and using narrative to explore alternative ways of expressing and dealing with them was healthier for girls than denying their existence.

I am an amateur student of animal behaviors. Among chimps and other nonhuman primates, some gender differences in social organization that are similar to the behaviors of humans can be observed. When journalists came to Purple Moon, our public relations person always swept the primate books off my shelves and hid them, afraid that fundamentalists might take offense. But much can be learned about human social behavior by observing our nearest genetic relatives. For example, one can see parallels between pygmy chimps and humans in the domain of grooming as behavior that helps to establish social order. The primacy of affiliation and exclusion as tools for organizing social relations is amply demonstrated by the behaviors of female primates in same-sex groups. Such observations confirm that these social tools are more than cultural epiphenomena, but are likely braided into our DNA. Seekings to reduce the pain experienced by young women who are emotionally buffeted by the operations of these social systems, requires calling upon conscious reflection—emotional rehearsal—to bring these hidden forces into the realm of consciousness and thus make them amenable to choice.

Good research is never done. Some things about people may remain constant throughout life—a love of music, for example, or a propensity for orderliness. But other aspects of people are changing all the time, as a result of aging, experience, and the changes in their cultural and personal contexts. When we started Purple Moon, for example, girls' interest in team sports was just beginning to gather momentum. Girls' sports heroes were most likely to be figure skaters or gymnasts. Then the WNBA emerged, and the U.S. women's soccer team captured the World Cup. We charted these changes in attitudes about sports and explored the experience of playing from a girls' perspective.

Our ongoing research enabled us to design *The Starfire Soccer Challenge*—our pioneering sports game just for girls.

Excerpted from Brenda Laurel (2001). *Utopian Entrepeneur.* Cambridge, Mass.: The MIT Press.

From the early days of "girl games"—the days of Girl Tech, Her Interactive, Purple Moon, and a host of others—the world has changed and changed and changed again. Despite Mattel's early attempt to take ownership of this burgeoning movement by acquiring everything that could be seen as competition (and killing most of it in the process), the number of games for girls and girls who game has grown and flourished. This book logs the amazing journeys of creative minds, engaged observers, and nervy companies that have run with the idea that there are distinct genres of games, interactive social spaces, and technology play that can bring delight to girls and women. The urgent need we felt in the early nineties to make an intervention in popular culture has been satisfied. Over the past decade, we have seen that once innovative people listen well and get to work, girls and women quickly take ownership of their own play space in the ever-broadening world of technology.

We win—and the game's not over!

3 Games and Technological Desire: Another Decade

Cornelia Brunner

A decade ago when *From Barbie to Mortal Kombat* came out (Cassell and Jenkins 1998), many of the book's authors were dreaming about technology that would connect us as well as empower us. Technologies we only dreamed of a decade ago are now practically ubiquitous. Everybody seems to be connected—sharing, communicating, and informing themselves and others. There are transactions happening over the Web, which push the boundaries of even the fantasies our most sophisticated high-tech respondents described twenty years ago. Game worlds have developed to the point where immersion experiences, involving both affective and cognitive capacities, are not only possible but are experienced by a growing number of players, both young and old. We now have successful life simulations, interpersonal worlds, and enormous resources for creative expression like *Second Life* in which residents purchase real estate and then build any world they can imagine on it (the vast multiplayer world is made up almost entirely of player-generated content). Yet the root metaphors used as narrative that surround most game worlds haven't changed all that much. They are still largely about epic struggles and use the same gender stereotypes. There are exceptions such as *The Sims*. Its success, especially in its second incarnation, *The Sims2,* which provides almost all the features and narratives we were asking for ten years ago, validates our call from a decade ago for gender-neutral games.

The affordances of new game engines, the power to simulate complex interactions, and the ability for players to create complex events and relationships are wondrous to someone of my generation. This was the stuff of magic in my childhood. If I had been invited to invent a magical toy, it would have been this incredible combination of 3D navigation in virtual worlds with real and imaginary people, with real and self-imposed rules, in which I could breathe life into any story I could make up just by selecting from a menu of choices!

Cornelia Brunner

I grew up with wooden puppets and a puppet theater consisting of the usual three wooden panels with a rectangular "stage" in the center. The good thing about this puppet theater was that it had curtains, which was very cool, and it also had a kind of wire frame around the top on which you could hang pictures as backdrops—but there was only enough room for two hands, so all performances were limited to two-puppet interactions. The cast of characters was known, much the way television characters are now. So inventing puppet plays was all about thinking up interesting variations on well-known themes. Sharing these inventions with others was an important component of the play activity. I spent many hours just playing with the puppets, imagining stories, but I also thought of this as leading to some kind of shared performance, not unlike sharing digital products with a wider audience. When I tried to introduce these puppets to my son at the appropriate age, they bombed. Action figures, which were much easier to handle, were available—and their backstory made sense to him (Star Wars and Camelot at that time) the way the adventures of Kasper (the puppet protagonist in German puppetry) made sense to me.

In the near future, I expect, digital dolls with programs that determine how they behave and material action figures with robotic features that permit meaningful interactions will blur the distinction between life on- and off-line and a whole new set of conventions and themes will make sense to our grandchildren. The power to tell dolls, virtual or material, what to do, to make them look any way one wants them to, and to put them into any setting one can think of, and then play with them together with friends, even when one's friends can't come over, which was only imaginable as magic when I was a child, is now available to kids when they play games or create their own.

Game worlds contain characters, whether licensed characters, whose personalities are predetermined, or neutral, new ones, who can be altered through almost infinite customization. In *The Sims2,* players can change every facial feature on a character—and players can create or buy a huge variety of outfits and objects to enhance their characters (see Kelleher, this volume, for an introduction to *The Sims* in a programming environment). Players can assign characteristics that create a specific personality with a specific set of predilections, ambitions, and memories. Players can make choices about where their characters go, whom they meet, and what they do, by choosing actions or behaviors. What they do can be entirely up to the players, or it can be a complex interaction between the attributes they have given their characters, the situation into which they place them, and the other characters or objects they encounter. There are backgrounds in game worlds that do more than indicate context but actually allow players to explore, wander around, and change the perspective from which they view the scene. That's a lot more exciting than a single hand-drawn watercolor backdrop of a castle or a forest we produced for our puppet plays. There are props that not only can do things but also can connect you to real people, real places in virtual space, real information, and real stories. These digital objects can be anything from puzzles or other games to video chats with live people in the physical world.

The most dramatic difference between my childhood puppets and the inhabitants of game worlds is in the nature of the narrative. Brenda Laurel calls interactive play "theater," a metaphor that makes perfect sense to the puppet-trained. Instead of spinning out variations on narratives within a known structure, as I did in the old 3D world, players are figuring out how to understand the rules of the game. Instead of plots and subplots, they are determining rules and states, triggers and actions. This offers a different way of playing. It has powerful implications for making games useful for education.

As information technology becomes increasingly ubiquitous in our lives, the number of women interested in IT, whether at the level of a programming course at school or preparing for the IT professions at university, has not kept pace. To interest young women, in particular, in the IT professions, we, at Education Development Center's Center for Children and Technology, have done a few studies in the past decade that investigated the potential of educational games from a gender perspective.

A disclaimer is needed here to address the issue of gender. I read too much about gender these days that still confuses it with sex—even when paying lip service to the idea that gender is a socially constructed concept. *Masculine* and *male* do not mean the same thing, and neither do *feminine* and *female*. Males can have a feminine perspective and females can have masculine preferences. In my community, the LBGTIQ (Lesbian, Gay, Bisexual, Transgender, Intersex, and Questioning) community, we have a useful concept to separate gender from sex: the *butch-femme continuum*. It is a simple reality, in our community, that both sides of the continuum apply equally to both sexes: there are lots of butch women and femme men, and (still less visible to the nonqueer world) there are just as many femme women and butch men. We thus understand *butch-femme* as a descriptive continuum, which captures culturally shared understandings about gender definitions we inherit, create, and discover. It is also understood that each of us, as an individual, has a mix of many butch as well as many femme characteristics, some are at the more extreme ends of the continuum and some are less distinctive, more at the gender-neutral middle—none of us is a stereotype. I propose to use *butch-femme* as a way to describe gendered voices in the hope of maintaining the distinction between sex and gender, which, after all, has been one of the main achievements of my generation of feminists.

In our studies at the Center for Children and Technology (CCT), we looked at two potentially powerful affordances of games, animation, and metaphor in an effort to understand how to consider and include the tastes and interests of diverse learners. The basic research underlying our theory of how gendered sensibilities differ when it comes to technology was conducted decades ago, but the findings have not been invalidated by recent advances in technology or in the social use of technology during this past decade. In essence, what we found then still seems to hold true: butch sensibility asks technology for ways to let humans transcend the limitations of time, space, and the physical body. Butch sensibility is relatively sanguine about the ability of new technology to solve unanticipated social, ecological, or biological problems created by new inventions. It is deeply interested in the machines themselves, in their power and speed. Femme sensibility, by contrast, still has more modest desires when it comes to technology. It wants small, flexible, multifunctional objects that allow us to share, communicate, and connect. It worries about the unanticipated consequences of new technologies on the human, social, and natural environment, and it is still far less interested in the machines that allow us such connectivity than in their function. Two images from a little study in which we asked students to draw their impressions of the Internet capture this difference between butch and femme perspectives on technology (see figure 3.1) (Brunner and Bennett 2002, pp. 74–75). The first image is of a browser, and the boy drawing it enumerated all the different kinds of information available on the Internet if one has this machine. The second image is by a girl and it is all about machines in the service of people connecting with each other. Evidently the gender differences we identified more than a decade ago still hold.

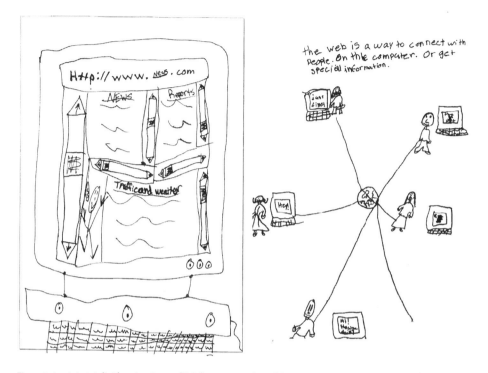

the web is a way to connect with people. On this computer. Or get special information.

Http://www. News.com

NEWS   Reports

Traffic and weather

Figure 3.1   A *butch* (left) and a *femme* (right) representation of the Internet.

Animation as a Form of Virtual Tinkering

We started looking at animation in design and construction environments more than a decade ago. The first in the series of National Science Foundation (NSF)–funded studies in this area was called Designing for Equity: A New Approach for Girls and Engineering. To stimulate girls' technological imaginations, in the early 1990s CCT created Imagine, a prototype graphics application that enables girls to create and animate machines that reflect their interests and perspectives. Imagine contained basic draw and paint tools as well as labeling and animation capabilities. Our pilot research revealed that Imagine was effective as a conceptual tinkering environment where girls were encouraged to create and elaborate on ideas for technological devices. Yet it was clear that children would benefit most if Imagine was part of a curricular context that helped foster children's thinking about design and invention in a safe and encouraging environment. In addition, we found girls needed more support in exploring and articulating different aspects of technological design, including relationships between parts and wholes, form and function of machines.

This research demonstrated that girls in particular responded well to activities that allowed them to explore relationships among familiar technologies and enabled them to investigate how technological design is related to the design process of artists, scientists, and other professionals. Girls were very interested in creating devices to solve problems that were personally relevant to them (Honey et al. 1991; Bennett 1996). Brainstorming and supporting activities that allowed girls to deal with common concerns about technological design, including ethical concerns about technology's impact on society, were successful. It was also clear that the girls benefited greatly from sharing their design ideas and concerns about technological decisions with peers and adults who could help facilitate such discussions (Honey et al. 1994).

To create a truly interactive online design space for girls, CCT collaborated with the Australian Children's Television Foundation to support design and invention activities within KAHooTZ—an Internet-based service for children. KAHooTZ is a multimedia construction environment that allows children to create computer games or stories, to show them to one another, and to talk about them (see figure 3.2).

The tools available in KAHooTZ included a large collection of clip art (including many categories of graphic stamps, backgrounds, and patterns), easy animation tools, and sound effects that allow the user to add simple sounds or to compose complex music.

With funding from NSF, CCT created a "channel" in the KAHooTZ world called Imagination Place!, where girls in particular—though not exclusively—were invited to join in a set of relatively structured design activities with other users to create fantastic inventions that solve problems they identify. We developed an additional set of graphics tools including art that girls could use as backdrops for their own illustrated stories, and a set of whimsical and evocative parts that children could use to construct complex, fantastic machines. We also produced carefully structured learning activities to foster girls' technological imagination. The activities invited girls to think about design in the real world, to imagine themselves as future designers and inventors, and to go through a process by using the KAHooTZ animation tools that helped

Figure 3.2   Activity starters in KAHooTZ's Imagination Place! (see color plate).

them think systematically—though not necessarily realistically—about creating their own inventions.

In many ways KAHooTZ proved to be a perfect vehicle for providing girls with opportunities to articulate their technological ideas. However, a set of interesting design issues that were particularly related to gender emerged. The KAHooTZ animation tools, for instance, did not allow an object to be moved along a user-defined path. Without the use of clever tricks, girls could not make something move from the front of their machines to the back of their machines and *then stop*. Instead, most of the animation tools only allowed objects to be moved across the screen in a prescribed set of patterns (e.g., in a ricochet or an up-and-down motion). We observed that these animation tools tended to work well for games that boys typically made in KAHooTZ, in which the action is essentially repetitive and involves shooting something, capturing it, or repeating the action while depleting the opponent's resources. It was not sufficient for the kinds of constructions we found that girls like to make, which focused on illustrating a process that has a beginning, middle, and end. As a result of this research, we developed not only additional images, more in keeping with girls' desire to invent machines that work in everyday settings, but also a new set of animation functions that supported a more narrative approach to design and inventing.

To make this construction world a place for femme play, a mechanism was also needed to connect the inhabitants, enabling girls to share their invention ideas and discuss some of the ethical concerns they typically have about technology. We observed in our research that girls often wanted to get to know the other KAHooTZ users before they published their inventions. They wanted to share their ideas with specific people, not with the world at large. These findings (Brunner and Bennett 2002) led us to develop design activities to help children think about how they might create an invention that others would like to see, and then to offer strategies for them to negotiate when they would chat, what about, and with whom. At the time, we were very taken with the chat interface in KAHooTZ because it was particularly well designed for supporting conversation about graphical ideas. Chats literally centered on graphical representations of inventions children created. In the chat room interface, children were represented by icons of their own making, distributed around the border of the window, while the center was taken up by the invention under discussion, fully animated. What the children wrote in the chat room appeared in speech balloons extending from their icons. By now this kind of interface for communicating with real people in a virtual space is quite commonplace, but at the time it seemed a major improvement on the confusing, linear presentation of most online chats, and much more suited to the kind of real connection with specific others girls were hoping for.

Many of the features and strategies that girls needed to engage in design and invention online are not very different from the kinds of tools that all children can benefit from. Using digital tools and virtual worlds to create narratives that express their knowledge and demonstrate their understanding of processes through animation is a powerful learning experience, which is further discussed in chapters throughout this book. Rather than creating more butch design and construction environments that privilege showing off how clever one is or how fast something can go, Imagination Place! demonstrated how such powerful environments can be designed to provide opportunities for femme children to collaborate and connect while sharing ideas.

Gender, Metaphor, and the IT Professions

Games serve as an entry point to the culture of computing and information technology. While we knew something about the general characteristics of games that appealed to girls and boys ten years ago (Cassell 1998; Huff and Cooper 1987; Inkpen et al. 1994; Miller, Chaika, and Groppe 1996), less was known about the relationship between specific design features and children's perceptions and understandings of information technology and related professions. To address this void, we conducted a study, Designing for Diversity, to examine how electronic games can facilitate positive understandings of IT professions among diverse groups of children, particularly girls.

The objective of the study was to investigate how narratives and activities in electronic games might be crafted to provide avenues for girls and boys to become interested in learning about the skills and problems involved in various IT professions and to understand more generally how to position IT to attract the interests of diverse middle-school students, particularly girls. Our hypothesis was that the prevailing ways IT is represented and described in schools is too exclusively butch, placing more emphasis on the machines rather than the problem solving, and that this emphasis contributes to girls' negative perceptions of the field. We speculated that electronic gaming environments, infused with appropriate narratives and activities, might be powerful vehicles for building girls' IT interests and knowledge.

The landscape of popular imagination about science, scientists, and technology has changed since the tremendous success of forensic dramas on television. Scientists are now portrayed as glamorous people, many of whom are attractive women, who investigate crime scenes and take evidence back to the lab to analyze. The technology used to do this is almost invisible—it is merely the container into which the scientists place their evidence to perform a confirming analysis to gather proof. Exactly how the technology works is rarely clear, however, even though there are some beautiful images of data and some interesting explanations of how the evidence constitutes proof. The narratives, which conform to the femme interests described in our work, are appealing because justice is achieved for the victims of crimes.

Information technology, on the other hand, plays a far more prominent role in shows about intelligence agencies and the military, where field agents are seamlessly connected to the home office through wireless PDAs and cell phones, and where the ability to find information in databases is prominent and highly prized. There are prominent women among the people who are shown to excel at this work, but the action is far more butch in flavor, filled with violent and epic struggles to save entire populations.

These shows have done a great deal to permit young women to imagine roles for themselves in the IT universe that appear rewarding, important, interesting, and even glamorous. This new familiarity with some of the ways IT professionals support and collaborate in solving mysteries provides a baseline for introducing the IT professions to young women in a new, more appealing manner. We have attractive, albeit fictional, role models now. We also have highly sophisticated game simulations, which allow us to create complex virtual explorations and adventures with appealing graphics and multiple paths of entry for players with diverse preferences, depths of domain knowledge, or levels of skill. The games allow sets of activities from collecting to puzzle solving, from designing characters or settings to having conversations and taking actions. Since these are often first-person games, the experience can be highly personal and intimate and allow young people from diverse backgrounds to identify with the protagonists of the games.

In our studies we learned what it might take to appeal to femme as well as butch sensibilities in games about IT professionals:

- Information technologists must be shown to possess a balance of people skills and technological skills to solve a broad range of human problems (e.g., from solving crimes to curing the sick).
- Femme narrative themes stay small but go deep—involving intimate, personal themes, not vast epic struggles. Femme game narratives stress the theme of reunification, whether of people or animals, families or friends. Butch narratives, by contrast, were typically about an epic struggle, with a mission to travel as global explorers and save the entire world. To appeal to both genders, the IT game should include travel in the service of some more direct, intimate connection with others.
- Narratives that focus on IT characters who were approachable, with whom the players could identify (not "know-it-alls"), were appealing to both genders. Femme stories more often included characters who worked as equal members of a team of people, whereas butch stories were more likely to be about the sole

hero or about the leader of a team. In an ungendered game, there would have to be some flexibility in defining the characters children could select to be, offering opportunities to be leaders as well as collaborators on a team.

- Unobtrusive and flexible game tools that are useful but neither intimidating nor lethal were popular in both femme and butch narratives. Femme tools were flexible. The challenge was in figuring out how to use them to solve a given problem rather than in having the right tool for the job. Butch games included the use of powerful tools, collecting them, and typically using them to destroy the enemy. In designing an ungendered game, tools can be prominent, but the emphasis should be on cleverly and flexibly exploring their uses rather than making them status symbols or tokens of strength and power.

- Femme game play involves complex interpersonal problem solving rather than cumulative conquest. In femme games, what players actually *do* when they are playing in the game world focuses on the rhythm and flow of working together to solve a meaningful problem and on the continuous effect choices have on the characters in need of help. By contrast, butch games measure how well the players are doing, how far they have come, and how many points they have earned along the way. To appeal to both genders, game play can involve solving complex puzzles, navigating tricky situations, and making risky choices, but successful use of tools, in these scenarios, comes as a result of creative thinking or clever guessing rather than from force, speed, or dexterity.

- In femme games, success means a positive resolution—justice restored, not victory or conquest. In an ungendered game, there can be plenty of action and suspense in which players can control aspects of the game through designing elements, features of many butch games. To invite femme players as well, however, the reward for playing must be the pleasure of the immediate personal relation-ship or the goal of improving someone's life or situation (see figure 3.3).

Conclusion

Game worlds can now provide a kind of scaffolding, a way to let young people experiment and discover without risk, provide an opportunity for apprenticeships that are both necessary in and well suited for the realities of the Information

Figure 3.3 *Butch* (left) and *femme* (right) versions of the same game idea.

Age. The possibilities of powerful new game worlds are striking—and contain the potential to create a world in which gender does not limit, but rather offers options. One can be butch and race around realistic streets in virtual cities on a variety of cool vehicles, but one can also be femme and create families of people or creatures. One can be butch and hunt a foe or drive a vehicle through an obstacle course, but one can also be femme and switch perspectives, see things from different angles, and zoom in or out. One can explore and inquire as well as build and share. One can search for objects that contain real, valuable information, from virtual treasure to streaming video of live events. One can explore the relationships between cause and effect, triggers and actions, properties and behaviors, states and interactions. One can go back and start over. One can vary things systematically and track the effects. One can compare alternatives. One can tell a story, construct images, make music, record movies, and converse with others. And one can do all of it in the safety of a virtual environment, which is rich with adventure and glory—as well as romance and intimacy. The Star Trek holodeck is here—and simulations will soon be the heart of the learning experience here as they are at the Star Fleet Academy.

Developments in information technology during the past decade have presented us with a technological universe that offers something for every gender: there are now ubiquitous femme tools that connect us and allow us to communicate—and that are butch enough to allow us to transcend time and space, reaching almost seamlessly across oceans and time zones. Playing in a current game world is far closer to playing with puppets of half a century ago than it is to playing some of the first generation of computer games. There are far fewer limits on the player's imagination. The possibilities for stories that allow young people to imagine themselves in adult roles, take risks, and try out personalities and fates are endless and inviting. The differences between virtual worlds and the real world must be explored, of course. Understanding the conceptual structure of a virtual world means understanding which kinds of variables were included in the simulation and which ones were left out—a component of media literacy. It also means understanding the rules that govern the virtual universe, which may be a very powerful educational opportunity. Understanding rules is a primary concern of preadolescent children—rules of behavior, rules of logic, and rules of social interaction.

Game worlds may well be the place where we can mine the potential of these technologies for learning. The world has always been too big for a kid to explore fully, and too much of what a kid has to understand has always been hidden from the naked eye and had to be learned to imagine it—from the ways of the gods to the structure of atoms and now the patterns of bytes. These new, attractive worlds give us a set of wonderful tools for taking apart and tinkering with the things we see around us, for imagining all the things we cannot see, and for sharing what we imagine with one another. What better learning environment, butch or femme, could there be?

Acknowledgment

The author would like to thank the National Science Foundation for its generous support across multiple research projects that contributed greatly to the author's understanding of the relationship among gaming, gender, and narrative environments. The views expressed are those of the author and do not necessarily represent the views of NSF.

References

Bennett, D. (1996, May). *Voices of Young Women in Engineering.* Research report. New York: Center for Children and Technology. http://cct.edc.org/report_summary .asp?numPublicationId=89.

Bennett, D., and C. Brunner (2000). The role of gender in the design of electronic learning environments for children. *Tech Learning's Well-Connected Educator Journal, 21.* http:// www.techlearning.com/db_area/archives/WCE/archives/bennett.html.

Brunner, C., and D. T. Bennett (2002). The feminization of technology. In N. Yelland and A. Rubin (eds.), *Ghosts in the Machine: Women Study Women and Technology* (pp. 71–96). New York: Peter Lang.

Brunner, C., D. Bennett, and M. Honey (1998). Girl games and technological desire. In J. Cassell and H. Jenkins (eds.), *From Barbie to Mortal Kombat: Gender and Computer Games* (pp. 72–87). Cambridge, Mass.: The MIT Press.

Cassell, J. (1998). Storytelling as a nexus for change in the relationship between gender and technology: A feminist approach to software design. In J. Cassell and H. Jenkins (eds.), *From Barbie to Mortal Kombat: Gender and Computer Games* (pp. 298–322). Cambridge, Mass.: The MIT Press.

Cassell, J., and H. Jenkins (eds.) (1998). *From Barbie to Mortal Kombat: Gender and Computer Games.* Cambridge, Mass.: The MIT Press.

Honey, M., B. Moeller, C. Brunner, D. Bennett, P. Clemens, and J. Hawkins (1991). *Girls and Design: Exploring the Question of Technological Imagination.* Research report. New York: Center for Children and Technology. http://cct.edc.org/report_summary .asp?numPublicationId=48.

Honey, M., C. Brunner, D. Bennett, T. Meade, and V. Tsen (1994). *Designing for Equity: A New Approach for Girls and Engineering.* Final report to the National Science Foundation. New York: Education Development Center's Center for Children and Technology.

Huff, C., and J. Cooper (1987). Sex bias in educational software: The effect of designer's stereotypes on the software they design. *Journal of Applied Social Psychology, 17*(6), 519–532.

Inkpen, K., R. Upitis, M. Klawe, J. Lawry, A. Anderson, M. Ndunda, K. Sedighian, S. Leroux, D. Hsu (1994). "We have never-forgetful flowers in our garden"; Girls' responses to electronic games. *Journal of Computers in Math and Science Teaching, 13*(4), 383–403.

Miller, L., M. Chaika, and L. Groppe (1996). Girls' preferences in software design: Insights from a focus group. *Interpersonal Computing and Technology: An Electronic Journal for the 21st Century, 4*(2), 27–36.

Part II Gaming Communities: Girls and Women as Players

For many years gaming has been associated with the near iconic image of a single player with a console in front of a television screen; this player was always a young boy or man. What this image failed to acknowledge is that gaming has always been a social enterprise for players exchanging strategies, providing assistance, and competing against one another. It is this world that girls and women have been mostly absent from but now are joining in large numbers. Thus our understanding of girls and women as gamers needs to move away from examining individual features and game mechanics to studying gaming cultures and genres. The chapters in this part aim to understand how women and girls become members of different gaming communities, whom they interact with, and how online and off-line spaces are structured to either welcome or hinder their entrance. The goal of this part is to unpack the multiple layers and structures that determine entry to gaming communities and spaces and distinguish between women and girl gaming communities. We were fortunate to include international observations from northern Europe and Asia to challenge universalities on what counts as relevant to women and girl gamers.

T. L. Taylor starts this part with "Becoming a Player: Networks, Structure, and Imagined Futures," examining how becoming a player takes place through a web of networks, practices, possibilities, and technologies. Understanding that assemblage, and how it relates to gender, is a challenging task. She argues that we need to be more careful to avoid conflating girls with women and oversimplifying the dynamic construction of gender as performed across the life cycle or within varying social contexts. For researchers, this also means we need better ways of researching gender, of recognizing that we and our participants are always—even at the very moment of trying to understand it—performing and enacting for one another particular identities that shape the research moment. Her research focuses on activist women gamer networks in Denmark that introduce women to game play but also provide key entry points to gaming communities. Most important, these networks render visible women as gamers and represent their interests at large gaming events.

From the vibrant game cultures in northern Europe, we move to the booming online gaming in South Korea, Taiwan, and other Asian countries. Holin Lin provides us with "Body, Space, and Gendered Gaming Experiences: A Cultural Geography of Gaming Experiences in Homes, Cybercafés, and Dormitories." She notes that in addition to playing console or PC games at home, Asian players—mostly young males—gather at cybercafés and turn them into online playgrounds. Her chapter focuses on gender differences in gaming experiences as shaped by both the virtual spaces created by games and the physical spaces where they are played. Young women's perceptions of risk and fear are deeply rooted in their bodies; they avoid what they perceive to be dangerous spaces in order to manage the risk of male violence. When they assume digital bodies in virtual space, female players are free to explore experiences of "meeting strangers in dangerous worlds." But as soon as they try to extend their interactions to the public playground, they must accept the regulations and constraints of the physical world, which explains why so few venture into the stigmatized environments of cybercafés. As a result, Taiwanese girls have very few opportunities to interact in the same physical space; female gamers' off-line communities remain small, and interactive layers are few. Another semipublic social space allows for investigations of female players' activities and autonomy: gender-segregated college dormitories. However, the pool of potential playing partners is much smaller than for males, and sensitivity to the gender-role expectations and schedules of roommates lead to a different set of self-regulating rules. The result: much lower profiles and greater constraints among dormitory-based female gamers.

These two chapters together with the chapter from Mizuko Ito introduce us to gaming cultures outside of the United States. Too much of the early research on games and gender is focused on activities in North America, and as gaming becomes global we need to pay close attention to local cultural norms that structure girls' and women's entrance into game spaces. Mizuko Ito's chapter on "Gender Dynamics of the Japanese Media Mix" is a case in point as she reviews electronic gaming in the post-*Pokémon* era where there is a growing role of gaming in girl-oriented media mixes. The stronger ties among media formats like comics and animation and video games have provided a conduit for girl-oriented content to make its way into an interactive format. Cute characters like those found in the Pokémon or Final Fantasy franchises have also provided avenues for girls to orient toward content that is marketed to both boys and girls. Finally, the popularity of portable gaming devices, particularly the Game Boy, has made electronic gaming more accessible to Japanese girls. While boys' content still defines the most cutting-edge developments in children's new media cultures, girls' content is also following.

Another chapter in this part examines the nature of and reasons for social interactions in game play by paying close attention to gender but also age and context. Nick Yee's chapter, "Maps of Digital Desires: Exploring the Topography of Gender and Play in Online Games," presents data from surveys of more than thirty thousand women and men online gamers. According to Yee, many observed gender differences in his data set can be attributed to age differences. The differences between older and younger players are far larger than the differences between male and female players. Moreover, to avoid mistakenly attributing the effects of contextual differences to intrinsic gender differences, we need to be aware of the myriad contextual differences under which men and women play video games. Finally, the experiences of current women gamers in online games suggest that it is not the game mechanics but the game culture that is the main deterrent to potential female gamers. These findings imply that the single-minded pursuit of gender differences in gaming may only serve to distract us from the goal of making games that are appealing to both men and women.

The final chapter in this part, "Gender Play in a Tween Gaming Club" by Yasmin Kafai, analyzes young players that frequent virtual communities such as *Habbo Hotel, Club Penguin,* and *Neopets. Whyville* at Whyville.net is an online community with more than 1.2 million registered players. Most research describes gaming communities where women and girls enter spaces, online and off-line, that are predominantly populated by boys and men. Whyville.net is particularly popular with teen girls ages ten to sixteen; more than 68 percent of its players are girls. We focus on two aspects of game play, gaining insider knowledge about secret places and avatar design, which are indicators of successful participation in gaming communities. Factors such as prior experience, proximity, and public play provide exception to gendered alliances. Players gain access to insider knowledge in multiple ways.

4 Becoming a Player: Networks, Structure, and Imagined Futures

T. L. Taylor

Computer games continue to gain attention not only in the popular press but within academic fields of study as well. While a large amount of research has been done on subjects like violence and game communities, one area remains relatively unexplored—the growing world of professional computer gaming. Though Johnathan "Fatal1ty" Wendel, one of the top pro gamers, was recently featured on the popular U.S. television news show *60 Minutes,* many are unaware of the growing number of people competing at a professional level in worldwide events for cash prizes. And, just as strikingly, increasing numbers of people are becoming avid spectators and amateur players within this scene. As researchers, we are especially fortunate when we encounter sites that let us inquire into broader trends and cultural debates. Pro gaming is such a space. As this nascent slice of play (and sports) culture takes shape, one of the most fascinating threads to emerge is tied to our larger cultural and research conversations about gender and games.

As I continue my research on professional gaming, I see recurring debates on gender and play emerge in evocative ways. The community continues to struggle with and debate whether or not men and woman can enjoyably and equitably play together. In the midst of the discussion we are seeing increasing gender segregation of pro players and growing structural stratification including single-sex teams (where there used to be more coed groups), higher prize winnings for male teams, and secondary status for women's competitions. Against these troubling developments is the simultaneous "glamorization" of women players à la the Ubisoft-sponsored Frag Dolls, the proposed reality-television show based on a Danish women's clan from the game *CounterStrike,* and the marketing and promotion of (some, and only some) women's teams.

These trends in pro gaming cannot be understood outside of a broader context and are instructive as a jumping-off point for a bigger discussion about the place for women and girls in gaming. At the same time that the pro scene is struggling with how to reconcile gender and play, the game industry is now more consistently asking, "What games do women want?" The assumption that there is a single answer (a single "woman") all too easily dovetails in unfortunate ways with the pernicious re-emergence—though maybe it never really abated—of notions of (bio-)gender difference underpinning how we understand play. Witness, for example, the myriad stories about women's aversion to competition or men being better at first-person shooter games due to their "historical" roots as the "hunters of the tribe."

This situation provides the foundation for my growing ambivalence and frustration about how to address gender within this field of scholarship. It is certainly an old and familiar struggle, one that extends far beyond the world of computer games. Suzanne de Castell and Mary Bryson (1998) argued in response to the 1990s girl games movement that we cannot untangle the production of such games from the very production of gender itself. They wrote:

> The question we urge is simply: Whose interests will be served in making use of these purportedly "essential" differences as a basis for creating "girl-friendly" computer-mediated environments? Most importantly, are we producing tools for girls, or are we producing girls themselves by, as Althusser (1984) would put it, "interpellating" the desire to become the girl? By playing with girlish toys, does the girl learn to become the kind of woman she was always already destined to become? (p. 251).

We can fruitfully repurpose their question, turning it back on ourselves who do work on gender and computer games, by asking, "How can we do research and write on the subject in ways that do not a priori essentialize or assume difference through the very construction of our projects, the formulation of our questions, the performance of our ethnographies and interviews? And what does research into gender and computer games look like if *from the outset* it reflectively and progressively confronts and deals with the *always present* production and performance of gender?"

My main concerns now are not only how to do research on gender and computer games but also how to write and tell stories about games that (1) are more resilient to conservative reappropriation, (2) do not by the fact of dealing with gender seem to assent by implication to problematic difference models, and (3) find methodological tools that upend the easy formulations we often re-create within the research moment itself. To that end, I am particularly interested in research that deals with gender across the life cycle and within a variety of contexts and demographics. There is no single construct of "woman" that we can describe, analyze, capture, and reproduce for the benefit of industry.

I continue also to be drawn to the women who *do* play as a way of better understanding something about game culture. Those who manage to inhabit that space tell us something useful about the paths into play. In this regard I find the work being done on the structural and contextual production of play to be a valuable contribution. And finally, my hope for the future lies in the activist work by a variety of small ongoing initiatives within the gaming scene.

Inhabiting Game Culture

The context of and structure around game play matter. Much of the previous research has had an individual-level focus and tried to identify core "feminine" traits (usually framed as a preference for indirect competition, socialization, and/or cooperation). However, a lesson we can learn from looking at women who inhabit game culture is that social networks and access (a category we need to understand in its broadest formulation) are core considerations for play. This is in fact often the case for men as well. Most people come into game culture through their networks and learn to be gamers within specific social contexts. For example, many of the women playing MMO games are introduced to them by a family member [see Taylor (2006) and Yee (this volume)], a friend, or a coworker. We should not overlook the power such introductions provide in both legitimating inhabitation of that space and providing the tools to stay. And we would be remiss in not recognizing that this is also the case for men. This is instructive because it means that paths into game culture are vital. For far too long we have had our eyes on the wrong target. We have looked to play *mechanics* as the explanation for who inhabits this space. But how people come to know about a game, get reviews of it (formal or informal), get their hands on it, are taught how to play it, and indeed have people to play with is deeply informed by their social networks.

Quite often women gamers are isolated and Web sites such as Womengamers.com show the power that a communal context for play holds. This social isolation may not always be, as it can appear at first glance, because they do not have women friends who play but because they do not *know* their friends play. Far too often we find that women gamers occupy a kind of closeted gamer identity. Holin Lin's work (this volume) on how Taiwanese woman negotiate revealing and hiding their game play is powerfully instructive here. Her work also points to the ways the physical and social settings in which play takes place can have a profound effect on one's interaction with games. The configuration of domestic and public space (does one have a space to play in and if not, can one comfortably access public sites), available resources (whose PC or console it is), and women's ongoing social negotiation around their desire to play need to be more centrally considered in our understanding of women as computer gamers (see also Bryce and Rutter 2003; Carr 2005; Kerr 2003; Schott and Horrell 2000). Considering the kind of structural barriers and social isolation women players often face, they actually are one of the most dedicated player demographics around.

This sidelining of women gamers in the general culture has, unfortunately, been mirrored far too often within industry and research communities. The population of women that does play games is frequently seen as an anomaly rather than taken as a prime informant for understanding how play works. Researchers, and people in the game industry, often talk about trying to capture that demographic of nonplaying "*Vogue* readers" to the exclusion of looking at the group that actually seems to be succeeding in inhabiting game culture *now*. At a recent conference on women and games I made this point and was told by an industry representative (one quite sympathetic to women gamers, no less) that current women players were the "low-hanging fruit" and thus didn't warrant our avid attention. But this kind of dismissal is incredibly shortsighted. The industry actively cultivates, indeed courts, their existing male demographic (to the point of ignoring others). Companies understand that part of playing games is being continually, actively, brought into game culture and told you have a rightful place there.

Part of the work of any leisure activity is coming to understand—practically and symbolically—that it is something you can do, that it is not at odds with your sense of self or your social world. The game industry (and, I would argue, the larger game community) knows this at some level and is constantly working to give players information about new games, where to get them, why they are fun, and how to play them. Just as powerfully, it is always mirroring back to boys and men that "this is your and your friends' play space" and "you belong here." Rarely are women gamers given this kind of attention. Indeed, when the game industry does try to make this kind of gesture it is regularly constrained to a slice of "girl games" or the now infamous single title that seems to have been legitimized for women, *The Sims*. If only we might critically untangle the causality loop at work in this game. How much of its popularity with women and girls is due to the way it has been, admirably, proactively shaped as a legitimate object of "feminine" play and leisure? I was struck by this thought while at the mall as I watched parents unhesitatingly usher their little girls to a promotional "child-size" cardboard Sims house to try out the newest expansion pack. Stories also abound of women who go into game shops looking for recommendations and are immediately directed to the game. Myriad newspaper articles have been written detailing the girls and women who love and play the game. It is far too easy to co-opt *The Sims'* success into an essentialist story about "dollhouses" and "noncompetitive" play, but we do so at the peril of overlooking the much more complex ways this game is framed, legitimized, and thus adopted.

On the research side, far too often we miss a prime opportunity to understand what it takes to inhabit gamer culture by seeing existing women or girl players as oddities, as if they cannot give us any real insight into the complex vertices of gender and play. Rather than turning our attention in earnest to current women gamers—a group that seems to be "making it"—an ever-illusive category of "girls who don't like computers" is regularly chased after. Of course I do not want to discount the value of researching this group. My intent is not to further render those girls invisible. Certainly we need research on the nonusers and nonplayers. But simultaneously we need to inquire critically about this persistent methodological turn. I would argue that the underlying decentralization of women gamers has at least some foothold in a very specific imagination of what a "real woman" is. For many research projects there is an a priori assumption about what constitutes core femininity, and current women and girl players often get defined out of projects from the outset. Current women players are regularly seen as anomalies and not of central research interest [see Taylor (2006) for more]. What this means, however, is that we tend to leave their pleasures, their strategies, their networks, their *play* always at the margins. We need to document the long—and strong—history of women players in everything from tabletop games to first-person shooter, multiplayer, and casual games.[1] They tell us a lot about the pleasures of game play and what it takes to get there. And for those interested in creating change, what better place to look than to the women and girls creating it now?

We also need to be much more reflective when we do research in this area to watch for the ways gender is always being produced and what this means to our "findings." As Caroline Pelletier notes (this volume) on her work with boys and girls, "The way these young people make sense of their experience as gamers is not wholly determined prior to the interview but enacted at particular times to achieve a social purpose within the group, namely to be recognized as gendered beings. The resources they have available in doing this are familiar discourses concerning gender, games and school, as well as their own unequal experiences, marked for example by disparity in levels of access to games" (p. 145). Within the research moment we are always participating in the construction of gendered identities—of ourselves and our participants—which includes formulations about play, enjoyment, competency, and preferences. And these performances are always in dialogue with the much larger cultural and local social conversations we are engaged in as individuals. We need greater reflectivity on this dynamic within our research processes and as we think about our data. Our repertoire of methodological tools sould be expanded to include field studies, life cycle analysis, cultural probes, contextual and natural situations, longitudinal work, and multidemographic considerations.

Gendered Technologies

Does this mean that there is nothing to be said about the gendered nature of gaming? Absolutely not. While I am sympathetic to many of the early attempts to understand the gendered status of computer games, I think they often missed the target. Game analysis requires a multilayered approach that looks at a variety of factors and their interrelations to one another. The attempt to categorize play *mechanics* as gendered (versus, for example, the broader context of the game or the technologies that support play) is misguided. We go much further in understanding some women's reticence toward computer games by situating their hesitations in relation to a particular construction of game culture or specific structural contexts. I mean something quite simple with this. It is not that women do not—or, just as often for those who have not yet had access to it, cannot—enjoy direct competition, power, fast action, or even violence or any of the other content or mechanics qualifiers we typically hear bracketed off as "masculine." But, in addition to the social network affordances I mention earlier, women also have to face a culture that works hard to keep them out by constructing particular technologies—consoles, graphics cards, software—as "for men" (see Kerr 2003; Schott 2004).

The (painful) irony of "girl games" is that they also serve to reify this very distinction. There is a web of practices, from advertising to reviews to game-store staffing and on and on, that constantly work to construct game artifacts as "not for girls" (or, conversely, mark only certain items as for them). And while a vast number of titles are notable for the way they do not build gender difference into the actual game mechanic (for example, in a game like *World of Warcraft* your character is no less strong if it is a female), art and marketing departments seem woefully behind on curve. I would argue the challenge lies not in trying to identify "feminine" game mechanics but in trying to make sense of the broader context, including the symbolics of the material world, in which games circulate.[2]

Game technologies are constructed within a framework that encompasses all kinds of entertainment and media devices. We can begin to see the widespread success of products like Apple's iPod or the saturation of mobile phones across genders and the ways game companies are influenced by innovations in product design. Most notable right now is the Nintendo DS Lite, the design of which borrows from a style that will be quite familiar for iBook and iPod owners (of which women certainly are), transforming the handheld game device from a fairly chunky silver brick into a smaller, sleeker device that looks like the playful cousin to the iPod. With such a design turn, products can begin to feel like natural companions to other devices we readily accept into our lives. Technologies, as objects, participate in our larger conversations about identity and gender and as such, we might consider how gaming devices—from consoles to graphics cards to computers—are always implicated in our discussions about who games and why.

My point here is not that simple changes in product design will suddenly bring women into computer gaming with ease (nor that there is some kind of "feminine" design template). But I do want to argue that play should be thought of as an assemblage in which content is only one component in dialogue with everything from very local social context to marketing, technical competency, and even broader understandings about the role of entertainment devices in our lives. Within this mix, people are always evaluating what play and leisure activities fit their view of themselves. This question of what people can imagine doing or trying is deeply socially informed and we need to pay careful attention to the ways leisure is socially sanctioned and regulated. Methodologically this means we need work on all these aspects and we should simultaneously be resistant to industry pressure to pinpoint a single (essential) factor (often boiled down to a game mechanic) that will capture some mythical "woman gamer."

Activist Interventions: Changing by Playing

In the course of my fieldwork on pro gaming I often find myself at gaming parties and competitions. I have been struck by an emerging scene (at least in Scandinavia) of hands-on activist groups directly involved in reshaping the politics of game culture. Projects like Edu-art (edu-art.dk), SuperMarit (supermarit.se), GrrlTech (grrltech.nu), and a variety of others point to the enthusiasm right now for engaging game space by ongoing interventionist projects. I was first alerted to this movement in 2005 when I attended DreamHack, a huge computer game fest in Sweden with more than seven thousand attendees over the course of a weekend. It brought together gamers and computer enthusiasts for a weekend of play, competitions, and demonstrations, and a general party atmosphere. At this event were at least five formal women's initiatives, which ranged from nonprofit groups like GrrlTech to women's pro-gaming teams. Their presence was notable (they all had special booths where people could visit for more information) and they were certainly making connections with the growing number of women (and teenage girls) turning up at the event. I am particularly inspired by the work these groups are doing in actively reshaping gamer culture through their initiatives and presence and I want to highlight one here.

Edu-art was started by Tina Lybæk and Emma Witkowski in 2005. Graduates of the IT University of Copenhagen, they were interested in taking the critical analysis they had done in their research (Lybæk 2005; Witkowski and Højrup 2004) and creating hands-on projects to effect change. They describe Edu-art as a project development team to "create activities that encourage women and girls to get involved with technology-based pastimes by means of shared experiences with computer games. Our vision is to make women visible as IT-users." While there is a fairly long history of creating girls' computer and technology clubs (often with the goal of training them for future use of technology), what I find particularly compelling about their formulation of action is that it focuses not only on building activities for shared experience but also on making women visible in the process. A large part of their work evokes what is sometimes called prefigurative politics—not just critiquing the current state of affairs but imagining and embodying better futures by enacting something different. For example, on International Women's Day they set up a happening at Fona (see figure 4.1), one of Denmark's large electronics stores, where they "took over all the gaming consoles and handhelds and took all the time needed to learn the various games functions. We continued to game, swapping the controls over to one another, even though others were watching/waiting for a turn" (Edu-art 2006a). Their work is deeply tied to demystifying play practices, providing embedded social support, and centralizing women as visible active participants. Rather than hiding in the margins, this is work that wants to authorize women as gamers to take up space and their rightful place in play culture.

In addition to this onetime event, they also run ongoing play sessions where they bring groups of women into net cafés and teach them to play computer games. Very important to this work is that quite often these are women who have some pre-existing social connection to one another. What this means is it is not just teaching a woman how to play a game and then sending her off into the private sphere but pulling in existing social networks that become play communities. This is of vital importance and mirrors one of the reasons many men can negotiate game culture—they inhabit it within a social context and derive support through those connections. If we look at the success many women MMO game players have with getting into, and staying in, that

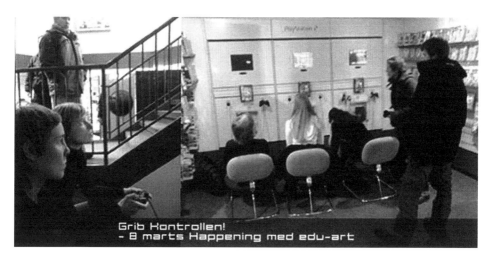

Figure 4.1 Edu-art takeover of Fona for International Women's Day (see color plate).

culture, it is tied to their being brought in by an off-line social connection and then extending their network once in the game.

But the other power of these events—of playing the demos in a store or going to a net café—is that, as I discuss earlier, they perform and make visible an identity typically hidden: woman as gamer. They are hitting on something with the ways this in turn legitimizes that behavior, and that identity, for women. Edu-art sponsors a series called Letz Play, which took their training/play sessions and extended them, culminating in a final competition that took place at Boomtown, one of the largest net cafés in Copenhagen. The goals of that event were to:

- participate in the development of girls' and women's IT skills by playing recreational computer gaming

- make women and girls visible in places where they, for the most, are not represented

- open up a space that provides the opportunity to create new networks outside of educational and family spaces

- give women and girls the opportunity to play with strategy, communication, leadership, and teamwork through recreational IT-based activities

- make net cafés interesting and accessible for women and girls as an alternative space for recreation

Letz Play supports women's and girls' IT-competencies and increases participants' computer confidence. This initiative offers the participants an opportunity that they were not aware they had. (Edu-art 2006b)

In addition to the value these initiatives bring to women wanting to try computer gaming, the symbolic importance, not only to the women themselves but also to the men and boys (and indeed other women) who happen into the space, should not be underestimated. Arriving at the site on the final day of the competition, the visitor saw a team of women DJing at the café entrance while other women played at tables in the main area (see figure 4.2). The other significant contribution initiatives like Edu-art provide go to a deeper methodological critique we need to reflect on as researchers. They are

Figure 4.2   Final day of the "Letz Play" event at Boomtown, Copenhagen (see color plate).
Photo by Emil Oustrup (edofoto.dk).

interested, as they put it, in giving participants "an opportunity that they were not aware they had." This is not minor when it comes to women and computer games. We should consider the ways women (and girls) may not yet know what they would enjoy in gaming and that it is all too easy to foreclose exploration through particular kinds of research questions or methods. For example, Diane Carr (2005) found in her work with a game club for girls that the stated preferences of the girls for particular titles was deeply situated in everything from the layout of the room to the social context in which a game might be played. As Carr notes, the "ability of the girls to recognize and actualize the pleasures promised by different games was enabled by their being literate in the forms of play available, and the kinds of experiences potentially on offer" (p. 376).

It is too often assumed that women who do not buy computer games or choose particular titles are making an informed decision—that is, a negative decision about a game or a play mechanic—rather than one in which they simply have not had the access to experiment and formulate tastes and preferences about genres and types of play. As stated earlier, many women have been given signals (from the broader culture and from the industry itself) that computer games are not meant for them, so it is no surprise that they may not have any real sense of what is out there or what they might enjoy doing if they had the chance. And far too often researchers misinterpret the behavior or comments common to new players as solely about gender. Knowledge of standard game mechanics, interface practices, and even genre conventions are powerful factors in computer game play and are regularly overlooked by researchers.[3] In fact, what often looks like a "women gamers" problem is very regularly a "newbie" issue. Initiatives like those done by Edu-art are about introducing women to games (and not special "women's" or "girls'" games) and, importantly, giving them the tools—technical, skill, *and* social—to play.

Future Studies

There is a strong body of research on gender and computer games that has emerged since the important work *From Barbie to Mortal Kombat*. This second wave of studies has provided critical pointers to the role that structure and contextual formulations of play can bring to our understanding of the issue. Rather than rely on stereotypical or essentializing stories of gender, we can see how becoming a player takes place through a web of networks, practices, possibilities, and technologies. We might also fruitfully consider how the work of scholars like Mizuko Ito (this volume) and Henry Jenkins (2006)—each of whom map out a much broader "media mix" that weaves together games with movies, animation, written work, and the like—can point to further paths of exploration and expanded understanding of play. Understanding this assemblage and how it relates to gender is the task ahead. This means we also need to be more careful to avoid conflating girls with women or oversimplifying the dynamic construction of gender as performed across the life cycle or within varying social contexts. We need better ways of researching gender, of recognizing that we and our participants are always—even at the very moment of trying to understand it—performing and enacting for one another particular identities that shape our understanding of the playful life.

Acknowledgments

A big thanks to all the participants of the UCLA workshop that inspired this collection but especially to my working group—Holin Lin, Mizuko Ito, Nick Yee, Pippin Barr, and Yasmin Kafai—for all the excellent feedback and a really great conversation about the issues. I also want to give a special thanks to Emma Witkowski and Tina Lybæk for their continued insights, good humor, and inspiring activity.

Notes

1. The work on gender and sports can also be useful in navigating these issues. We can see there the long battle over not simply women playing but about what *kind of play* they should engage in. See, for example, Bolin and Granskog (2003), Cahn (1994), Hargreaves (1994), and Lawler (2002).

2. I find Judith Halberstam's (1998) provocative claim that "at least early on in life, girls should avoid femininity" fairly compelling (p. 269). She argues that the costs that come with "excessive conventional femininity" (such as passivity, inactivity, and "unhealthy body manipulations") should prompt us to consider the positive potential subjectivities like the tomboy hold. While this approach has some resonance with Cornelia Brunner's proposal in this volume, I remain somewhat ambivalent about the rhetorical potential of asking people to suddenly think of themselves as "masculine women" or "feminine men" rather than reconfiguring what we understand as potential identities that men and women, boys and girls, can legitimately inhabit (and term whatever they are most comfortable with). Though I have a great deal of sympathy for the long-term project the language of "female masculinities" evokes, I worry about its practical deployment in the short term versus simply broadening the domain of the "feminine" or "masculine."

3. I eagerly await the study, for example, that finally controls for genre knowledge. How often do we read yet another article showing that women prefer stories or puzzles in computer games without any attention to the fact that these are deep genre conventions that they are well familiar with outside of the digital realm and that that very familiarity may play a strong role in how preference and pleasure gets mapped out?

References

Bolin, A., and J. Granskog (eds.). (2003). *Athletic Intruders: Ethnographic Research on Women, Culture, and Exercise.* Albany: State University of New York Publishing.

Bryce, J., and J. Rutter (2003). The gendering of computer gaming: Experience and space. In S. Fleming and I. Jones (eds.), *Leisure Cultures: Investigations in Sport, Media, and Technology.* Eastbourned, UK: Leisure Studies Association.

Cahn, S. (1994). *Coming On Strong: Gender and Sexuality in Twentieth-Century Women's Sport.* Cambridge, Mass.: Harvard University Press.

Carr, D. (2005). Contexts, pleasures and preferences: Girls playing computer games. In S. de Castell and J. Jenson (eds.), *Changing Views: Worlds in Play.* DiGRA Conference Proceedings. Vancouver, Canada.

de Castell, S., and M. Bryson (1998). Retooling play: Dystopia, dysphoria, and difference. In J. Cassell and H. Jenkins (eds.), *From Barbie to Mortal Kombat: Gender and Computer Games.* Cambridge, Mass.: The MIT Press.

Edu-art. 2006a. http://www.edu-art.dk/html/index_UK.htm.

Edu-art. 2006b. http://www.edu-art.dk/html/let_play.htm.

Halberstam, J. (1998). *Female Masculinity.* Durham: Duke University Press.

Hargreaves, J. (1994). *Sporting Females: Critical Issues in the History and Sociology of Women's Sports.* London: Routledge.

Jenkins, H. (2006). *Convergence Culture: Where Old and New Media Collide.* New York: New York University Press.

Kennedy, H. (2002). Lara Croft: Feminist icon or cyberbimbo. *Game Studies,* vol. 2, issue 2.

Kerr, A. (2003). Women just want to have fun: A study of adult female players of digital games. In M. Copier and J. Raessens (eds.), *Level Up Conference Proceedings.* Utrecht: Universiteit Utrect.

Krzywinksa, T. (2005). Demon girl power: Regimes of form and force in videogames Primal and Buffy the Vampire Slayer. Women in Games Conference. Dundee.

Lawler, J. (2002). *Punch! Why Women Participate in Violent Sports.* Terre Haute, Ind.: Wish Publishing.

Lybæk, T. (2005). Women's right to a gamer identity. MsC Thesis, IT University of Copenhagen, Denmark.

Schott, G. (2004). "For men": Examining female reactions to Nintendo's marketing for Game Boy Advance SP. *New Zealand Game Developer's Conference.* Dunedin.

Schott, G., and K. R. Horrell (2000). Girl gamers and their relationship with the gaming culture. *Convergence,* 6 (4).

Taylor, T. L. (2006). *Play between Worlds: Exploring Online Game Culture.* Cambridge, Mass.: The MIT Press.

Witkowski, E. and S. Højrup (2004). Accessing space, barriers of entrance: Females and the Counter-Strike universe. MsC Thesis, IT University of Copenhagen, Denmark.

5 Body, Space, and Gendered Gaming Experiences: A Cultural Geography of Homes, Cybercafés, and Dormitories

Holin Lin

As massively multiplayer online games (MMOs) have started to catch up with video games as a favored leisure activity among adolescents, gender and game studies researchers have shown greater interest in issues involving place and space. In addition to the implications of leisure spaces and game content, recent efforts have focused on online role-playing and gender-based interaction. Virtual space is now considered an important arena for analysis, but it is important to remember that online activities are only one part of the gaming experience. Other important elements include such off-line experiences as discussing and sharing game expertise, competition, and making personal connections as a result of online game activities. In game worlds, social relations exist among avatars, among players, and between avatars and players.

Due to the strong influences of culture, understanding the social experience of gaming requires consideration of two factors: social relations among avatar representations and social relations among player embodiments in digital and physical spaces. This is especially important when analyzing the relationship between gender and gaming, since physical bodies and places are gendered. Women's fear and perceptions of risk are deeply rooted in their bodies, and avoiding dangerous places is a common practice for managing the fear of male violence. In contrast, no threat of physical harm exists for players wearing either female or male avatar bodies. For this reason, I call my research a cultural geography because online gaming and travel have similarities. Both involve activities in unfamiliar spaces, pretrip (pregame) research on locations to visit, decisions about whether or not to have travel partners, and the recording and sharing of experiences through conversations, journals, photos, or videos. When travelers and gamers return to their daily routines, they are eager to share their adventures with people who may or may not have played in or traveled to the same places. An online gamer may begin playing due to an introduction from an acquaintance and subsequently encourage other friends to explore game worlds. In the same manner that friends made while traveling can become lifelong influences, online acquaintances have the potential to become continuing off-line friends.

Leisure researchers have long noted differences in access to public spaces between males and females (Green, Hebron, and Woodward 1990; Shaw 1994; Skeggs 1999). In addition to accepting the exclusive male use of many public spaces (Seabrook and Green 2004), women now face reduced leisure opportunities in the private spaces that they have traditionally dominated as young males increasingly withdraw into home domains to play video games (Flynn 2001). The expanded use of computer games in domestic spaces has also placed children's leisure activities under greater parental supervision (Jenkins 1998).

Studies on gaming space (e.g., Bryce and Rutter 2003a,b; Flynn 2001; McNamee 1998) have identified the importance of physical spaces in which games are actually played. The rapid spread of online gaming has made the issue more complex, thus raising questions on game resource redistribution. Do the spaces created by games and in which they are played have common characteristics? If so, do they share those characteristics across different games? If virtual game world experiences constitute the most important factor among players, should we consider the spaces where computer terminals are located as mere portals or real play spaces? At the core of this issue is whether physical space is losing meaning among youth who are active in virtual gaming cultures.

Online gaming researchers (e.g., Taylor 2002; Wright, Boria, and Breidenbach 2002; Bartle 2003; Turkle 1997) suggest that experiences in virtual game worlds and bodily experiences in physical places set aside for game playing are interwoven in complex ways. Gaming spaces and the gaming networks embedded within them can exert profound and multifaceted influences on gaming experiences. How much do gamers want to play? When and under what conditions can they play? For how long? What types of games should or are allowed to be played? How can they be played safely and/or appropriately? What characteristics of fun and risk are experienced while playing? In addition to gender, these issues are tied to social networks that emerge from different game spaces. Young female and male players are subject to different social perceptions and face different situations when they share the same game space;

consequently, game space characteristics produce gender-specific differences in gaming experiences.

In this chapter, I explore the cultural geography of online gaming in three spaces where Taiwanese children and youth—especially young females—are subject to regulating forces. First, parents supervise children's computer usage and play activities at home. Second, in Taiwan, many local, regional, and national governments are acting to regulate cybercafés, places many view as the contemporary equivalent of playgrounds. Although proposed and enacted regulations are not gender-specific, they have added to the stigma of cybercafés as dangerous places where girls and young women are at particular risk. Combined with parental and other social constraints, these attempts to regulate the leisure activities of youth reflect culturally bound gender role expectations that restrict the number of opportunities for girls to play together in the same physical space. The third space is college dormitories, where social restrictions become increasingly important among females. As young girls grow into young women and become more resourceful, they gain more autonomy in game playing, but restrictions on women's social gaming experience never fully cease to exist. However, based on my observations I have concluded that young female game players should not be viewed as passive objects of social regulation, since there is plenty of evidence in support of their agency. In the face of material constraints, they adopt strategies, mobilize available resources for negotiation, and evade or resist surveillance and regulations so as to expand their autonomy in terms of playing online games.

The data used in this study came from three sources. First, field notes on participant observations were collected in sixteen Internet cafés in the Taipei metropolitan area during a three-week period. Observations lasted for at least one hour per café; in several cases, second and third visits were required at different times of the day to gather sufficient data. The cafés varied in size, price, and location. Observations were primarily focused on space layout, the age and gender distribution of customers, major activities, and social interactions. Second, interviews were conducted with forty-three individual game players and nine focus groups consisting of players and members of their families—a total of seventy-nine interviewees, thirty-five of whom were female.[1] Purposive snowball sampling[2] was used to ensure diversity in terms of age, educational background, and geographic location. Interviewee ages ranged from eleven to fifty-four. Third, the author's personal experiences and observations from more than five hundred hours of online gaming have resulted in a basic understanding of the gaming community.

From Virtual Space to the Physical World

This research focuses on social networks, which are known to impact behavior via four psychosocial mechanisms: social support, social influence, social engagement and attachment, and access to material resources (Berkman et al. 2000). Online game players interact within a minimum of three observable networks: social relations among game-world avatars, off-line social circles consisting of fellow players and family members, and off-line interactions among players who originally meet online. Player interactions in virtual spaces occur via digital bodies, therefore female players do not feel physically threatened while exploring game-world spaces—regardless of the gender of their avatars. The act of exploration can result in liberating experiences of "meeting strangers in a dangerous world" minus exposure to real risks. However, once a female player's real-world social networks and connections between online and off-line relationships are taken into account, her freedom of movement is clearly influenced by various constraints.

Gender plays a pivotal role in social interactions in Taiwanese online game worlds (Lin and Sun 2003). Almost all the interviewees stated that playing as a female character has many benefits. Male players are generally more willing to guide, teach, and help female avatars and to give them valuable gifts. But female avatars are also more likely to be targets of verbal harassment, flirtation, surveillance, and endless efforts to determine the player's real gender and age. Other players may canvass their networks or arrange off-line gatherings for the specific purpose of confirming the off-line gender of an online female avatar. The online treatment of female players reflects the off-line dominance of traditional gender-based roles in heterosexual relationships: males as providers and females as dependents. Male players using female avatars are generally stigmatized as "girlboys" by gaming communities because they are viewed as taking advantage of role-playing opportunities to harvest benefits they don't deserve.

Once a female player's identity and gender are confirmed, the chances of her being asked to meet with other players off-line increases. I was told that a small number of female players trade information about themselves to get dates, but the large majority generally enjoy their online adventures while maintaining strict boundaries in terms of revealing their real identities and contact information. Female players are much more conscientious and vigilant about these issues compared with their male counterparts, who are more likely to reveal the names of their schools, if not their phone numbers or addresses. For a female player willing to develop a friendship beyond game boundaries, her first step is usually to give her MSN instant messaging address, then she gives her phone number, and finally she agrees to a face-to-face meeting. She is very cautious at each stage.

Physical Space

In Taiwan, the off-line networks of young female players primarily consist of siblings and the few female friends and classmates who play the same online game. Girls with game-playing siblings have more opportunities to be exposed to games, but siblings are less likely to play together due to competition for limited gaming resources at home and other aspects of sibling rivalries. Since they have few chances to play with classmates in person after school, the sharing of game experiences is usually limited to exchanges regarding game tactics. The possibility of girls playing in cybercafés exists but is restrained by a combination of self-surveillance and family regulation. Accordingly, the size of young female off-line game communities tends to be small, with many fewer layers of game sharing and interaction than in male communities. This is especially true for the youngest female players, who have weaker social relations and fewer material resources, and who are subject to much greater parental regulations of contact with strangers in public places.

Domestic Space

Game researchers have long known that leisure space and time access is very different for girls and boys (Bunton, Green, and Mitchell 2004). Girls are socially excluded from many public leisure spaces, making their homes their primary play locations by parental edict if not by personal choice. Thus, playing in supervised and regulated home environments represents the primary playing experiences for the large majority of Taiwanese girls. Such traits may be more disturbing to online game players than to video game players, since the first involves large amounts of social interaction.

Another important issue involves how computers are perceived. Parents view them as "educational devices" that facilitate their children's learning

(Selwyn 2003), but children view them primarily as game-playing devices, thus setting the stage for conflict. Based on the parental belief that they must constantly monitor their children's computer usage, home computers are commonly placed in such areas as the living room or parents' bedroom. Taiwanese parents frequently use gaming time as a reward for academic performance. Some parents protect their home computers with passwords and others block access for a set period of time when their children violate agreements on computer game playing.

On the other hand, playing computer games at home has some advantages, especially for the children of parents who hold lenient attitudes toward game playing. The most important is that they have no need to worry about cybercafé costs or safety issues associated with staying out late. Still, parental surveillance is the most common complaint among children and adolescents who play games at home. Parents feel the need to constantly check on their children to make sure rules are followed, which creates an atmosphere of surveillance and generates arguments over privacy. Playing on a home computer also entails interruptions to meet the demands of daily family routines. This is especially true for young female players who live with their parents. They are frequently sent to run errands, ordered to help with household chores, or simply nagged about the "uselessness" of playing online games. Besides, gaming at home usually involves very few or no coplayers.

The control of gaming time and access is further complicated by negotiations with other family members over computer ownership and use. When Taiwanese siblings must share a computer, boys are more likely to enjoy greater access, regardless of their position in order of age. Still, I have observed many girls showing equal enthusiasm as boys for online games and using a broad range of strategies and tricks to get playing time—for example, threatening to change their brothers' passwords or reporting instances of unauthorized playing to their parents.

Cybercafés

In Taiwan, cybercafés are synonymous with computer game playgrounds—places where friends play online games, exchange tactics, help one another with strategies, and make new gaming friends (see figure 5.1). They currently attract a disproportionate amount of local media coverage and are frequently portrayed as dens of depravation where teenagers cannot help but get involved

Figure 5.1   A typical late-night scene in a Taipei cybercafé (see color plate).

in all kinds of criminal and deviant behaviors related to the Internet. Such descriptions trigger reactions similar to those traditionally associated with amusement arcades (Fisher 1995) and pool halls. Few Taiwanese cybercafé owners make any effort to ameliorate their images: the majority of the cybercafés I observed were smoky and noisy, their computer keyboards were usually sticky, and their bathrooms were often dirty. The customers I spoke with frequently expressed concern over gaming security—specifically that their passwords could be stolen by Trojan horse programs or onlookers.

Local, regional, and national government bodies in Taiwan have passed various measures to regulate the teen and preteen patronage of cybercafés,[3] yet even casual observers can quickly note the significant presence of students by their school uniforms—despite the risk of local police reporting their "delinquent behavior" to their parents. Taiwanese parents and schools are pushing for tighter restrictions on underage access to cybercafés based on wild rumors about the cybercafés' detrimental influences on young gamers. One of the most intriguing comments I heard came from an eleven-year-old girl: "The air conditioning is spiked with heroin or something like that, so when we inhale it we become addicted and buy drugs from the people who run the cybercafés."

The girls I interviewed expressed keen awareness of the great imbalance in the gender ratios at cybercafés. The layouts of some cybercafés serve as gender barriers: girls must pass through a room full of pool tables to access the back spaces that are reserved for computers. Most girls are not willing to subject themselves to the scrutiny of and comments made by the pool players, and therefore only enter when accompanied by male friends. "The men all turned to look at me as I entered," one female interviewee complained. A small number of girls grew accustomed to the attention they attracted after several visits. During a focus-group interview, a group of high-school friends expressed genuine shock in reaction to a quiet girl who admitted that she paid regular visits to cybercafés on her own. Their surprise was based on the generally accepted belief that "good girls do not go to cybercafés alone." This explains why in Taiwan, females account for 41 percent of all gamers but less than 20 percent of cybercafé patrons (Insight Xplorer Marketing Research Company 2004). And more often than not, young female players feel the need to go to cybercafés with their friends.

If cybercafés are considered dangerous for girls and dirty and unpleasant for boys, why do players bother going? Cited reasons include superior equipment, uninterrupted playing time, and convenience for group playing. The most popular games played in cybercafés are online role-playing, real-time shooting, and strategy games. Players prefer the instant communication that accompanies playing in the same physical space. As with all adolescent activities, just hanging out with friends and being with other players are essential attractions. As one teen told me, "The feeling I get from playing with my friends in a cybercafé, the whole atmosphere, it makes me feel high with excitement." (See figure 5.2.)

College Dormitories

Girls gain greater autonomy when they leave home to attend college, therefore the characteristics of game playing in college dormitories can aid in our understanding of the role of gender in online game playing. Staying up all night playing online games is now considered a common experience for college students in Taiwanese dormitories, but there is little support for the assump-

Figure 5.2   Sharing exciting moments in a cybercafé (see color plate).

tion that young females have more opportunities on campuses to form social gaming networks in shared physical spaces. The physical layout of many dormitories, lack of existing networks for young female players, and differences in gender-specific peer cultures make gaming in college dormitories more of a solitary and isolated experience for interested female college students.

In male dormitories (Taiwanese college dorms are strictly gender-segregated), online gaming is a popular activity that is both highly competitive and performance-centered. Students from different floors or wings organize teams to play against one another. Games can attract large crowds of onlookers who cheer as advancements are made or victories won. Male dormitory life presents many opportunities for students to spend long hours playing computer and online games. In contrast, gamers in female dormitories have much lower profiles and greater difficulty finding other players. Game playing is discouraged by roommates who complain about noise or insist that "game-playing is for boys."[4]

One female interviewee said she played video games continuously throughout her college years. Upon reflection, she expressed guilt for disturbing others' study or rest time. Although she did her best to minimize her disturbances (e.g., using earphones to mute the sound track and a special keyboard to reduce noise), she described having feelings of regret over opening and shutting the dorm door to use the toilet and taking a shower at hours when her roommates were asleep. One of her roommates put up a curtain between their desks to reduce the potential for distraction (see figure 5.3). The interviewee felt that it was perfectly legitimate for her roommates to do whatever was necessary to protect their spaces. When her roommates complained that her game playing interfered with their schedules and argued that it wasn't good for her health, she felt a strong sense of guilt. She also stated that she did not regard herself as a legitimate part of her dormitory group "because others did not play."

Other dormitory situations marked by more independent living quarters give female gamers greater autonomy, yet most still end up playing by themselves.[5] The small number and low profile of female players contribute to a generally invisible gaming culture in female dorms. Due to the large number of game players in most male dorms, there is little sense of embarrassment over

Figure 5.3   Playing under restrictions in a female college dormitory (see color plate).

playing late at night or making lots of noise. Those who have never played before can watch, learn, and be invited by friends to join in. Those who don't want to play usually see the futility of complaining and either accept the noisy environment or rent apartments off-campus. As members of a small minority, female gamers must be more sensitive to their roommates' reactions. Instead of inviting roommates to join them, they play alone and try to cause as little disturbance as possible. Many decide that it is better to quit playing than to face further peer pressure. As a result, in college dormitories the male majorities tend to expand and the female minorities tend to shrink.

Gaming community size exerts an impact on game selection, with team competition being the most influential factor. Players in male dormitories prefer team games (three on three or four on four) and can always find enough teammates regardless of the length of a gaming session. Once a team shooting or action game begins, it is very difficult for individual players to quit before the game ends, since doing so causes major imbalances. Male interviewees reported that once a game starts, they tend to become so absorbed in the activity that they play for many hours beyond their original intent. Male players who do not want to play for prolonged sessions therefore choose real-time strategy games that last for as little as ten minutes, which therefore provide frequent opportunities to stop playing and find replacements without disappointing other players. Female players in dormitories do not enjoy the same flexibility in choosing game genres. Since team games are not an option for them, their remaining options most likely are self-paced online role-playing games, puzzles, or emulated video games.

Above all other factors, gender culture plays a crucial role in shaping gaming dynamics in Taiwanese college dormitories. Being mindful of the needs of others is considered an important feminine virtue, whereas competitiveness and aggressiveness are considered male values. Male college student interviewees expressed a very different sense from female students of what constitutes legitimate behavior. None of the male students considered it a big deal to play noisy games while their roommates tried to study or rest. The respective ways that male and female students act and describe their distinctive game playing activities are examples of what Pelletier (this volume) refers to as "doing gender"—that is, ways in which young people construct their gender identities by making sense of the games they play, interpret, and produce.

Conclusion

In this chapter I identify factors that shape the cultural geography of online gaming spaces, which in turn shape the gender-specific experiences of young Taiwanese game players. These factors include differential parental supervision at home, governmental regulation of public leisure spaces, stigmas attached to public game playgrounds and their male-dominated atmospheres, game place site design, and group dynamics of male and female gamer communities. Links between the politics of game spaces and player behaviors in those spaces enhance our understanding of the complex context of young female gaming behaviors. They should not be regarded as the simple result of girls' autonomous, well-informed, rational calculations for self-preservation nor as submissive responses to material restrictions imposed on young female players. The girls I spoke with actively invent strategies to evade parental supervision and compete with their brothers for opportunities to play at home, and a small but growing number are willing to visit cybercafés after school. When girl gamers go to college, they seek out other female game lovers but face a different set of restrictions supported by their peers and roommates. As Taylor notes in this volume, if we take into account the structural and social isolation that female players often face, they can be considered the most dedicated group of online game players.

I stress the importance of an otherwise neglected culture in the social construction of gender and gaming, trying to show how a competitive gaming culture regarded as more legitimate for aggressive young males sets the tone for gendered gaming behaviors. As Ito notes in another chapter in this volume, in Japanese *otaku* (computer geek) culture, intense involvement in fantasy-oriented games is generally deemed as acceptable or cool for boys but marginal for girls. Not only are relationships between computer games and gender roles defined by larger cultural constraints, but game choice and play are themselves acts of gender identity construction. Future researchers may be interested in making comparisons of gender and gaming construction in different cultural contexts.

Access to public game space is also determined by economic resources (fees for access) and age (parental and governmental rules). Unlike young adults, adolescents and preadolescents have fewer options for alternative game spaces such as friends' homes or school dormitories. These factors serve as particularly powerful barriers for young girls. Other factors tied to complex life changes among females require further exploration.

Player experiences and feelings of risk and pleasure are socially, economically, and culturally grounded in local contexts. In Taiwan, social rules, parental regulation, and differences in risk perceptions and economic resources affect gender-based behavioral choices and access to cybercafés. But despite the lack of comfort and expense involved, the use of cybercafés as online playgrounds pays off in other ways. The collective aspect of online role-playing games involves ongoing collaborations with team members and conversations with friends and playing partners. These features make scheduling and privacy more important factors for online game players than for video game players and make parental surveillance and restrictions on playing time more unbearable. For Taiwanese girls these factors result in fewer opportunities than for boys to play in public, play with others in the same physical space, or play at home if their parents require them to share in domestic responsibilities.

Online role-playing games have created new virtual spaces for girls to experiment with exploratory behaviors without worrying about physical danger or other consequences. They can safely move through virtual worlds as long as they don't transfer their online friendships off-line. The geographic dispersion of game players exerts a subtle influence on female players' constant need to remain alert so as to avoid accidentally giving off-line contact information during online interactions. As for physical play spaces, Taiwanese cybercafés serve as modern playgrounds for boys, but whereas physical playgrounds reinforce the sense of male-only spaces, in online game worlds boys are allowed to play with girls—or at least to assume that they are playing with girls. Cultural constructions of gender are ubiquitous and therefore hard to remove from any analytical interpretation of gender issues in computer gaming.

Acknowledgments

This research was supported by the Republic of China National Science Council (nos. NSC-93-2412-H002-008 and NSC-94-2412-H002-001). I wish to thank Yasmin Kafai, Carrie Heeter, Debbie Fields, Mizuko Ito, T. L. Taylor, Nick Yee, and Pippin Barr for their valuable comments on earlier drafts of this chapter, as well as Chuen-Tsai Sun for his help and support.

Notes

1. The final sample consisted of twelve primary school students, eight junior high school students, nineteen senior high school students (including one dropout and one preparing to retake the national university entrance examination), twenty-six college students, eight graduate students, two journalists, two housewives, one social worker, and one junior high school teacher.

2. In snowball sampling, participants are asked to recommend other potential interviewees, who are also asked to make recommendations (Babbie, 1995).

3. For example, children and teenagers are prohibited from entering cybercafés during school hours and after designated times at night (ranging from 10 to midnight, depending on the night of the week and geographic area). A proposal under consideration in the national legislature would forbid the operation of cybercafés within two hundred meters of any elementary, junior, or senior high school.

4. Dormitory residents of three national universities were interviewed.

5. None of the five female interviewees living on campus had ever participated in group play with other females living in the same dormitory.

References

Babbie, E. (1995). *The Practice of Social Research*. Belmont: Wadsworth Publishing Co.

Bartle, R. (2003). *A Self of Sense*. http://www.mud.co.uk/richard/selfware.htm.

Berkman, L. F., T. Glass, I. Brissete, and T. E. Seeman (2000). From social integration to health: Durkheim in the new millennium. *Social Science and Medicine, 51,* 843–857.

Bryce, J., and J. Rutter (2003a). Gender dynamics and the social and spatial organization of computer gaming. *Leisure Studies, 22,* 1–15.

Bryce, J., and J. Rutter (2003b). The gendering of computer gaming: Experience and space. In S. Fleming and I. Jones (eds.), *Leisure Cultures: Investigations in Sport, Media and Technology* (pp. 3–22). Eastbourne, UK: Leisure Studies Association.

Bunton, R., E. Green, and W. Mitchell (2004). Introduction: Young people, risk and leisure, an overview. In W. Mitchell, R. Bunton, and E. Green (eds.), *Young People, Risk and Leisure: Constructing Identities in Everyday Life* (pp. 1–23). New York: Palgrave Macmillan.

Fisher, S. (1995). The amusement arcade as a social space for adolescents: An empirical study. *Journal of Adolescence, 18,* 71–86.

Flynn, B. (2001). Video games and the new look domesticity. *Bad Subjects,* (57). http://bad.eserver.org/issues/2001/57/flynn.html.

Green, E., S. Hebron, and D. Woodward (1990). *Women's Leisure, What Leisure?* Basingstoke. NJ: Ablex.

Insight Xplorer Marketing Research Company (2004). *Annual Research on the Internet and Life in Taiwan.* Taipei: Insight Xplorer Marketing Research Company.

Jenkins, H. (1998). "Complete freedom of movement": Video games as gendered play spaces. In J. Cassell and H. Jenkins (eds.), *From Barbie to Mortal Kombat: Gender and Computer Games* (pp. 262–297). Cambridge, Mass.: The MIT Press.

Lin, H., and Chuen-Tsai Sun (2003). Problems in simulating social reality: Observations on a MUD construction. *Simulation & Gaming, 34*(1), 69–88.

McNamee, S. (1998). The home: Youth, gender and video games: Power and control in the home. In T. Skelton and G. Valentine (eds.), *Cool Place: Geographies of Youth Culture* (pp. 195–206). London: Routledge.

Seabrook, T., and E. Green (2004). Streetwise or safe? Girls negotiating time and space. In W. Mitchell, R. Bunton, and E. Green (eds.), *Young People, Risk and Leisure: Constructing Identities in Everyday Life* (pp. 129–141). New York: Palgrave Macmillan.

Selwyn, N. (2003). "Doing it for the kids": Re-examining children, computers and the "Information Society." *Media, Culture & Society, 25,* 351–378.

Shaw, S. M. (1994). Gender, leisure and constraint: Towards a framework for the analysis of women's leisure. *Journal of Leisure Research, 26,* 8–23.

Skeggs, B. (1999). Matter out of place: Visibility and sexualities in leisure spaces. *Leisure Studies, 18*(3), 213–32.

Taylor, T. L. (2002). Living digitally: Embodiment in virtual worlds. In R. Schroeder (ed.), *The Social Life of Avatars: Presence and Interaction In Shared Virtual Environment* (pp. 40–62). London: Springer-Verlag.

Turkle, S. (1997). Constructions and reconstructions of self in virtual reality: Playing in the MUDs. In S. Kiesler (ed.), *Culture of the Internet* (pp.143–155). Mahwah, N.J.: Erlbaum.

Wright, T., E. Boria, and P. Breidenbach (2002). Creative player actions in FPS online video games playing Counter-Strike. *Game Studies, 2*(2). http://www.gamestudies.org/0202/wright.

6 Maps of Digital Desires: Exploring the Topography of Gender and Play in Online Games

Nick Yee

In one corner of the game *World of Warcraft*, forty players have just gathered in Molten Core to begin their weekly raid. Every Friday night, these players spend five to ten hours working together to defeat the same series of increasingly difficult monsters. Tonight, a sixty-year-old female player is raiding with her granddaughter on her lap and the baby's gurgles are heard over the VoIP channel amid commands to "hold aggro dammit." Over in the game *Eve Online*, infiltrators inside a leading corporation are moments away from assassinating the CEO and emptying the resource and equipment stores in a synchronized heist (Francis 2006). And in a small, undecorated room in the Chinese province of Fuzhou, four teenage boys are rushing to meet their daily quota of virtual gold while evading the systematic harassment from Western players who have branded them as "Chinese gold farmers." These are a few glimpses of the structured and emergent play in the digital constructs known as massively multiplayer online role-playing games (MMORPGs, or MMOs for short).

In talking about gender and gaming, we often hear assumptions that men and women simply prefer different kinds of games. These assumptions echo a growing body of literature suggesting that our evolutionary past has engineered much of our current social behavior (e.g., Diamond 1998; Wright 1995), including why we play games (Steen and Owens 2001). These accounts also tend to propose hardwired biological differences stemming from different challenges for men and women in our evolutionary past (Low 2001). Indeed, game designer Chris Crawford (2005) explicitly argued that men and women prefer different kinds of video games because of how we lived in the Pleistocene savannas. These arguments lead us to believe that creating games for the "female brain" is the only sensible solution to attracting women to play video games; there is a particular set of "feminine" game mechanics that we simply haven't found or perfected yet.

In this chapter, I offer data from a study of MMO players that challenge this assumption. Talking about game play simply as a function of desire ignores the fact that legitimate social access to video gaming differs for men and women. In fact, particularly for multiplayer games, game mechanics may not be the main problem at all. Women in many MMOs perceive the game culture rather than the game mechanics to be the primary deterrent to potential female gamers.

The Survey Study

The data presented here were collected from a series of ongoing online surveys as part of The Daedalus Project (Yee 2007a). Links to these surveys are publicized on Web portals catering to specific games and portals catering to MMO gamers in general. Respondents from past surveys are also notified of the available surveys. Most of the surveys contain both open-ended and multiple-choice questions and usually take about five to ten minutes to complete. Approximately two thousand to four thousand respondents participate in each survey phase. The more popular MMOs were targeted over the past six years, which have included games such as *Ultima Online, EverQuest, Dark Age of Camelot, Star Wars Galaxies, City of Heroes,* and *World of Warcraft.* Over the past six years, more than forty thousand MMO players have participated in the study.

The Physical and Social Context of Play

The topography of play in MMOs is multilayered; it is a dynamic territory shaped by social and physical access, individual motivations, and other in-game and out-of-game contexts, creating an uneven terrain that presents different navigational challenges depending on the player. As Carr (2005) has noted, "preferences are an assemblage, made up of past access and positive experiences, and subject to situation and context." Thus, play isn't simply about what players like to do in the game, but also about what constrains their access to games, how they were introduced to the game, and whom they play with. As Lin (this volume) describes, we need to take into account the external physical and social context of online play because sometimes these locations constrain whether we can play at all. Kafai (this volume) intentionally blurs the boundaries between virtual and physical play by bringing kids together in an after-school club to play online in *Whyville*. Our social contexts constrain how we play, with whom we play, and what we play. I use the survey data to describe the demographic profile of MMO players. In particular, I articulate out-of-game contextual gender differences such as how men and women gain social access to MMOs.

Basic Demographics

According to the survey's responses, the large majority of MMO players are male (85.4%). The average age is twenty-six; the median is twenty-five, with a range from eleven to sixty-eight. Female players are considerably older than male players in MMOs. Forty-four percent of male players are age twenty-two or younger, compared with 20 percent of female players. Overall, about 50 percent of MMO players work full-time, and 36 percent are married. About 80 percent of female players and 60 percent of male players indicated that they were in a stable romantic relationship in real life (i.e., dating, engaged, or married). What these numbers show is that the overall demographic composition of MMO users is relatively diverse (except for gender), and does not consist primarily of adolescents. In fact, it also includes college students, early adult professionals, middle-aged homemakers, as well as retirees. On average, respondents spend twenty-two hours each week in an MMO. The median was twenty hours per week—the equivalent of half a workweek. There were no significant gender or age differences in usage patterns; players over the age of forty play on average just as much as players under the age of twenty.

Introduction to Games

While women are severely underrepresented in MMOs, women who play MMOs play for the same amount of time as men do. One potential reason for the underrepresentation of female players in MMOs may be social context including limited social access points to introduce women to MMOs as well as social dynamics within the game (how female players are treated). Social norms and perceptions may govern access to video games for women in ways that are different from men. The following analyses reveal how access points to these games may be different for men and women. Earlier, we note that female players in MMOs are older than male players. One possible explanation for this age difference may lie in how players are introduced to MMOs. While about 27 percent of female players were introduced to the game by a romantic partner, only 1 percent of male players were introduced in this way. If we assume that people in stable romantic relationships tend to be older, and a romantic partner who plays is a primary mechanism for introducing women to MMOs, this helps to explain why there are fewer young female players.

Playing Together

A related difference can be seen in the number of players who play an MMO with someone they know in real life. Overall, about 25 percent of players play an MMO with their romantic partner. Female players are more likely to be playing with a romantic partner than male players (see figure 6.1). About two-thirds of female gamers are playing with a romantic partner, while less than one-fifth of male gamers are.

These survey findings resonate with those from ethnographic data research by Jenson and de Castell (2005) where initial trends suggested that "for most women, transgressing gender 'norms' in relation to playing games, occurs most frequently when it is legitimated by male relations (boyfriends, cousins, brothers and fathers)" (p. 4). The survey findings are congruent with this observation. Some women gain legitimate initial social access points into MMOs and allocate time toward MMO play via male relations. Responses

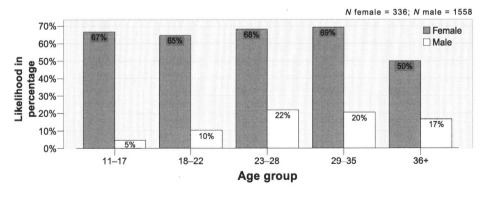

Figure 6.1   Likelihood of playing with a romantic partner (by age and gender).

from female gamers to open-ended questions in the surveys also suggest that female gamers are very aware of the legitimizing effects of male relations.

> I find that most people do not think female players in game are really female unless you have your significant other (husband, boyfriend, roommate) playing the game, too. I think most people in game assume that 98% of all players are male and the other 2% are girlfriends/wives who were dragged along into the game—that it's not something a girl would want to do. (*World of Warcraft,* female, 38)

> Many also seem to assume that I play with my boyfriend or husband, and are surprised when I tell them that I played MMOs long before my former boyfriend started playing City of Heroes, and that he doesn't play EQ at all. (*EverQuest,* female, 24)

These two anecdotes, examples of many similar comments, highlight that acceptable social access to online games differs considerably between men and women. Men are allowed relatively free access to online games, but a woman's presence in an online game is seen as legitimate only if it occurs via a relationship with a man. Other male players use a female player's relationship with a man as a means to legitimate her actual biological sex, to know whether a player claiming to be female is indeed a woman in real life. Playing an MMO as part of a romantic relationship also helps female players justify long hours spent playing; she is nurturing her romantic relationship as well as (presumably) having fun. Thus, these male relations legitimate both their initial entry and ongoing presence in an MMO. This parallels one of Lin's observations of cybercafés in Taiwan (this volume); most girls are unwilling to enter a cybercafé unless accompanied by a male friend. Together, these stories imply that physical and social barriers to entry for women become misinterpreted as a lack of desire to play video games. The twisted logic legitimates both the *want* and the *should* of playing MMOs for female players, but this logic is ultimately predicated on the assumption that women neither inherently want to play or should be playing MMOs on their own. Under this logic, the "unnatural" phenomenon of women wanting to play video games for many hours a week occurs as a side effect of their male relations. This mind-set is probably not very appealing to female gamers who want to enter these gaming spaces.

Thus, playing a game isn't simply about what we want to play; it's about how we gain initial and ongoing access to these spaces because men and women have very different legitimate social access points to online games and these determine quite frequently what each of them will play.

Co-located Play

Finally, there is also a significant difference in the physical play settings of male and female gamers that ties into the general trends we have seen so far. Female gamers are about twice as likely to be playing with someone else in the same room than are male gamers (see figure 6.2). Men are more likely to be playing alone.

These findings illustrate that context matters when we talk about gender and gaming. Gaming isn't simply about what we want to play, but it also depends on what social access points are available to us. It is also important to keep in mind that these contextual differences in turn shape how we play. Playing with your romantic partner at your side might encourage more social-oriented play than playing alone. Or, for example, men who introduce their girlfriends to the game might encourage them to play support roles (e.g., healers) to facilitate their own game play. Studying current male and female gamers to understand what games may appeal to female gamers might inadvertently lead us to mistake the *how* for the *why*.

Moreover, the emphasis on creating games for the "female brain" ignores the fact that desire is not the only factor in what games we play. The above

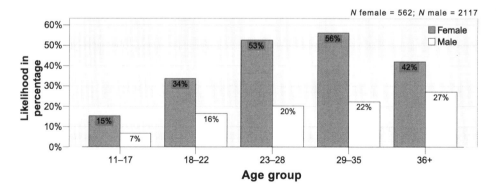

Figure 6.2   Likelihood of co-located play (by age and gender).

survey data of MMO players suggest that access points into online games can be incredibly gendered. And perhaps women are underrepresented in certain game genres not because they don't like those games but because male players who dominate many physical and social access points actively discourage women from entering. As the following incident illustrates, homes are not the only places where constraints to social access occur. At the workshop for this book at University of California, Los Angeles, Ubisoft's Frag Dolls' Morgan Romine, a professional woman gamer, described walking into the local EB Games to pick up a new Nintendo DS game. When Romine approached the counter, the cashier asked, "So who are you getting this for?" She recalled a similar experience when she was preordering *Halo 2*. After the clerk chatted with her a bit, he exclaimed, "Wait—you're ordering this for yourself?" It is ironic that the game industry is trying so hard to appeal to female gamers even as they remain so adamant that women don't play video games.

Motivations for Play in MMOs

Many people assume that men and women prefer different kinds of game play. In this section, I present data on motivations for play among MMO gamers that challenge the assumption that there are dramatic differences between men and women in terms of what games they might enjoy playing. Over the years, I've noticed that when MMO players are asked why they play, the responses reveal a large array of varied motivations. Indeed, this variation suggests that one reason why MMOs are so popular may be that there are many subgames embedded within a larger system.

> After many weeks of watching I found myself interested in the interactions between people in the game, it was totally absorbing! The fact that I was able to immerse myself in the game and relate to other people or just listen in to the "chatter" was appealing. (*Dark Age of Camelot*, female, 34)

> There's a certain satisfaction to be had from leveling, I find. While there ARE things much more enriching and rewarding than mindless leveling, there's a certain . . . feeling of zen to be found in the grind. I've spent hours on end in the same area, doing the same thing over and over,

watching the exp bar creep slowly upwards . . . Just soloing, just me and the monsters. (*City of Heroes,* female, 22)

Currently, I am trying to establish a working corporation within the economic boundaries of the virtual world. Primarily, to learn more about how real world social theories play out in a virtual economy. (*Eve Online,* male, 30)

Being able to articulate these underlying motivational differences is the precursor to exploring more complex behaviors and interactions in these environments. For example, are certain kinds of players more likely to become guild leaders? Or are certain players more likely to develop problematic usage patterns? To create an empirical framework of motivations for play among MMO gamers, I used a factor-analytic approach, which yielded ten motivations (see table 6.1) grouped into achievement, social, and immersion components (Yee, 2007b).

Examining Gender Differences

This resulting framework reveals the diversity of play in MMOs. There is no one kind of MMO player. The same model emerges whether we include the whole sample, or perform the analysis separately for male and female players. As Taylor has noted (2003), women (and men) play MMOs for many

Table 6.1 Factor Analysis Framework for MMO Play Motivations

Achievement	Social	Immersion
Advancement progress, power, accumulation, status	**Socializing** casual chat, helping others, making friends	**Discovery** exploration, lore, finding hidden things
Mechanics numbers, optimization, templating, analysis	**Relationship** personal, self-disclosure, find and give support	**Role-Playing** story line, character history, roles, fantasy
Competition challenging others, provocation, domination	**Teamwork** collaboration, groups, group achievements	**Customization** appearances, accessories, style, color schemes
		Escapism relax, escape from real life, avoiding real-life problems

reasons. It isn't the case that women play only for socializing or that men play only to kill monsters. On the other hand, there are gender differences in these self-identified motivations. Male players score higher in the Advancement, Mechanics, and Competition motivations, while female players score higher in the Relationship and Customization motivations. There were very small or no gender differences in the other five motivations—Socializing, Teamwork, Discovery, Role-Playing, and Escapism. Even though statistical differences emerged, the data show that there are far more commonalities than differences. It is important to remember that significant differences on Gaussian distributions nevertheless usually imply a large overlap range. For example, even in the motivation with the largest statistical gender difference (Mechanics), the overlap between men and women was 66 percent. The average gender overlap across all the listed motivations was actually 87 percent: the overwhelming majority of men and women like to do the same kinds of things in online games. An attempt to identify play motivations that appeal to the "female brain" might be solving a problem that doesn't actually exist.

The results of the factor analysis also reveal that assumed gender differences should be largely attributed to other factors. For example, men are stereotyped as being more achievement-oriented than women in video games. Within this MMO study, the desire to achieve in games is in fact better explained by age than by gender. A multiple regression reveals that age accounts for significantly more variation in the achievement motivation than gender does. What the multiple regression shows is that differences in how competitive or power-driven a player is are better explained by age than gender. Players are less likely to be achievement-driven in video games as they get older. As we see in the previous section, female players in MMOs tend to be older than male players. Thus, a pure gender comparison without taking into account the underlying age differences between male and female players would have inflated the apparent gender difference. Given the nontrivial role that age plays in motivations for playing MMOs, it is ironic that so much attention has focused on gender alone.

Other interesting findings also emerge from the data set. For example, whereas one might have expected a large gender difference in the Socializing motivation, the results show a small difference. Men like to chat, gossip, and talk just as much in these games as women do. The same is true for the Role-Playing motivation. Some researchers had identified storytelling and character investment as important forms of play for women (Brunner, Bennett, and Honey 1998), but this motivation is only slightly more important for women than it is for men. And as we've noted, even where we do see gender differences, such as in the Achievement component, these differences are in fact more strongly driven by age than gender.

Thoughts from current female MMO players on gendered motivations for playing these games dovetail with the results presented here. The main theme that emerged was that MMOs offer such varied styles of play that there is bound to be something for most players.

> I think that there is a very definite difference in the way that men and women approach online games. However, the games themselves tend to be so flexible that all styles can be accommodated quite easily. (*Eve Online,* female, 35)

Others commented that the beauty of MMOs is that these games may hook in new players for stereotypical gendered reasons, but once players are there, they may be tempted to try out and enjoy the other things these games offer. In other words, MMOs have the potential to broaden game playing for both men and women.

> I know plenty of females that wouldn't consider themselves gamers that easily pick up (and get addicted to) these games. I think that's also why WoW is starting to gain female gamers: some come for the socialization aspect, and stay for the fun. :) (*World of Warcraft,* female, 24)

One central dilemma for the girl games movement is figuring out how to get there from here without only creating stereotypically gendered games and perpetuating gender stereotypes. While some have suggested that MMOs may be more appealing to women because of the storytelling or socialization elements, I'd argue that the importance of MMOs lies in their ability to potentially broaden the game-playing scope of its players. Once committed to playing, women who initially play to chat may eventually find slaying dragons enjoyable. And men who initially play to slaughter innocent rabbits may eventually find sustaining social relationships enjoyable. MMOs are thus potential gateways for both male and female players.

Social and Cultural Deterrents in MMOs

Playing a video game isn't only about desire; playing a game is always shaped by our physical and social access points (whether that game is football or *World of Warcraft*). And even if gaming were simply a matter of desire, men and women actually share roughly the same desires. The burden now falls on me to explain why the current games aren't attracting more women. After all, if it's not an issue of motivation, then why do female players only account for 15 percent of the MMO population? Unfortunately, current MMOs are not gender-inclusive utopias. There are many social and cultural constraints for women who enter these spaces. In a recent survey, I asked female gamers about what they saw as potential deterrents to female gamers in the MMO they played. Almost every respondent cited the proportions and clothing options of the female avatars as problematic.

> The only really off-putting detail is that it's ludicrous that every time my elf fights, her breasts stick out to the side repeatedly. It is a constant reminder to me that this game is made for 13 year old boys, or men who still think like them. (*World of Warcraft,* female, 42)

To a certain extent, this encourages players to think about women as token spectacles rather than actual players. In fact, players are often assumed to be men unless proven otherwise. As we've noted, however, the legitimacy of a player's real-life gender is a by-product of male relations. Thus, many female players described experiences where other players simply did not believe they were actually female.

> But every once in a while, I seem to meet someone who wants to violently deny that I am who I am. And how am I supposed to respond to a charge of "You are not a girl!"—I can't exactly flash ID or body parts to prove it. (*World of Warcraft,* female, 36)

For many of these female players, the problem with being in an MMO is that they are constantly reminded of the intended male subject position they are trespassing upon. On top of this, the male-dominated player culture itself becomes a deterrent—something that isn't an issue in single-player games.

There are things that happen in-game that make me embarrassed, as a woman and as a person who tries to be socially responsible, to be playing. For example, male players will talk about getting "raped" without really thinking about it, things that happen will be referred to as "gay," which is offensive, people do crude things to player corpses in PvP [Player vs. Player settings], etc. (*World of Warcraft*, female, 29)

More important, many female players have learned that it is dangerous to reveal your real-life gender in MMOs because they will be branded as incompetent and constantly propositioned; In other words, they must either accept the male-subject position silently, or risk constant discrimination and harassment if they reveal that they are female.

When I played EQ, I was so sick and tired of being treated like a moron or hit on 24–7 that I made a male character. The way people treat female chars and males in EQ was drastic, I had immediate respect. When on a female char, men think you don't know how to play, cant be hardcore, and try to give you things to hit on you. Its annoying to say the least. (*World of Warcraft*, female, 35)

It is unfortunate that much of what has been brought up in this section has little to do with the game mechanics themselves. Desire isn't the only thing that brings someone to play a game. And mismatched desire is not the only thing that keeps them away. It isn't the achievement-oriented game play that drives women away from MMOs as much as the player culture itself—elements of the metagame rather than the game code.

Conclusion

Focusing on desire in game play sidelines important elements while privileging factors that may be simply distracting. My surveys of current MMO players, as well as the research conducted by Lin and Kafai (this volume), suggest that online play is always a contextual combination of social and physical access. The reality is that those men and women who currently play online games are overwhelmingly similar in terms of what they like to do in them. And stereotypical assumptions of gendered motivations are either nonsignificant (i.e., Socializing), or are dwarfed by differences in age (as in the case of the Achievement motivation). Attention should be paid to including game mechanics appealing to older and younger players, in addition to masculine and feminine motivations.

And finally, the emphasis on finding an inclusive set of game mechanics that appeal to and can be enjoyed by female and male gamers ignores other more important deterrents from current games. As the narratives from current female MMO players illustrate, gender bias can be coded into games and perpetuated via the game culture in ways that have nothing to do with actual game-play mechanics. Understanding why there aren't more women in gaming cannot be answered by questions that simply focus on game mechanics.

Ultimately, MMOs are an interesting game genre to think about not because of the particular game-play styles they provide but for the breadth of styles that can coexist in the same system. These environments make it possible to shift from combat to customization to socialization in a coherent way. Thus, it's interesting to think of MMOs as being able to broaden the scope of gamers' play motivations—for both men and women. Also, there are very few other places (in physical or virtual worlds) where high-school students are collaborating with professors, retired war veterans, and stay-at-home moms. Despite the constraints of our current MMOs, I am hopeful that future iterations will help foster a more gender-inclusive sensibility by encouraging gamers to broaden their perspectives and desires.

References

Brunner, C., Bennett, D., and Honey, M. (1998). Girl games and technological desire. In J. Cassell and H. Jenkins (eds.), *From Barbie to Mortal Kombat: Gender and Computer Games* (pp. 72–88). Cambridge: The MIT Press.

Carr, D. (2005). Contexts, Pleasures and Preferences: Girls Playing Computer Games. Paper presented at the DiGRA, Vancouver.

Crawford, C. (2005). Women in games. *The Escapist, 17,* 3–9.

Diamond, J. (1998). Why Is Sex Fun?: The Evolution of Human Sexuality. New York: Basic Books.

Francis, T. (2006). Murder incorporated. *PC Gamer, 13*(1), 90–93.

Jenson, J., and de Castell, S. (2005). *Her Own Boss: Gender and the Pursuit of Incompetent Play.* Paper presented at the DiGRA, Vancouver.

Low, B. (2001). *Why Sex Matters: A Darwinian Look at Human Behavior.* Princeton, N.J.: Princeton University Press.

Steen, F., and Owens, S. (2001). Evolution's pedagogy: An adaptationist model of pretense and entertainment. *Journal of Cognition and Culture, 1,* 289–321.

Taylor, T. L. (2003). Multiple pleasures: Women and online gaming. *Convergence, 9,* 21–46.

Wright, R. (1995). The Moral Animal: Why We Are the Way We Are: The New Science of Evolutionary Psychology. New York: Vintage.

Yee, N. (2007a). The Daedalus Project. Retrieved October 17, 2007. http://www.nickyee .com/daedalus.

Yee, N. (2007b). Motivations for play in online games. *Journal of CyberPsychology and Behavior, 9,* 772–775.

Mizuko Ito

Although never characterized as a social movement, Japanese gaming culture has produced highly successful games that have crossed gender boundaries. Japanese games such as *Pac-Man, Donkey Kong, Dig Dug,* and *PaRappa The Rapper* provided alternatives to shooting, fighting, and racing as idioms for game play. Further, across game genres, many Japanese games have been characterized by relatively girl-friendly cute characters derived from Japanese animation. Many of the most memorable characters in Japanese gaming—Mario, Yoshi, Baby Kong, and the early *Dragon Quest* and *Final Fantasy* characters—have been depicted with big eyes and cute childlike proportions. More recently, Pikachu demonstrated on a global scale that cute characters and (relatively) nonviolent game play idioms appeal to both boys and girls. Although gaming culture in Japan is still dominated by boys, the post-*Pokémon* gaming landscape has a strong presence of girls' games and gamers. The percentage of gamers who are female has been steadily increasing from about 15 percent a decade ago to 30 percent in 2005 (CESA 2005). In 2006, one of the most popular arcade games in Japan was *Oshare Majo,* a fashion game oriented to young girls; the super-cute *Tamagotchi* game for Nintendo DS topped the sales charts that same year; and *Brain Age* is being touted as a breakthrough game in crossing boundaries of both age and gender. This chapter describes some historical and ethnographic cases of Japanese games as examples of gender politics of gaming that differ from what we find in the United States.

The role of Japanese gaming in bringing girls into electronic gaming should not be overlooked. *Barbie Fashion Designer* and *The Sims* are generally cited as key milestones in bringing women and girls into gaming, but *Pokémon* has been at least as influential in attracting girls in both Japan and the United States. The contemporary post-*Pokémon* Japanese media mix embodies representational and structural features that suggest a certain fluidity in how gender is coded. These features of Japanese gaming have proven to be attractive to both boys and girls in a wide range of cultural contexts. Japanese media complicate Euro-American understandings of how representations and play mechanics get identified as masculine or feminine. They also complicate any lingering assumptions we might have about whether boys can identify with cute and girls can identify with geek cultural forms. A close look at the cultural context and content of Japanese games can denaturalize (Yanagisako and Delaney 1995), or make less commonsensical, some of our assumptions about gender representation. In this chapter I first describe some cultural and historical contexts of Japanese gaming including media mixing, cute culture, and *otaku* culture. I then describe the gender dynamics of two media mixes, *Yu-Gi-Oh!* and *Hamtaro.*

Contexts of Japanese Gaming Cultures

Japanese games and media mixes grow out of social and cultural contexts closely connected but distinct from the U.S. gaming scene. Just as Holin Lin (this volume) argues for the important influence of cultural norms and physical settings of play, I argue that Japanese games grow out of and play out in specific social and cultural contexts. The gender dynamics of Japanese gaming cannot be read from the representational content of the game without first understanding how that content is embedded within a broader media ecology and certain crosscutting social and cultural structures. As T. L. Taylor (this volume) states, "context and structure matter"; the content of media has a privileged but not fully determining effect on social and cultural dynamics of play. Before discussing the cases of *Yu-Gi-Oh!* and *Hamtaro,* I describe some of the key contextual features of Japanese gaming: the mixing and cross-referencing among media types, cultures of cute, and *otaku.*

The Media Mix

Electronic gaming in Japan is one component of a broader media ecology that includes anime (Japanese animation), manga (Japanese comics and graphic novels), trading card games, toys, and character merchandise. I borrow the native industry term *media mix* to describe this linked character-based media system. Japan has a more integrated and synergistic relationship among media types than one tends to see in the case of U.S. children's culture. Popular series will make their way to all the different platforms of the media mix and each plays off the strengths of the other. Weekly or monthly manga magazines provide the serialized narrative foundation for the series, as well as a venue for disseminating information about new game and toy releases, strategy, and tournaments. Television series provide a focus for younger children, a broader casual audience, and a marketing channel. Games then incorporate that same content into an interactive form, building on existing recognition of character and backstory established through the narrative media. The synergies among the different media have grown from the postwar period to the present, beginning with manga in the fifties, and then incorporating the anime and toy industries in the sixties and seventies. While electronic gaming was in a somewhat separate domain through the eighties, by the nineties it was well integrated with the overall media mix of manga and anime characters, aided by the popularity of game-origin characters such as Mario and Pikachu.

The Japanese media mix is also distinctive because of the centrality of serialized print media. Manga are generally (but not always) the primary texts of the media mix, generating the characters and narrative that go on to populate anime and games. The Japanese manga industry is unique in that it constitutes about 38 percent of all printed matter in Japan (Schodt 1996) and spans a much wider range of genres and topics than in other countries. Topics taken up by manga include fictional and nonfictional topics that are generally not published in comic books elsewhere, for example, romance, pornography, business, child rearing, mah-jongg, sports, and historical fiction. Today, manga are enjoyed by all age groups in Japan and are generally the primary literacy experiences for children. Manga are such a central fixture of Japanese childhood that one editor asked me with puzzlement after our interview, "What do American children *do* without manga?" Serialized manga, printed vastly and diversely on cheap newsprint, are a way for content industries to test the market. When a series takes off, it can be simultaneously released in an integrated way throughout the other avenues in the media mix ecology. This base in popular, serialized print media can support long-running, complex narratives that can be easily revisited and mined by other media platforms.

This media mix ecology means that within a given content series there are multiple forms of participation and multiple avenues to different modes of engagement and play. The barriers to initial entry are very low in the case of television and manga content, and allow a mechanism for maintaining casual engagement with a series or sparking an interest in interactive gaming. This parallels what Nick Yee (this volume) describes in the case of MMOs as "sub-games embedded in a larger system." A player who might be drawn initially to the social dimensions of MMOs can develop an interest in the hard mastery of the game and vice versa. As Lin and Taylor (this volume) argue, one reason why women don't game is because they lack social networks and settings for learning about gaming. In Japan, some of this function of exposing new players to gaming is performed through the linkage between different media formats. Avenues to gaming are more widely distributed across different social settings, including settings and practices that are more accessible to girls.

Cultures of Cute

Japanese media mix content is also distinctive because of the centrality of *kawaii* (cute) culture epitomized by characters like Hello Kitty and Pikachu. Sharon Kinsella (1995) describes kawaii culture as one of the dominant forms of Japanese popular culture in the eighties and beyond. "Kawaii or 'cute' essentially means childlike; it celebrates sweet, adorable, innocent, pure, simple, genuine, gentle, vulnerable, weak and inexperienced social behaviour and physical appearances" (p. 220). It is a cultural style that manifests in domains including pop idols, handwriting, fashion, speech, music, and food, but has its most iconic manifestations in media mix characters. Kinsella (1995; 2000) suggests that girl-identified cultures of cute operate from a marginalized position of resistance and irresponsibility, cut off from mainstream sources of power. She echoes the arguments of Lise Skov and Brian Moeran (1995) when they describe how Japanese women came to take a central role in the domains of popular culture and consumption, reflecting their disenfranchised role in production. In the cultural logic of Japanese childhood, kawaii is located in opposition to the *kakkoii* (cool) kids culture of boy-oriented superheroes, fighting games, and robots. But while kakkoii is a frequently used adjective, it is a less clearly defined cultural style than kawaii culture. Although there are notable crossovers in genres such as *kowa-kawa* (scary-cute) or *kimo-kawa* (gross cute), or in series such as *Pokémon,* typically kawaii and kakkoii have distinctive genre conventions that mark them as culturally in tension.

Although kawaii is a marginal cultural form, identified as feminine and childlike, it can be adopted to some extent by people of all ages and genders.

It is quite unremarkable to see characters such as Miffy or Snoopy advertising adult-oriented services such as travel agencies and insurance policies. Popular culture aimed at very young boys is overwhelmingly kawaii, and even young men are often fans of kawaii idols and anime characters, adopt cute fashion, and buy character goods. More controversially, schoolgirls and childlike manga characters are frequently depicted as objects of adult male desire. Trade shows like the annual Character Show are oriented primarily to the young adult male, and one sees erotic images of young anime girl characters alongside booths selling Snoopy pencils and hamster note pads. Although a limited market overseas, *bishoujo* (beautiful girl) genres of manga and games are a sizeable portion of the Japanese market, often featuring cute but sexy girl characters. The "dating sim" genre, feature narratives for getting to know bishoujo, has barely registered in the United States, but constitutes about a quarter of the market for Japanese electronic games.

Although kawaii culture has found a large international audience, its cultural influence is something that is still relatively distinctive to Japan. As in most Euro-American contexts, it is culturally acceptable for girls to adopt kakkoii boys' culture to some extent. But unlike U.S. girlie culture of pink ponies and Barbie dolls, kawaii culture is not as strongly ghettoized as *just* for young girls. Not only is kawaii and children's culture fetishized as something unique, pure, and special—a tendency common to most cultures with modern notions of childhood—but kawaii culture is also seen as something that people with diverse gender and age identities can adopt and emulate.

Otaku

In addition to kawaii culture, Japan is also home to the distinctive subculture of *otaku,* a term that can be roughly translated as "media geek." In the mainstream, *otaku* is a pejorative label attached to young men and women who are avid fans of media mix content, and who go one step further to remake and traffic in the elements of that culture (Eng 2001). Otaku culture is important to the discussion here because it represents a relationship to technology and media that moves beyond casual consumption into the more activist and expert identities associated with creative production. Otaku are not casual consumers of media and technology; they are experts, connoisseurs, enthusiasts, and hackers of media culture. Hard technical mastery in games and computers also has an inextricable tie to otaku culture; game geeking is probably the most stereotypical of otaku-identified practices. In an essay on otaku culture, I argue that otaku embody the ethic of amateur cultural production, remix, and connoisseurship increasingly central to media literacy in a digital age (Ito 2006).

How otaku identities play out in different cultural domains has implications for how girls and boys engage with technology. Just as in the United States, information technology geekdom tends to be coded as male, socially challenged, and unwelcoming to girls. Otaku-like engagement with media is culturally acceptable for young boys who spend hours at their game consoles or playing trading card games, but girls who are highly involved in media mix content tend to be more socially marginalized. In my fieldwork with elementary-aged boys and girls in Japan, I found that it was generally cool for elementary-aged boys to have an intense interest in media culture and games, but the most popular girls tended to be focused more on real-life friendships than fantasy-oriented play.

Girls who do have otaku leanings tend to gravitate to media formats that are less technology intensive. The two arenas of otaku practices that historically have been dominated by girls are the relatively low-tech practices of *doujinshi* (amateur manga) and *cosplay* (costume play). Although nearly invisible to the mainstream in Japan, the otaku subculture of amateur comics is immense. The biannual Comic Market, dominated by young working-class women, is the largest convention in Japan, convening more than five hundred thousand people buying and selling doujinshi. Men tend to create and consume doujinshi depicting cute girls or beautiful women characters. The most popular genre of doujinshi created by young women is of the *yaoi* and *bishounen* (beautiful boy) variety, which is analogous to slash in the United States. Popular male characters from *shounen* (boys) comics are rendered in alternative and often sexually explicit narratives of boy-boy affection (McLelland 2001). In cosplay, young women dress up as both boy and girl characters often in a performative version of yaoi counter-narratives. Yaoi narratives produced by girls for girls give voice to women's and girls' fantasies, objectifying beautiful boy characters and using them to depict forms of intimacy that are a far cry from their real-life experiences of gender and sexuality. Although yaoi subcultures are not yet strongly represented in electronic gaming, they are indicative of alternative forms of content and activist media production driven by the interests of young women (Flanagan and Nissenbaum this volume; Taylor this volume).

Today's Media Mix

The media mix platform, cultures of cute, and cultures of otaku are some of the social contexts that structure children's engagements with new media in Japan. More specifically, in recent history, the contemporary media mix for children must be understood in relation to *Pokémon,* a breakthrough media form that has informed all subsequent media mix series. *Pokémon* pushed the media mix equation into new directions. Rather than being pursued serially, as in the case of manga being converted into anime, the media mix of *Pokémon* developed the more integrated and synergistic media mix that we see today. *Pokémon* also set the precedent of locating the portable media formats of trading cards and handheld networked game play at the center rather than at the periphery of the media ecology. This had the effect of channeling media engagement into collective social settings both within and outside the home as kids looked for opportunities to link up their game devices and play with and trade their Pokémon cards. Trading cards, Game Boys, and character merchandise create what Anne Allison (2004) has called "pocket fantasies," "digitized icons . . . that children carry with them wherever they go" and "that straddle the border between phantasm and everyday life" (p. 42).

Pokémon broke new ground by hybridizing styles and game play that crossed gender lines. Its large pantheon meant that its developers could include creatures that were both kakkoii and kawaii, but by and large the monsters embody the kawaii aesthetic. The game mechanic is also hybrid, including competitive battles between the monsters, as well as a dimension of pet care, nurturing, and social networking with more feminine overtones. The main character in the original series was a boy, but one of his close companions is a preadolescent girl Pokémon trainer. The current television series has a girl trainer as a main character on par with Ash (the main protagonist of the series), indicating that girls are increasingly seen as the target demographic. Part of *Pokémon*'s success was based on its ability to appeal to girls as well as boys. Given that Game Boy gaming was so central to *Pokémon,* it also had the side effect of drawing girls to gaming in large numbers. The dominance of the Game Boy as the preferred platform for girls persists to this day.

My research in Japan was conducted in the wake of the *Pokémon* phenomenon. From 1998 to 2002, I conducted fieldwork in the greater Tokyo area among children, parents, and media industrialists at the height of *Yu-Gi-Oh!*'s popularity. My research focused on *Yu-Gi-Oh!* as a case study, as it was the most popular series in currency at the time (see figure 7.1). My description is drawn from interviews with these parties involved with *Yu-Gi-Oh!*, my own engagements with the various media forms, and participant observation at sites of player activity including weekly tournaments at card shops, trade shows, homes, and an after-school center for elementary-aged children. Among girls, *Hamtaro* was the most popular children's series at the time, so it became a secondary focus for my research (see figure 7.2). I also conducted research that was not content-specific, interviewing parents, observing a wide range of activities at the after-school center, and reviewing diverse children's media. I turn now to descriptions of *Yu-Gi-Oh!* and *Hamtaro* and the gender dynamics surrounding these two series.

Yu-Gi-Oh!

Like other media mixes, Yu-Gi-Oh! relies on cross-referencing between serialized manga, a television anime series, a card game, video games, occasional movie releases, and a plethora of character merchandise. The manga ran for 343 installments between 1996 and 2004 in the weekly magazine *Shonen Jump* and is still continuing as an animated series and in spin-off manga series. In 2001 the anime and card game was released in the United States, and soon after in the UK and other parts of the world. The series centers on a boy, Mutoh Yugi, who is a game master, and gets involved in various adventures with a small cohort of friends and rivals. The narrative focuses on long sequences of card game duels, stitched together by an adventure narrative. Yugi and his friends engage in a card game derivative of the U.S. card game Magic: The Gathering. The series is devoted to duels that explicate the detailed esoterica of the games, such as strategies and rules of game play, properties of cards, and fine points of card collecting and trading. Although embellished with fantastic characters and narratives, the manga and anime function as game-play tutorials and marketing for the Yu-Gi-Oh! card game. The height of Yu-Gi-Oh!'s popularity in Japan was between 1999 and 2001. A 2000 survey of three hundred students in a Kyoto elementary school indicated that by the third grade *every* student owned some Yu-Gi-Oh! cards (Asahi Shinbun 2001).

Unlike *Pokémon* and *Digimon, Yu-Gi-Oh!* has relied more heavily on aesthetics and play mechanics more tied to kakkoii cultures. Although some of the characters are kawaii (most notably Yugi), the series overall is based on

Figure 7.1   *Yu-Gi-Oh!* (see color plate). © 1996 Kazuki Takahashi.

a dark, occult-like theme and does not rely as strongly on the bright colors so characteristic of *Pokémon*. Unlike the cuddly Pokémon and Digimon, the monsters in *Yu-Gi-Oh!* are mostly kakkoii, scary and ferocious (e.g., Blue-Eyes White Dragon, Dark Magician), with just a few exceptions (e.g., Time Wizard, Baby Dragon, Dark Magician Girl) that seem designed as small concessions to girls. When I spoke to girls about their favorite card characters, they tended to list these cuter ones. Unlike *Pokémon*'s Misty, who is an accomplished Pokémon trainer, Yugi's girl companion is a mediocre duelist and takes on a spectator, victim, and support role. The series is also more closely tied to competitive

Figure 7.2   Hamtaro and friends (from left to right: Oxnard, Hamtaro, Bijou, and Boss) (see color plate). © R. Kawai / 2000, 2006 Shogakukan, SMDE, TV Tokyo. All rights reserved.

game play and the narrative tends to focus on Yugi's progression through different competitive scenarios like tournaments or the hostile incursions of evil duelists. These features of *Yu-Gi-Oh!* have coded it as much less girl-friendly than *Pokémon* or *Digimon*.

At the same time, it was such a central part of children's popular culture during the peak years that girls couldn't avoid it. Almost all girls owned some *Yu-Gi-Oh!* cards and watched the anime at least sporadically. When *Yu-Gi-Oh!* tournaments were held at the after-school center I observed, a handful of girls participated, but they tended to watch in the sidelines even though they likely had their own stash of cards. When the girls did participate, they seemed well versed in the characters and idioms of game play, attesting to their ongoing role as spectators in the series. *Yu-Gi-Oh!* has also been popular fodder for yaoi doujinshi, fan fiction, and cosplay, depicting tender intimacy that women readers see as a homoerotic subtext to the narrative of competition. Popular couplings include romance between the rivals Kaiba and Yugi, or best friends Joey and Yugi. Even with a series that seems clearly marked as boys' culture, the actual gender dynamics as it gets taken up in everyday contexts of play can be unexpectedly complex.

Hamtaro

As we saw with many of the media mix franchises that followed *Pokémon*— *Yu-Gi-Oh!*, *Beyblade*, *Duel Masters*, *Mushiking*—for content that centers on gaming, boys' culture is still central. It sets the trends in media mixing that girls' content follows. But girls' content *is* following. The trend is slower, but as of the late nineties most popular girls' content will find its way to Game Boy, though not usually to platforms like Nintendo consoles or PlayStation. Otaku-like forms of character development and multiyear and multithreaded narrative arcs are also becoming more common in series oriented toward girls. Ever since *Sailor Moon,* it has also become more common for girl-oriented series to include action and violent conflict that was historically more associated with boys' content. Series like *Cardcaptor Sakura, Corrector Yui,* and *Angelic Layer* relied on boyish idioms of action and battle but were rendered in the *shojo* (young girl) style of manga. Although the main characters in these series were girls, they appealed to both girls and boys. One example of how the dynamics of new media mixes is making its way into girls content is the case of *Tottoko Hamutarou* (or *Hamtaro,* as it is known in English), the series that was most popular among girls during the period of my fieldwork.

Hamtaro is an intrepid hamster owned by a little girl. The story originated in picture-book form in the late nineties and became an animated series that aired 296 episodes from 2000 to 2006, and continues in a short five-minute episode format. After being released as a television anime, Hamtaro attracted a wide following, quickly becoming the most popular licensed character for girls. It was released in the United States, the UK, and other parts of the world in 2002. Hamtaro is an interesting case because it is clearly coded as girls' content, and the human protagonist is a girl. But the central character, Hamtaro, is a boy. The character has attracted a fairly wide following among boys as well as girls, though it was dwarfed by Yu-Gi-Oh! in the boys' market during the time I was conducting my fieldwork. The story makes use of a formula that was developed by *Pokémon,* which is of a proliferating set of characters that create esoteric knowledge and domains of expertise. While not nearly as extensive as the Pokémon pantheon or Yu-Gi-Oh! cards, Hamtaro is part of a group of about twenty hamster friends, each of which has a distinct personality and life situation. To date the series has introduced more than fifty quirky hamster characters, and complex narratives of relationships, compatibilities, antagonisms, and rivalries. The formula is quite different from the classic one for girls' manga or anime that has tended to have shorter runs and is tightly focused on a small band of characters including the heroine, friend, love interest, and rival. Instead, Hamtaro is a curious blend of multiyear soap opera and media mix esoterica, blending the girlie focus on friendship and romance with otaku-like attention to details and a character-based knowledge industry.

In addition to the narrative and character development that follows some of the formulas established by *Pokémon,* the series also exhibits the convergent characteristics of the contemporary media mix. Hamtaro's commercial success hinges on an incredibly wide array of licensed products that make him an intimate presence in girls' lives even when he is not on the screen. These products include board games, clothing, curry packages and corn soup in addition to the usual battery of pencils, stationery, stickers, toys, and stuffed animals. Another important element of the Hamtaro media mix is Game Boy games. Five have been released so far. The first (never released overseas), *Tomodachi Daisakusen Dechu (The Great Friendship Plan),* was heavily promoted on television. Unlike most game commercials that focus on the content of the game, the spot featured two girls sitting on a bed with their Game Boys, discussing the game. The game blends the traditionally girlie content of relationships and fortune-telling with certain formulas around collection and exchange developed in the boys' media mix. Girls collect data on their friends and input their birthdays. The game then generates a match with a particular hamster character, and then predicts certain personality traits from that. The game allows players to predict whether different people will get along as friends or as couples as well. Girls can also exchange data between Game Boy cartridges. The game builds on a model of collection and exchange that was established in the industry since *Pokémon,* but applied to a less overtly competitive girl-oriented exchange system.

Conclusion

In this chapter I provide some historical background and a description of Japanese media mixes to describe game-related gender dynamics in another culture. While gender differences are resilient in Japan as elsewhere, there are also points of fluidity and crossover that differ from what we see in the United States. Japanese media mix cultures are increasingly influential overseas, and cannot be dismissed as informative but irrelevant oddities. Culturally engrained assumptions about what boys and girls like can stand in the way of alternative gender politics and representations. The case of Japanese media mixes challenges culturally specific assumptions about the relations between feminine and masculine culture, boys and girls, in the following four ways:

First, kawaii cultures provide an example of feminine forms of representations that are not ghettoized as only for girls. Although gaming, particularly action genres, is still dominated by kakkoii cultures, there is a stronger presence of kawaii cultures in the gaming mainstream than what we see in Euro-American gaming. Although boys do tend to engage with kakkoii culture and vice versa, it also can be culturally appropriate for boys and girls to consume both kakkoii and kawaii forms of gaming culture.

Second, hybrid media formats such as the Japanese media mix can lead to a more socially distributed set of pathways into gaming cultures. If popular content in television and print media makes its way regularly into games and vice versa, it provides multiple avenues for translating both girl-oriented and boy-oriented culture into interactive and digital formats.

Third, amateur and otaku subcultures of youth media production in Japan depict alternative gender representations that are in demand among young people but are underrepresented within commercial media. Although gaming culture has relied heavily on sexualized and submissive representations of women, it has done much less to objectify male characters for a female gaze. The immense appeal of yaoi boy-love fantasies in Japan, and increasingly abroad, indicate a latent demand for representations of feminized, sexualized, and sensitive male characters. It may be time for a women's gaming movement to listen to these voices. Otaku cultures are an important example of player- and youth-driven innovation in gender representation.

Finally, feminine and masculine cultural forms get taken up and reshaped within different contexts of play in unpredictable ways. Boys can engage with kawaii cultural forms if they are given appropriate cultural warrants for play, and vice versa. This dynamic operates when action-oriented play mechanics are depicted in a kawaii cultural style, or when fans find a homoerotic subtext of boy love in a kakkoii manga series. Despite the resilience of gender-differentiated social and cultural structure in Japan, the on-the-ground dynamics of media mixing, media engagement, and play are evidence of a shifting set of gender dynamics intersecting with gaming cultures.

Acknowledgments

The research and writing for this chapter was funded by a postdoctoral fellowship from the Japan Society for the Promotion of Science, the Abe Fellowship, the Annenberg Center for Communication at the University of Southern California, and a grant from the MacArthur Foundation. My research assistants in Japan were Tomoko Kawamura and Kyoko Sekizuka. This chapter has benefited from comments from Pippin Barr, Yasmin Kafai, Holin Lee, T. L. Taylor, and Nick Yee.

References

Allison, A. (2004). Cuteness and Japan's millennial product. In J. Tobin (ed.), *Pikachu's Global Adventure: The Rise and Fall of Pokémon* (pp. 34–52). Durham: Duke University Press.

Asahi Shinbun. (2001). Otousan datte Hamaru. In *Asahi Shinbun* (p. 24). Tokyo.

CESA (2005). 2005 CESA Ippan Seikatsu Chousa Houkokusho. Computer Entertainment Suppliers Association, Tokyo.

Eng, L. (2001). The politics of otaku. http://www.cjas.org/~leng/otaku-p.htm.

Ito, M. (2006). Japanese media mixes and amateur cultural exchange. In D. Buckingham and R. Willett (eds.), *Digital Generations*. Lawrence Erlbaum.

Kinsella, S. (2000). Adult Manga: Culture and Power in Contemporary Japanese Society. Honolulu: University of Hawaii Press.

Kinsella, S. (1995). Cuties in Japan. In L. Skov and B. Moeran (eds.), *Women, Media, and Consumption in Japan* (pp. 220–254). Honolulu: University of Hawaii Press.

McLelland, M. (2001). Local meanings in global space: A case study of women's "Boy Love" Web sites in Japanese and English. *Mots Pluriels.*

Schodt, F. L. (1996). *Dreamland Japan: Writings on Modern Manga.* Berkeley: Stonebridge.

Skov, L., and B. Moeran (1995). Hiding in the light: From Oshin to Yoshimoto Banana. In L. Skov and B. Moeran (eds.), *Woman Media and Consumption in Japan* (pp. 1–74). Honolulu: University of Hawaii Press.

Yanagisako, S., and C. Delaney (1995). *Naturalizing Power: Essays in Feminist Cultural Analysis.* New York: Routledge.

8   Gender Play in a Tween Gaming Club

Yasmin B. Kafai

Much of current research on adult gaming has focused on why and how women join online role-playing games and what their experiences in these game communities and spaces are (see Lin this volume; Taylor this volume; and Yee this volume). It is only recently that our attention has turned to younger online players. Being online is an increasingly important part of teen social life in which teens initiate and develop relationships through e-mail, chats, blogs, and virtual worlds. Gaming is still considered a male-dominated domain; studies have shown how girls position themselves as game players by either challenging or conforming to gender conventions (Pelletier this volume; Schott and Kambouri 2003).

As Taylor (this volume) has argued, it is crucial to understand how players inhabit gaming cultures to understand the complex interactions between gender and play. Those few studies that have examined the relationship between girls and gaming focus on how girls play games popular with boys (Carr 2005), how girls compete in teams against boys (Beavis 2005), or how girls at home negotiate access to games with male family members (Schott and Horrell 2000). A common factor in all this research is that girls' access and participation to gaming is studied in relation to male-dominated games and contexts. To expand our discussions, it may be helpful to examine participation in game spaces known to be popular with girls. For instance, Beavis and Charles (2005) found that boys' approaches to playing *The Sims* provided critical insights into the gendering of gaming practices.

In this chapter I examine gaming practices in a virtual world called *Whyville*. More than 68 percent of its registered players are girls, ages ten to sixteen (Aschbacher 2003; see also Kafai and Giang 2007). At the time of this study, *Whyville* counted more than 1.2 million registered users logging more than 50 million page views per year to explore topics in science, economics, and citizenship. Players, known as Whyvillians, become part of *Whyville*'s community by creating their own avatar-based personas composed of different face parts. Through participation in science activities, Whyvillians can earn at every log-in a regular salary in "clams," the virtual currency. In addition, Whyvillians can design, sell, and trade face parts for their avatars and projectiles for play activities. On a typical day, players log in to *Whyville* and check their y-mail accounts (the name of the e-mail system used in *Whyville*) for new messages and review their clam salary ledgers for current account status. Whyvillians then head out to popular places such as the beach, or one of the planetary colonies, to chat with others. They also meet to play checker games or complete more science activities to increase their salaries. Frequently, one will find them at the virtual mall called Akbar's, browsing through the latest offerings of face parts for eyes, hair, lips, clothes, or other accessories before deciding on a purchase (see figure 8.1).

Whyville is what Danah Boyd calls a digital public (2006) that provides tweens and teens with a "youth space, a place to gather and see and be seen by peers. Publics are critical to the coming-of-age narrative because they provide the framework for building cultural knowledge." In *Whyville,* players can create their own online representations, and socialize with other players by chatting, hanging out, cruising around, or playing games. These types of digital publics have become very popular among youth, as indicated by the growing memberships in virtual worlds such as *Club Penguin, Habbo Hotel, Virtual Laguna Beach,* or *Teen Second Life.* Previous research in public spaces such as lunchrooms and on school yards used the idea of gender play to help us understand the purposes and contexts in which girls and boys experience and construct gender. Barrie Thorne's (1993; 2005) work, which inspired the title of this chapter, emphasizes gender play as social construction by examining the actions youth take to affirm or negate differences. She also recognized the complexities of gender relations, meaning that gender might not always be in the foreground of interactions, can fluctuate, and gives room for possibilities of change.

The location for our study in *Whyville* was an after-school club in an elementary school. About twenty girls and boys between the ages of ten and twelve participated over a seven-week period; some teens came regularly for an hour while others dropped in and out. We were able to observe, interview, and track tweens' interactions online in our data collections (Kafai et al. 2007). We

Figure 8.1   Different Whyville activities: trading post (top) and beach (bottom) (see color plate).

were interested in the many ways boys and girls inhabit and share the boundaries between the virtual world of *Whyville* and the physical location of the after-school club, following Thorne's (1993) suggestion that research should start "with a sense of the whole rather than with the assumption of gender as separate and different" (p. 108) and focus on context in our analyses to cross the gender divide.

In this study we focused on game play in *Whyville* in an after-school club because it allowed us to observe tweens' online and off-line interactions designing avatars and learning teleporting. We know from our analyses of data that all *Whyville* players participate in these activities (Kafai et al. 2007). Previous research has shown that becoming a proficient gamer is a complex enterprise that involves peer networks (Gee 2003). In our observations of the *Whyville* club, we found that most boys and girls preferred playing together in all-female or all-male groups of two or three around one computer to sitting with someone of the opposite sex. These gender play patterns are fairly typical of what has been observed in other public spaces such as school yards, lunchrooms, and classrooms (Thorne 1993). We identified three exceptions that facilitated peer networking and teaching across gender boundaries: prior experience, proximity, and public play. In the following sections, I present examples of how these three aspects come into play when learning teleporting and designing avatars.

Multiple Access Points to Insider Knowledge

Insider knowledge, or as Consalvo (2007) called it, "gaming capital," is at the core of gaming, which players either discover through trial and error or interacting with others. We selected the two activities of designing avatars (Kafai, Fields, and Cook 2007) and traveling to secret places (Fields and Kafai 2007a) because both illustrate key aspects of becoming and being a player in *Whyville* and are of relevance to the field of game studies. Like most of *Whyville*'s activities, both involve multiple types of logistical and cultural knowledge. For instance, designing the look of one's avatar is a common practice that is easily visible to all on *Whyville*. But there is still a lot to be learned about the cultural practices of how to assemble an attractive and interesting avatar in this world. In contrast, traveling to a secret place, such as the planet system in *Whyville*, is an activity that cannot be observed directly in people's online interactions because the typed command is only visible to the player outside of *Whyville*. Most other sites in *Whyville* can be selected from a pull-down menu that allows players to navigate between different sites.

Teleporting

Like all other games, *Whyville* has its share of secret commands and places. We selected a simple command, called teleporting, which when typed in a player's chat automatically transports the player to social places not listed in the destination menu on *Whyville* (e.g., "teleport moon" takes a player to a space in *Whyville* called the Moon not accessible in any other manner). We focused on how club members learned about this command that one cannot observe in others' chats (the typed command "teleport moon" is not visible to others) unless people are publicly discussing a social gathering at one of the teleport locations (see figure 8.2a). The only exception to this can be found on select cheat sites where instructions on teleporting are included in tips for new players (see also Fields and Kafai 2007b).

For most club members, information about teleporting spreads along gender lines. For example, one experienced club member liked to throw projectiles with three other boys, Gabe, Aidan, and Kyle, so it is not surprising that all of them would learn in quick succession how to teleport. We observed the same pattern of knowledge sharing in a group of girls. But we also noticed how proximity in seating and prior experience provided exceptions to these more typical forms of distribution along gender lines. Some club members learned how to teleport in the club by asking other club members physically sitting next to them. Gabe learned from Briana while they were working on separate computers side by side. Gabe learned to teleport in the context of a social need to meet his friend Marv, a classmate who did not participate in the after-school club. In addition, since he was sitting next to Briana, she was able to observe him typing and corrected his initial mistake of typing "teleport to moon" instead of "teleport moon," a mistake that she made frequently when she learned how to teleport on *Whyville* earlier that day.

Club members with some *Whyville* experience took the lead in learning about teleporting and our analyses indicate that this applied to all six boys and girls. These teens had more opportunities to be on *Whyville* during the day than other club members. While it is not clear how the sixth graders were introduced to teleporting during that time, it seems natural that these would

Figure 8.2   Teleporting (top) and Saturn (bottom) (see color plate).

be among the first club members to use teleport. We know that two among the first youth to teleport found out on *Whyville* by asking questions online. This is perhaps the easiest learning method to identify since it is literally spelled out in the text. Consider one club member with the screen name "bluwave" who on the third day of the club sought online advice on a lot of things including whispering, making friends, dancing, and teleporting. Like many of the club members, bluwave did not ask how to teleport but how to get to the moon. She tried asking anonymous people several times before getting the answers she needed. What's important here is that familiarity with the world and knowledge of how to gather information in *Whyville* played an important role in how she gained access to this insider knowledge.

Over time, teleporting became a much more public activity, with youths yelling across the room to one another to "meet me at the Moon!" This probably allowed other youth to overhear their conversations. In addition, as more youths teleported, others could glance at computer screens while wandering the room and see places like the Moon. The rest discovered a particular teleport location, Saturn, in an unusual clubwide social incident five weeks into the project. On this day, Leslie, who had learned about Saturn through experimentation a few days earlier, organized a get-together with Marissa, Ulani, and Isabel on that planet, inviting them by y-mail to meet her at Saturn. This invitation seems to have provided the instigation for Marissa and Ulani to teleport for the first time, and while Isabel knew how to teleport to the Moon, Mars, and Earth, she had not been to Saturn before that day. While at Saturn, a Whyvillian who was not part of the club insulted Ulani, who yelled out to the club that someone had insulted her on Saturn. Immediately several other club members teleported to Saturn, two for the first time (they had to ask how to spell it), and threw projectiles at the offender. By the end of the day, almost all the club members had been to Saturn, doubling the daily average of Saturn visits by club members, a trend that continued through the remainder of the week.

While our initial expectations—based on teens' self-chosen arrangements—would predict that insider knowledge would stay within gender boundaries, our observations indicate otherwise. Proximity as prior experience and public play were equally important avenues for sharing insider knowledge across gender boundaries. In fact, one could argue that the club setting facilitates a sharing across gender boundaries as the last incident illustrates when all club members, girls and boys, rallied around Ulani. This illustrates the passing between outsider and insider status in both the physically and virtually located communities of our study (Fields and Kafai 2007a).

Avatar Design

In *Whyville,* players have the ability to customize their avatars with various two-dimensional face parts and accessories; more than thirty thousand elements have been drawn and sold by other players. Perhaps no other aspect of game research has focused more on issues of gender stereotyping than players' representation and choices of avatars. Taylor (2003) illustrates how different factors and values about immersion, identity, and legitimacy determine in which ways game designers structure virtual environments and content available to players. Most commercial games provide players with menus of choices for selecting avatar types and for customizing clothing, hair, and other features of their appearance. In contrast to these select-from-a-menu choices of most multiplayer online games, virtual worlds such as *Teen Second Life* and *Whyville* are entirely based on player-generated content. These avatars are not ephemeral and spurious creations: players spend considerable time selecting and customizing them and then interacting with others online.

All girls and boys in the club, with no exception, were engaged in designing and accessorizing their avatars. In fact, activities involving the design, selection, sale, and sharing of face parts are among the most popular in *Whyville* (Feldon and Kafai in press). We also know from the repository of the *Whyville Times* (*Whyville*'s weekly citizen-written newspaper) that online representation is of interest to all *Whyville* players: close to six hundred articles refer to face parts and about three hundred articles openly share opinions about how to look good, where to shop, and how *not* to dress. One of the reasons why this might be the case is that all players are given the same avatar when they join *Whyville:* their faces are ovals only furnished with a set of eyes and a mouth, signaling newcomer status. While avatar looks can be copied by buying face parts, players need to learn how to earn clams that provide the funds for purchases. Players also need to select the face parts among the thousands of available offerings and establish what might make them look attractive, which involves a complex mix of personal choices, observations of other avatars, and reading the online newspaper (see figure 8.3).

Figure 8.3 Choosing a nose in *Whyville*—a sequence of face changes (see color plate).

Girls' and boys' engagement with avatars did not change during the seven weeks of the club. Club members would invite same-sex peers to comment on their avatars. For instance, when Marissa called to Molly, "Do you want to see me with earrings?" Molly came around the desk to look at Marissa's screen, and then said, "They look so pretty!" Marissa smiled and said, "Thank you," and the two girls continued to look at the screen. When Paul, Ethan, and Blake found Alex online, Paul called, "He's ugly. Alex, you're ugly!" His tone was light and cheerful, but one boy called back across the room, "Look who's talking, Paul!" Many of these exchanges happened on a daily basis with club members in close proximity.

Boys would also often create affinity looks where two or more players would have coordinated face parts for group ventures into *Whyville*. A primary motivation for a particular avatar look was to affiliate with something or someone they liked, such as a video game character, relative, hobby, or nationality. For instance, one boy created his avatar because "I like Dragon Ball Z and he looks like someone from Dragon Ball Z." This young man made his entire character to look like a favorite video game hero. In contrast, another teen in this category would pick a single part that showed an affinity, like a baseball bat for a love of baseball or a shirt with a sister's name on it. We know that these displays of affinity sometimes led to friendships on *Whyville*—conversations would start based on observations of shared interest in something displayed on a player's avatar.

Both girls and boys talked about avatars being "hot," "ugly," or "cute" when talking about their online appearance and often collaborated with opposite-sex peers when searching new face parts for their avatars or friends. For example, Jill appraised the "bling" (the name of the accessory) necklace that Cole was buying for his girlfriend. She also offered her accessories for free but declined when Cole wanted to have all of them, even if they're "girlie," for his girlfriend. She then moved on to critique with Cole his avatar's looks and accessories including the lip piercing. One could argue that club members considered one another experts in avatar design, especially when purchases or trades were for the opposite gender.

All these examples showcase players designing avatars of the same gender. While we did not find references to gender-swapping in the context of daily club interactions (Berman and Bruckman 2001), some teens revealed in interviews that they had multiple accounts allowing them to earn several salaries, as in the case of one sixth-grade girl named Bev: "[My second account] is a boy! And it's called cuteguy and I just made it for more clams, but sometimes when I am bored I hang out in that account." Besides making her second account a boy, Bev also claimed to create an entirely different look for cuteboy than her primary avatar. A sixth-grade boy named Walter used his second account as a disguise: "Well actually [my second account] is a girl account that I use to trick people that I don't like on *Whyville*. So if they mess with me, I, um—I don't know, I do something to them." These justifications provide some interesting insights on how tweens used gender in their avatar designs other than to accessorize their looks.

Discussion

In this chapter I aim to understand how tweens gain access to insider knowledge in virtual worlds by observing girls and boys in an after-school gaming club. Our gaming context, however, was different from previous research: Whyville.net is a virtual world in which more than two-thirds of registered players are girls. A visit any time during the day would confirm that the majority of avatars visible on the screen are female. One of our initial concerns was whether boys would be interested at all in joining the *Whyville* club—a concern that was quickly dispelled through boys' active engagement and continuous visits to the *Whyville* club and the online space.

In our analysis, we focus on two key aspects of gaming in *Whyville*: designing avatars and teleporting to secret places. We observed some fairly typical gender divisions in who talked to whom in the club, but we also found quite a number of instances where gender boundaries were crossed. We examined the social interactions that contributed to the distribution of gaming expertise. Our example of teleporting is only a small facet of what is needed to become a competent player in *Whyville,* but it allowed us to track on multiple levels different forms of and access to knowledge distribution. While there are situations in which boys or girls choose to organize their play along gender lines, we also have as many examples where other factors structure participation. Prior familiarity such as the daytime playing of sixth graders creates shared experiences, and collaborative play informs others about teleporting. At other times, proximity allows other players to see what's happening or to ask for assistance. We see these different forms of participation as illustrations of the social networking that goes on in gaming communities.

It is possible that the avatar design in *Whyville* creates a more equitable game space. As the interviews with club members reveal, *all* boys and girls were invested in customizing their avatars. It is worthwhile to illustrate in more detail the different intentions that covered aesthetics, coolness, and functionality. Many of the teens would experiment with different themes to design their avatar, in part as a challenge: "I try to pick themes and sometimes they are dorky I think, but I just try to have fun and change it." Some teens did make their avatars similar to themselves either in physical appearance or in personality while others tried to have a certain look or develop a sense of belonging that they could not have in "real" life. Describing his avatar, one boy said, "I want to get a haircut like that but my mom won't let me." Similarly, a girl remarked while discussing her avatar, "I wish I had black hair . . . [and] I don't have really pretty lips like she does." Much as some people peruse magazines or fashion sites for looks to imitate, youths also copied other people's looks, seeing a face part on one Whyvillian and searching for it in Akbar's to put on their own face: "I take their looks and then if I see somebody I like again then I copy them. . . . we were taking people's looks." One boy defined himself against the trend: "I wanted to look different from other people." What these statements reveal is that *Whyville* not only offers room for customizing avatars but also provides room for different purposes of doing so.

This range of avatar customization is rather extensive and unique to *Whyville* when compared to the choices provided in most commercial video and role-playing games. Such game worlds are designed with particular story lines and thus the constraints imposed on the diversity of virtual characters ensure that the play experience stays within the boundaries of the fantasy world. By contrasting, in *Whyville* the provision of all avatar content and interactions resides in the hands of players. Thus the purposes for creating avatars differ from other games; the primary purpose is to enhance socialization between players, a primary activity among teens. In fact, one could say that play in *Whyville* is avatar design because it occupies a considerable amount of time spent in *Whyville*.

These findings provide at least some initial pointers on how avatar customization in virtual worlds can structure access and participation of players. The current success of online role-playing games that allow players not only to select their roles but also their forms of participation seem to provide further support. Gender play in public spaces, as Thorne defined it, is about the possibilities of affirming or opposing differences and with that, giving room for change. The new digital publics can be seen as a crucial context for youth development as teens decide which groups they identify with, what kind of people they wish to be within those groups, and what is required to be those people (Bers 2006). But it also leaves us with many other issues. For instance, this incredible range of customization led to a number of social issues in regard to avatars—class stratification (newbie vs. oldbie), pressure to fit in with the latest trend, and even inequitable racial representation (see Kafai, Cook, and Fields 2007). Further research is needed on how individuals use the broad resources of this environment to play and experiment with appearances, even to the point of transgressing situated social boundaries including flirting, cross-dressing, and supposed anonymity.

Acknowledgments

The work reported in this chapter has been supported by a grant from the National Science Foundation. The opinions presented in this article are those of the author and do not reflect those of the supporting agency. Linda Kao helped document club activities in field notes, and Deborah Fields and Melissa Cook participated in the analyses. Many thanks also to Jill Denner, Carrie Heeter, Deborah Fields, Kylie Peppler, and Joshua Danish for comments on earlier drafts of this chapter.

References

Aschbacher, P. (2003). *Gender Differences in the Perception and Use of an Informal Science Learning Website.* Grant funded by National Science Foundation, PGE-0086338. Arlington, Va.

Beavis, C., and C. Charles (2005). Challenging notions of gendered game play: Teenagers playing the Sims. *Discourse: Studies in the Cultural Politics of Education, 26*(3), 355–367.

Beavis, C. (2005). Pretty good for a girl: Gender, identity, and computer games. Paper presented at DiGRA conference in Vancouver, Canada. http://www.digra.org/dl/db/ 06276.30483.pdf.

Berman, J., and A. Bruckman (2001). The Turing game: Exploring identity in an Online Environment. *Convergence, 7*(3), 83–102.

Bers, M. (2006). The role of new technologies to foster positive youth development. *Applied Developmental Science, 10*(4), 200–219.

Boyd, D. (2006). *Identity Productions in a Networked Culture: Why Youth Heart MySpace.* American Association for the Advancement of Science, St. Louis, Mo. February 19. http:// www.danah.org/papers/AAAS2006.html.

Carr, D. (2005). Context, pleasures, and preferences: Girls playing computer games. Paper presented at DiGRA conference in Vancouver, Canada. http://www.digra.org/dl/db/ 06278.08421.pdf.

Consalvo, M. (2007). *Cheating: Gaining Advantage in VideogGames.* Cambridge, Mass.: The MIT Press.

Feldon, D., and Y.B. Kafai (in press). Mixed methods for mixed realities: understanding users' avatar activities in virtual worlds. *ETR&D.*

Fields, D. A., and Y. B. Kafai (2007a). Tracing insider knowledge across time and spaces: A connective ethnography in a teen online game world. Paper to be presented at the 8th Conference on Computer Supported Collaborative Learning, New Brunswick, N.J.

Fields, D. A., and Y. B. Kafai (2007b). Stealing from Grandma or generating cultural knowledge? Contestations and effects of cheats in a teen virtual world. Paper to be presented at DiGRA in Tokyo, Japan.

Gee, J. (2003). *What Videogames Have to Teach Us about Learning and Literacy.* New York: Palgrave.

Kafai, Y. B., M. Cook, and D. A. Fields (2007). "Blacks deserve bodies too": Design and discussion about race and diversity in a teen virtual world. Paper to be presented at DiGRA in Tokyo, Japan.

Kafai, Y. B., D. Feldon, D. Fields, M. Giang, and M. Quintero (2007). *Life in the Times of Whypox: A Virtual Epidemic as a Community Event.* In C. Steinfeld, B. Pentland, M. Ackermann, and N. Contractor (eds.), *Proceedings of the Third International Conference on Communities and Technology.* New York: Springer.

Kafai, Y. B., D. A. Fields, and M. Cook (2007). Your second selves: Avatar design and identity play in a teen virtual world. Paper to be presented at DiGRA in Tokyo, Japan.

Kafai, Y. B., and M. T. Giang (2007). New virtual playgrounds: Children's multi-user virtual environments for playing and learning with science. In T. Willoughby and E. Wood (eds.), *Children's Learning in a Digital World* (pp. 196–217). Oxford, UK: Blackwell Publishing.

Schott, G., and K. R. Horrell (2000). Girls' gamers and their relationship with the gaming culture. *Convergence, 6*(4), 36–53.

Schott, G., and M. Kambouri (2003). Moving between the spectral and material plane: Interactivity in social play with computer games. *Convergence, 9*(3), 42–55.

Taylor, T. L. (2003). Multiple pleasures: Women and online gaming. *Convergence, 9*(1), 21–46.

Thorne, B. (2005). Unpacking school lunchtime: Structure, practice, and the negotiation of differences. In C. R. Cooper, C. T. G. Coll, W. T. Bartko, H. Davis, and C. Chatman (eds.), *Developmental Pathways through Middle Childhood* (pp. 63–87). Mahwah, N.J.: Lawrence Erlbaum Associates.

Thorne, B. (1993). *Gender Play: Boys and Girls in School.* Brunswick, N.J.: Rutgers University Press.

Part III Girls and Women as Game Designers

A much-heralded strategy for increasing the diversity of games is to increase the number of females who are involved in all aspects of game design and production. The hope is that if girls and women are involved not only in the design but in the programming part of game building, the games they make will be more appealing to players like themselves. The four chapters in this third part, "Girls and Women as Game Designers," describe what happens when girls and women fill these roles. The chapters identify both the potential and the challenges of making females across a range of ages and settings full participants in how games are designed and created. They also challenge the simplistic idea that there is a certain kind of game that all females like, and that simply putting a female on a design team will lead to a game that will appeal to all girls and women.

The four chapters also focus on the importance of understanding and transforming the cultural context of game design. Others (Yates and Littleton 2001) have noted the importance of describing the constraints of the system and environment on how a player interacts with a game. However, most conversations about game play ignore the context in which it occurs, and instead focus on the player's abilities or interests. Similarly, most of the dialogue about game design has been about what kinds of games would most appeal to girls and women. The chapters in this part move the conversation to a new level by focusing on how the circumstances in which game design occurs have a powerful influence on the kinds of games that are made, regardless of the biological sex of the people creating them. And they suggest ways to transform game design workplaces in order to increase the diversity of game play options.

In "What Games Made by Girls Can Tell Us," researcher Jill Denner and educator Shannon Campe describe the computer games made in an all-female after-school program they developed for middle-school girls in California.

These games show that we need to move beyond asking "What do girls want in a game?" because this question leads us to focus on narrow definitions of female-friendly games. The girls in this study did not simply replicate their favorite games. Rather, the games they envisioned had different content from that of typical board games or electronic games. For example, the girls used game design not only to depict, but also to play with gender stereotypical subject matter like social dilemmas, boys, and clothing. Many of the games played with gender role stereotypes by challenging authority figures and social taboos, using humor, and proposing innovative strategies for working through moral decisions in real-world settings. Unlike the most popular console games today, most of the girls' games were not about dominating others, and few used violent feedback. This chapter shows how putting girls in the role of game designer and programmer in an all-female setting can result in new types of games that go beyond simple gender stereotypes.

In "Gaming in Context: How Young People Construct Their Gendered Identities in Playing and Making Games," Caroline Pelletier, a researcher at the London Knowledge Lab, University of London, examined how children in London talk about and design games. She describes how gender is produced in relation to social norms. For example, over time and in different settings, many students made contradictory statements, such as saying they like to play *The Sims* and then saying that they find it boring. Some said they like action games with fighting and killing, and then later said they only like to play simulations like *The Sims*. Pelletier also examined how in making games, children come to identify themselves as gendered. The students used a new software tool to make three-dimensional game worlds with the capacity to include features such as an inventory with indicators of health, strength, and nutritional levels of the play. By comparing the findings in the focus groups with the kinds of games that boys and girls created using this tool, she sheds light on the process of socialization and children's culture.

Despite the use of different software and the very different settings for game design, there are some similarities across the games in these two chapters. In particular, both challenge narrow stereotypes about what girls want. Pelletier highlights one girl's game that uses a psychological narrative—the goal is to find out why the female character committed suicide. There are helpful tips and warnings throughout, which guide the player toward solving the mystery. Like the games in Denner and Campe, this game provides an opportunity for the player to learn how to negotiate challenging social situations and learn the negative consequences to the player's health for bad choices. The findings from both chapters suggest that certain game design settings will result in more games that allow girls to experiment with a range of gender identities, and new ways to negotiate fears in realistic rather than fantasy settings. Until recently, games have served to reinforce traditional gender stereotypes and alienate females from the potential benefits of gaming. The findings suggest one way that new contexts of game design can result in opportunities to rethink gender stereotypes and gaming.

To involve girls and women in game design, it is important to understand the factors that engage and motivate them, and the contextual barriers to sustaining their involvement. The two final chapters in this part address this issue. As part of their work with Ludica, a women and games collaborative, Tracy Fullerton, Janine Fron, Celia Pearce, and Jacki Morie describe in "Getting Girls into the Game: Toward a 'Virtuous Cycle'" how women's participation is critical to developing more games that reach a broad audience, like *The Sims* in which 50 percent of its designers and 40 percent of its producers are female. Based on their experience both in and outside the game industry, they make the case that the current cultures of game making and game play have discouraged girls and women from participating in either one. They describe efforts to change that culture, including how to motivate and engage women in the game-making process. For example, academic programs and workshops can provide a setting in which to go beyond the gender dichotomies that pervade most games. Mentoring has provided the background and support for women to pursue and persist in the game industry.

Mia Consalvo, a professor of telecommunications at Ohio University, describes in "Crunched by Passion: Women Game Developers and Workplace Challenges" the importance of not just increasing diversity in the game industry, but also changing organizational structures in order to maintain it. Based on interviews with female game developers, she finds that the demands of "crunch time," the weeks or months right before a game is released when final creative and technical challenges are resolved, have led many women to leave the business. Crunch periods often require seventy- to eighty-hour workweeks, and this is more difficult for women, who still shoulder the bulk of the responsibility for managing family life. The people who stay in the industry attribute their persistence to both their passion and a supportive work setting.

Consalvo argues that the high rate of staff turnover in the game industry can have a cost to both profits and to products. Both these chapters show the importance of creating work environments that allow employees to balance home and work, and support a diversity of perspectives in the game design and production process.

Reference

Yates, S. J., and K. Littleton (2001). Understanding computer game cultures: A situated approach. In E. Green and A. Adam (eds.), *Virtual Gender: Technology, Consumption, and Identity* (pp. 103–123). London: Routledge.

9 What Games Made by Girls Can Tell Us

Jill Denner and Shannon Campe

In the past, both the production and consumption of video games were enjoyed mostly by boys and men, and console and computer games dominated the market. The most popular console games today have larger-than-life settings and the goal is to win through individual or team dominance (like overcoming an enemy) rather than through building relationships or experiencing new cultures. These games allow the player to act out fantasies, which include becoming a successful football player in the NFL, being a professional skateboarder, or testing one's prowess as a soldier fighting a powerful enemy. In 1998, Brunner, Bennett, and Honey concluded that most popular computer games emphasized "victory over justice, competition over collaboration, speed over flexibility, transcendence over empathy, control over communication, and force over facilitation" (pp. 81–82). These qualities continue to pervade the most popular games and generate a mostly male audience for console games. With such an exclusive focus on games for boys and men, many suggest that to attract girls and women, a different and less stereotypically male game is needed. This chapter explores what kinds of games are designed and programmed by girls in an all-female design setting, and whether girls create highly gendered games.

What Games Do Girls Play?

In the 1990s, many games were designed and marketed specifically for girls. The success of *Barbie Fashion Designer* was attributed not only to the mass market appeal of the Barbie franchise but also to the problem solving and sense of accomplishment associated with making a real-world product—clothes (Subrahmanyam and Greenfield 1998). Most games that targeted girls had character-centered plots, dealt with friendship issues and social relations, and featured brightly colored graphics (Cassell and Jenkins 1998). These games continue to attract some, but not all, girls. A growing body of research goes beyond a focus on girl-specific games to describe games with a broader range of features, which may attract girls to gaming. These features include competition and conflict alternatives, real-world settings, and opportunities to explore a range of identities. Below we review what others have found to appeal to girls. This is followed by our more recent findings on the kinds of games created by girls in an all-female setting.

Cooperation or Competition?

Studies suggest that games are likely to attract girls when games are cooperative, have a narrative and characters girls can relate to, show little meaningless violence, have rich audio and images, and include multiple ways to win (Children Now 2001; Gorriz and Medina 2002; Laurel 1998; Rubin et al. 1997). For games to be more inclusive, there must be ways to resolve conflicts that do not require one person to win and everyone else to lose (Ray 2004), and winning and losing must be meaningful (Brunner, Bennett, and Honey 1998). For example, opportunities for personal triumph could be balanced with opportunities to help others or learn a lesson. Other features that attract girls include creative components, puzzle elements, tips, positive unsolicited feedback, a slow or variable pace, clear and predictable rules, and the absence of violence, killing, or evil characters (Cassell and Jenkins 1998; Kafai 1995). This includes games where the goal is to outsmart instead of overcome (Roberts et al. 1999). While young boys design adventure games with violent feedback in which players "get" something (i.e., win), girls are more likely to make skill or learning games (Kafai 1998).

Real-World Applications

Research suggests that girls like to play games in which they work through real-life problems or challenges they expect to face in the future. For example, many girls like games that allow them to work through social issues with stories, or narrative (Brunner, Bennett, and Honey 1998; Gorriz and Medina 2002), especially when the story involves character development and characters they can identify with. Girls like to design everyday living spaces, practice working through complex social relationships, and examine situations from different perspectives (Brunner, Bennett, and Honey 1998). For example, Kafai (1995) found that girls were more likely than boys to create mathematics games that take place in real-life settings, while boys were more likely to create games in fantasy settings. Interestingly, in her study there were fewer gender differences in settings chosen for games about science.

Challenges to Gender Roles

Girls have expressed dislike for games where female characters are sexualized or portrayed as victims and not heroes. Most games that target girls involve "good" girls who get along with their friends and do well in school. But games that include humor are one way to play with gendered identities (Brunner, Bennett, and Honey 1998). Studies suggest that girls want games in which they can try out different identities, exploring what it means to be female (AAUW 2000; Kinder 1998). To attract, engage, and sustain the interests of girls in gaming, it is important to increase the depth of games available (Hayes this volume; Jenson and de Castell 2002). Culp and Honey (2002) challenged us to create "less gendered game worlds" that go beyond the dichotomy of gender-focused versus genderless games and instead allow the player to define the role or importance of gender and how it is enacted. The more recent games that have been popular with girls have done this by offering opportunities to use a range of play styles, try out different identities, and explore various relationships. Popular multi- and single-player games include *Whyville* (Numedeon), *RuneScape* (Jagex), and *The Sims* (EA/Maxis). Games that are most popular with female players include role-playing games, narrative adventures, puzzles, life simulations, and driving games (Entertainment and Leisure Software Publishers Association 2004). But what remains unclear is what girls themselves would create if given the tools to make their own games.

There are limits to simply asking girls what they want in a game. Pelletier (this volume) shows how the answers that children give to questions about game-play behaviors, likes, and dislikes change depending on the social context in which they are asked. Studying games girls actually create, not what they talk about, can reveal interests. In a recent empirical study, Heeter and colleagues (2005) found that girls ranked games envisioned by all-girl design teams significantly higher than games envisioned by all-boy teams, even without knowing the sex of the team members. Pelletier's and Heeter's findings add credence to the utility of looking more deeply into games that girls design as a source of understanding their gaming preferences. In this chapter, we describe games made by girls, and address this question: Are girl game designs closer to predictions of highly gendered play, or are they more consistent with typical commercial games, which if anything are more male-oriented?

The Girls Creating Games Program

The Girls Creating Games (GCG) program was designed to test game creation as a strategy to increase girls' interest, confidence, and skills with computer technology. The program was also a research platform to examine how girls engage with computers and what kinds of games they would construct. The girls met for twenty-three sessions either after school or during the summer and learned to design and program a digital game using Macromedia's Flash™ software program. Building on research that shows the benefits of collaborative learning structures for female students (Light et al. 2000; Werner, Hanks, and McDowell 2005), the girls worked in pairs to both write and program their stories. More detail about the activities in the GCG program can be found in Denner and colleagues (2005).

The girls were required to create interactive, story-based, choose-your-own-adventure games. This format was a practical constraint in response to the complexity of the authoring software, plus it was consistent with previous studies that found that storytelling can be used to interest girls in programming (Kelleher this volume) and offers opportunities to transform the relation between gender and technology (Cassell 1998). Although the mechanics are the same in all games, each is unique in its themes, stories, characters, and game features.

The 126 girls who made the 45 games were in sixth (52%), seventh (24%), and eighth (22%) grades, and ranged in age from 11 to 14. The girls' race/ethnicity was 31 percent Latina and 60 percent white; at the time they enrolled in the program, 90 percent said they had a computer at home they could use.

The game content was coded as a way to identify repeating themes. Building on the work of Kafai (1995), two researchers reviewed the finished games and identified twelve subcategories grouped within three main themes: competition and conflict, real-world applications, and challenges to gender stereotypes.

What Kinds of Games Do Girls Make?

We use one game to illustrate the findings reported here. All games began with a welcome page, like the one shown in figure 9.1, where the player has the option of clicking on the Play button, or the Credits button. The image on the welcome page is of a male coach, even though the coach in the story is female. The Flash library offered female images but no female coach. This is an example of the limitations of the Flash images library, although the students had the option to download other images from the Internet.

On the first page of the game, the player is given a choice: "Today is your first day of Jr. Guards. You have a chance to skip or stay. Choose one of the buttons below. Remember, don't get caught!" One button says "stay" while a much larger button says "skip skip skip skip skip." Right away, the player faces a dilemma between accepting and defying responsibility. The Skip button leads the player to punishment with this ending: "You got caught. Your coach saw you running into a stall. She didn't tell your mom but you had to do 100,000,000,000 push-ups!"

If the player chooses the Stay button, the player faces a series of choices that lead to four possible endings. In one, the player sees an image of a woman

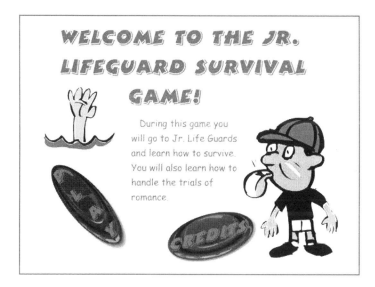

Figure 9.1   Screen shot of welcome page from *Jr. Lifeguard* (see color plate).

in a wedding dress and a famous guy; the text says: "You live happily ever after . . . Oh great, now I sound like Jiminy Cricket." If the player says no to the cute boy's invitation to lunch, she is socially ostracized. This ending reads: "What have you done? You rejected the hottest guy in Jr. Guards. Oh well, your loss. Look at his face! He's devastated. Now everyone hates your guts. Even the counselors. They even kicked you out of Jr. Guards. So I guess it's good-bye . . . traitor!" The player is not ostracized, however, if she goes on the date but says no to the wedding proposal. In this scenario, the game ends with the guy saying, "Fine!! But I'm outa here!!!" In yet another ending, the player competes in a foot race but falls and fractures her pelvis and cannot participate in Jr. Guards for the rest of the season. This game provides an example of how players must negotiate social challenges, how triumph and hardship were balanced with humor, and how a single game offers a range of gendered roles for girls to choose from.

Most of the girls' games offered the player the chance to either win or lose the game; 18 percent had endings where the player could only win or only lose (for an overview see table 9.1). Winning often involved getting an A on a test, getting a trip to an exotic place, becoming friends with an enemy, or getting a boy. Ways of losing the game included school detention, getting hurt, or losing friends. Violent feedback occurred in less than one-third of the games and included getting hurt or killed (e.g., getting sucked into the Bermuda Triangle). More than half the games provided opportunities for personal triumph such as making a sports team or doing well in school. These examples of personal triumph are not triumph over everyone else (being the star of the team or the best in the class), echoing Heeter and Winn's (this volume) thoughts about different male and female perspectives on competition. Only a few games offered opportunities to help others, including saving animals and saving students at the school from evil forces. This was in contrast to other studies that find that girls see technology as a tool to help others (Brunner, Bennett, and Honey 1998). It is even more surprising, given that instructors encouraged the girls to make games to help other students.

The girls' games support previous assertions that girls are interested in games based on real-world situations (Subrahmanyam and Greenfield 1998). A prominent theme that emerged from the girls' games (in 99%) was how they expressed and worked through fears in their stories, which is consistent with previous studies that find girls are more likely than boys to use technol-

Table 9.1 Results of Coding Games

Categories	Percent of games
Competition and conflict	
Opportunity to win and lose	82%
Opportunity for personal triumph	51%
Violent feedback	24%
Opportunity to help others	15%
Real-world applications	
Addresses social issues	99%
Deals with fears	99%
Real-world settings	71%
Teaches a prosocial lesson	53%
Challenges gender stereotypes	
Defyies authority	64%
Reinforces gender stereotypes	58%
Uses humor	35%
Has female authority figures	33%

ogy to solve real-world problems (Brunner, Bennett, and Honey 1998). In their games, the fears were about getting into trouble (50%), the threat of violence (34%), negative repercussions for relationships (20%), and school failure (11%) (the total adds up to more than 100 percent because some games included more than one type of fear). Fears about getting into trouble included getting detention from a school authority, being grounded by parents, or getting kicked off a sports team, as in the game *Soccer Fever*. Fears that focused on the threat of violence included being chased by a bear in the game *Getting Lost*. Fears also involved relationships such as concerns about social exclusion and judgment as a result of peer pressure to skip school, sneak out of the house, or listen to certain kinds of music, as in the *Music Mania* game. Fears were also grounded in fantasy characters (e.g., Big Foot) that lived in realistic worlds.

Most games addressed social issues that are on the minds of teen girls. In 57 percent of the games, the player must deal with authorities and in 45 percent they must make moral decisions, as in the game *My Big School Test*. Many of the authority decisions involved choices such as whether or not to tell Mom the truth. Moral decisions involved making choices about hard work (especially in school) versus having fun, such as in *To Go to School or Not to Go to School*. Decisions about moral issues also revolved around hiding from attackers versus helping others. For example, in the game *A Horrifying Alienistic Experience,* aliens invade the school and turn students into pigs. The player must decide whether to confront the aliens and help her classmates—putting herself at risk—or run away. Other social issues involved romantic relationships (20%), peers and parties (18%), sports (16%), animals (11%), and media (7%). Examples of games with animals include *Welcome to the Great Cat Rescue* and *Me and My Ape,* where a player brings her pet to school.

Most of the games that girls built took place in real-world settings such as schools, homes, or the beaches near their houses. However, despite previous research that suggests girls use technology to help others, only 53 percent used a social issue to teach a lesson or take a moral stand. Those games that did attempt to teach a lesson tended to focus on how to behave or succeed at school, or on how to be a moral person by showing the negative consequences of lying or sneaking out of the house.

Some of the games challenged or reinforced gender stereotypes. Examples of challenging stereotypes take the form of social taboos such as rejecting the good-girl image by defying authority, or having two male characters live together as a couple. Two-thirds of the games included opportunities to defy authority by cutting school, sneaking into the principal's office, or yelling at a teacher. However, stereotypical female gender roles were narrated in several of the story lines. In the game *Cruise Line* the characters end up dancing with boys at a party. In *Fashion Emergency* the character's reputation and whether or not she gets in trouble with the school principal depends on her choosing the right outfit. Games about boys included *The Day I Got Paired Up with the Hottie* and *Dreams Come True,* where the dream is to go to the school dance with the cutest boy at school.

More than half the games used humor in their stories, which was a way to play with gender role stereotypes and adult expectations about behavior. For example, in the game featuring a fictitious game show called *Who Is Your Dream Date?,* the character must choose among different types of dates (e.g., the romantic guy, the funny guy, or the quiet, mature guy). The player can win silk pajamas, and if she chooses the funny guy, she is told "he doesn't mind be-

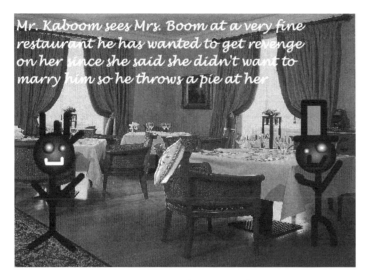

Mr. Kaboom sees Mrs. Boom at a very fine restaurant he has wanted to get revenge on her since she said she didn't want to marry him so he throws a pie at her

Figure 9.2   Screen shot from *Mr. Kaboom* (see color plate).

Table 9.2 Main Characters

Categories	Percent of games
Allows player to choose sex	42%
Female main characters	22%
Mixed main characters	15%
Gender-neutral or unclear	13%

ing a little loud, just like you." Another example of humor was the pie thrown at the character Ms. Boom when she refused a marriage proposition in the game *The Story of Mr. Kaboom* (see figure 9.2).

Slightly less than half of the games gave the player an option to choose the character's sex by filling in the name of the character (for a summary, see table 9.2). A small percentage of the games had female main characters only, and two games had male main characters only. Notably, 13 percent did not designate a gender category; this was most common when the characters were animals.

Authority figures were the most popular characters, and these varied in whether they played a supportive or disciplinary role (see table 9.3). Of the

Table 9.3 Gender of Characters

	Percent of games		
	Females	Males	Nonspecified
Authority figures	20%	27%	17%
Parents	20%	2%	4%
Nonhumans (e.g., animals, ghosts)	2%	4%	20%
Schoolchildren	24%	13%	4%
Friends	—	—	18%
Romantic attractions	0%	9%	2%
Service workers	2%	7%	0%

Table 9.4 Additional Images

	Percent of games	
	Females	Males
Regular children	31%	35%
Authorities	27%	27%
Stylish clothes	15%	2%
Needs help	13%	7%
Sexy clothes	11%	7%
Bathing suit	11%	4%
Superhuman	9%	7%
Athlete	4%	20%
Brides	4%	—

nine games that had a female authority character, four were disciplinarians, three were helpful, and two played both roles depending on what the player chose to do. Of the twelve games that had male authority characters, four were disciplinarians, four were helpful, three had both roles, and one offered a reward. In a challenge to traditional expectations about gender roles, when parents were combined with other authority figures, there were more female than male authority figures in the games (40% vs. 29%). These included mothers (22%) and females in institutions, such as female teachers (13%).

Other games featured male authorities in institutions, such as male coaches or principals (29%).

In addition to story characters, other visual images that were included in the games were coded (see table 9.4). Those coded as authorities included adults, while images coded "needs help" showed a person in distress.

Regular children and authorities were the most common images. Pictures of females were more likely to feature a teen in a stylish dress, or to appear to need help, while male images were more likely to be athletes. The predominance of male athletes was due in part to the lack of female athletes in the Flash library of images.

Conclusions

It has been more than ten years since Kafai (1995) published her findings on what children create when given the tools to program a computer game. In this chapter, we describe the first known study to replicate her approach and extend it to girls in an all-female after-school program. The girls' games were quite varied, despite the limitations placed on their designs by the instructors. They were different from the most popular games on the market today, but did not always support what previous research says girls like about games. Most stories took place in realistic settings, and most did not provide violent feedback. Games focused on the fears and social issues that girls face (or expect to face) in their lives. Very few games on the market today allow players to express and work through fears about getting in trouble or doing well in school or sports. In addition, few games provide opportunities to make moral decisions and to challenge the authority figures that children encounter in their daily lives.

As expected, there were few games that included violent feedback and only half that offered opportunities for personal triumph. In contrast to popular games, the violence was often comic, such as throwing a pie in someone's face, and the personal triumph focused mostly on the school or after-school setting rather than on saving the world. This finding is in stark contrast to the vast majority of games created by the male-dominated computer game industry, which feature violent play in which the player can kill and die (see Lazzaro this volume).

Most of the girls' games had bright and vivid colors, rather than the dark, gloomy worlds of many of the most popular computer games sold today. However, the games challenge several assumptions about what girls want. Others have suggested that girls are motivated to use technology as a tool to improve the world, but despite being encouraged to make a game that would help other students, only half actually used their game to teach something to the player, and even fewer included opportunities for the character to help others. It has also been suggested that girls like games that involve puzzles and trivia questions, and while these elements did not appear in the girls' games, this was probably due in part to the limited game structure and software skills they learned.

These findings also challenge the assumption that girls are satisfied with games that allow them to explore, and that it is not important to girls to have opportunities to win and lose. All games had at least three different endings, and most had both positive and negative endings. However, unlike most popular games, the girls created opportunities for winning that were not at the expense of someone else losing. Consistent with what others have recommended for games that target girls, winning often entailed accomplishing something meaningful, such as succeeding at school or having your pets love you.

Despite the fact that girls created the games, there was not an overwhelming focus on female characters: less than one-quarter of the games had only female main characters. Instead, almost half the games allowed the player to name the character—and thus to choose the gender—which supports research that says girls want games that allow them to play with identities. An alternate explanation for girls' inclusion of a choice of character gender is that they wanted boys to be able to play their game, too. In addition, in many games, the gender of the main and other characters was ambiguous, which reflects one strategy of creating a gender-neutral game space. Similarly, Kafai (1998) found that girls were more likely than boys to create characters that were gender-neutral. For new games to speak to girls' experience, the industry might consider increasing player choice of character, including more mother figures as characters, and allowing the player to determine whether the authority is a helper or a disciplinarian.

There are several factors that might have affected the kinds of games the girls created. First, most of the games were done in pairs. Although Kelleher (this volume) found that pairing girls undermined their productivity in a three-hour work session, many of the pairs in the twenty-three-hour session GCG went beyond their individual skill levels when working with a partner. This was because our program provided both training and ongoing support for how to work effectively with another person. However, working with a partner may result in games that do not reflect the design preferences of any particular individual. Second, the girls were not asked to create the kind of game they would like to play; we are assuming that they created a game that they liked. Third, the interactive story structure of the game limited the type of game the girls could create. Finally, thirty-three of the games were created in an after-school program where the school administration asked the students to limit swearing and any sexualized images that might be considered offensive.

These findings have implications for understanding the intersection of gender and computer gaming. When given the opportunity, girls in an all-female setting designed game content that challenges the current thematic trends in the gaming industry. In particular, they used humor and defiance of familiar authority to play with gender stereotypes and reject the expectation that girls are always well behaved. The games highlight new ways to think about game design. In particular, the games address the issues and problems that affect girls' lives and what they think about. We can use this information to make games that will engage a broader range of girls in game playing. The girls in this study created games that have content and elements that could engage girls and boys in gaming, such as dealing with authority, doing well at school, opportunities to both win and lose, and a chance to experience personal triumph.

Finally, our research demonstrates the ways that game production can be a site of resisting and transforming traditional gender role expectations. Consistent with previous research, the findings suggest that game design in an all-female setting allowed girls to create games that offer opportunities to experiment with different notions of femininity (Brunner, Bennett, and Honey 1998) and experiment with identifying and resolving fears. In many games, the player is given the option to test out different and sometimes conflicting gender roles. In addition, looking at the games the girls built suggests that girls seek to explore different identities in realistic rather than fantasy settings (Jenkins 1998). Until now, games have served to reinforce traditional gender stereotypes and alienate females from the potential benefits of gaming. Our findings suggest a clear opportunity to use this powerful medium to engage a more diverse group of people in game design and play.

Acknowledgments

This material is based upon work supported by the National Science Foundation under grant 0217221. Any opinions, findings, and conclusions or recommendations expressed in this material are those of the authors and do not necessarily reflect the views of the National Science Foundation. The authors thank Steve Bean, Linda Werner, Audrey Blumeneau, Cathy Tyner, and Gail Levine for helping to create and run the program; Pamela Anderson for game coding; and the girls for making the games.

References

AAUW (2000). *Tech-Savvy: Educating Girls in the New Computer Age.* Washington, D.C., American Association of University Women.

Brunner, C., D. Bennett, and M. Honey (1998). Girl games and technological desire. In J. Cassell and H. Jenkins (eds.), *From Barbie to Mortal Kombat: Gender and Computer Games* (pp. 72–79). Cambridge, Mass.: The MIT Press.

Cassell, J. (1998). Storytelling as a nexus of change in the relationship between gender and technology: A feminist approach to software design. In J. Cassell and H. Jenkins (eds.), *From Barbie to Mortal Kombat: Gender and Computer Games* (pp. 298–327). Cambridge, Mass.: The MIT Press.

Cassell, J., and H. Jenkins (1998). Chess for girls? Feminism and computer games. In J.Cassell and H Jenkins (eds.), *From Barbie to Mortal Kombat: Gender and Computer Games* (pp. 2–45). Cambridge, Mass.: The MIT Press.

Children Now (2001). *Fair Play: Violence, Gender and Race in Video Games.* Oakland, Calif.

Culp, K. M., and M. Honey (2002). Imagining less-gendered game worlds. In N. Yelland and A. Rubin (ed.), *Ghosts in the Machine: Women's Voices in Research with Technology* (pp. 33–54). New York: Lang.

Denner, J., L. Werner, S. Bean, and S. Campe (2005). The Girls Creating Games program: Strategies for engaging middle school girls in information technology. *Frontiers: A Journal of Women's Studies. Special Issue on Gender and IT,* 26, 90–98.

Entertainment and Leisure Software Publishers Association (2004). Chicks and joysticks: An exploration of women and gaming. White paper. http://www.elspa.com/assets/files/c/chicksandjoysticksanexplorationofwomenandgaming_176.pdf.

Girard, N. (2006). Explaining disconnect between women, video games. http://www.news.com/Explaining-disconnect-between-women%2C-video-games/2100-1043_3-6082459.html?tag=item.

Gorriz, C.M., and C. Medina (2002). Engaging girls with computers through software games. *Communications of the Association for Computing Machinery,* 43, 42–49.

Greenfield, P. M., and R. R. Cocking (eds.) (1996). *Interacting with Video, Vol. 11, Advances in Applied Developmental Psychology.* Norwood, N.J.: Ablex Publishing Corp.

Heeter, C., K. Chu, R. Egidio, P. Mishra, and L. Graves-Wolf (2005). *Do Girls Prefer Games Designed by Girls?* New York: International Communication Association.

Jenkins, H. (1998). Complete freedom of movement: Video games as gendered play spaces. In J. Cassell and H. Jenkins (eds.), *From Barbie to Mortal Kombat: Gender and Computer Games* (pp. 262–297). Cambridge, Mass.: The MIT Press.

Jenson, J., and S. de Castell (2002). Serious play: Challenges of educational game design. Paper presented at the annual meeting of the American Educational Research Association.

Kafai, Y. B. (1998). Video game designs by girls and boys: Variability and consistency of gender differences. In J. Cassell and H. Jenkins (eds.), *From Barbie to Mortal Kombat: Gender and Computer Games* (pp. 90–114). Cambridge, Mass.: The MIT Press.

Kafai, Y. B. (1995). *Minds in Play: Computer Game Design as a Context for Children's Learning.* Mahwah, N.J.: Erlbaum.

Kafai, Y. B., and M. Resnick (1996). Introduction. In Y. Kafai and M. Resnick (eds.), *Constructionism in Practice: Designing, Thinking, and Learning in a Digital World* (pp. 1–8). Mahwah, N.J.: Erlbaum.

Kinder, M. (1998). An interview with Marsha Kinder. In J. Cassell and H. Jenkins (eds.), *From Barbie to Mortal Kombat: Gender and Computer Games* (pp. 214–230). Cambridge, Mass.: The MIT Press.

Laurel, B. (1998). An interview with Brenda Laurel. In J. Cassell and H. Jenkins (eds.), *From Barbie to Mortal Kombat: Gender and Computer Games* (pp. 118–135). Cambridge, Mass.: The MIT Press.

Light, P., K. Littleton, S. Bale, R. Joiner, and D. Messer (2000). Gender and social comparison effects in computer-based problem solving. *Learning and Instruction, 10,* 483–496.

Ray, S. G. (2004). *Gender Inclusive Game Design: Expanding the Market.* Hingham, Mass.: Charles River Media, Inc.

Roberts, D. F., U. G. Foehr, V. J. Rideout, and M. Brodie (1999). *Kids & Media @ the New Millennium: A Comprehensive National Analysis of Children's Media Use.* Menlo Park, Calif.: Kaiser Family Foundation. http://www.kff.org/entmedia/1535-index.cfm.

Rubin, A., M. Murray, K. O'Neil, and J. Ashley (1997). What kind of educational computer games would girls like? Paper presented at the annual meeting of the American Educational Research Association.

Subrahmanyam, K., and P. M. Greenfield (1998). Computer games for girls: What makes them play? In J. Cassell and H. Jenkins (eds.), *From Barbie to Mortal Kombat: Gender and Computer Games* (pp. 46–71). Cambridge, Mass.: The MIT Press.

Werner, L., B. Hanks, and C. McDowell (2005). Female computer science students who pair program persist. *ACM Journal of Educational Resources in Computing.* http://www.cse.ucsc.edu/~charlie/pubs/jeric2005.pdf.

10 Gaming in Context: How Young People Construct Their Gendered Identities in Playing and Making Games

Caroline Pelletier

Gender is a fundamental aspect of identity, one which people wish to assert and protect by emphasizing difference. Discussions about gender and computer games have tended to focus on preferences in game play and content. This chapter aims to open up this discussion by examining how players use game play and game design to construct their own identities, including their gendered identities. The primary goal is to show that the ways in which young people make sense of games, the ways in which they interpret them, and the way they make their own games is related to how they construct a sense of their self in a social and cultural context. This is important for two reasons. First, it highlights the role games have in processes of socialization—how they are used by young people to establish relations with others. Second, it indicates how games become meaningful. The meaning of a game is not contained within the game itself. The social context in which games are played, interpreted, and produced strongly shapes how players make sense of the games. Context refers to the characteristics of the social situation in which people find themselves at any one time; this situation, however, is always framed by broad trends and relationships, which can be referred to in terms of *culture* or *society*.

This chapter is based on two sources of evidence collected at a co-educational school in the UK: a focus group of students talking about the games they play at home and two games made at an after-school club. A brief comparison is made at the end of the chapter with similar data collected in a girls' school. The analysis indicates that in contexts where gender can be purposefully invoked to mark difference from some and create social bonds with others, young people construct games as gendered in order to construct themselves as gendered, as divided or united by gender. In contexts where gender differences assume less significance, games are interpreted and produced according to different criteria. A number of chapters in this volume examine how the meaning that games have to players relates to the context in which they are played (see Lin this volume; Taylor this volume; Ito this volume). This chapter similarly emphasizes that the relationship between gender and gaming is a function of context, precisely because different contexts offer different resources with which to construct an identity.

The data in this chapter were drawn from a research and development project called Making Games, with researchers from the Centre for the Study of Children, Youth, and Media, University of London, in collaboration with Immersive Education, a UK software company. The purpose of the partnership was to develop a production tool for young people to make their own computer games, as well as teaching strategies for use in English and media education classrooms. The educational rationale for game authoring by young people is that games are a significant cultural phenomenon that have an important role in processes of socialization. To participate more fully in game culture, young people should be able to produce games and not only play them (Pelletier 2005). For the industry partner (Immersive Education), the project created the opportunity to design software in collaboration with researchers, teachers, and young people. Over the course of three years, successive prototypes were released for use in classrooms, after-school clubs, and students' homes. Feedback and design ideas were collected to inform the development of the next prototype. In this way, young people were involved as codesigners of the software.

Although we collaborated with more than one hundred students and a dozen teachers over the course of the project, we worked particularly intensively with two small groups of eight students, one group in a coed and the other in a girls' school. The decision to work in a girls' school was taken in the light of concerns regarding the marginalization of women in game-related social practices (Cassell and Jenkins 2000; see also chapters by Denner and Campe, Consalvo, and Fullerton et al. in this volume for details of other efforts to address this). Although the coed school also included girls, we wanted to work in an environment in which we could research the interests of girls without pointedly excluding boys and thereby defining, for the students' benefit, the terms of participation in terms of gender (as opposed to school).

In analyzing the role of gender in the interpretation and production of games over the course of this study, Judith Butler's work (1993, 1999, 2004) has been particularly useful. Butler is a constructivist, which means that she is interested in how concepts and ideas emerge and evolve historically (Andersen 2003). This has implications for how research questions are formulated. Rather than ask what women want, for example, she asks how and for what purposes do people classify interests and actions (including their own) as distinctly female. Rather than assume that the categories "boy" and "girl" are fixed and known variables, she asks how such categories become validated over time as "ideological understandings," to borrow Consalvo's phrase (this volume). Butler argues that gender is a set of norms that are performed and worked at every day, and not something people are simply born with or socialized into at an early age. Gender is never a settled identity but an incessant activity, an outcome of people's continuous efforts. Gender in this sense is individually authored; it is something people construct for themselves. But the terms that make a gendered identity possible are social; they are defined in social norms (or, in Consalvo's terms, "institutional practices") and the contexts in which such norms are instantiated. As a result, one determines one's own sense of gender to the extent that social norms exist that enable particular gendered identities.

Constructing Gender through Talk: Discussing Computer Games

Following a media studies lesson with a class of twelve- to thirteen-year-olds, we asked for six volunteers who were keen game players to talk to us about how they would approach game design. Much of this discussion (see table 10.1) at first glance seems to confirm research indicating that access, preferences, and choice of platform are differentiated by gender (Cassell and Jenkins 2000). The girls' preferences support arguments that girls tend to play "improving games" in the home (mainly on the PC), with parents (particularly fathers) distancing their daughters from "masculine" technologies and interests (Thomas and Walkerdine 2000). However, as the interview developed, contradictions appeared in the students' answers, which suggest that gender is not the cause of these preferences in a straightforward way, but precisely their outcome; gender is what is produced as an effect of their statements. I will focus on the pattern of Sarah's responses, as she seemed to be the most experienced player.

Table 10.1 Interview Transcript

Speaker	Dialogue
female interviewer	What kind of computer games do you play?
male interviewer	Shall we go straight 'round? Yeah.
Sarah	I just play . . . I don't really play action. I just play things like *The Sims* and just things that you can rule their lives and just make . . . just have fun with.
Kate	And I play with *The Sims* as well.
Jo	And me. Yeah. I play *The Sims* on my . . . My dad has a different range of . . . He has our computer and a PlayStation and when I'm with my dad I play like . . . usually *Lord of the Rings* and *Harry Potter* and sort of known games, like, not sort of . . . Games that have got books as well or films or TV programs that I know of.
female interviewer	Is that why you choose them?
Jo	Sort of. I'm quite fussy and when I do read books, I can't read books that I haven't heard of. And so, that's probably why I choose them.
Joshua	I play action adventure, shoot-'em-ups, fighting games, on PS2.
female interviewer	Have you tried any other platforms as well?
Joshua	Like *The Sims*?
female interviewer	Like the Xbox or PC?
Joshua	Oh, I've played on the Xbox and the GameCube, PlayStation1.
male interviewer	So you've not played on a PC?
Joshua	Well, I haven't really got a PC. I have consoles instead.
Simon	I play adventure and strategy games. I hate racing games. *Formula One* is probably the only racing game I like. I have a PC if the PlayStation isn't working.
male interviewer	Can you name the titles of some games you play?
Simon	*Spiderman. Crash Bandicoot. Silent Hill. Silent Hill* is a horror game. I like adventure for my PC. We get to buy some from the Internet.
male interviewer	Do you play any online games?
Simon	Yeah. Loads. *Age of Empires.* Some take up one-fifth of my computer space, they are so huge. And *Star Quest,* and I've forgotten what other games I've got.

Table 10.1 (continued)

Speaker	Dialogue
Jak	I like more strategy computer games like *Red Alert* and *Age of Empires* because I like the idea of building moon bases, going out killing people, and that. Yeah.
Simon	Yeah.
Jak	I play *Red Alert* on PC, which is good. It's better than Play-Station because it's got better graphics. You've got more options on what you can play. And I like extreme sport games as well. I like *Tony Hawks*.

Shortly after the moment in the interview transcribed above, Sarah states she plays games on the PC. When asked whether she has a console at home, she adds that she has a PlayStation on which she plays racing games. When asked about the PC's merits, she answers: "Well on the PC you are not as into it as on the PlayStation, I find. Because I play *Tony Hawks* on the PlayStation and I just got into it a lot more than when I play on *The Sims* or the Internet or anything."

When the group is prompted again about what PC games they have played, Sarah interjects that she plays mainly on the PlayStation. The discussion then shifts to how games are designed, and Sarah comments: "I've looked around shops and I've looked for things for my age and for me and I can't really find anything. I find racing and that, but my brother would just buy that sort of thing." Here, the racing games are identified as her brother's, the implication being that she plays them on a compromise basis, as an exception in a general rule.

Toward the end of the conversation, she adds: "I think some games are quite good when it's all about the same thing like fighting and killing. . . . If it's a boxing match and then you walk around town and kill people, it's not very good. But some games you have to have a bit of difference, like you can drive a car one minute, then walk the other."

Her comments suggest she has played games that involve fighting and killing, and furthermore, that she has played a wide enough range of those kinds of games as well as other genres to comment on some broad design principles. At that point, her concern is with quality of design, not nature of game play—in contrast to her first remark (line 4).

The range of her gaming interests is confirmed by questionnaire data collected four weeks after the group interview. Here, Sarah lists *GTA: Vice City* as her favorite game. When she is asked to draw a screenshot of a game she would ideally like to create, she represents a racing game. The racing games may be her brother's, but they would seem to provide sufficient enjoyment for Sarah to consider creating her own.

There is similar, if less pronounced, movement in the other students' responses. In the questionnaire, Jo lists *Tomb Raider* as a favorite game, and indicates that she has a Game Boy. In a subsequent interview, Kate says she has played "*The Sims* and *Harry Potter* and other things"—the "other things" belonging to her father or to her friends. Although Joshua initially denies all knowledge of PC gaming, he later offers an evaluation of it, arguing that its value lies in the quality of its graphics. Simon initially says he only plays on the PC when his PlayStation is broken, but when pressed, he emphasizes how much space online games take up on his computer. In the questionnaire, Simon lists platform games as among his favorite, although they are not mentioned in the interview. Jak similarly lists *Spiro* as one of his favorite games, which is more of an adventure than a strategy or extreme sports game.

From the discussions presented here, it is clear that the games with which students claim familiarity, as well as how they evaluate those games, change over time. Next we examine what might explain these variations.

Strategies Motivating Shifts in Students' Positions

There is no reason to believe students are deliberately misleading the researchers. Instead, it appears that at different times, students understand their own experience as gamers differently. How they discuss their knowledge and experience of games depends on the context, including the ways in which the discussion develops. This raises some questions: What factors lead students to make particular selections from their experience as gamers? Is there a pattern to their answers that might explain what motivates them?

One striking feature of both girls' and boys' answers is that they present their game playing in terms of difference—often pointing out what it is not. Sarah starts by describing what she does *not* play (line 3). Her remarks divide games, and by implication game players, into two kinds: *The Sims* and other simulation games where people have fun, and "action" games associated with other kinds of motives (which are not described but by implication seem less wholesome and lighthearted than the idea of "fun").

When Jo goes on to mention other games apart from *The Sims* (which the two girls have already mentioned), she makes clear that she only plays them with her father (line 9), as part of her wider engagement with media, and upon the recommendation of others (line 16). She presents her game playing in terms of social interactions away from the console, and therefore not as a lonely or obsessive interest. Jo's remarks, like Sarah's, construct games as divided into two kinds; those whose quality is ensured by others (other media, other people) and those that have no such "independent" guarantee. Game players are constructed as either those who carefully select games or those who play indiscriminately. Game platforms are also divided into two kinds. The use of the word *our* (line 8) presents the PC as the family's technology but the console (she uses *a,* line 8) as her father's personal platform.

The repetition of *and* at the beginning of Kate's and Jo's responses (lines 6 and 7) suggests they want to make clear they share similar tastes. In effect, they are creating a norm—one, I would argue, that is based on gender lines. The logic of the dichotomies that Sarah and Jo establish is not contained in the oppositions themselves but in the values attached to them, which reflect certain popularly held notions surrounding games and gender—games are boys' toys, played by antisocial and addicted geeks on dedicated technologies. This portrayal of games cannot simply be understood in terms of the girls' pattern of access to games—rather the meanings they attach to games and game play are selected to present a particular identity, defined in the first part of this interview in terms of gender.

The boys use very similar strategies to describe their own preferences, by opposing their experiences to that of the girls'. In effect, they describe their own experiences in such a way as to make clear "we aren't girls," while also seeking to protect themselves from some of the negative discourses surrounding men and gaming. For example, Joshua, Simon, and Jak describe their gaming habits in terms of genres (lines 18, 19, 27, 28, 33, 40, 48) and a broad range of individual titles. The genre categories they use are also used by the game industry to market titles to different kinds of audiences. By using them, the boys identify themselves as a target audience, as gamers, and therefore as authorities on the subject of the interview. Simon's confirmation of Jak's tastes (line 44) is similar to the girls' use of *and* (lines 6 and 7), presenting tastes as shared among the three boys. The boys do not talk about games that may be seen to appeal to women (platform and adventure games), although these are mentioned in their questionnaires.

Conceptualizing Gendered Identity in Game Culture

Statements about gaming preferences are not stable across time and context. They are therefore not a reflection of some inner essence but rather a way of situating oneself in relation to others in a particular situation. This is not to argue that students are deceptively strategic, but that they come to recognize or to know their own preferences in social contexts. For example, in the interview situation, students seek to give credibility to their answers and thereby justify their inclusion in the focus group. The way these students describe their experiences and demonstrate knowledge of games cannot be extricated from their desire to establish social bonds. This is not to suggest they are somehow hiding what they really think at any point but that thought emerges in relation to social identity. It is when the interview questions start to focus on characteristics of good game design that Sarah, for example, displays knowledge of a much wider range of games. At this point, she abandons her earlier position in order to give credibility to her statements about how good games are designed and thereby warrant expert status in the focus group.

Sarah and Joshua have played and enjoyed many of the same games. But in the focus-group interview, the differing representations they produce of their gaming experience and how they make sense of their experience as gamers are some of the ways in which they signify their gender (as well as their age, expertise, etc.), to themselves and to others.

Constructing Gender through Design: Making Computer Games

A new game-authoring tool was developed to enable young people not only to play and talk about play but also to design games. In this section, I discuss games made by two students, from the same class we worked with previously, in an after-school club eighteen months after the focus-group discussion. First, I briefly outline the software used to make these games.

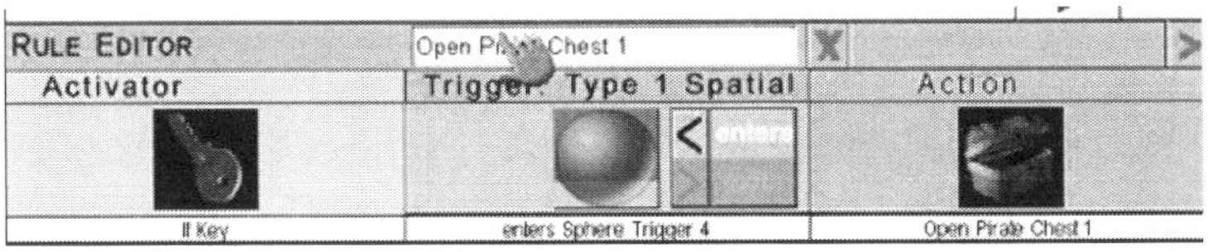

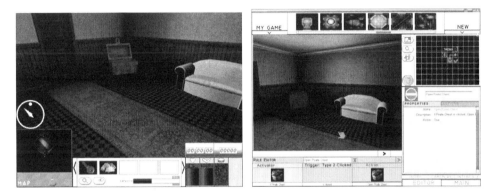

Figure 10.1 Students make rules by deciding which objects with which properties to put into the three-part rule system (see color plate).

Figure 10.2 Screen shots from Alice's game: player mode (left) and designer mode (right) (see color plate).

The game-authoring software consists of a number of ready-made assets including locations (rooms and corridors), props, characters, pick-ups (objects the player can pick up and examine), triggers (which trigger an action), and media (sound and still images—these can be imported from external sources also). These assets are organized into classes, which determine the assets' properties. Rules are written by defining the conditions under which an object changes its properties (see figure 10.1). For example, "if the player picks up the cockroach, the player gets 50 points."

Designing a game within this software means organizing relations between objects rather than producing the objects themselves or the classes within which such objects are organized. The emphasis is on designing a game rather than on producing the raw materials for presentation (see figure 10.2).

The after-school club initially consisted of twelve students and was gender balanced. Over the first few weeks, the number dropped off to about eight regulars, only two of which were girls. Below, two games are compared in order to explore how gender-based considerations seem to have influenced their design.

Alice's Game

Alice started her game with two friends who subsequently stopped coming to the club. The game is set up as a mystery for the player to resolve. Much of the game involves working out significant from insignificant objects (objects that delay or do not enhance the player's progress through the game). A series of apples left in a corridor are identified as being either healthy or unhealthy, with the player asked to "choose wisely." The reference to wisdom here is suggestive of a coming-of-age story in which the player learns how to act and behave appropriately within a particular environment.

The written messages in the game provide explanations of objects and of the conditions under which the player is acting. For example, upon finding a dagger, the player can examine it to reveal the message: "Lady Hosiepol committed suicide with this very knife and now haunts this house . . . WATCH OUT!!!!" The message forewarns of danger but does not state what it might consist of, creating a level of suspense while also giving information. Playing the game therefore involves acting with the aid of a friendly presence that helps the player. The implied in-game character and player character are positioned as being equally fearful of the dangers ahead, and one knows only a little more than the other.

Alice's game draws on a fictional form often targeted toward young women—the murder mystery featuring a young heroic detective, such as is featured in the Nancy Drew series. The narrative is unusual for a game—it is psychological rather than action-based (the aim is to find out why a woman committed suicide). The genre of narrative that Alice draws on is found across media platforms, rather than primarily in games. This is somewhat reminiscent of Jo's remark in the focus groups that she played only games based on other media franchises.

Alice goes to some length to suggest the presence of a helper character. The nature of this relationship enacts familiar conventions about male and female relations—none of the boys had a message with a helpful, convivial tone in his game. In her choice of narrative genre and creation of mood, Alice is constructing her player as female, and in so doing, positioning herself also as a female designer. This process is not unconscious, or simply a consequence of Alice's experience of games—she was a keen game player, particularly interested in platform games, but with a wide repertoire of gaming experiences to draw on. In taking from this experience to inform design work, she emphasized features that defined her audience in terms of gender.

Simon's Game

In configuring his game, Simon stated he drew inspiration from one of his favorite games at the time, *Silent Hill,* which he liked because of its near-impossible puzzles. The opening message tells the player they have been imprisoned by a maniac, but the story line is not developed. In the first half of the game, however, explicit instructions are often given to the player on what to do—click on this, use this here. The player is thereby given help on how to progress, but rather than suggesting a helper character, as Alice did, Simon frames the first section of his game as a "training level," with the player given instructions on what actions to perform. However, the second level does not draw on the skills acquired in the training level; to emulate the complexity of *Silent Hill,* Simon designs challenges for which the player cannot be prepared.

The game is structurally organized to reference a range of game conventions. The weapons are spaced out from small (a knife) to large (a mine), the sequence indicating increasing firepower. Similarly, the obstacles to be overcome are organized to suggest a progressively increasing level of difficulty. Simon here draws on the convention whereby computer games initiate players into the rules of play and then become increasingly difficult, while providing increasingly larger weapons to overcome challenges.

The basis on which Simon organizes his game positions him as a game fan in a gendered way. He emphasizes those aspects that are often said to appeal to dedicated male gamers (see Jenkins this volume): the fearsome weapons, the fantasy-based action, the high binary stakes (win or lose). Simon could have drawn on any aspect of the *Silent Hill* games including the highly developed narrative, which is de-emphasized in favor of fearsomely challenging puzzles. It would be simplistic to deduce from this that Simon is not interested in well-developed narrative or believable characters—in fact, his list of favorite games is dominated by games with these two elements, unlike Alice's list. Rather, the basis on which Simon configures his game is designed to establish a particular social identity in the group—the knowledgeable, well-experienced gamer. It is precisely because members of the group will recognize and acknowledge an interest in weapons and ludic design as "male" interests, according to prevalent social norms, that Simon's game is effective as a statement of gendered identity. It is precisely because these social norms exist that they are drawn on by students to establish themselves as gendered.

Challenging or Perpetuating Stereotypes?

Alice and Simon make games that identify each author's gender in normative ways. So in giving students game-authoring tools in a mixed setting, were we simply giving them resources to perpetuate existing stereotypes about games for girls and games for boys?

I would say not, for the following reasons: Game-authoring is a new representational resource, which allows young people to express themselves through a medium (game design) that was previously inaccessible to them. Alice and Simon are drawing on their knowledge of games in producing their own games—this is how their games are comprehensible and playable. The reason their games reenact game-based gender norms is that it is precisely in relation to such norms (either for or against them) that games are intelligible (see Taylor this volume). However, norms are never simply maintained but always remade—or made anew—in new games and new situations. So making a game means designing in conventional ways in order to be understood, but also appropriating such conventions and adapting them to one's particular situation—and therefore, in effect, changing such conventions (Kress 2003).

In addition, the process of making a game means that Alice and Simon are not simply interpreting or talking about conventions of design; they are following the process by which such conventions become established. Alice's use of sound to distinguish among apples is not a copy of an established convention. Rather it indicates that she has learned the generative rules whereby conventions become meaningful, enabling players to act in particular ways. In effect, Alice and Simon have learned what it means to design. They draw on established conventions, but the bigger issue is that they are in a position to reshape design patterns. In reference to Consalvo's work, however, it is important to qualify this by emphasizing that women's ability to shape the development of games and, more generally, engage in important social practices, is a function of particular institutions. Challenging the marginalization of women in social practices cannot be achieved without also challenging how institutions work.

Working in a Girls' School

Our understanding of the data collected in the coed school was influenced by our experience of working in a girls' school. I make only a couple of points about this here. Carr (2005) has an excellent paper about this site of research, which explores the issues it raised more fully.

In the girls' school, students claimed to play games across the range of genres. This suggested that they attached a different meaning to their experience as gamers compared to girls in the coed school. Given that gender was not a source of difference among students, they constituted their identities along other axes such as their fandom of *Harry Potter,* their maturity in liking more adult-oriented games, their preference for anime, and so on. The students did not understand their needs in terms of being female players or designers but rather as *Star Wars* or *Buffy* fans. In designing games, students often borrowed from the narratives of films and books and targeted an audience of fellow fans on the basis of their knowledge of a story rather than their gender. It is not that their games were dramatically different from Simon's and Alice's in terms of play mechanics, but that features were not made significant in terms of gender.

This aspect of the research study suggested that in a social context where gender identity did not need to be established through difference (boy vs. girl), the way girls discussed, interpreted, and designed games was not used to achieve a gendered identity but rather other aspects of their identity. I do not wish to suggest by this that issues pertaining to gender were eliminated from game playing and design activities—the students' experience of different media was clearly shaped by material differences in society relating to gender. However, the ways in which students transformed their experience of these media in designing games were not motivated by their need to establish themselves as distinctively female designers. Norms are therefore not simply imposed on people but used actively to construct identity. These students drew on different descriptive norms than the girls in the coed school because classifying games (including their own) in terms of their "gender orientation" served limited purpose.

Conclusions

These findings indicate the importance of recognizing the role of social context in how students discuss and make games [see Fullerton et al. (this volume) and Consalvo (this volume) on the importance of crafting environments that support women]. The software design was informed by the finding that it is less important to provide girl- or boy-friendly assets, and more important to focus on maximizing the opportunities for students to define the meanings of those assets themselves. In practice, this meant creating an authoring tool that allowed for extensive personalization of assets and design patterns so that students had extensive control over the genre of game they made and the events that took place within it.

Differences in the way young people make sense of games are better explained in terms of how they construct their identity in a broad cultural context as well as in specific situations rather than relying on essentialist definitions of identity that seek to pin down *boy* or *girl* to fixed positions. It is precisely because the students are highly aware of norms relating to gender that they remain effective (from their point of view) in enabling them to assume an identity. As Taylor suggests, research that uses *boy* or *girl* as natural variables should be wary of tautologically "discovering" the very norms its research questions assume and uphold.

However, to enable more equitable access to the pleasures and benefits of gaming, it is also insufficient to simply critique existing social norms in game-related social practices. The point is to change them. This is the potential value of developing game design tools, so that game design can become an everyday, domestic leisure activity. By widening the range of people who make games, and democratizing access to game design tools, new forms of representation, game play, and participatory activities can emerge. As a result, new resources for constituting a gendered identity can also become available.

This chapter shows the value of exploring the different and variable ways in which people make sense of games, according to why and where they are playing, discussing, or making them. If we wish to reformulate the norms that distinguish gamers on the basis of gender, we need to understand how games are involved in social relations and people's sense of self.

Acknowledgment

This research is generously supported by the Paccit Link program: www.paccit.gla.ac.uk.

References

Andersen, N. A. (2003) *Discursive Analytical Strategies: Understanding Foucault, Koselleck, Laclau, Luhman.* London: Polity Press.

Butler, J. (2004) *Undoing Gender.* London: Routledge.

Butler, J. (1999). *Gender Trouble: Feminism and the Subversion of Identity* (2nd edition). London: Routledge.

Butler, J. (1993). *Bodies That Matter: On the Discursive Limits of Sex.* London: Routledge.

Carr, D. (2005) Contexts, gaming pleasures, and gendered preferences. *Simulation and Gaming* 36(4), 464–482. www.childrenyouthandmediacentre.co.uk/Pics/SimAndGameCarr.pdf.

Cassell, J., and Jenkins, H. (eds.). (2000). *From Barbie to Mortal Kombat: Gender and Computer Games.* Cambridge, Mass.: The MIT Press.

Kress, G. (2003). *Literacy in the New Media Age.* London: Routledge.

Pelletier, C. (2005). The uses of literacy in studying computer games: Comparing students' oral and visual representation of games. *English Teaching: Practice and Critique* 4(1), 40–59. http://education.waikato.ac.nz/journal/english_journal/uploads/files/2005v4n1art3.pdf.

Thomas, A., and V. Walkerdine (2000). The girl as a cyberchild Paper presented at the Association of Internet Researchers' Conference, Kansas, United States.

11 Getting Girls into the Game: Toward a "Virtuous Cycle"

Tracy Fullerton, Janine Fron, Celia Pearce, and Jacki Morie (Ludica)

This chapter challenges employers, educators, and game designers to recognize and change the ways in which current cultures of game making and game play discourage women and girls from interest and participation in the field. Based on our professional experience and conversations with female game students, faculty, and designers, we propose the "ideal" work environment and describe the historical and continuing disparities that inhibit women from becoming motivated and engaged in both the game playing and making processes, which we argue are highly connected. Our goal is to create a "virtuous cycle" that draws more women into game creation through more inclusive learning, play, and work environments.

Background

This chapter was authored by Ludica, a game design and art collective devoted to developing innovative design concepts that explore the potential of games to express women's narratives, aesthetics, culture, and play. Ludica's members combine experience in virtual reality, art and technology collaboration, game design, computer science, academic research, the game and theme park industries, fine art, photography, and graphic design. A critical component of Ludica's mission is to identify and develop methodologies and organizational contexts that provide more inclusive and productive environments in which women can actively contribute to the game design process. In this chapter, we bring to bear our own experience as designers, authors, researchers, and teachers, as well as conversations with women in industry, academia, and current and former students, to outline a vision for a future in which the culture of game design is more conducive to female participation.

Imagine a job description that looked like this:

Wanted: Talented game designers. We have your ideal job in the perfect workplace!

Our environment: A casual yet intimate setting, with lots of floor space and comfortable open areas designed to encourage spontaneous brainstorming sessions. Semiprivate office spaces surround these areas and allow for reflective or focused working time. Décor includes abundant plants, windows, and lots of light with fun accents including a display of historic games from across the centuries. Group gathering areas for eating and talking boast comfortable, fun, and sometimes wacky seating arrangements. Outside garden seating area also available and a variety of nutritious food is brought in for purchase daily.

We pride ourselves on creating excellent products in a collaborative development environment. Overtime is kept to a minimum by setting realistic production schedules. Several excellent child-care and elder-care facilities are located nearby.

Our people: Talented, passionate, good communicators, respectful of others' ideas, and supportive. They offer constructive, helpful criticism that challenges rather than intimidates. We look for self-motivated, intelligent, intellectually curious talent that is diverse, both in ethnicity, gender, background, expertise, breadth, and ideas. Applicants should have a great sense of humor and be tolerant, empathetic, and nonjudgmental. Supervisors are encouraged to offer guidance and feedback but also to listen and help draw out creative ideas from their team members. We expect a mutually supportive environment with time for both group and individual work and contributions.

Our philosophy includes emphasis on methods to do the following:

- Empower people to act on their ideas.
- Relieve the creative team from administrative details so they can focus, without locking them out of the decision process.
- Challenge everyone to rise beyond ordinary expectations of competency and achievement.

Tracy Fullerton, Janine Fron, Celia Pearce, and Jacki Morie

- Build time into the workweek for experimentation and learning.
- Support conference travel; encourage presenting and publishing work, if possible.
- Promote personal and professional development.
- Encourage everyone to suggest ideas and try their hand at different roles or projects to stay fresh.
- Focus on quality of work and the workplace as critical elements of quality of life.

The ideal work environment described was assembled based our own professional experience as well as qualitative interviews with women in game-related industries, arts, and academia. We asked them what inspired their interest in game design and asked them to describe their ideal work environment for game creation. In our conversations with female game-design students and game designers we also identified the chicken-and-egg problem that more girls and women would be interested in games if more games existed that girls and women liked to play and if work environments could be found that were more supportive of their values and work styles. Far from being an academic exercise, we see this description as a goal that industry must aspire to in order to increase the appeal of games to a broader audience. Consalvo (this volume) describes the distressing state of working conditions in the gaming industry, in dramatic contrast to the idealistic vision here. Here we provide evidence that the ideal working environment does not currently exist, describe some of the reasons why, and highlight how this state of affairs has implications for women's involvement in gaming.

The Current Industry Scenario

Women are the fastest-growing group of video and computer game consumers, making up an estimated 43 percent of players (ESA 2005). A recent study by the Consumer Electronics Association (Brightman 2006) found that in the twenty-four-to-thirty-five-year-old age group, women outnumber male players by a factor of nearly two to one, largely based on the growing popularity of Web and downloadable (casual) games. Yet a survey by the International

Game Developers Association found that only 11.5 percent of the digital game industry workforce in North America is female. What's more, while 30 percent of game writers are female, women's roles tend to be weighted heavily toward operations and human resources (47%), public relations and marketing (25%), and production (21%). In the roles of executive, artist, designer, and audio producer, women occupy 10 to 12 percent of roles, while they constitute a mere 5 percent of programmers; in the UK this figure is even lower (Haines 2004). The IGDA report also found that women earn on average $9,000 less than their male counterparts, even with equivalent tenure in the industry. The low representation of female programmers and the salary discrepancy are consistent with national data.

Both the IGDA and the Haines reports cited here, as well as Consalvo (this volume), identify a number of factors relevant to the disparity in female participation in the game industry, especially in creative and technical fields. These include extreme working conditions and poor quality of life, a misconception that girls don't play games, the industry practice of making games that makers (most of whom are men) like to play, an unfriendly workplace environment and "garage hacker" culture, and alienating business practices such as "booth babes" at trade shows. Both reports also noted a general decline in female participation within the IT industry. (In the UK, only 22 percent of IT workers were female in 2004, as opposed to 50 percent in 1960.) Based on these reports, it would seem that girls and women are less interested in pursuing computers and games as a career because they seek a more balanced lifestyle and are not as willing to work the long hours that have become standard in the game industry.

Comments culled from the IGDA and Haines studies suggest a general tenor of apathy among the majority of the largely male practitioners of the game industry. Respondents to the IGDA survey, 88.5 percent of whom were male, felt that diversity was not an issue; more important was a "good quality team" or "creating a good quality game," the definition of which is driven by the current workforce makeup. A female game industry worker in the UK reported a manager stating that women were "more trouble than they're worth" (Haines 2004). Many men in both reports asserted that they were "gender neutral," even though the data regarding hiring, promotion, and salaries suggest otherwise. They also argued that since the target market is largely male, an assertion we now know to be untrue, it is appropriate that the designers should be male.

Improving working conditions in the game industry would benefit male and female workers alike. And if it attracts more females to the game industry, it will lead to expanding the nature of games, the breadth of their appeal, and the size of the market.

How to Get More Women in the Game: A Roadmap

Perhaps the largest hurdle for greater gender equity in game creation is that women would aspire to be game designers more frequently if there were more games available they enjoyed. In our interviews, as well as in our experiences with our students, we identified this as a classic chicken-and-egg, or as we like to term it, hen-and-egg, problem. Although research in this topic is limited, current evidence suggests that inclusion of female game designers tends to result in game designs that appeal to females. In an empirical study, Heeter and colleagues (2005) found that girls rate games envisioned by all-girl teams more favorably than games envisioned by all-male teams, without knowing the gender of the design team. Commercial game design teams that included more women in key design and production roles have produced products that women enjoy. For example, one of our interview subjects employed at Maxis, makers of *The Sims,* a game estimated to have between 40 and 50 percent female players (Becker 2001; Dickey and Summers 2005), described it this way:

> On the original Sims game (February 2000), 50% of the people credited as designers are female (2 of 4). 40% of the people credited as producers are female (4 of 10 producers).
>
> Since then, The Sims development teams tend to have more women on average than other teams here at EA. After the base game, I think lots of women were drawn to work for Maxis (myself included) because we like The Sims. It is a cycle: make a game that appeals to women, draw more women to work on games, make more games that appeal to women.

We refer to this cycle as the "virtuous cycle." In this case, we conflate women and girls because our experience with our students shows that women

Tracy Fullerton, Janine Fron, Celia Pearce, and Jacki Morie

who pursue the study of game design typically played games as children and teenagers.

Through our experience and conversations, we have identified the presence of a tipping point that attracts women to game design: this is the notion of games as "entertainment plus." Without discounting the notion of pure entertainment or "escape from reality," games and play can also have other values. The power of play to change the world and have a positive impact on society as a whole can inspire a generation of game designers. For instance, cognitive and educational possibilities of games appeal to female game design students, as do games that allow for altered states of consciousness. This perspective is consistent with Margolis and Fisher's research on female computer science majors—that helping the world rather than just learning algorithms is most motivating to female students (2002). One interesting example of this is Susana Ruiz, who created the game *Darfur Is Dying* as her graduate thesis at University of Southern California's Interactive Media program. Ruiz entered the program with a focus on interactive documentary, not game design, but quickly realized the power of games to effect social change and she became interested in the form. Based on the success of the *Darfur* game, Ruiz and her classmate Ashley York, producer of *Darfur Is Dying,* started a company focused specifically on socially relevant game design.

In addition to social relevance, our discussions revealed that female (and male) students are often inspired to create games because doing so provides the opportunity to explore, experiment, and fail safely. They typically enjoy the game development process, describing it as being challenging, interdisciplinary, and collaborative; engaging diverse skills; and integrating creativity with structure. One interview subject, a student, described the practice of making games as

> an odd amalgam of all disciplines and knowledge sets. They mix creativity and technology to form something that can transport people to other worlds, convey deep messages, and cause real emotion in people for little more than sprites on a screen.

In the context of university programs, students and professors tend to view game design as a kind of renaissance discipline that requires not only artistic and technical aptitude but also higher orders of thinking that integrate disciplines from mathematics to sociology to history to visual arts.

Thus it would appear that for women, games and game design provide a challenging form of interdisciplinary expression that combine imagination, creativity, and social interaction, and can also have cultural, educational, or personal value in addition to games' merits as entertainment.

The Importance of Early Experience

An interest in designing games and playful products can often be traced back to positive early experiences of play with family, friends, and peers. For many girls, fantasy and imagination often spring from role-playing with dolls, re-enacting scenes from treasured books, and creating festive events including tea parties and playing dress-up. In many cases, girls devise their own games. Pamela Dell, creator of the Purple Moon characters, recalls spending

> long unsupervised summer days outside (and sometimes inside) creating games by myself or with my sisters and a few neighborhood kids. We imagined ourselves into all kinds of worlds, making props from whatever we had on hand and playing various roles depending on the game and who was available to join in.

Barbara Stafford, curator and author of *Devices of Wonder*, acknowledges "Games of make-believe provide opportunities for risk taking, pattern making, puzzle solving, as well as offering powerful models for the child's future self" (Stafford, Terpak, and Poggi 2001).

Most of the women we interviewed remembered playing video games, such as *Pong* and *Zork*, with their families. Similarly, in *Joystick Nation*, dedicated to her "vidkid little brother," author J. C. Herz states: "When it comes to videogames, teenage boys are the ones with positive female role models. It's painful to say this, but boys' games have the only female characters worth playing. They always get the cool stuff first" (Herz 1997). Elina Ollila, a game designer from Nokia Research Center, recalls:

> When I was a kid, even single-player computer gaming was quite social. Our friends did not have computers, so often it was me and

my brother and sometimes his friends sitting around the computer and watching one person playing and others commenting. I did not know any girls who played computer games. When I was a teen, I started to play more pen & paper RPGs [role-playing games] (again with boys) and then later started to play more computer games again.

Another game designer recalls:

> Some of my best memories are of hanging out in the arcade, playing *Galaga* while holding an ice cream in one hand, roller-skating from game to game. It was great. Later, I got into *D&D* [*Dungeons and Dragons*], and was the only girl "allowed" to play in our group.

These early experiences pave the way to an interest in game development, but male-dominated environments can limit girls' involvement. In fact, computer labs in schools or clubhouses are often dominated by boys, who tend to elbow out the girls and take control of the equipment. (Margolis and Fisher 2002)

The male-dominated environment can serve as an incentive to some, at least initially. Rebecca Allen, a pioneer of computer graphics and game design, comments in *Women, Art, and Technology:*

> I always like to go where I am not supposed to be. I was very much a part of the computer graphics research community, but I did not see why I shouldn't go to this very commercial "low" art form and find out what was driving it. . . . I also thought that maybe I could change some of the video games and make them more artistic, but 3D games were so expensive to build that the industry did not want to experiment. They wanted to play it very safe, imitating *Doom*-like games that were already popular. When I first started at Virgin Interactive Entertainment, there was a lot of potential for new and different ideas, but it changed quickly; I lost my interest because I knew there was no way to really express my ideas. (Allen and Huhtamo 2003)

Allen went on to become an artist and college professor, a career that afforded her more creative freedom.

The Role of Education in Getting Women into the Game

Recently, a number of universities have begun to offer both graduate and undergraduate degrees in game design and development. Although the game industry has not traditionally looked to academia for new talent, that trend is beginning to change because of these programs. Electronic Arts (EA), the largest employer in the game industry today, has said that they plan to dramatically increase their university hires over the next several years. University of Southern California's Interactive Media program and Georgia Tech's Digital Media program partner regularly with EA and other game companies on research projects, classes, conferences, and internship programs. What this means for young women interested in the game industry is that academia now offers a potential entry path to industry via internships and recruitment relationships. Currently, the primary path of entry to the game industry is to take a junior position as a game tester, a job that requires being a "hard-core gamer," thus ruling out most women. This new academic entry point has had the effect of offering young women improved opportunities for employment because they can prove themselves on student development teams, build confidence and skill sets, and explore their own creative interests and insights in game design in the academic environment before trying to break into the game industry. Thus educational programs can serve to attract young women to the field, help them to gain employment and train them to contribute effectively once they have entered the game industry. Of course, these programs offer the same advantages to male students who want to get into the industry; however, if properly leveraged, the effect on young women could be far greater. Although women come to the subject with equal interest and talent, they often lack confidence in their ability to gain access to a male-dominated industry. This is where academic and educational institutions can make a significant impact on shifting the "vicious cycle," or hen-and-egg syndrome mentioned previously, creating a bridge between aspiring female game designers and the game industry clubhouse.

The following are several brief case studies of young women who have graduated from some of these programs and are currently making their mark in the game industry:

JEN HOLLCROFT   BA in East Asian languages and cultures with a double minor in game design and development and in game programming at USC. "I came

Tracy Fullerton, Janine Fron, Celia Pearce, and Jacki Morie

into college with very little understanding of what I wanted to do," says Holl-croft. "I was a bit interested in everything." Hollcroft found herself interested in "physics, chemistry, programming, calculus, English, Spanish, Japanese, his-tory, electronic music, etc." In her junior year she decided to take a game design class. "The concepts really were interesting," she says, "and I found it quickly became my favorite class. It fascinated me to study the way games worked, and to come up with game concepts of my own. . . . After that class, nearly all the classes I took were related to game design. The more I studied, the clearer it became that this was the right fit for me." Hollcroft is currently interning at Electronic Arts helping to define concepts and prototypes for an as-yet-unannounced project. Although she had the technical and creative talent to work in the game industry, the classes in game design were what offered her an entry point to the game industry as a career choice, via an industry internship.

KELLEE SANTIAGO   MFA in interactive media at USC. As producer of the student research project *Cloud* (figure 11.1), Santiago was part of a team dedicated to creating an emotionally rich, age- and genderless game experience. The over-arching design goal for *Cloud* was to create a game that would reach out to

Figure 11.1   *Cloud* is a student research project created at the EA Game Innovation Lab at USC. It exemplifies an "ageless and genderless" game design (see color plate).

gamers and nongamers alike and expand the potential market as well as emotional palette for games. After graduation, Santiago and classmate Jenova Chen formed thatgamecompany and produced yet another rich, age- and genderless game experience—*flOw* for the PS3. These young designers are challenging the industry's expectations of what makes great game play, and who plays games, by example.

Vivian Tam   BA in studio art, University of California, Irvine. An avid gamer since childhood, Tam was already computer-savvy by the time she entered the university. In determining her career plans, Tam asked to meet with her game design professor, a woman. Even though she really wanted to become a game designer, she expressed concern that as a woman it would be too much of a struggle to take on a career in the game industry. One reason was that there were few companies she would want to work at. Another was she was concerned that the industry was too challenging for females. Her professor helped her get a summer internship at Whyville.net, a massively multiplayer online world consisting of science games, which transformed into a full-time job. The lead designer at Whyville.net is a woman, and 60 percent of its players are girls. (Whyville.net's Jennifer Sun is also a contributor to this volume.)

In the background of these case studies are several women professors who recognized these students' talent and took deliberate steps toward helping them succeed. It is this type of difference that academia can make for young women who may have all the same skills and talent as the young men who aspire to be game designers and yet don't believe this career is open to them.

But can these academic programs offer more than just an environment that will attract female students to the current game industry? Can they also provide an environment for these young women to experiment creatively, to question accepted wisdom about what games are, and to imagine not only a game industry in which they can participate but also a range of games that addresses these young women's unique interests and perspectives? Or do they merely provide female game students with an opportunity to experience firsthand the same lack of diversity that currently exists in the game industry before embarking on their careers? Of all the game design students we interviewed, not one had taken a class or had an assignment or exercise that dealt specifically with gender in terms of design process, workplace environment, team dynamics, or inspiration. Hollcroft says, "It seems to me to be a gross oversight in the curriculum and the industry, even taking into account that it's a male-dominated field." Estefania Pickens, a graduate student from the Entertainment Technology Center at Carnegie Mellon University now working at Disney Imagineering, says, "Most of the females at the ETC complained that there was nothing at all addressing gender issues within our program or the industry. How are we ever going to get it to change if we don't address it at the academic level?"

The eventual effect of academic programs on the overall number of women in the industry remains to be seen. However, these new design programs provide several promising elements. The first is a comfortable place for those with interdisciplinary interests to coalesce those interests into an industrial perspective. Course work provides young women important opportunities to "prove themselves" as valuable team members. They encourage a dialog about critical recognition and analysis of gender issues in games. And perhaps most important, they present girls with positive role models and mentorships. For example, one of the coauthors, Tracy Fullerton, teaches game play mechanics and design that surmount gender stratification to get at the heart of what games can offer. Another coauthor, Celia Pearce, gives her students assignments that constrain them from using some of the classic themes of violence and killing that alienate many female players. Many of our interview subjects pointed at mentors, including Fullerton and Pearce, as providing the necessary support to encourage them to go for their dreams.

Margolis and Fisher (2002) call upon educational institutions to take concrete action to address such gender issues:

> Our analysis of the nexus of confidence and interest leads to an emphasis on institutional responsibility. We do not blame the student or expect her to toughen up, turn a blind eye, or adjust. We believe that educational institutions and their culture, curriculum, faculty-student relations, norms, and standards must change.

Thus, academics are in the unique position of training the next-generation game professional, and can potentially influence *all* their students both male *and* female to critique, reconsider, and possibly reconstruct the status quo of

Figure 11.2   Ludica game design events that seek to create a more female-friendly ethos for game creation (see color plate). Photo: Ivana Murder.

male domination in the game industry. The authors of this chapter, all "culture workers" (Laurel 2001) who have worked in industry, academia, and the arts, feel it is critical to provide positive models for students and faculty alike, and have hosted a number of workshops to this end (figure 11.2).

Positive Steps: Games that Motivate Women to Make Games

The Sims is cited earlier as an example of a game that could counter the vicious cycle (of women being disinterested in game play, thus, disinterested in game design) with a virtuous cycle: girls who like to play *The Sims* were inspired to design games. Next we provide examples of projects specifically designed to re-configure game play paradigms, representation, and even game creation itself, to inspire girls to engage with the game development workforce. The number of such projects is beginning to grow, and it is our hope that their presence will have a positive influence on the paths games will take.

Brenda Laurel (whose work is included in this volume), a long-time pioneer of computing, interface design, and game design who has worked at both Apple and Atari and introduced the notion of "computers as theater," has been a pioneer in this area. In the mid-1990s, she launched Purple Moon Software, producing interactive games designed specifically for tween girls. Laurel describes some of the challenges of creating games that are innovative and that address the real-world concerns of contemporary girls:

> At Purple Moon we played with various structures for interactive narrative and tried to do positive work for girls in the context of popular culture. I took a lot of heat from some people who call themselves feminists for portraying girl characters who cared about such things as appearance, popularity, belonging, betrayal, and all the other strum und drang of preadolescent friendship. Some people thought I shouldn't do that because girls shouldn't behave in this way. Bu they do, you see. And who they become depends a great deal on how they manage their transit through the narrows of girlhood.
>
> When we had to choose, we sacrificed political correctness in order to meet girls where they were, in the realities of their own lives. (Laurel 2001)

Meeting girls "in the realities of their own lives" is exactly what is needed still today. More recently, Mary Flanagan (another contributor to this volume) has been awarded grants from the National Science Foundation to create games that rethink girls' relationship to science and technology. About her series of Web-based games for girls, *The Adventures of Josie True,* Flanagan states: "representing adventurous, smart, and scientific women of color is very important to enhancing all players' exposure to what constitutes a hero." (Flanagan/Leccetti Interview 2006)

Flanagan's newest project, *RAPUNSEL,* is a game that teaches tween girls how to program by developing dance steps for their game characters.

> Instead of matters of representation . . . my attention has turned toward thinking and reworking computer-media specific things such as "game goals" and "architectures" as important sites for social change and ac-

tivism. How we participate in digital culture, how we are framed—as consumers or as producers—is fundamental to this notion.

Other pioneers, such as Kelleher, Hayes, Denner and Campe, and Pelletier (contributors to this volume) are developing new methods and settings to expand girls' and young women's interests in game creation.

There is much work to be done and we hope the points made here will help guide the way toward solutions. It is a multidimensional challenge, targeted in part by the words of Flanagan:

> My belief is that by changing who authors systems, there may be some kind of change, at least through empowering and sharing knowledge. In part IT is a knowledge economy. Therefore, this certainly means networking women together to support their success in technological arenas as much as possible as they become authors. I think it also means shifting how we teach technology, as well as who designs hardware and even programming languages, too.
> (Flanagan as quoted by Laccetti 2006)

Conclusion

The job description that introduces this chapter is a way to begin a dialog about how to draw women into game creation. We identify some of the challenges, and begin to point out some of the solutions. We have consistently heard the industry lament, "We would include more women in the game development process; we just don't get qualified applications." Our "ideal" job environment serves as an initial vision that both teachers and industry can use to begin to craft an environment that is more female-friendly. In addition, as we point out, creating more games that appeal to girls and women will help to create a "virtuous cycle" to draw more women into game creation. This includes games that meet them where they live, and by doing so brings them into the process of future creation.

It is this "virtuous cycle" that we encourage educators, mentors, employers, and game designers of all genders to make the rule and not the exception.

Tracy Fullerton, Janine Fron, Celia Pearce, and Jacki Morie

Acknowledgments

Ludica would like to thank all the women who participated in the interviews that were referenced in this chapter; also a special thanks to Mary Flanagan for her support with this research.

References

Allen, R., and Erkki Huhtamo (2003). In J. Malloy (ed.), *Women, Art, and Technology.* Cambridge, Mass.: The MIT Press.

Becker, D. (2001). Newsmaker: The secret behind "The Sims." CNET News.com. http://news.com.com/2008-1082-254218.html.

Brightman, J. (2006). Study: Women gamers outnumber men in 25–34 age group. *GameDailyBiz.* http://biz.gamedaily.com/industry/feature/?id=12424.

Dickey, C., and N. Summers (2005). A female sensibility: Videogame makers have ignored half their potential market. Now they're having a second look, and altering the possibilities of gaming. *Newsweek International.* http://www.msnbc.msn.com/id/9378641/site/newsweek.

Entertainment Software Association (2005). *2005 Essential Facts about the Computer and Video Game Industry.* Washington, D.C.: The ESA.

Haines, L. (2004). *Why Are There So Few Women in Games?* Manchester: Media Training Northwest.

Heeter, C., K. Chu, R. Egidio, and P. Mishra (2005). Do girls prefer games designed by girls? Proceedings from ISA: *55th Annual Conference of the International Communication Association,* June, 2005, New York.

Herz, J. C. (1997). *Joystick Nation: How Videogames Ate Our Quarters, Won Our Hearts, and Rewired Our Minds.* New York: Little, Brown & Company.

IGDA (2005). *Game Developer Demographics: An Exploration of Workforce Diversity.* San Francisco: International Game Developers Association.

Laccetti, J. (2006). Interview with Mary Flanagan. Furtherfield.org. http://www.furtherfield.org/displayreview.php?From=Index&review_id=179.

Laurel, B. (2001). *Utopian Entrepreneur.* Cambridge, Mass.: The MIT Press.

Margolis, J., A. Fisher (2002). *Unlocking the Clubhouse: Women in Computing.* Cambridge, Mass.: The MIT Press.

Stafford, B. M., F. Terpak, and I. Poggi (2001). *Devices of Wonder: From the World in a Box to Images on a Screen.* Los Angeles: Getty Trust Publications.

12 Crunched by Passion: Women Game Developers and Workplace Challenges

Mia Consalvo

This chapter describes women's experiences in the game industry—why they stay and why they leave. Recruiting and retaining more women in the game industry is central to the call for getting more girls to play digital games. Although no one has yet shown causal data, anecdotal evidence does suggest a more diverse workforce can lead to a more diverse game-playing audience. For example, 40 percent of the development team for *The Sims Online* are female, and 60 percent of the players of *The Sims Online* are female (Hanman 2005). Likewise, the early arcade game *Centipede* had a female developer, and was quite popular with female players (Chen 2006). Additionally, there are several prominent female alternate-reality game (ARG) developers as well as greater gender diversity in the ARG development community, and the player base for ARGs is gender balanced as well (Phillips 2005).

Creating and maintaining a more diverse workforce, it seems, could result in games that are more gender inclusive, and that better reflect game play styles and content that would interest a broader population of gamers. Proponents of such a strategy also argue that the current console market demographic has tapped out young adult men and boys and needs to seek new populations in order to grow. Successes include the explosion of the casual games market, which includes online sites such as Pogo and MSN Games, as well as downloadable games like *Yohoho! Puzzle Pirates* (Taylor 2006). Likewise, the success of games like the UK-released *Singstar,* and the PlayStation2 peripheral controller EyeToy, suggest that women and girls can be appealed to, even with console games.

Yet, maintaining women's active participation in the game industry on a consistent basis has met with many challenges. Beyond design elements, factors involving marketing disconnects, structural sexism, and resistance to change continue to drive many women away. This chapter explores that terrain, describing why women remain or leave jobs in game development. In particular, I argue that programs, pipelines, and curricula meant to encourage girls and women to enter this industry will have little long-term impact if women leave the industry in a decade or less, as recent reports have suggested (IGDA 2004).

Bringing Women into Games: Programmatic Efforts and Challenges

What do women like about working in the game industry? In her ethnographic work exploring the players and world of *EverQuest,* T. L. Taylor argues for considering the interests and pleasures of women as central to understanding the game, rather than seeing them as the "exceptions, data points that are outliers to be written off" (2006, p. 94; see also Taylor this volume). And when asked what they find pleasurable about the game, they report not only the expected social factors involved but also the importance of mastery, exploration, and displays of power that the game enables for them.

In this chapter, I take Taylor's strategy of making women's views central, and apply it to a study of the game development industry. There has been increasing attention in the past few years to quality of life issues in the digital game industry. Although women make up a small percentage of developers (even smaller than the proportion of women who play games), by taking their concerns and challenges as central issues to explore, we can arrive at a better understanding of who "fits" in the industry and who does not, how women are fighting to keep their seat at this table, and how they experience the structural aspects of this world.

Studies suggest that one barrier to girls' participation in information technology careers is that girls hold negative beliefs about those careers. But efforts to increase women's participation in the tech field (including game development) have typically ignored or denied the reality of the work environments. Along with private individuals and companies that have made games that target certain girls (such as Brenda Laurel with Purple Moon, and Her Interactive with the *Nancy Drew* series), there has also been research designed to address the gender imbalance in this area. Along with smaller-scale research exploring game play preferences and styles (see Cunningham 2000; Kerr 2003; Schott and Horrell 2000), the federal government has directed significant amounts of money toward increasing the number of women participating in science, technology, engineering, and math (STEM) fields (AAUW 2004) with specific projects focused on having girls design, program, or modify games (see also chapters by Flanagan and Nissenbaum, Kelleher, Heeter and Winn, and Denner and Campe in this volume). Research studies by the American Association of University Women (2000), Brown (2001), Silverman and Pritchard (1996), and Smith (2000), for example, have all explored similar questions about attempts to attract girls into fields that are traditionally male dominated and have resisted integration, unlike areas such as law and medicine.

My focus here is on what happens if these efforts are successful—what kinds of work environments those future professionals are entering. The structure and functioning of the digital game industry needs greater exploration, as it is the future workplace for those girls who will be shaping the products that are ultimately circulated and used as marketing devices to further (or diminish) other individuals' interests in entering the field. As with any creative industry, it is important to understand how industry and professional constraints, biases, affordances, and practices all shape not only the products that are created but also the living conditions within that industry, and perceptions and beliefs about its processes and practices. I should also clarify that my argument is not that we can simply add more women to the industry and make it better—there are particular constraints currently built into organizational, everyday work practices that make it difficult for most workers, and in particular female workers, to survive and potentially thrive in this industry.

Models for Understanding Digital Game Industry Practices

There has been some attention from media and cultural studies scholars related to studying the means of production, such as daily work practices in organizations and how economic considerations limit the choices that consumers are presented with. Most of this work has come from political economy scholars (Meehan and Riordan 2002; Garnham 2000). Yet we need to consider not only how media industries make their profits and how media audiences are turned into products (such as desirable demographic groups) to be sold to advertisers but also how the structure of an industry limits the types of commodities or products that it produces. Past work done in this area relates to the news (Tuchman 1978) and the television industries (Gitlin 1983). More specifically, focused work by Julie D'Acci explored how the production process constrained ideas about feminism and femininity on the television show

Cagney & Lacey (1994), and more recently, Kristal Brent Zook has explored how the Fox television network created an (early) identity appealing to African-American viewers (1999). Yet much of this work has provided little guidance about how to explore other industries, or specific instances, beyond case studies.

One potential model, however, is offered in Stuart Hall's encoding/decoding theory of media production and reception. Encoding occurs during the production of a media message and involves choices about how to make sense of an event or what to include or exclude in a message. While most scholars have focused on Hall's three audience viewing/decoding positions (dominant, resistant, and negotiated), Hall also argued for the importance of the encoding process on shaping audience readings, as well as the specific elements making up that production process. He writes,

> production, here, constructs the message. . . . Of course, the production process is not without its "discursive" aspect: it, too, is framed throughout by meanings and ideas: knowledge-in-use concerning the routines of production, historically defined technical skills, professional ideologies, institutional knowledge, definitions and assumptions, assumptions about the audience and so on frame the constitution of the programme through this production structure. (2001, 1980, p. 167)

There are many avenues offered in Hall's description of what constitutes the production process, but here I focus on routines of production and professional ideologies, and how they function within the digital game industry, particularly in relation to gender.

It is important to recognize that both routines and ideologies are mutually constituted, and are contextually and materially bound. So while practices are often put in place due to particular ideological beliefs, likewise ideologies themselves can arise from practices that become entrenched or come to seem as second nature in the workplace. Thus, while certain practices may not arise from sexist (or racist) ideologies, a sexist institution can arise, due to particular practices being valued and sustained, rather than alternate practices.

This chapter explores some of the practices of the digital game industry, both in the daily functioning of the development cycle, as well as particular activities such as the production of industry workload reports that attempt to spur change in the industry as a whole. By studying both, we can see how practices inform ideologies, and ideologies inform practices. Likewise, Hall mentions "institutional knowledge" as another element informing the encoding/production process. At the end of this chapter I explore briefly how current game industry practices and ideologies have led to a certain *lack* of institutional knowledge, which is itself a value that must be deconstructed and explored.

Sources of Data

This chapter draws on several sources of information. These include my experiences working with the Women in Game Development Special Interest Group (WiGD SIG) that formed as a part of the International Game Developers Association (IGDA) in 2001. One of the more active elements of WiGD is the e-mail list, which I have subscribed to since 2002 and which generates, on average, between ten and fifty posts per day. I have also attended and spoken at the Game Developers Conference since 2002, been on the steering committee that ran the first Women's Game Conference in Austin, Texas, in 2004, and am now on the steering committee of Women in Games International, which puts on regional conferences as well as promotes the advancement of women in the game industry generally.

Additionally, I bring in data from two specific sources. One is the raw data from the IGDA's Quality of Life survey of game developers, done in 2004. That data include responses from 994 respondents, 7.1 percent of whom are women. The survey asked about such things as work environment, time spent on the job, crunch time, family life, attitudes toward work, and future expectations about employment. In addition, I have supplemented that quantitative data with in-depth interviews of ten women currently working in different types of positions within the industry including game design, programming, art, and animation. These interviews explore in greater detail their daily duties, their feelings about working in the industry, and their future plans. That data provides a deeper understanding of what the broader survey results hint at.

Practices and Routines that Discourage Women's Participation in the Game Industry

Game design has changed in major ways from the beginnings of the industry in the 1970s and 1980s. During the time of the Atari 2600 console, one person could develop and code an entire game in the period of about six months

(Robinett 2003, pp. xviii–xix). Today, production teams for "triple-A" games (which are expected to sell more than 2.5 million units[1]) can run in the triple digits themselves, with development cycles of eighteen to twenty-four months, and budgets between $10 and 50 million. Along with those increases in scale has come a division of labor, with game development being sliced into distinct areas including (at the broadest level) programming, art, animation, audio, production, and design.

Most teams work full-time for game development companies, which may or may not be owned by the company publishing the game. That work is project-based, and most often planned to conclude with the game's release during the most important buying time for any seller: the fourth-quarter Christmas rush. Game development is then a continual battle between what is (the majority of the time) a hard deadline for launch, and a series of creative, technical, and social challenges to meet in the process of developing a game. The result is an industry that often relies on "crunch time" and "passion" to shape artistic endeavors into business-shaped bottles.

Most game developers,[2] when interviewed, talked to casually, or heard in conversation, will admit to seeing some of these challenges. As an example that illustrates larger issucs, I want to focus on the notion of crunch time, and how it arises from industry-instituted practices such as milestones and the division of labor due to job specialization now present in most companies.

In my interviews with female game developers, I asked about the quality of their lives and what was the biggest challenge they had to deal with. The most frequent concern mentioned was crunch time. Game development projects, as mentioned previously, stretch over many months and can involve the development of new game engines, libraries of assets, and considerable (and unpredictable) creative work. Much of that work, while budgeted for in game design documents and production planning, is unpredictable. Yet even as programmers encounter bugs and level designers create new features, developers must meet deadlines to complete specific portions of the game in order to be paid by publishers.

To meet those outside deadlines, crunch time is employed in varying degrees across most of the game industry. Crunch time is so ingrained in the work culture that most individuals report feeling "lucky" if they only have to work a standard forty- to fifty-hour week. Much more common, for periods lasting from two weeks to several months, are weekly periods of fifty to one hundred hours. Both male and female workers are subject to crunch time, but the women I spoke with raised specific concerns about working extremely long hours that are tied in to commitments to their families.

For example, at one smaller development house, Barbara[3] worked seventy-hour weeks as a lead designer in the final weeks before the product shipped. She explains, "It never starts out like that. The project is coming close to an end, you need to finish, the project slips, and you need to crunch." Although that house was not known for its overuse of crunch, Barbara eventually left the industry because

> it would have been nice if I'd felt I had a choice to be a lead and a good mom. I wouldn't be abusive but I wouldn't be there [for my children].

Even larger companies, which should be in a better position to add staff or plan for extra time, do not shy away from crunching. For example, Sylvia recently quit working for a large development company where crunch time was the norm for the last four months she was employed there:

> We had minimum 12-hour days, 14 hours preferred. Permission was required to leave the building. They wanted to make sure we'd finished or if we needed to leave we had to check. . . . They let us out one Sunday after eight hours, and told us we should be grateful we didn't have to stay for twelve.

While Sylvia left the commercial game industry to work for a small defense contractor making serious games, a few women have found game companies that let them maintain a balance between work and personal life. Eleanor left a midsized developer to work for a larger company for just that reason. Her prior employer

> had crunch time for several months, with a mandatory 60+ hours per week. This was a company that regularly had extended crunch times of 70 to 80 hours a week, over several months. There was, in fact, a fair amount of disdain from some of the company's management over the

fact that the team wasn't willing to do more than 60 hours a week, and some team members resented even that. I'm no longer with that company, obviously.

Eleanor's story also points to the fact that it isn't only women working in the industry who have a problem with crunch time. Yet some data show that they are more likely to plan to leave the industry than their male counterparts. For example, in the Quality of Life survey conducted by the IGDA, 49 percent of men responded that they planned to stay in the game industry for their entire career, while only 34 percent of women said the same (IGDA 2004). We can view these women, then, as the bellwethers for assessing the health of the overall industry and what workers will tolerate and what they will not.

These stories illustrate what other data confirm. The 2004 survey conducted by the IGDA on quality of life issues reports that 51.7 percent of both women and men said "management sees crunch as a normal part of doing business in the game industry" (2004, p. 19). Only 2.4 percent said their company "never has any crunch at all" (p. 18). Such concerns reached a flashpoint of sorts with the publication of the much-talked-about blog entry by "EA Spouse," which confirms the view that large, very successful game developers also employ such practices, even when they have the resources to reduce the load on their employees (EA Spouse 2004). She writes:

> The current mandatory hours are 9am to 10pm—seven days a week—with the occasional Saturday evening off for good behavior (at 6:30pm). This averages out to an eighty-five hour workweek.

Such practices are widespread enough that companies are considered unusual if they don't practice crunch time. For example, in explaining her average workweek of about forty-five hours, Laura says, "I work for a company that's a quality of life advocate so I feel I'm perhaps luckier than many in the industry." Similarly, Joanna reports in relation to her new employer, "whatever 'crunch time' is asked of us, we are given an equivalent amount of freedom to schedule our lives so that, IMHO,[4] it is more than made up for."

These stories work to construct ideological understandings of what it means to work in the digital game industry. Through repeated practice, crunching is discursively constructed as normal, or routine. It is the odd company that does *not* crunch, whether because they can't afford not to do so, or they simply choose not to.

For the digital game industry (as with any industry), work practices are ideological, and norms are created and maintained through repetition over time. Additionally, given that the majority of game developers work on a salary basis rather than hourly, this means that overtime generally is not compensated, and hours are not considered when setting general work or individual schedules.

What Keeps Women in the Game Industry

When asked what keeps individuals working under such conditions, most of the women I interviewed used one word—*passion*. While passion isn't a work routine, it does serve as a unifying ideology from which development companies can draw in order to justify various practices that might be considered exploitative in other industries. Thus, it is the passion for games that leads people into the industry, and the passion that keeps them going through long days, little time off, and relatively low pay.[5] Companies know this, and can trade on that passion to increase output.

The passion for making games is such an important part of one's attitude that it is often listed by game companies as a critical element when hiring potential employees. For example, in a search of job opportunities in game development studios on the Web and through Gamasutra, companies as diverse as Blizzard Entertainment, Bungie Studios, PopCap Games, Ubisoft, Radical Entertainment, Gas-Powered Games, and Collision Studios all listed a "passion for games" in either their job requirements or general job or company description. Blizzard begins its "Employment Opportunities" page with the question "Do you have the passion to create, and the will to forge, great games?" (Blizzard 2006). And under job requirements for the position of Games Lab Coordinator, Ubisoft lists as its ninth qualification "has passion and strong interest & desire in console games and PC" (Gamasutra 2006).

Likewise, studio executives have argued that passion is necessary because "people with passion don't need to be clocked. We all work on a level to make it great until we are done" (IGDA 2005). However, even some executives are beginning to acknowledge that "we're faced with fading passion due to crunch, so we must find a way to protect it and manage it" (Allard, quoted in IGDA

2005). Yet notice that while crunch time might need to be reduced, *passion* is still maintained as a central requirement for working in the industry.

Although passion continues to be cited as a necessity for working in the industry, of the women I interviewed, many (especially those who had been in the industry for ten or more years) had come from different businesses. They had not known game development was a viable career choice (and for some women when they started it truly wasn't) and thus had not planned for it. Even relative newcomers didn't always dream of working in game development. Alice, who has worked in the industry for three years, explained, "before starting [in game development] I didn't have any interest in the industry." But even if women had not developed a passion for working in the industry prior to entering it, they did generally cite a passion for playing games as helping them to make their choice. As Sylvia explained, "it was the only way I could put playing fifteen years of D&D[6] experience on my resume." Such stories suggest that for women as well as men, a "passion" for game playing is constructed as a necessity to work in the game development industry, potentially keeping away those (particularly women) who do not share the same interests in development or game play yet might still have valuable skills or ideas to contribute.

And that love of games has kept women there, sometimes working in ways they do not enjoy. Yet when some finally did leave, or considered leaving, it was still the passion that made it difficult to break away. Eleanor confirms that while she is still in the industry and has found a company that meets her needs, "I've tried to quit the game industry in the past, and returned to it. It's too addictive to work on games." Likewise, Sylvia states that her move out of the commercial game industry is probably not permanent because she can't stand to be away from making games: "I love the industry. I'm a consummate game designer. I can't *not* think about design. But it [the industry] just chews people up." Barbara relates how even two years ago she didn't see herself leaving the industry because it "has an odd vortex effect. The pull is constantly there to go work on a game. It feels very weird."

Passion is a strong ideological driver for the game industry. The ideal worker is constructed as someone possessing a "passion for games," and that passion is used to help maintain work practices that may ultimately kill the passion. Crunch time is normalized and seen as a necessary part of work, what "passionate" workers would endure to stay within the industry that means so much to them. And it does, as these interviews show. Frances, a woman working in game industry recruiting, reinforced those stories, explaining that in her opinion, "the game industry is far more exploitive of its talent than any other entertainment discipline that I've ever seen."

Additionally, as Sylvia details, "it's a glamour industry. Their answer is 'I've got 16 applications on my desk. I don't need you. I've got all these other people who want to come work for me.'" So even as the passion may fade for some workers, or not be enough to keep them in the industry, there are plenty of other passionate potential workers to take up the slack, much as EA Spouse's significant other did. To help keep women passionate about their jobs, a better balance between work and personal life is necessary.

Beyond Passion and Crunch: Institutional Knowledge or Lack Thereof

To succeed, businesses must innovate and also discard what doesn't work. To that end, they must develop norms that help them function and find ways to retain that knowledge often accumulated informally through long-standing employees. In the game industry, that institutional knowledge could include a better sense of budgeting time for game development, as well as how to effectively manage teams composed of artists and programmers, for example. While some skills may be learned prior to employment, there are certain job skills, particularly in management, that are gained only through years of experience. And without such knowledge or its individual carriers, practices that discourage women from remaining in the digital game industry will likely continue.

In the digital game industry, that institutional knowledge is constantly being lost due to the rapid turnover. For example, the IGDA Quality of Life survey found that "fewer than one lead developer in 10 has over ten years of experience" (2004, p. 16). Furthermore, more than half the respondents (51.2%) expected to leave the game industry within ten years. As the report itself states, "for the industry as a whole, such a high turnover rate is nothing short of catastrophic, and it goes a long way toward explaining our difficulty in ensuring that our projects run smoothly" (p. 16).

For this industry, then, there seems to be a greater emphasis on institutional shortsightedness than institutional memory or knowledge. Such situations have real consequences for those who work in the industry, and what kind of experience they can fall back on. As Eleanor says, we have a steady influx of young talent, but the veterans, who are the repository of collective information about how projects can succeed or fail, the ones who the executives can trust with the multi-million dollar wagers on high-end titles, aren't going to be as willing to put up with this nonsense forever. They'll leave the industry, and that's a real loss.

Yet that seems to be exactly what's happening. Sylvia explains, "It's a self-perpetuating problem. We've got people in this industry with two and three years experience heading up multi-million dollar projects." So as institutional memory fades or disappears for the long term, work routines and practices become standardized in the short term as rapid turnover, retention problems, and a work culture that valorizes youth, passion, and long hours over maturity and experience.

Reshaping the Wheel: Roundtables and White Papers

These activities and practices have not gone unnoticed by those in the game industry, as evidenced by the fact that much of this data is drawn from industry sources. One of the advocacy groups for game developers, the IGDA, has been quite active about making quality of life an important issue at the forefront of developers' attention. Likewise, women game developers have been quite active in promoting hiring practices that encourage more women to apply, and work practices that will not actively discourage them from sticking around (see Fullerton et al. this volume). Yet, as we can see, there are powerful institutional, ideological, and practical barriers that are in place that challenge such efforts.

Much of what I write about here could apply to male as well as female game developers. However, I feel it is especially important to present this argument with the female perspective as central. Women do bring some special demands to the table, whatever their family roles or obligations or personal interests may be. As part of a minority group in most development studios, they often express frustration at having to "fit in" to a masculine culture, or worse, feel that they are being "treated differently" simply because they are women. Adding those concerns to the already difficult work hours and never-ending demand for passion in their approach can leave some feeling burned out and ready to move on to other fields.

Where does this leave us? To return to Hall for a moment, it is important to investigate the production process in media companies to see how work practices and ideologies can help perpetuate systems that we find troublesome as well as beneficial. The game industry sees "passion" as a central component of the ideal worker, and uses that element to help ensure that regular practices such as crunch time are not overly protested. Yet that passion comes at a price. If a majority of workers, both women and men, plan to leave the game industry in the next decade, we should ask if the burnout and long hours are too much, and how helpful passion truly is when considering humane work practices.

If we are serious about encouraging girls and women to enter the diverse fields associated with game development, we should also take pause and consider what we are asking them to do. It may be beneficial to challenge the current work systems in addition to encouraging girls to seek employment there. One way to do that is to encourage more girls and women to work up to be studio heads and executives, who are in positions of power and are able to set policies to encourage healthy work practices.[7] With such systems in place, it is possible that new institutional memories and knowledge can develop, which can challenge the more damaging ideologies and practices we now witness in the contemporary games industry.

Notes

1. The figure of 2.5 million units is for console games only, with PC games expected to sell around 1 million for the same title. Personal communication, Eric Marcoullier, April 12, 2006.

2. In this chapter I use the term *game developer* to refer to my informants, but that use is generic, referring to anyone who is involved in the production of digital games.

3. For this project, pseudonyms are used for the women interviewed as well as the names of their current or prior companies.

4. IMHO stands for "in my humble opinion."

5. For example, beginning programmers can expect to make around $53,000 yearly, but artists including animators and designers average only about $45,000 (Duffy 2006).

6. D&D is short for *Dungeons & Dragons,* a popular tabletop fantasy-themed game played with dice, a map, a leader (Dungeon Master) and a group of players who together create adventures that can last for hours, days, or years.

7. It would be valuable to compare male- and female-led game development studios to determine if better workplace practices are found in the latter. However, I personally know of no such companies, and did not seek to compare such companies (if found) with male-led studios. That would certainly be a valuable follow-up study to conduct. Anecdotal stories of the game industry suggest that studios with greater numbers of women tend to make games that are more appealing to women, such as Maxis Studio (maker of *The Sims*), but that is the extent of information I have about the relationship between women in a game company and any possible differences in products or workplace practices.

References

AAUW (2004). *Under the Microscope: A Decade of Gender Equity Projects in the Sciences*. Washington, D.C.: American Association of University Women Educational Foundation. http://www.aauw.org/research/underthemicroscope.pdf.

AAUW Educational Foundation Commission on Technology, Gender, and Teacher Education (2000). *Tech-Savvy: Educating Girls in the New Computer Age*. Washington, D.C.: American Association of University Women Educational Foundation. http://www.aauw.org/research/girls_education/techsavvy.cfm.

Blizzard Entertainment. (2006). Employment Opportunities. Blizzard Entertainment. http://www.blizzard.com/jobopp/

Brown, B. L. (2001). Women and minorities in high-tech careers. *ERIC Digest* no. 226. http://www.eric.ed.gov/ERICDocs/data/ericdocs2sql/content_storage_01/0000019b/80/16/fc/9e.pdf

Chen, S. (2006). The rise of the woman gamer. Fierce Mobile Content. http://www.fiercemobilecontent.com/story/feature-the-rise-of-the-woman-gamer/2006-07-21.

Cunningham, H. (2000). Mortal Kombat and computer game girls. In J. Caldwell (ed.), *Electronic Media and Technoculture* (pp. 213–226). New Brunswick: Rutgers.

D'Acci, J. (1994). *Defining Women: Television and the Case of Cagney & Lacey*. Chapel Hill, N.C.: University of North Carolina Press.

Duffy. J. (2006). Are you in demand? 2006 game industry salary survey. Game Career Guide. http://gamecareerguide.com/features/266/index.php?page=1.

EA Spouse (2004). EA: The human story. http://ea-spouse.livejournal.com/.

Gamasutra (2006). Enhanced job search listing. http://www.gamasutra.com/php-bin/jobs_display.php?job_id=9535.

Garnham, N. (2000). *Emancipation, the Media, and Modernity: Arguments about the Media and Social Theory*. Oxford: Oxford University Press.

Gitlin, T. (1983). *Inside Prime Time.* New York: Pantheon Books.

Hall, S. (2001, 1980). Encoding/decoding. In M. Durham and D. Kellner (eds.), *Media and Cultural Studies: Keyworks* (pp. 166–176). Malden, Mass.: Blackwell Publishers.

Hanman, N. (2005). Jobs for the girls. *Guardian Unlimited.* http://technology.guardian .co.uk/online/story/0,3605,1511985,00.html.

IGDA (2005). International Game Developers Association Quality of Life Summit Proceedings, Game Developers Conference, San Francisco, California. http://www.igda.org/ qol/IGDA_2005_QoLSummit_Proceedings.pdf.

IGDA. (2004). Quality of life in the game industry: Challenges and best practices. Mt. Royal, N.J.: International Game Developers Association. http://www.igda.org/qol/.

Kerr, A. (2003). Women just want to have fun: A study of adult female players of digital games. In M. Copier and J. Raessens (eds.), *Level Up: Digital Games Research Conference* (pp. 270–285). Utrecht, the Netherlands: Universiteit Utrecht.

Meehan, E., and E. Riordan (eds.) (2002). *Sex & Money: Feminism and Political Economy.* Minneapolis, Minn.: University of Minnesota Press.

Phillips, A. (2005). Soapbox: ARGs and how to appeal to female gamers. Gamasutra. http:// www.gamasutra.com/features/20051129/phillips_pfv.htm.

Robinett, W. (2003). Foreword. In M. Wolf and B. Perron (eds.), *The Videogame Theory Reader* (pp. vii–xix). New York: Routledge.

Schott, G., and K. Horrell (2000). Girl gamers and their relationship with the gaming culture. *Convergence* 6(4) 36–53.

Silverman, S., and A. Pritchard (1996). Building their future: Girls and technology education in Connecticut. *Journal of Technology Education* 7(2): 41–54.

Smith, L. (2000). The socialization of females with regard to a technology-related career: Recommendations for change. *Meridian: A Middle School Computer Technologies Journal* 3(2): 2–30.

Taylor, T. L. (2006). *Play between Worlds: Exploring Online Game Culture.* Cambridge, Mass.: The MIT Press.

Tuchman, G. (1978). *Making News: A Study in the Construction of Reality.* New York: Free Press.

Zook, K. B. (1999). *Color by Fox: The Fox network and the revolution in black television.* New York: Oxford University Press.

Part IV Changing Girls, Changing Games

The authors of our fourth part, "Changing Girls, Changing Games," have strong ideas about how games could be different and are working toward realizing those visions. They apply a plethora of formative design research techniques to understanding player motivations and to designing games that achieve the designers' goals. We want to empower girls to become technological superheroes. We want to change games, diversifying and enhancing the play and learning experience. Our motivations vary, from practical perspectives on how to make games more fun and sell to larger markets, to gender equity concerns about increasing girls' and women's information technology powers, to designing games for learning that engage and teach gamers and nongamers, girls and boys. We hope that the next generation of game designers will read these chapters and as a result, will approach their own future game designs with more gender-conscious perspectives. We hope game designers will be inspired to focus on game and player goals throughout the design process, informed by their own and others' design research.

Industry consultant Nicole Lazzaro, president of XEODesign, starts this part with a delightful reframing of the often-asked question: Are games designed just for girls necessary? Necessary for what depends on who is asking the question. For example, game companies that hope to expand their market wonder whether girl games are the best way to sell games to female consumers. And activists who hope games will be a means to technological empowerment wonder whether girl games are the best way to entice girls to learn and love technology. On the other hand, in her chapter, "Are Boy Games Even Necessary?," Lazzaro questions whether the game industry should continue creating games for boys. She argues that the industry remains stuck designing for a niche market: the once adolescent but now aging males who were the original consumers of console first-person shooter, war, and sports games. Segmenting the game market by sex, and developing for a narrow, extreme subset of either males or females limits market size. Designing games that are strongly "male" typed (or strongly "female" typed) limits the appeal of a game. Extreme male games and extreme female games are probably not extremely fun games. Lazzaro argues, and her company's research shows, that what is fun for both sexes is more similar than different. She points the way to a game design approach based on what players want rather than what women or men want. Best-selling games accommodate more different forms of fun and allow for a wider range of play styles.

Elisabeth Hayes, professor with the University of Wisconsin Games, Learning, and Society Research Group, wants girls to play games that encourage technological mastery. She doesn't want them to play just any game; it has to be games that help girls develop tech-savvy abilities, attitudes, and identities. In her chapter, "Girls, Gaming, and Trajectories of IT Expertise," Hayes acknowledges girls are not technophobic; they do play games and in fact surpass boys in some uses of computer technology such as blogging. But for Hayes, just playing games is not enough. It matters what games girls choose, and she wants girls to move beyond being players to engage in game-related practices such as creating in-game and game-related content. These kinds of activities develop domains of IT expertise and problem solving that translate easily into careers in programming and computer science and other fields that rely on technologies. Hayes considers strategies to intentionally foster girls' deeper participation in game-related constructive activities, reminding us that *fun* is one of the primary underlying reasons that people want to play games.

The authors of the next three chapters are each leading large-scale projects aimed at getting girls interested in and teaching them about computer programming or technology. Because women are an underrepresented group in science, technology, engineering, and math graduate education and careers, the National Science Foundation (NSF) provides funding to find ways to broaden their participation in these fields. All three projects (*Click! Urban Adventure,* Storytelling Alice, and *RAPUNSEL*) as well as *Life Preservers* (chapter 18) were funded by the NSF and designed for middle-school girls. Research has shown middle school to be a critical period when girls' educational and career choices related to computers as well as science are formed. These games represent a new branch of what David Shaffer calls "monument games"—heavily researched prototypical game examples, in this case exploring how games might target, teach, and interest girls. NSF has funded a series of girl games created at universities, often led by a female university faculty member, applying in-depth design research methods with the intent of creating a game to engage girls, teach them, and interest them in programming, technology, and science.

In "Design to Promote Girls' Agency through Educational Games: *The Click! Urban Adventure*," Kristin Hughes outlines the design process of creating *Click!*, a role-playing science adventure game for middle-school girls. Hughes is on the faculty at the Carnegie Mellon University School of Design, which is well known for innovation and excellence in design research. Her chapter is a fascinating case study detailing a four-semester exploratory and discovery phase of researching how to use games to change middle-school girls' antipathy toward STEM (science, technology, engineering, and math) careers. The process itself, the insights gained about middle-school girls, and the resulting product will inspire others working in this domain. Early in the design research process, the designers noticed that boy and girl players took very different approaches, and furthermore that when girls and boys played together, girls ended up in support roles. Because the project's explicit goal was to increase girls' agency with science and technology, they decided to create a girls-only experience. The discovery process applied a sequence of qualitative and quantitative research activities contributing to the design team's understanding of the types of play experience that would excite and sustain girls' interests. *Click!* is a mixed-reality story-based multiplayer team mystery game involving five weeks of training to prepare for game day. The first test of the final game, conducted with one hundred girls, succeeded in its goal of promoting girls' sense of agency in relation to STEM. Refinements and larger community deployment are underway.

The next author, Caitlin Kelleher, grew up interested and skilled in computer science. She earned a doctorate in computer science at Carnegie Mellon University without the benefit of the software that she designed to help interest girls in computer programming. Her chapter, "Using Storytelling to Introduce Girls to Computer Programming," describes a multiyear iterative process of design, user testing, and refinement. Kelleher had worked with "Alice," a programming environment designed by Randy Pausch and colleagues at Carnegie Mellon University that enables novice programmers to create high quality animations. Knowing how to program computers unlocks the power to create simulations, games, communication systems, and other information systems. Women are strongly underrepresented in computer science and their absence holds back not only individual careers but also inclusion of other-than-male perspectives in the day-to-day creation of computer-based experiences. Because Kelleher believed that storytelling and sharing stories would provide stronger inherent motivation for girls to want to learn programming than would animation alone, she adapted Alice to create Storytelling Alice. She began with the hunch that programming as a means to tell stories would attract girls. Over a three-year period she prototyped, tested, and revised her design. She then conducted a trial of Storytelling Alice involving forty-three girls. The trial showed that Storytelling Alice was more successful than Alice at engaging middle-school girls. The success of her program will grow with the donation by Electronic Arts of *The Sims2* character library to be integrated into Alice and Storytelling Alice.

In "Design Heuristics for Activist Games," academic, activist, and former commercial game designer Mary Flanagan and philosopher colleague Helen Nissenbaum propose a design heuristic for embedding activist values in a game. They draw examples from *RAPUNSEL,* a game designed to engage inner-city girls and teach them programming. Their Values at Play method involves three often-overlapping phases: discovery, translation, and verification. The goal of discovery is to identify relevant values. Translation operationalizes the values, transforming them into game features. Verification checks to see that the intended value goals are actually achieved. This process is applied each time the game design iterates. They advocate conscious consideration of values throughout the design process, from the definition of a project, to specification of game mechanics, to safeguarding critical values-rich design features during implementation and revision. V.A.P. provides an added layer of design methodology, to be applied in conjunction with whatever process game designers currently use. Flanagan and Nissenbaum describe the overriding social value of *RAPUNSEL,* a game designed to teach girls to program, as "gender equity." The game itself is based on girls' preferences and interests. *RAPUNSEL* addresses the goal of gender equity not within the confines of the game (which intentionally privileges girls' preferences) but within the larger societal perspective because of the extreme underrepresentation of women in game design and computer science. *RAPUNSEL* also embodies values such as cooperation, sharing, and fair representation. Whether makers of media experiences intend to do so or not, they transmit values through their designs. Flanagan and Nissenbaum provide game designers with tools to appreciate and consciously apply the subtle power of this medium to embody and reinforce activist (or socially responsible) values.

In "Gender Identity, Play Style, and the Design of Games for Classroom Learning," serious game designers Carrie Heeter and Brian Winn anticipate that educational games used in the context of classroom learning will trigger players' cultural expectations about gender. Playing games is still a predominantly male pastime, resulting in an ever-increasing game experience gap between girls and boys. Research has shown that girls are reluctant to use technology or game in public, mixed-gender contexts. Furthermore, females and males approach competition differently. Among males, keeping score and competing is natural and expected. For females, trying to win is only one of several options. Consistent with Lazzaro, Heeter and Winn advocate designing for diverse play styles to incorporate what different players (including boys and girls) find fun. They created *Life Preservers,* a game to teach adaptation and evolution and to serve as the basis for an experiment comparing the effects of rewarding speedy play versus rewarding exploration on play style and learning. Play styles were significantly different for girls and boys as well as for gamers and nongamers. Girls and boys were both responsive to bonus points. When speedy play was rewarded, girls played faster and made more mistakes. When exploration was rewarded, boys slowed down and made fewer mistakes. Whether a player was male or female was a more significant predictor of play style than how often they played games.

This part begins with persuasive arguments for why to design for players rather than for extreme male or female play preferences. Designing for players will result in more satisfying, more fun, and more widely appealing games. Games are assumed to be powerful, designed experiences able to engage and change players. Experiences can be improved upon, made more powerful or more fun, through a combination of carefully held design objectives and design research techniques. The authors' belief in the potential power of games underlies their attempts to use games to engage and empower girls to themselves someday wield this power. Three chapters describe the design of games specifically for a female audience. This approach is less contradictory of Lazzaro's chapter than it may seem because the authors' works are based on design research. Although they only consider girls' interests and preferences, the question they ask is not "What do girls want?" but "How do we understand and engage our (girl) audience?" Their goal is not to create games that are extreme girl games. They are trying to create games that are extremely appealing to girl players. We would expect that their games already accommodate a diversity of play styles, though slanted toward more feminine play styles. Games for classroom learning are likely to trigger players' awareness of cultural expectations about how their gender performs. Designing for diverse play styles and considering the impact of reward structures on play style may help mitigate this divide. The potential power of games to change players, for better or for worse, motivates both hope and concern. Games for girls continue to attract the attention and energy of academics and game designers.

13 Are Boy Games Even Necessary?

Nicole Lazzaro

Why are boy games even necessary? They are violent. They chase an increasingly narrow demographic. They require a lot of energy, time, and skill to learn how to play and offer a limited range of emotions. They copy one another and hog shelf space, limiting new types of player experiences. While they are enjoyed by millions of players around the globe and rival Hollywood for revenue and media attention, their narrow range of offerings attracts a smaller audience than possible.

In an industry driven by novelty, publishers find themselves pursuing the extreme end of a single demographic. If a game does not involve war, sports or Tolkien, it is hard to find at retail. Last year the twenty top-selling titles made most of the money for PC, console, as well as handheld games (NPD 2006). In these best-sellers there were essentially four types of games for sale: role-playing fighting games, war simulation games, racing games, and sports games. Why are there so many very "boy" play pattern games with very mature themes? Why are there so few games for women? Or for men who are bored with playing Rambo?

Not only have commercial games targeted the tastes and interests of a narrow range of potential players, the games are quickly exhausting the creative possibilities of their main themes of fighting, warfare, sports, and racing. This is like walking into a toy store that only offered G. I. Joes, Dungeons and Dragons, RISK, football, and Hot Wheels. It is a paradox that video games target this narrow segment of an aging population when a greater percentage of younger players have grown up playing games. This raises the question: Are boy games necessary?

Only the top titles sell in enough volume for retailers to stock them. The ones that do sell cater to extreme male tastes. "Mature" games offer a narrow range of adult themes mapped onto children's games treated with childlike

Table 13.1 The twenty best-selling games in each of three platforms in 2005 are really just the same four games. More imitation = less novelty and more sequels; more licenses = less fun.

Type	No. of Titles	Percent	Definition	Example games
Role-playing and fighting	31	52%	Games where the primary interaction is fighting one-on-one or in small groups with a gun or fists	*World of Warcraft, Guild Wars, Star Wars: Battlefront II*
War strategy	5	8%	Games that simulate warfare where the player manages a whole battlefield of fighters	*Age of Empires, Civilization IV, Rome: Total War*
Sports	9	9%	Games that simulate a real-world sport such as basketball or football	*Madden NFL, NCAA Football, NBA Live*
Racing	5	5%	Games where players compete by driving or flying	*Gran Turismo, Need for Speed, Mario Kart*
Other	10	10%	Games where players build or manage people and their relationships or run a business such as a theme park or zoo	*The Sims2, Roller Coaster Tycoon, Zoo Tycoon*
Total	60	84%		

Source: NPD FunWorld, Top 60 Selling PC, Console, and Handheld Games 2005

boyish simplicity. Such "boy games" offer a narrow range of options, saturate the industry's early-adopter market, and limit the industry's growth potential. In competing for the top-selling spots, many in the industry have been misled by focusing more on market data sorted by biological sex instead of how players like to have fun. This in turn leads to designs that target gender identity rather than fun because they mostly offer gender-stereotyped play. To make matters worse, traditional, outdated notions of gender identity heavily influence the conclusions drawn from such market research. Yet this is the data used by designers to create new titles, as well as the data used to green-light projects (see table 13.1).

At its formation, the game industry used traditional market research data to understand and segment the market. They came up with their target customer: a twenty-three-year-old single male technophile. The vast majority of computer games still focus on the tastes and preferences of the industry's first adopter, chasing him as he gets older. Because the average game player is now thirty-three years old (ESA 2006), games offer ever more mature themes, lifting experiences from R-rated movies like *Rambo*. Televised sports spawn sequels that are ever more realistic. Of course, this niche is still financially successful; these players buy multiple titles per year. But growth in the market is slowing as publishers rely on imitating past successes instead of broadening the customer base. A lot of money is left on the table by an industry obsessed with a narrow emotional range of extreme male-stereotyped play patterns. But female and male gamers of all ages just want to have fun.

Why the Game Industry Uses Demographics

The game industry uses demographic data to segment the market because it is the easiest data to use. Sorting survey responses by the sex of the player is cheaper than analyzing behavioral preference data. Plus there is a fifty-year tradition of advertising that offers techniques to measure taste and preference for different slices of the American population. Segmenting the market targets specific groups' interests and tastes. This works in advertising and marketing. Because such data contains no information on play styles, it does little to inform game design.

Traditional market research does not focus on understanding gamers and their behavior. Rather than understanding what is unique about gamers and why they play, marketing segmentation efforts rest on identifying gamers' sex, age, and income demographics, and making assumptions about their gaming preferences based on sex-stereotyped interests and tastes. Unlike other consumer products, games are used for the experience of play. Soap manufacturers can target half the market because everyone still gets clean in roughly the same way. With games, not everyone seeks the same game play or the same themes.

Another example of demographic segmentation influencing design is the trend to identify the most important concerns of a particular age group and create content that targets this. People have shared concerns at different stages of their lives, or share interests surrounding a hobby like photography or hunting. Magazine content and style geared to a certain sex, age, lifestyle, or hobby works because the magazine interactive experience of turning pages, reading articles, and looking at images remains constant. Segmenting by content preference does not succeed as well for games. Topics that pop to the top of an age category, like "planning for retirement" for fifty- to fifty-five-year-old men or "researching consumer information" for thirty- to thirty-five-year-old women, do not necessarily map to great game play. Game designers need a different approach to segmentation to find out what makes great games.

Highly Gendered Design Ignores What Makes Games Fun

To expand the industry, games need to attract more players, get players to make bigger purchases, and get players to buy more often. The current approach to demographic design reduces market size. Demographic design fails when virtually an entire industry focuses on a small segment of potential customers. Making games for "hard-core gamers" (those who play today's commercial games the most) perpetuates the practice of ignoring the tastes and preferences of the mass market (Moore 1991). For instance, it bypasses what motivates the new generation of young gamers and what motivates older female gamers who have been playing *Solitaire* since it first shipped on Windows.

Design that emphasizes stereotyped sex-based preferences ignores what people like the most about play. What players find the most fun about games transcends the gender continuum. To segment the market along gender stereotypes results in creating only martial arts or marital relations games (figure 13.1).

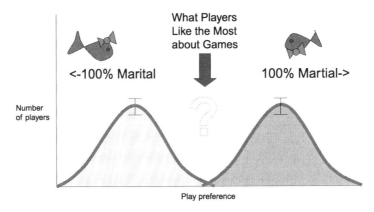

Figure 13.1   Designing for an extreme gender identity excludes more than half the market for a game.

Demographics and Design

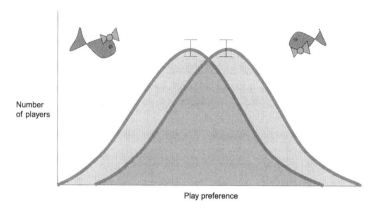

Number
of players

Play preference

Figure 13.2   Play preferences for males and females often overlap more than they
exclude.

Designing games based on extreme stereotypical preferences leaves out
most of what boys, and girls, find fun. In comparing what boys and girls find
most fun in games, the distribution curves overlap more than they exclude
(figure 13.2) (Lazzaro 2004).

Therefore, to maximize the number of potential players, the area under
the curves matters more than the peak. Finding play patterns that appeal to
both males and females maximizes the market. Marketing to one gender only
can reduce the market for a game by 30 to 40 percent. Two of the most successful games of all time, *The Sims* and *Myst,* offer a wide range of ways of
playing and things to do in the game that appeal to the interests of both men
and women.

Few Connections between Demographic Data and Play Styles

Today's gamers have a wide variety of tastes and play styles that traditional
market research can neither touch nor see. To design a new type of game,
more important than gamers' sex, age, and income demographics is why they
like to play games. Copying the features of last year's hit game and adding one
innovation does not copy the fun. Not all innovations make better games. To

Demographics and Design
Area under the Curve Matters

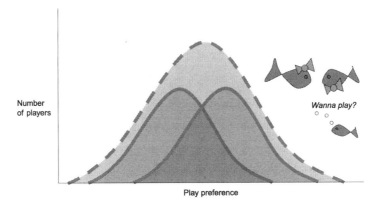

Figure 13.3   Best-selling games capture more players by maximizing the area under both curves appealing to both genders.

succeed, developers need to know which innovations their customers think are more fun to play (figure 13.3).

Designing a better game is often about making it more fun. Instead of making the same few games over and over, the industry needs a deeper understanding of its current and potential customers and why they play. The proper customer insight, vocabulary, and tools broaden the audience and deepen the appeal. Those who understand the player's response gain control over it and can innovate with less risk. For example, only part of *Halo*'s and *World of Warcraft*'s success comes from what is easy to see from a focus group or survey. Direct observation of new types of play leads to more innovations than rehashing old ideas designed to appeal to a certain demographic.

Women Play a Wider Variety of Roles

The 1903 handbook *The Child Housekeeper* offered play activities for girls to increase interest in domestic tasks, thereby increasing their skills and chances to become wives, mothers, and housekeepers (figure 13.4). Many strongly stereotyped female play activities such as playing with dolls and playing house prepare female children for a future role as domestic adults (Colsor and Gansevort Chittenden 1903).

> The Child Housekeeper: Unlike fantasy role-playing games, this handbook was created to instill the importance of domestic industry in young females. The texts with lessons, games and illustrations place the child in the role of a "housewife" in preparation for domestic service of wife and motherhood. (Cornell 1994)

Women's roles in society changed dramatically when in 1920, nearly twenty years after the handbook was printed, women got the right to vote in the United States. As a result, compared to twenty or even ten years ago, far more women assume high-profile, prominent roles. The woman lawmaker, CEO, or soldier is no longer a rarity. Not only do female enrollments exceed those of males at college, women now also outperform men in academic achievement (Lewin 2006). In 1999, astronaut Eileen Collins became the first female

Figure 13.4   Highly gender-stereotyped toys for girls prepare girls for the roles of wife, mother, and housekeeper (see color plate).

Space Shuttle commander. In 2006 Nancy Pelosi became the first speaker of the House. In fact, for today's women, the world is running out of firsts.

Women's changing role in society is reflected in sports as well as in business. In part due to Title 9 (U.S. federal legislation that required the funding of women's sports teams), more women play sports with more passion. It is now common to see photos of female athletes in the sports section and female teams on television. Sports heroes such as Venus and Serena Williams share equal time with their male tennis counterparts. Race-car driver Katherine Legge now competes in the San José Grand Prix. Golfer Michelle Wie has her eyes on being the first woman to compete in the British Open and becoming the next Tiger Woods.

Signifying that more roles and attitudes are open to women beyond Barbie, a University of California, Berkeley, women's basketball team photo dropped the feminine posture and instead adopted body language to state that they've got game. The photo captures a hard-playing attitude. Rolled-up shirtsleeves, pulled-back hair, and sweat-beaded arms communicate athletic prowess and trump any conscious display of "female" good looks.

None of these professions or sports roles is modeled in the strongly female-stereotyped play recommended to girls from early childhood. While domestic roles are important for women, they reflect only part of their identities and interests as adults. Girl-stereotyped play patterns are a poor model for today's younger gamers. What girls need are a wide variety of play experiences that reflect their diverse interests and that prepare this next generation for expanded roles in society.

Gender Definitions Are Diverse and Fluid

Today both girls and boys bend traditional gender norms as they grow up. Men and women under thirty have a less traditional gender identity than those over thirty. In a sense, today people experiment with the middle. Both men and women remove body hair, exfoliate, and sport ponytails and jewelry. Men are increasingly concerned about their appearance, even to the point of wearing makeup. Skirts for guys, such as the Utilikilt, have made brief appearances as men play with the boundaries.

This spills into their gaming habits. Women under thirty, this next generation of gamers, are more computer-savvy, play more commercial video games, and have different play preferences than women over thirty. Women use and consume more technologically advanced products such as computers, cell phones, digital cameras, and cars. In entertainment, Saturday morning cartoons such as *Dora the Explorer* and *Kim Possible* provide new, active role models for young girls unavailable to previous generations. In 2006, eighty-five years after women got the right to vote, ABC aired *Commander in Chief,* the first television series depicting a female president.

Women and girls construct their own unique gender identities and preferred play patterns. Computer game teams made up of professional women such as the Frag Dolls, Ubisoft's professional all-women computer game team, combine top-level gaming skills with come-hither looks. Unlike the UC Berkeley women's basketball team, the Frag Dolls send a clear message with a bent-at-the-knees-and-waist pose in their promotional material—We're hot and we can kick your butt.

Men under thirty are also much more tech-savvy than their elders. They have played games for longer and have changing attitudes about gender. The popularity of metrosexuals is rising, as indicated by the high ratings of television shows such as *Queer Eye for the Straight Guy.* Like dandies at the turn of the century, men care more about their appearance. The focus on achievement and status as well as sex without intimacy is fading in popularity with younger men. More men try to be more open emotionally than their fathers were and want to have deeper relationships with their children than they had with their dad when they were growing up (Simpson 1994; St. John 2003).

This increasingly diverse array of interests and roles makes one's position on the gender continuum hard to pin down. Everything depends on the questions one asks. A thirty-year-old who has won medals for martial arts and marksmanship with a .45-caliber gun would be positioned at the far end of the boys' scale. This same person may have also purchased a scented spa product in the past thirty days, placing that person on the far end of the women's scale. An expert analyst might triangulate what magazine this person reads, but nothing in the data reveals how he or she likes to play.

Demographic marketing will be more challenging with the upcoming generation. Not only do young people have more role model choices than superhero or supermodel; those under thirty have grown up with games and have more diverse and fluid gender identities. This effects how and what they want to game.

Demographic Design: The Failure of Girl Games

Why did most girl games fail? Designing a game around strongly gender-stereotyped data only succeeds if the strongly gendered aspects are what players find the most fun about playing games. Developers were unable to combine extreme gender-stereotyped themes with interesting game play. Strongly gendered game designs still need to be fun. They will not be played for their gender-typing alone.

This is why the market for games for girls never really took off. To set themselves apart from boy games, developers focused on what was different about girls before they targeted what girls found the most fun. These games for girls focused on the extreme end of female characteristics such as hairstyles and makeup. *Barbie Fashion Designer* was the best-selling game for the holiday season in 1996. *Cosmopolitan Virtual Makeover* did well enough to spawn several sequels, including version two designed by XEODesign. But these turned out to be the exceptions. There are many reasons for this, but from a player's perspective, games for girls drew inspiration from what was different about girls and not what girls (and boys) found the most fun. They pursued what made their niche *niche* rather than what made their niche *fun*.

XEODesign's research showed that what people enjoy the most about games spans the gender continuum (Lazzaro 2004). Ignoring what males and females both enjoy limits designer options. So by focusing the design on what appeals to only one sex, designers sacrificed the game play that has most mass-market appeal. Looking for sex differences pulls resources away from core game design features that everyone would enjoy.

Extreme Male Titles Limit Appeal

Likewise, the area with the most growth potential in games for guys is not at the extreme end of the "male" spectrum. Designing for the extreme end of the testosterone-charged, muscle-bound gunslingers misses out on men who want to play with their smarts rather than their fists. And popular triple-A titles that target the middle of what appeals to men may capture most of the male gamer market but not the market as a whole.

The video game market has been chasing the same core gamer they originally attracted—the twenty-three-year-old male social recluse—by offering more and more mature themes. It has gone with the assumption that more violence and realistic gore equals more fun. This is true to a certain extent. Violation of social norms creates emotions (Ekman 2003). And a game suspends consequences by eliminating the penalty for these violations. But violation of norms is not necessarily what players enjoy most about play. Plus, as the industry pursues more realistic graphics, there is a diminishing return. Those boy games that attempt to create new experiences by becoming even more violent—well past the amount of violence that appeals to most boys—will only appeal to the extreme tail end of the bell curve.

The Solution

Instead of offering more games based on game play that appeal to an extreme on the gender continuum, reaching new players requires mastery of why we play games. Is the solution to make *Halo* a love story?

Video games that succeed in the new mass market will focus on what players find most fun. New methods to research and understand the customer and how games create enjoyment provide the essential development tools to make more appealing products. Beyond age, weight, and shoe size, new criteria for understanding customers will define and target types of player experiences they most enjoy.

Differences in play styles between males and females are easier to talk about; however, design around what is fun about games sells to the true mass market. The solution is to offer new types of gender-inclusive play based on what gamers like the most. This requires more than traditional market research methods. Research should first focus on updating the image of who a gamer is, and then discover what players like best about game play. The objective is to identify game play characteristics that create mass appeal.

There is more going on in best-selling titles than fighting and violence. In a study we ran of thirty game players, violence and war themes were not listed as what they liked most about play. For example, emotions such as *fiero* (Italian for personal triumph over adversity), curiosity, and relaxation are found in abundance in hit game experiences whether it is a shooter like *Halo* or a match-3 game like *Bejeweled* (Lazzaro 2004).

Game designers need to undertake design research to understand what makes great games. Instead of including the "must have" features of last year's best-selling fighting game, developers can create new types of games. Games create strong player emotions that traditional marketing research cannot measure; other research methods such as those developed by XEODesign can. Developers that have access to player emotions can innovate with less risk. By focusing on what players like the most in games, developers can create new ways to deliver these types of experiences instead of copying the features and themes of previous games.

Looking only at preference differences based on demographics, it is easy to assume men and women would want very different things from games. Reinforced by cultural stereotypes, it is easier to think that men would like difficult games where as women would be more into social ones. What we found were striking similarities at the heart of game play. Both genders found challenge appealing, whether it was in *Halo* or the speed mode of *Tetris*. What differed was the appeal of violence. Best-selling games like *The Sims, Myst,* and *World of Warcraft* manage to pull in a large female audience by offering many opportunities for play that tapped into these types of fun (Lazzaro 2004).

Themes are important for market appeal; these maintain interest and are part of Easy Fun, or aspects that motivate play by inspiring curiosity and exploration outside of the game's main challenge. What makes a game a game, however, is also how well it offers goals, obstacles, and opportunities for new strategy. None of these is tracked in traditional market research and by definition is not a demographic. Many other forms of entertainment go for a more gender-neutral approach. Most board games target families rather than gender, as do many Hollywood movies. The first *Star Trek* television series improved its ratings once it alternated space battle scenes with relationship scenes between characters, thereby attracting both male and female viewers. Record-setting best-selling games of all time like *Myst* and *The Sims* took a more balanced approach and appealed across the gender divide. Both *Myst* and *The Sims* attract large female audiences by including playing patterns that women enjoy. It turns out that these playing patterns also appeal to a lot of guys as well (just don't tell them). *The Sims* was initially code-named "the Dollhouse." The working name was changed to "Home Tactics Experimental Domestic Simulation" to better target the intended initial market: players of *SIM City,* which in 2002 were 75 percent male (Bradshaw 2002, 2007). Marketers deliberately avoided calling it a doll house because this would repel male gamers. In

Myst, players solve a mystery without killing anyone. Some games like *World of Warcraft* accommodate play styles that offer a little something to both extremes of the gender continuum. For example, in *World of Warcraft* players can take on roles of healers instead of killers. They also have gathering and helping quests or tasks in addition to fighting. The quest descriptions in *World of Warcraft* always provide a motivation for the violence such as how hunting wolves will restore the balance of nature. Adding these elements greatly increases appeal to women.

Incorporating a diversity of play-style opportunities within a game allows male and female players to choose where on the gender continuum and other continuums they want to focus their play at any given time. In spite of many differences between men and women the core of what they both enjoy about game play is surprisingly the same. These similarities are what we call the Four Fun Keys (Lazzaro 2007). XEODesign's observational research of thirty people (twenty-three male and seven female) and interviews with fifteen others who were present in the home environment with the player identified a surprising amount of overlap in what male and female players enjoyed about games. From XEODesign's research to develop the Four Fun Keys, we can say four things about what all gamers want. They want the opportunity for mastery (Hard Fun); aspects that inspire curiosity (Easy Fun); a method to change how they think, feel, or behave (Serious Fun); and an excuse to hang out with their friends (People Fun) (figure 13.5). When asked what they liked most about play, male and female players use many of the same words. None of these aspects that players like most about games requires strongly sex-stereotyped themes or game play.

When designing from stereotypes, it is tempting to think that men like difficult games and women prefer to socialize and avoid challenge. However, this belief is not supported by our research. Women like to be challenged and achieve a level of mastery that comes only from overcoming difficulty. They are not looking for an easier time. For example, much of the appeal of the best-selling game *Diner Dash* comes from making the levels challenging. Designer Nick Fortugno was concerned about making the levels too hard, but found that women really liked the difficulty. For *Diner Dash,* he also focused on emotions that women were familiar with rather than the emotions found in a war game. What made the game even more successful was that there were

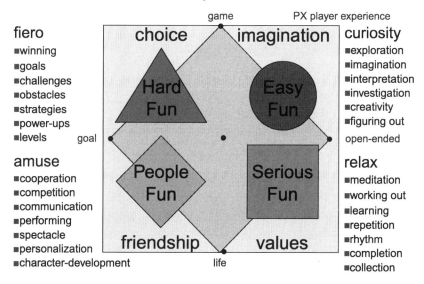

The Four Fun Keys to Next Gen PX

Figure 13.5   The Four Fun Keys. Hard Fun: achieve, challenge, strategize. Easy Fun: experiment, explore fantasy role-play. Serious Fun: change thoughts, feelings, and behaviors. People Fun: socialize, spend time with friends (see color plate).

few games offering this emotional experience (Lazzaro 2005). Women tend to play in shorter time periods than core gamers, but they play as many hours per week as men. Where women differ is in the amount of experience they have in different game genres (ESA 2006).

More can be gained by bringing the market together than by splitting it apart by sex. While many males enjoy blowing up their friends and rivals, what players enjoy most about games is not the violence. XEODesign's research also found that a lot of men liked People Fun—because they liked to hang out with their friends. Many of these social gamers thought it would be strange to play games all by themselves. Likewise, men like social interaction in popular games that arises from competition and cooperative game play. What they enjoy the most is surprisingly similar to women.

Instead of the challenge of pulling a trigger or raiding an enemy base, truly mass-market games offer other opportunities for Hard Fun, such as running a restaurant as in *Diner Dash*. Instead of offering roles only of soldier, general, race-car driver, or sports hero, games could offer other opportunities for fantasy and exploration, such as astronaut, undersea explorer, or archaeologist. More games could offer the Serious Fun of solving a crime such as *Mystery Case Files: Huntsville.* In addition to head-to-head competition, games could offer other two-player emotions such as gratitude and generosity. Focusing on these four elements of fun unlocks the hidden emotional potential for games.

XEODesign's analysis of best-selling games showed that these games all supported at least three of the Four Fun Keys that crossed all gender boundaries. Hits such as *Halo* outperformed their imitators because the clones copied only one type of fun from the Four Fun Keys. *CounterStrike,* a modification of the game *Half-Life,* by adding more types of fun became more popular than the original because it offered the ability to modify levels, publish, and play with friends. A successful game such as *Zuma* faces stiff competition when close rivals such as *Tumblebugs* master several types of fun.

Games focusing on the Four Fun Keys that cross sex boundaries present huge opportunities for growth as the rest of the market chases heavily male-stereotyped play. What we need is the relationship between game play and emotion. How do gamers and potential gamers (our new customers) want to feel as they play? Play is both an emotional and cognitive experience. It absorbs our attention in ways that life often does not. It brings us experiences we could never have, and lets us learn from them and enjoy the thrill of the fantasy while suspending the consequences.

Conclusion

The risks of continuing to invest large budgets only in boy games are severe. Game publishers could become caught in a stereotype like the American comic industry, trapped in a narrow range of boy themes and situations that can be drawn and published cheaply. Comic art forms in other countries, most notably Japan, offer a wide selection of graphic novels for many different tastes.

Focusing games on this core of early adopters excludes potential players, leaving a lot of money on the table. Unless developers broaden the appeal beyond early adopters, the industry will be unable to cross this chasm to become mass-market (Moore 1991) and fail to take its place alongside film and television as an entertainment medium for all to enjoy.

Nicole Lazzaro

Companies that recognize this growth opportunity of providing games for broader audiences will flourish and become market leaders. Rather than trying to convince all gamers to become hard-core, where players' lives revolve around a single choice of entertainment, the industry will be healthier if it offers more content with broad appeal. To do that, developers need to move away from reliance on outmoded demographics and embrace new concepts of what appeals to both genders. In short, they need to put the fun back in to games.

Acknowledgments

Joseph Olin, president of Academy of Interactive Arts and Sciences, Carrie Heeter, Jill Denner, Nick Fortugno, and Jane Booth provided useful guidance and suggestions in the preparation of this chapter.

References

Bradshaw, L. (2007). The secret of the SIMS success. Keynote speech to the Women in Games International Conference, San Francisco.

Bradshaw, L. (2002). SIM City. Markel forum on Children and Media. http://www.cat.nyu.edu/current/news/media/marklesimcity.pdf.

Colsor, E., and A. Gansevort Chittenden (1903). *The Child Housekeeper: Simple Lessons, with Songs, Stories and Games.* New York: A. S. Barns and Company.

Cornell University Division of Rare and Manuscript Collections (1994). *Pastimes and Paradigms.* http://rmc.library.cornell.edu/games/playing/4.html.

Ekman, P. (2003). *Emotions Revealed.* New York: Times Books Henry Hold and Company.

ESA (2006). Game Player Data. Washington, D.C.: Electronic Software Association. http://www.theesa.com/facts/gamer_data.php.

Lazzaro, N. (2005) Diner Dash and the People Factor. www.xeodesign.com/whyweplaygames.html.

Lazzaro, N. (2004). Why we play games: Four keys to more emotion in player experiences. *Proceedings of the Game Developers Conference.* San Jose, Calif., gdconf.com. www.xeodesign.com/whyweplaygames.html.

Lazzaro, N. (2007). Why we play: Affect and the fun of games. Designing emotions for games, entertainment interfaces and interactive products. In J. Jako and A. Sears (eds.), *Human-Computer Interaction Handbook*. Mawhaw, N.J.: Lawrence Erlbaum and Associates.

Lewin, T. (2006). At Colleges, women are leaving men in the dust. *New York Times,* July 9.

Moore, G. (1991). *Crossing the Chasm: Marketing and Selling High-Tech Products to Mainstream Customers.* New York: HarperBusiness.

NPD (2006). *NPD Top Selling Games for 2005.* Port Washington, N.Y.: NPD Funworld.

Simpson, M. (1994). Here come the mirror men. *The Independent London,* Nov. 15, p. 22.

St. John, W. (2003). *New York Times,* June 23, section 9, p. 1.

14 Girls, Gaming, and Trajectories of IT Expertise

Elisabeth Hayes

Why should we care whether more girls and women play video and computer games, or about what kind of games they play? As a woman who has devoted considerable time to gaming over the past few years, I could build an argument around the many ways that playing well-designed games can be life-enhancing: how games can immerse you in compelling and often visually stunning worlds, the sense of mastery and control derived from successfully solving complex problems, the pleasure of taking on new identities, and in multiplayer games the chance to build relationships and achieve social recognition for skillful performance. Many children's games and toys are strongly identified with one or the other gender (Blakemore and Centers 2005). The positive qualities of gaming might lead us to object to gender-typing games as a boys' medium and to ask why should girls and women be less able or less likely to have such gaming experiences than boys and men?

As important as such an argument may be, I discuss here the claim that gaming can be a gateway to mastery of a broader range of digital tools, to trajectories of information technology (IT) expertise. The need to engage more girls in particular with IT is typically cast in terms of increasing their interest and aptitude for jobs in computer science and aligned fields. In addition, using and creating with digital tools is rapidly becoming central to many occupations, and lack of experience or comfort with these tools can be problematic. Learning, in and out of formal education, is increasingly mediated by one's ability to use various forms of IT. Participating in local and global communities is also facilitated by technologies, whether it be for professional, political, social, or cultural ends.

We have anecdotal evidence from male players that games can serve as a focal point for acquiring distinctive modes of IT expertise through built-in tools such as options for customization and modding. Present-day games offer features far beyond anything in games from the past decade (foreword and introduction in this volume), considerably enhancing the ability of even novice players to engage in productive IT practices as part of gaming. IT expertise also can be acquired through practices that extend beyond the game, for example, creating video clips of game play, creating and contributing to fan sites, and redesigning characters and levels, as well as through acquiring and using specialized technical language and interacting with other players. These kinds of expertise can become the basis for further learning and productive participation in a wide range of academic, professional, and community-related practices. In the rush to develop educational and commercial games that appeal to girls and women, we have tended to ignore a crucial question, and one that often motivates efforts to involve girls in gaming to begin with: to what extent do such games—and the communities and practices associated with them—offer affordances for developing domains of IT expertise? This expertise includes not only mastery of technical skills but also modes of problem solving, specialist language, design knowledge, and the appropriation of tech-savvy identities. We need to find ways to involve more girls and women not simply in playing games but in practices associated with gaming that help them develop such tech-savvy abilities, attitudes, and identities.

I end this section with a disclaimer of sorts. A theme throughout this volume is the importance of acknowledging diversity among girls' and women's identities, preferences, and experiences, and of avoiding sweeping generalizations about differences between men and women. In this chapter I refer to general trends among girls and boys, or women and men, not to any absolute differences. While certain forms of gaming and certain forms of IT expertise are considered to be "masculine," there are women who play these games and develop these forms of expertise, while at the same time there are many men who do not. Factors such as socioeconomic status, race, culture, and individual experience all have a role in shaping people's access to certain practices and identities, that may, as Cornelia Brunner points out (this volume), reflect both masculine and feminine attributes. Trends such as those described below are important in suggesting *patterns* of difference in experience that continue to restrict women's overall participation in IT.

How Do Girls Currently Use IT?

Girls certainly are not technophobic, and general experience with computers among boys and girls has equalized (Girl Scout Research Institute 2001; Roberts, Foehr, and Rideout 2005; Subrahmanyam et al. 2000). Girls engage in certain IT-related practices such as using the Internet at comparable rates to boys (Becker 2000; Roberts, Foehr, and Rideout 2005), and their use of computer technology for some practices such as e-mail and blogging has actually surpassed that of boys (Lenhart and Madden 2005).

However, there is still a gap between the degree of technology use among young girls and these girls' subsequent educational and career choices related to technology. Girls are less likely to take computer courses in high school and college, to take the Advanced Placement Computer Science test, and to participate in science fairs (National Center for Women and Information Technology 2005). Women who do enroll in computer science courses in college are more likely than men to drop out (Margolis and Fisher 2002). While both women and men may acquire IT expertise through other routes, such as informal learning or certificate programs, less academic preparation is a factor in the small percentage of women in computer science–related careers. Differences in IT expertise may have other, less-documented consequences for women. They may be at a disadvantage in other fields that rely on technologies such as simulation and computer modeling, particularly the sciences and engineering, and women may not be as prepared to use complex digital technologies for personal, family, and community-related purposes.

Women's lower participation rates in academic and professional computer science–related domains can be attributed in part to an unsupportive and even hostile masculine culture including persistent beliefs that women are less capable of mastering complex technologies (Ramsey and McCorduck 2005). Girls tend to have little knowledge of occupations that require IT expertise, viewing them as the realm of male "geeks" (Kekelis 2005). Interestingly, boys also tend to have limited knowledge about these occupations, yet that does not seem to be as much of a deterrent without the gender barrier.

Informal experience with computer technologies seems to be a critical factor in young people's interest and success in academic computer science, as well as their general attitudes toward computers. Differences in how girls and boys use computers may contribute to girls' lack of interest in computer science, to their identities as IT users, and to differences in the extent of their IT expertise. Boys are more likely to own personal media than girls are, including handheld and console games, televisions, VCR or DVD players, and computers, and are more likely to have Internet connections (Roberts, Foehr, and Rideout 2005). Although boys and girls are equally likely to use computers, and for similar amounts of time, they use computers for different things. Middle school seems to be a crucial point at which differences in girls' and boys' patterns of computer usage accentuate, seemingly due to girls' greater orientation toward social interaction and their immersion in the culture of beauty and romance, which leads them to seek sources of self-esteem and identity that lie more in relationships and attractiveness than in IT expertise. Throughout these crucial years of development, girls increasingly tend to use digital technologies for communication, such as for e-mail and instant messaging, while they are less likely than boys to engage in IT practices associated with entertainment and recreation, such as playing games or downloading music and videos (Girl Scout Research Institute 2001; Lenhart, Rainie, and Lewis 2001). In general, boys engage in more "productive" computer-related experiences than girls; as a result, boys continue to gain more out-of-school knowledge of computing and programming concepts than do girls (Barron 2004). Not surprisingly, students with such experience are more confident and more successful in introductory IT courses than are their inexperienced peers.

Gaming is a particularly significant source of productive computer experience for boys (Kersteen et al. 1998; Taylor and Mounfield 1994). Gaming also is instrumental in helping boys develop personal goals and motivations for their academic study of computer science and related domains. Playing and modding computer games are often reported as a trigger for boys' continuing interest in computer science (Tillberg and Cohoon 2005). For example, Margolis and Fisher (2002) found that male computer science majors reported that family- and peer-based experience playing games was a significant reason for their sense of IT competence.

While girls now play games in increasing numbers, they spend less time playing games than boys do (Roberts, Foehr, and Rideout 2005) and they play different kinds of games, factors that likely influence their motivation and opportunity to engage in technology-based practices associated with gaming.

Social norms identified by children a decade ago still are likely to be in place today: it is more socially acceptable for boys to play a lot of video games than for girls, and certain games, particularly games that emphasize fighting, are assumed to be inappropriate for girls (Funk and Buchman 1996a,b). Despite the existence of some high-profile, hard-core "girl gamers" (Morgan Romine interview in this volume), as well as the increasingly widespread popularity of gaming, stereotypes of gamers as teenage male geeks persist. Thus, it still is not socially rewarding for females to identify themselves as gamers (Griffiths 1997), and they may miss opportunities to participate in gaming communities that can support their development of related IT expertise.

Of course, gaming is only one potential path to IT expertise; new online communities and practices may offer girls as well as boys alternative routes to such expertise. MySpace, for example, has surfaced as a widely popular site for young women as well as men to share information and construct identities, often through the use of digital photos, art, and other computer applications. However, gaming still offers some particularly powerful affordances for technology-related learning, as I discuss in the following sections.

How Can Gaming Be a Route to IT Expertise?

If we hope that gaming can serve as one entrée to various kinds of IT expertise for girls, getting girls to play more games is a partial solution at best. They need to play games that have the most potential for sparking interest in and providing opportunities for learning skills, new ways of thinking, and developing identities associated with IT expertise. Girls also need to participate in the social practices that have evolved around gaming, which support and motivate technology learning, as well as develop skills such as collaborative problem-solving and collective knowledge-building. Though designing games that girls want to play is of course important, and designing games intended to increase girls' IT expertise can help girls who encounter those games (Hughes this volume; Kelleher this volume; Flanagan and Nissenbaum this volume), the crucial issue with the greatest possible payoff is how to leverage commercial games to contribute to IT expertise goals. We need to identify the valued skills and practices associated with IT expertise, explain how learning these skills and practices can be initiated and scaffolded through gaming and gaming communities, and find ways to provide girls (and more boys) with opportunities to engage with these games and participate in these communities. I provide just a sketch of relevant ideas in the following sections.

Why might *games* be particularly powerful starting points for trajectories of IT expertise? At first glance, games might seem a rather unlikely source of IT expertise after all. While many games now offer in-game tools that enable players to personalize avatars or create customized game scenarios, gaming itself doesn't require much algorithmic thinking, programming, or even mastery of presumably important applications like spreadsheets or e-mail. What games (at least good ones) offer, perhaps most significantly, are incredibly immersive, rich, challenging, and emotionally charged experiences, along with the ability to take on new and compelling identities. Of course, these experiences currently appear to be highly motivating primarily for male players, though we can find examples of games that have such attraction for women as well. These experiences are what prompt (mostly male) players' desire to document their gaming through screenshots, *machinima* (video clips made with IT tools available in games), and storytelling; to extend game play through creating new levels and scenarios; to further improve on their game play by modding everything from interface layouts to the eye color of an avatar; and to enhance the visual effects of the game by figuring out how to install the latest graphics card. These experiences prompt players to participate in gaming communities, seek and offer assistance, and share accomplishments and mods, which also support their development of specialist language, the ability to leverage distributed expertise, and so forth.

We have little specific or systematic documentation of individual players' trajectories of learning and development of expertise—which games are more likely to trigger such learning, which players engage in such practices, or what conditions seem to be important in supporting this trajectory of expertise. The literature on out-of-school learning, particularly as it relates to children's and adults' acquisition of expertise, can be a starting point for identifying what factors might be important.

Some children, even at very young ages, develop "centers of expertise" (Gee 2004; Crowley and Jacobs 2002), consisting of extensive knowledge about quite specialized topics. Crowley and Jacobs (2002) provide examples of how young children develop an interest in dinosaurs, which becomes a starting point for their development of complex language and conceptual understandings. While the child's initial interest in a topic sparks the development of such expertise, his or her learning is typically scaffolded through interactions with knowledgeable adults such as parents, who provide experiences, and resources, which extend the child's expertise. Parents scaffold the child's learning, in part, by engaging them in forms of talk and reasoning that mirror more formal academic discourse. Centers of expertise thus can lead to initial mastery of academic language and forms of thinking, as well as the acquisition of expert identities, that serve as building blocks to success in school and professional disciplines.

Applying centers of expertise to IT-related learning, we can argue that gaming, for some boys, is a center of expertise that with the combination of individual motivation and outside scaffolding gradually encompasses various forms of IT fluency. Parents may play a role in this scaffolding by providing boys with their own computers and additional technology, engaging them in talk, and encouraging them to pursue academic studies. In the case of gaming, more knowledgeable peers also play an important role, perhaps more important in some cases than parents. We know that out-of-school learning occurs through actual participation in valued cultural practices (Lave and Wenger 1991; Rogoff et al. 2003; Wenger 1998). Through guided or peripheral participation, learning takes place on multiple levels; in addition to specific practices, the learner acquires ways of viewing the world, valuing, and relating to others in the community. To understand how gaming contributes to IT expertise, we need to take into account the social communities—be they virtual or face-to-face—that surround gaming and give certain IT practices value and significance.

How Do Boys and Girls Differ in Gaming-Related IT Expertise?

While we don't have much information about how gaming contributes to IT expertise, we do have evidence of how players are using technologies to create game-related content, to participate in technology-mediated social practices, to engage in gaming-related problem solving and reasoning, and in general to use technologies to be active participants and producers in game-related communities. It is easy to identify IT-based practices motivated by or associated with gaming that suggest the development of IT fluencies. A selective listing includes (1) built-in editing and design tools such as level editors, avatar design and customization tools, game feature customization tools, and screenshot and photo tools, and (2) game-related technology practices such as fan site creation and design, machinima production, interface modding, computer art design, learning about computer hardware and software, troubleshooting technical problems, and collective problem solving (i.e., with friends or online forums). A more comprehensive analysis would likely yield many more examples.

I included a few questions about such practices in a recent survey of students in a local school district (Schell 2006). The questionnaire, intended to gather data on a wide range of students' technology-related practices, was administered to more than 1,400 students in grades four through twelve in an affluent, predominantly white suburb. While this group is not representative, it offers some insight into the practices of economically advantaged young people who are likely to have access to technology resources at home as well as in school. Notably, 92 percent of both girls and boys indicated that they played computer games now or in the past, consistent with other research that suggests the vast majority of children have some computer gaming experience (Roberts, Foehr, and Rideout 2005). Girls were much less likely to report engagement in related IT-based practices, either using in-game tools or creating game-related content (see tables 14.1 and 14.2).

The disparities are striking, though not surprising given what we know about differences in girls' and boys' gaming practices overall. There are many possible explanations for such differences; for example, boys tend to spend more time on gaming, or girl gaming drops off at what may be a critical age for playing more sophisticated games or acquiring more sophisticated IT skills (such as modding). The disparities are also likely due to factors such as that girls, regardless of age, are playing games that do not have the same affordances for technology-related learning that games played by boys do, that girls do not participate in gaming communities in similar ways, or that girls do not get similar social rewards for such practices.

I've taken an informal look at some prominent games designed for girls, or that seem to be favored by girls, and what I found was not encouraging in terms of opportunities for or evidence of technology-related learning. Let's start with puzzle-type or casual games such as *Tetris, Bejeweled, Snood,* or *Zuma.* These games require considerable mental acuity and problem-solving ability, and some can be played competitively with like-minded players. However, they haven't prompted the development of many fan sites, videos, mods, or interface designs. It's not impossible to imagine such things, but these games simply don't have the complexity or the affordances to encourage such activity.

Table 14.1 In-Game Content Creation

Have you ever created the following in-game content?	Female (*N* = 628)	Male (*N* = 727)
New game levels or scenarios	6.2%	22%
Game characters, clothes, or other items	18.5%	30.1%
Interface mods or other add-ons	1.6%	14.2%
Cheat codes	14.6%	36.2%
None of the above	76.3%	53.5%

Table 14.2 Game-Related Content Creation

Have you ever created the following game-related content?	Female (*N* = 633)	Male (*N* = 718)
Video clips	6.8%	17.5%
Fan fiction	1.9%	7.1%
Screen shots	3.8%	15.9%
Walk-throughs	2.5%	11%
Fan art	3.9%	7.4%
None of the above	90.5%	73.5%

I turned to the *Nancy Drew* series, assuming I would find more evidence of player use of productive technologies. Her Interactive's *Nancy Drew* Web site (herinteractive.com/prod/index.shtml) offeres game information, downloads, player forums, tech support, and links to other sites (Megan Gaiser interview in this volume).

Downloads for recent games included only wallpaper and printable bookmarks. The player forums consisted almost entirely of requests for assistance with solving specific puzzles in the games. The majority of links were to sites emphasizing the "empowerment" of girls, including their participation in science and technology-related fields, which seemed to be created by adults and mostly aimed at an adult audience. I was excited to see a link for players who wanted to create movies based on *Nancy Drew* games, but the link was to a site selling costumes. I searched in vain for *Nancy Drew* fan sites. I found only one, Nancy Drew Fun, (s6.invisionfree.com/Nancy_Drew_Fun) that encouraged designing and posting user creations such as avatars and graphical signatures, and the site seemed to be for the most part inactive. Many girls who play *Nancy Drew* games are quite young, and perhaps not ready to master new forms of IT expertise. Quite a few girls seem to play with their parents, as suggested by the number of postings from moms and dads. The games do provide opportunities for adult-scaffolded conversation and problem solving, and it would be useful to investigate the nature of such interactions in future research.

To find extensive evidence of technology-related practices, I turned to a game that attracts large numbers of both male and female players: *The Sims.* While *The Sims* has been overused as a positive example of a "female-friendly" game, it is a good example of a game that has many features supporting player engagement in practices contributing to IT expertise. An integral part of the game itself, of course, is the design of avatars, home décor, buildings, and landscapes, using built-in tools. Electronic Arts (EA) encourages players to experiment and share their creations through a variety of mechanisms. For example, the EA site for *The Sims2* includes a section where players can post and download user-created objects, avatars, lots, and stories (thesims2.ea.com/exchange/). The site has simple tools that users can download and use to manage new content, design and import new textures into their game, and create customized Sims movies, among other creations. A huge fan community has grown around The Sims franchise, reflected in a myriad of player-created Web sites and content. In March 2006, EA's *The Sims2* site had links to two hundred general fan sites, with additional downloads, news, fiction, cheat codes, and a myriad of other resources. Women are well represented among the players who created content, Web sites, and so forth. The virtual world *Second Life* also has attracted a number of women who have mastered complex graphic design tools to create everything from avatars to virtual architecture. *Second Life* and *The Sims* would be good starting points for further investigation of how women might already be developing some forms of IT expertise through gaming.

How Do We Develop Tech-Savvy Girl Gamers?

How might we engage more girls and women in such productive IT practices associated with gaming? This is a question that should be of great interest to educators, parents, game manufacturers, and the gaming community at large.

The first issue is how to involve more girls in playing games that support the acquisition of IT expertise. One approach is to rethink our conception of "girl games." If evidence continues to suggest that some girls and women prefer games with features that differ from those that appeal to boys, we need to design such games in ways that ensure they also incorporate opportunities for IT-related learning. Most certainly, we can't give girls games that are overly superficial, simplistic, or emotionally lackluster. *The Sims* seems to be a promising example, but other types of games can be designed to include tools for level design, avatar customization, and other productive practices. For example, a *Nancy Drew*–type adventure game could include a scenario editor that allows players to modify or create a scenario with new puzzles, narratives, or characters.

Another approach is to involve girls in currently more male-dominated games that support such IT practices. Multiplayer games like *World of Warcraft* are proving to be appealing to many women (Yee this volume), and they offer many opportunities for technology-related learning. My own research suggests that women may come to enjoy male-typed games if given the time and support to master them (Hayes 2005a,b). As Jenkins (2003) notes, games enjoyed by men often have features, such as avatar customization, that appeal to presumably "female" sensibilities. (In turn, boys' delight in designing and dressing their avatars suggests that boys might like to play dress-up with dolls just as much as girls, given socially acceptable conditions.) As Lazzaro (this volume) points out, there is far more overlap than difference in male and female game-play preferences. Games that appeal to both male and female play preferences may be the most effective for involving a wider and diverse group of players in IT-related learning.

This leads to the issue of how we can encourage girls' and women's participation in communities of players that support technology-related learning. This is a question of how we might intentionally foster such communities primarily for girls, as well as how current gaming communities can better support girls' engagement in highly valued technology-related practices. Given that girls currently may lag behind boys in their IT skills, all-girl groups can be important as incubators for girls' initial development of IT skills through gaming (see also Taylor in this volume). In designing such tech-savvy girl gamer communities, we can draw on insights from prior efforts to attract girls to computer science (which include a number of projects incorporating games), as well as from online girl-gamer communities created by fans themselves. Such communities, online as well as face-to-face, would provide opportunities for girls to develop multiple dimensions of IT expertise: not just technology skills, but also intellectual capabilities, conceptual understanding, social engagement practices (including collective knowledge building and use of specialist language), and design knowledge. To accomplish these goals, communities need to be structured in ways to support multiple forms of legitimate participation, scaffolding not only in the use of tools but also in ways of thinking and problem solving by more experienced peers or adults, and lots of talk to develop fluency in communicating ideas, mastering specialist language, and generally acquiring the identity of a "tech-savvy" individual. A particularly important aspect of these communities for girls is the opportunity to engage in "identity play," finding ways to challenge their prior assumptions about the identities associated with IT expertise, to help them expand their conceptions of desirable "feminine" identities and practices, and to provide social recognition and legitimacy for these new identities.

One last thought: In designing ways to use gaming as a starting point for IT expertise, we must not lose sight of a key reason that gaming might motivate such learning: games, or at least good games, are fun. Raph Koster (2005) has written an entire book on how fun in games arises from mastery, or, in other words, from learning. There's an obvious danger in trying to coopt any form of popular culture for more overt educational purposes, because educators have a tendency to ignore fun in favor of more "serious" things like curriculum objectives or standards. The projects discussed in the following chapters (Hughes, Kelleher, and Flanagan and Nissenbaum) provide examples of games that were designed to be both enjoyable and educational. We can learn much from their efforts about how games of all sorts, commercial as well as educational, can help girls build technological as well as scientific skills and aptitudes. If gaming is to help girls not only master new skills and knowledge but also unlearn negative attitudes and associations acquired through stereotypes and popular beliefs, gaming must become a source of pleasure, mastery, and identity for girls.

References

AAUW Educational Foundation Commission on Technology, Gender, and Teacher Education (2000). *Tech-Savvy: Educating Girls in the New Computer Age.* Washington, D.C.: American Association of University Women Educational Foundation.

Barron, B. (2004). Learning ecologies for technological fluency: Gender and experience differences. *Journal of Educational Computing Research, 31*(1), 1–36.

Becker, H. J. (2000). Who's wired and who's not: Children's access to and use of computer technology. *Children and Computer Technology, 10*(2), 44–75.

Blakemore, J. E. O., and R. E. Centers (2005). Characteristics of boys' and girls' toys. *Sex Roles, 53*, 619–633.

Crowley, K., and M. Jacobs (2002). Islands of expertise and the development of family scientific literacy. In G. Leinhardt, K. Crowley, and K. Knutson (eds.)., *Learning Conversations in Museums* (pp. 333–356). Mahwah, N.J.: Lawrence Erlbaum.

Funk, J. B., and D. D. Buchman (1996a). Playing violent video and computer games and adolescent self-concept. *Journal of Communication 46*(2): 19–32.

Funk, J. B., and D. D. Buchman (1996b). Children's perceptions of gender differences in social approval for playing electronic games. *Sex Roles, 35*(3/4), 219–231.

Gee, J. P. (2004). *Situated Language and Learning: A Critique of Traditional Schooling.* London: Routledge.

Girl Scout Research Institute (2001). *The Girl Difference: Short-Circuiting the Myth of the Technophobic Girl.* New York: Girl Scouts of the USA.

Griffiths, M. D. (1997). Computer game playing in early adolescence, *Youth & Society, 29,* 2, 223–236.

Hayes, E. (2005a). Gendered identities at play. Paper presented at the Games, Learning, & Society Conference, Madison, Wis., June 23–24.

Hayes, E. (2005b). Women, video gaming, & learning: Beyond stereotypes. *TechTrends,* 49(5), 23–28.

Jenkins, H. (2003) From Barbie to Mortal Kombat: Further reflections. In A. Everett and J. T. Caldwell (eds.), *New Media (AFI Reader).* New York: Routledge.

Kekelis, L. (2005). Hurdles in the pipeline: Girls and technology careers. *Frontiers, 26*(1), 99–109.

Kersteen, Z., M. Linn, M. Clancy, and C. Hardyck (1998). Previous experience and the learning of computer programming: The computer helps those who help themselves. *Journal of Educational Computing Research, 4,* 321–333.

Koster, R. (2005). *A Theory of Fun.* Scottsdale, Ariz.: Paraglyph Press.

Lave, J., and E. Wenger (1991). *Situated Learning: Legitimate Peripheral Participation.* New York: Cambridge University Press.

Lenhart, A., and M. Madden (2005). *Teen Content Creators and Consumers.* Washington, D.C.: Pew Internet & American Life Project.

Lenhart, A., L. Rainie, and O. Lewis (2001). *Teenage Life Online: The Rise of the Instant-Message Generation and the Internet's Impact on Friendships and Family Relationships.* Washington, D.C.: Pew Internet & American Life Project.

Margolis, J., and A. Fisher (2002). *Unlocking the Clubhouse: Women in Computing.* Cambridge: The MIT Press.

National Center for Women and Information Technology (2005). *Women and Information Technology: By the Numbers.* Washington, D.C.: National Center for Women and Information Technology.

Ramsey, N., and P. McCorduck (2005). *Where Are the Women in Information Technology?* Boulder, Colo.: National Center for Women & Information Technology.

Roberts, D. F., U. G. Foehr, and V. Rideout (2005). *Generation M: Media in the Lives of 8- to 18-Year-Olds.* Menlo Park, Calif.: Kaiser Family Foundation Study.

Rogoff, B., R. Paradise, R. Mejía Arauz, M. Correa-Chávez, and C. Angelillo (2003). First-hand learning by intent participation. *Annual Review of Psychology, 54,* 175–203.

Schell, T. (2006). *2006 Student Technology Survey.* Waunakee, Wis.: Waunakee School District.

Subrahmanyam, K., R. E. Kraut, P. M. Greenfield, and E. F. Gross (2000). The impact of home computer use on children's activities and development. *Children and Computer Technology, 10*(2), 123–144.

Taylor, H. G., and L. C. Mounfield (1994). Exploration of the relationship between prior computing experience and gender on success in college computer science. *Journal of Educational Computing Research, 11,* 291–306.

Tillberg, H. K., and J. M. Cohoon (2005). Attracting women to the CS major. *Frontiers: A Journal of Women Studies, 26*(1), 126–140

Wenger, E. (1998). *Communities of Practice: Learning, Meaning, and Identity.* New York: Cambridge University Press.

Plate 1   Activity starters in KAHooTZ's Imagination Place! (chapter 3).

Plate 2   Edu-art takeover of Fona for International Women's Day (chapter 4).

Plate 3   Final day of the "Letz Play" event at Boomtown, Copenhagen (chapter 4). Photo by Emil Oustrup (edofoto.dk).

Plate 21   Click! agents in the field (chapter 15).

Plate 22   Storytelling Alice scene (left) and "Crazy go nuts" robot (right) (chapter 16).

Plate 23 Alice characters (top) and Sims characters (bottom) (chapter 16).

Plate 24 Designing for cooperation: in *RAPUNSEL*, players can choose to chat or use chat interaction to swap bits of computer code for points and recognition (chapter 17).

Plate 25 Iterations of the *RAPUNSEL* interface (chapter 17).

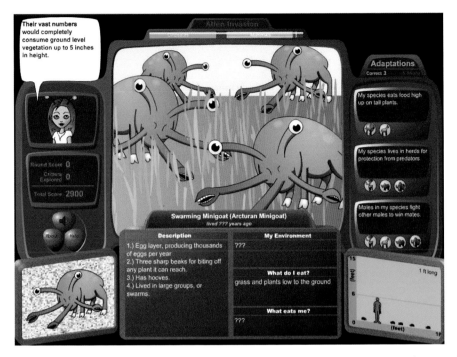

Plate 26   *Life Preservers* evolution game interface showing swarming mini-goat invasive species (chapter 18).

Plate 27   Frag Dolls (Ubisoft): Team of professional women gamers.

Plate 28   Workshop meeting in May 2006 at UCLA.

Plate 29   Girls 'n' Games conference in May 2006 at UCLA.

Plate 30   E3 visit in Los Angeles in May 2006.

Plate 31   Booth babes at E3 in 2006.

15   Design to Promote Girls' Agency through Educational Games: The Click! Urban Adventure

Kristin Hughes

In the past decade, tremendous effort has gone into creating experiences that nurture girls' sense of curiosity while building their technological and scientific skills and competencies (AAUW 2004). This chapter outlines the design process of creating *Click!*, a role-playing science adventure game for middle-school girls. It exemplifies an approach for creating experiences that promote agency and that share impressions and insights to inform the development of gaming experiences designed to help increase middle-schools girls' interest and participation in science, technology, engineering, and math (STEM).

Exploring, Discovering, and Making: The Design Process

The design process encompasses all aspects of a given problem, creating a catalyst for product development and innovation. Design research methods employed at the exploratory and generative phase (at the front end) of product development help to contextualize and frame the problem through the lens of the participant. Time spent in the early stages of product development ensures that the needs and desires of the audience are accounted for. This interaction with the participant at the front end not only helps break down assumptions on the part of the development team but also allows for the participant to become a cocreator in the product's conception (Sanders and William 2001). Cocreation helps to inform things like aesthetics, usability, and language.

Changing Middle-School Girls' Perceptions toward STEM Careers

Research has shown that girls are as adept as boys at grasping scientific and technical subjects, but during their formative school years middle-school girls are more likely to choose nonscience- and nontechnology-related career paths (see Hayes this volume). Studies, including our own, confirm that many girls assume that only men enjoy science or are proficient with computers. Science and technology, then, are often approached by girls as things that exist outside themselves. Girls develop a negative attitude toward science and computer technologies. People proficient in these areas are attributed with characteristics girls regard as negative (Parikh 2004). This implies that girls' lack of desire and failure to incorporate the skills, tools, and physical attributes associated with STEM fields are due to their negative perceptions and stereotypes of these fields (AAUW 2004).

The exploratory phase of our project began by investigating how to use games to change middle-school girls' antipathy toward STEM careers. The inquiry began with an investigation into the world of middle-school girls and their relationship to STEM, popular culture, and social and peer networks. We found that fashion and music trends, technological devices, television shows, and friends are ever-changing in the lives of middle-school girls, resulting in an exclusive subculture of their own. Middle-school girls are especially impressionable and react to popular culture and trends as they begin to form identities and awareness of the world around them. We also found that girls who are a part of a peer community use that community as the basis for negotiation and problem solving before transferring those skills to everyday settings.

Knowing that this particular demographic of girls responds to popular culture and trends helps us to conceptualize ways that we can introduce to girls desirable impressions and characteristics of women in science. During this vulnerable adolescent period of development, participating in meaningful, educational play that mirrors the existing culture but provides counterstereotypical, appealing role models can be the catalyst needed to redirect girls' attitudes toward a more positive view of women in science (Girl Scouts 2003). If we work to support and reinforce future interests and choices, countering negative career perceptions and trends, we can perhaps modify behavior and patterns that currently exist within this particular demographic. To this end, it is critical to promote girls' sense of agency.

Albert Bandura defines *agency* as the capacity of humans to exercise control over the nature and quality of their lives. Given the appropriate skills and tools, individuals can reshape and change their behaviors and patterns. Designing a community experience around these skills and tools provides opportunities for change for the entire community (Bandura 2001). Exploring Bandura's theory helped us to articulate the type of play experience we needed to create to hold girls' interests. *Click!* was designed to have the credibility to gain a foothold in the subculture, and survive once there. The play experience also needed to have all the skills and tools embedded in it to empower girls to interact on their own and to discover ways STEM could be used in their everyday experiences. In short, *Click!* was designed to build a strong sense of agency in the girls.

The Click! Team

The Click! Team was an interdisciplinary group that consisted of interaction designers, a writer, visual designers, a programmer, public school teachers, a cognitive psychologist, informal education research assistants, a sociologist, and a full-time project manager. The project was developed, designed, and implemented by Carnegie Mellon's School of Design and the University of Pittsburgh's Learning Research Development Center. It spanned four semesters, with classes taught simultaneously and collaboratively at both universities. We worked with approximately four hundred girls from diverse backgrounds over the course of the project. Organizations like the Boys and Girls Clubs of America, the Girl Scouts, YWCA, and the Pittsburgh Public Schools were key to the success of our program. This chapter discusses the design research methods used during the front-end development of the project. It details several tools, activities, and prototypes that helped us design the game.

Discovering, Observing, and Learning about Our Audience

Our project team saw a need to develop a multiplayer, team-based game, rich with tools and activities that would be fun, would resonate with girls' interests, and would sustain their long-term interest in STEM, without reminding them of science lessons from school (Cassell and Jenkins 1998). Some of the various research activities used in the exploratory phase included observing, surveying, and interviewing middle-school girls, teachers, and parents; reviewing magazines and literature; playing games; having the girls create an inventory of the popular culture; having the girls create journals and photo books; and spending a day in the girls' lives, shadowing them. These various activities helped break down our assumptions and let us see the problem through the lenses of the girls (Dewalt and Dewalt 2002). Every person on the team had a very different take on what they learned, so we shared knowledge and observations, found overlaps, and began to formulate the problem.

Generative Tools: Audience Participation

Design research methods have the capacity to support and manage a given problem from multiple perspectives and vantage points. It is a holistic process and, when used correctly, it purposefully addresses and serves the divergent needs of a particular user group and offers opportunities for meaningful interactions and exchanges. These methods are participatory activities done with the user group and development team and are often referred to as generative (or make) tools (Sanders and William 2001). Generative tools and activities covered the gamut of empirical quantitative and qualitative methods and helped us gain deeper insights into the girls' lives and their interests, dreams, and fears. They also set the stage for further discussions on the value of a design framework as integral to understanding the way girls solve problems and learn in informal settings. Discovering middle-school girls' likes and dislikes and observing how they interacted with their peers helped us design our first set of generative tools as we sought to discover what type of play experience would excite and sustain girls' interests.

The Cream Pie Mystery Game, one of our first activities, was a week-long interactive display at the Science and Technology Festival, held at the Carnegie Science Center in Pittsburgh. Festival attendees (more than two hundred boys and girls) were invited to help solve the mystery of Dr. Lamb's missing revolutionary recipe for cream pie that does not spoil. Participants encountered two distinct game elements embedded in the activities: role-playing and problem solving. The display represented the fictional lab of Dr. Lamb and asked for help with five key problem-solving, science-based tasks to discover which of the three suspects was guilty and where to find him or her. Before beginning the game, we asked the participants to select an ID badge with one of ten female characters (including Kim Possible, Lara Croft, and Hermione Granger), and then to complete the badge with additional information including their assumed name, job title, special skills, and favorite tools. Participants adopted stereotypical characteristics that were reflective of what a crime-scene investigator, detective, or scientist might use. Participants were also offered a choice to wear lab coats and protective eyewear to help them role-play as forensic scientists.

Significant developments in the game design were based upon this research. One example came about when we noted that although the activity was designed for an individual experience the girls played all aspects of the gamelike activity collaboratively. They filled out their forms, reviewed their choices, and conducted the labs together. The male participants were very different in their approach, not sharing their answers, trying to be the first to participate, and instilling a competitive aspect into the activity. When girls and boys played together, girls took on the role of note-takers while boys did the lab experiments, handing dirty test tubes to the girls. At the end of the five tasks, girls on mixed teams were unable to piece together the mystery, making it almost impossible for them to solve the crime. At this point, based on these observations, we decided to make a girls-only game. In addition, we decided to allow girls to play with their friends. Although we anticipated the name badges to be popular, the props (lab coats, protective glass) allowed for the participants to further immerse themselves and held their attention through the activities. Participants who did not fully engage in role-playing lost interest more quickly.

Had we not taken the time to design this preliminary game and get girls to provide feedback on ways to make it a richer experience, we would have lost an opportunity to learn what the narrative types, science-related tasks, tools and technologies, characters, and personas should be in the final game. The activities like the one just discussed, although time consuming, helped us to engage the girls in exercising their voices and exploring issues surrounding identity and self-perception. Redefining and creating new ways to engage girls during the generative research phase is imperative. During this activity the research team was able to ask participants questions, have them read from the worksheets and talk out loud when solving science-specific tasks, and observe peer-to-peer interactions. Although not explicit, the participants were cocreators in our process, helping us further facilitate the design of the larger game.

Another informative tool was called *mini-missions*, designed to teach us what the girls' interests were. Mini-missions, given to girls once a week over five weeks (figure 15.1), had activities, questions, and games related to science

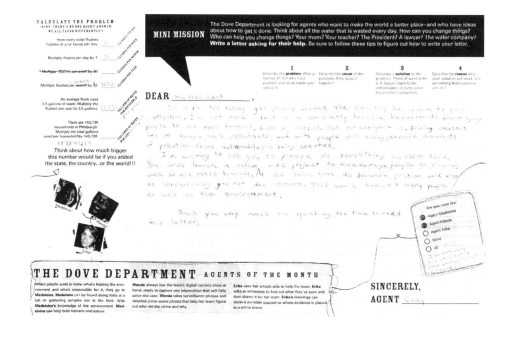

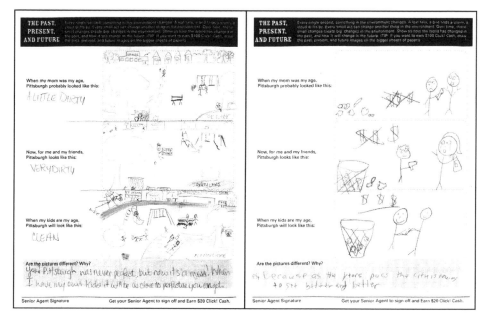

Figure 15.1 Examples of take-home assignments called mini-missions (see color plate).

and technology. Participants were diligent about completing them and turning them in the following week. One parent commented that his daughter "hid her mini-mission under her pillow until Wednesday evening, when she and her fellow agents would lock themselves in her bedroom to work on the case." Solving the mini-missions required many kinds of problem-solving skills such as testing ideas, research, observation, and invention.

The mini-missions became a tool (one of many) that facilitated the development team's understanding of our target audience. Careful planning and design of these tools worked to authenticate the game experience for the girls. The mini-missions were designed to give the girls an opportunity for fun, unstructured, nonjudgmental activities, much like those they engaged in during their private time. Girls revealed aspects of their personal life that in turn helped us understand their needs as participants in the game (Sanders and William 2001). In this case the mini-missions taught us how to better create a story that would inspire girls, including suspects and other *Click!* agents.

At the core of *Click!* is storytelling, so we created another front-end tool to help us develop the *Click!* narrative. This approach is consistent with Kelleher's research on girls' interest in storytelling and programming with Storytelling Alice (this volume). The aspects of storytelling that make a narrative successful are plot, interesting characters, engaging interactions, and details that allow the readers to imagine and project themselves into a particular scenario. After the Cream Pie Mystery Game at the Science Center, we decided to design a narrative-based mystery game that gave girls the opportunity to imagine themselves as characters within the story.

Girls were asked to imagine themselves as special agents charged with the task of solving a mystery. We provided a loose framework for the mystery but asked girls to develop their own personas, agent names, outfits, and the tools that they would need for their adventure. They also decided on the places they would visit on the mission. We provided stickers with images of Pittsburgh locations, tools, and outfits for their personas so the girls could apply these visual aids to paper as they played, and thus complete the story. In the process of creating agent profiles they began to share with us, through storytelling, their personal goals and aspirations. These findings helped us develop details for the narrative and the characters in the story, and to begin to identify and construct basic science- and math-related tasks and activities in locations that girls found appealing.

Making, Prototyping, and Testing the *Click! Urban Adventure*

In July 2004, we ran a small prototype of our first science and technology role-play adventure game based on a crime scene investigation (CSI) theme. The participants were eight middle-school girls from a middle-class Pittsburgh suburb. Realizing that the girls would be unable to tackle most of the tasks in the game without additional training in these fields, we added a session before the game called Agency Training. Education professionals introduced girls to the basics of physics, technology, the Global Positioning System (GPS), and environmental science.

The adventure game prototype (the Roxy Robin kidnapping case) took place the next day with one team participating in the morning and one team in the afternoon. The girls began the game with a briefing by the narrative developer who played the role of Inspector Kate Muth, a police officer looking for their help to solve the kidnapping of fictional local pop star Roxy Robin. The girls then viewed a video featuring VJ Carnival Wilson (VJ Carnie), who happened to be at the right spot to videotape Roxy Robin's abduction. The girls viewed the video and other evidence provided by Inspector Kate. After completing a series of science tasks, collecting clues in the community, and interviewing witnesses (who were design team members acting out the roles), the girls returned to headquarters. They then decided which suspects to interview. During the interview phase girls spent time interrogating team members acting as suspects and found the final, crucial pieces of evidence that would solve the case, leading them to arrest the criminal. Researchers acted as characters within the scenario, allowing the girls to seamlessly enter and leave the game space while making observations about game play and player interactions and reactions.

After the Roxy Robin kidnapping prototype test, the development team expanded the crime scene investigation into a full-scale mystery that could support five teams (twenty girls). The story was made more complex with a larger number of clues and characters. From this point on, the development path for the game involved creating numerous prototypes that took on multiple forms including card games, game boards, and role-playing games.

Card Game

The initial development sessions leading up to this game examined the narrative as a card game. The background information on the mystery was provided orally. The girls then randomly chose sites at which they would find their first clues and were given cards with detailed instruction as to where the evidence would be. After visiting three or four of the six locations, each girl was asked how she would solve the mystery, what she thought was going on, who was involved, and why. The card game broke down the narrative structure, characters, locations, and science content, allowing the research team to identify confusing or overly complex concepts that could potentially disengage girls when playing the game in real time and space.

Game Board

The final two development sessions examined the narrative as a more intricate game involving a game board, a casebook, clue cards, and community/location cards. The girls played on teams of four. The basic clue-gathering structure worked the same as in the CSI mystery. The players moved game pieces to locations on the game board and gathered the clues at that location. This version of the game introduced the idea of "special clue cards." There were seven of these cards in five locations. When a girl visited a location she could keep only one special clue card from that place. Once all the special clue cards had been collected, the game moved into its second phase where the teams of girls worked together. Each team was asked to write down their speculation about how to solve the mystery. The special clues were introduced to allow every team access to the content needed to be successful in solving the mystery.

The development and observation of game play with these smaller games helped us to better understand the level of complexity needed when constructing the narrative for the larger game. Several key observations were noted while the girls were playing. Verbally introducing the game rules and the mystery provided more information than the girls needed, making it difficult for them to remember key aspects of game play. When the girls became lost or confused they looked to the instructor for confirmation rather than relying on the clue cards or other team members. The clue cards contained complex information about the narrative and suspects, but because of the amount of information presented on each card, players could not synthesize what each card meant within the context of the larger story. We anticipated this as a potential problem and provided a casebook for the girls to record notes about the clues they collected.

With the game board the narrative structure was enhanced to provide more information about character relationships and plot. The girls were able to identify suspects, motive, and the overall plot. But they had trouble understanding exactly how the plot was carried out and the big picture of how the clues worked together. To improve the game efficiency in a later prototype, the casebook was modified to provide a unified suspect sheet and condensed space for recording clues.

The Game: *Click! Urban Adventure 1.0*

Building on the prototypes, we created a play experience that the girls would find enticing and would want to be a part of. The final game was designed for one hundred girls (twenty-five teams). *Click!* provided a context for what the girls were doing as they played and motivated themselves to chart their paths between locations where they found important clues, interacted with other players, and met characters. The fictional story and all its parts were located in a real city environment with its own set of rules, clues, and characters.

Our design process revealed the need for a five-week Click! Agency training component, which was critical not only to teach players the necessary basic science and technology skills but also to get the girls' buy-in so they would want to be a part of the game's culture. Girls who joined *Click!* understood that they would be in "training" for five weeks, after which they would be called on to test their skills (on game day) and advance to Level One Agents. The training and game focused on science-related activities, and role-playing scenarios were coupled with supportive technology tools such as laptop computers, GPS devices, and cameras.

Each girl joined *Click!* with three friends and was assigned an adult Senior Agent (a female science, technology, engineering, or math college student) who stayed with the team during training and throughout the game. Contextual inquiry determined that girls enjoy taking quizzes not only because they are fun but also because they indirectly allow for self-assessment. Because of this, we designed a Persona Builder, essentially a personality quiz that suggested compatible roles and department fits within the Agency. The Persona Builder helped girls' discover new STEM interests. Once the girls' took the personality quiz, the quiz delivered results in the form of suggested compatible roles. The reason for this multiplicity in compatibility is to reinforce the concept that every girl has the potential to engage many types of career opportunities. For example, scoring well in the math-oriented roles should not bar her from engaging in more technological roles. By identifying several roles that girls are naturally inclined toward, the fit between personality and the roles will have a higher likelihood of transferring to her life subsequent to the game (as suggested by Nguyen and Hughes 2005).

Our analysis of the Persona Builder personality quiz identified the following roles: Team Sketch Artist, Environmental Specialist, Forensic Specialist, Profiler, Code Maker and Breaker, Mission Specialist, Navigation Specialist, and Gear Guru. The roles and personas in the game were tied to visual imagery, vocabulary, and activities that intended to reshape the girls' preconceptions about STEM professions.

Game Day

After five weeks of training, all Click! Agents were called to the Carnegie Science Center to help solve a mystery. The 2005 mystery was focused on how to remotely control pollution in Pittsburgh's rivers as a means of politically influencing a mayoral election. The game was dispersed over six locations within walking distance of the Science Center where the teams could find clues and/or suspects.

Once the teams entered the clues they found (e.g., evidence, suspects, notes) into their laptop computer, the software prompted them to enter information about the evidence or to move on to another task. We also incorporated a mapping feature to encourage social networking with other teams. This feature allowed girls to track their own progress as well as that of other teams, send messages, and mark the map when they found one of the five "key" clues necessary to solve the crime. Each location had a wireless hotspot that allowed the girls to access messages throughout the day (figure 15.2).

When all five "key" clues had been collected, the teams were called back to Click! Headquarters. Here they interrogated suspects and analyzed evidence as they created a Click! Case File. This detailed who was involved in the mystery, why they were involved, and how the plot was being carried out. In addition to clues, teams sometimes encountered different characters as they

Figure 15.2   Click! agents in the field (see color plate).

moved around the game space. These characters could be suspects or supporting characters who simply provided information related to the story.

Once all the teams had built their cases, they were combined into three groups and each team made an argument and provided evidence for who was guilty of the crime, why they did it, and how. Each of the three groups voted on the best team in their group and on the following day the three chosen teams presented their final cases.

The first full version of *Click! Urban Adventure* was run in June 2005. Girls were recruited from all over Pittsburgh, and although the game was designed to support one hundred girls, due to financial constraints we allowed only eighty-four girls to sign on as Click! Agents. Of the participants, 86 percent came from public schools and 53 percent were minorities. Prior to training, the girls were asked about their previous knowledge and interest in STEM, characteristics of their friends, what it meant for them to be a part of a subculture like *Click!,* and their future aspirations. These data were compared against the girls' perceptions and attitudes after they played *Click!*

Outcomes

Click! asks important questions, such as whether it is possible to design educational games that can change, promote, and sustain agency within a particular culture. Our data suggest positive influences and tools that help shape and validate girls' empowerment. Within the context of *Click!,* girls were able to learn skills, research methodologies, and collaborative approaches, as well as develop a sense of autonomy and responsibility in relation to the project. We also found that girls who participated in *Click!* developed a more open and confident attitude toward their own participation in STEM-oriented fields. Interviews with *Click!* participants revealed that agency was one of the overall recurring themes that players talked about when asked what they gained by playing the game, as illustrated in the following quotes.

> Agent 1: I think *Click!* is a way to learn more math and science and about our environment. And to learn about new people and new chances to do stuff so that like, like let's say my friend, Asia, she goes to Robert, I mean Roger's. And I'm going to Roger's next year so I met her and I met

Brittany. So I met a lot of new people. (Interviewer: Oh good.) And it's fun cause I'm making new friends. They're very cool, very cool. They're like me.

Agent 2: (Interviewer: Okay, and what do you want to do as a career?) I want to work in the Click! Agency. (Interviewer: In the Click! Agency?) (Agent 2 nods) (Interviewer: Okay, and do you think you'll need to learn more science and technology to do that?) Yeah. (Interviewer: So, why do you want to work in the Click! agency?) 'Cause it's fun and I think it will be better than working at any other job.

Most educational games do not have the luxury of multiweek training and game play, university faculty and student researchers, and extensive design research. Nonetheless, game designers may benefit from some of our findings, from the general approach and philosophy of design research, and from some of the front-end techniques we employed.

As we refine *Click! Urban Adventure* and design other educational games, we have the opportunity to better understand how gaming can create meaningful play experiences. The fact that middle-school girls took ownership of the game culture was key to sustaining their interests. Based on our findings at the exploratory and generative phase of the project's development, we chose to emphasize a more humanistic, holistic view of science. The real-world setting engaged the girls, pushed them to think in deeper, more critically reflexive ways about the social and political forces constructing their communities. Choosing a role-playing narrative-driven game was another way to make science more girl-friendly. The structure of the game gave the girls an immediate way to participate in STEM-oriented problems. Moreover, the game's narratives engaged the girls in learning, igniting their imaginations in a way that the conventional classroom cannot. The narratives we developed also allowed the girls an opportunity to envision career possibilities and options. Including only girls in the game defined *Click!* and the activities associated with playing *Click!* as girl-appropriate activities. Most important, *Click!* provided the participants with a play space they could create and sustain on their own.

Game design is an invaluable way of developing new pedagogical methods—especially in the STEM fields. Design research is paramount to the acceptance or rejection of a learning game by its participants; designers must think of how to engage the audience from the bottom up, rather than from the top down. Iterations encountered during the design process drive the product's sustainability, educational outcomes, and innovation. Finally, the design of educational games is one of the most exciting ventures to enter the pedagogical sphere. It creates new categories of meaning such as community knowledge and civic engagement. Because front-end research gives game designers a glimpse into the world of the people for whom they are designing, it generates a shift in point of view. It grounds the design in the participants' world. In this way these research methods are relevant and necessary for creating quality educational games that make a difference.

Acknowledgments

A special thank-you to our funders, the National Science Foundation under grant 0217033, and the Heinz Endowments. Also thanks to my colleagues Janet Stocks at Carnegie Mellon and Kevin Crowley at the University of Pittsburgh Learning Research Development Center, various student groups for their individual contributions, and Betsy DiSalvo for her guidance in managing the project.

References

AAUW (2004). *Tech-Savvy: Educating Girls in the New Computer Age*. Washington, D.C.: American Association of University Women.

Bandura, A. (2001). Social cognitive theory: An agentic perspective. *Annual Review of Psychology*, 52, 1–26.

Cassell, J., and H. Jenkins (1998). Chess for girls? Feminism and computer games. In J. Cassell and H. Jenkins (eds.), *From Barbie to Mortal Kombat: Gender and Computer Games*. Cambridge, Mass.: The MIT Press.

Dewalt, K., and B. Dewalt (2002). *Participant Observation: A Guide for Fieldworkers*. Walnut Creek, Calif.: Altamira Press.

Girl Scouts of the USA (2003). *The Ten Emerging Truths: New Directions for Girls 11–17: Executive Summary*. New York: Girls Scouts of the USA.

Nguyen, S., and K. Hughes (2005). From role-playing to personality development: Designing the preadolescent identity. In *Nordic Design Research Proceedings*. Copenhagen, Denmark.

Parikh, A. (2004). How personal identity, motivation, interest and outside expectations affect the way science and technology is viewed: A case study of six middle school girls. Unpublished master's thesis, University of Pittsburgh.

Sanders, E. (2005). Information, inspiration and co-creation. Presented at the International Conference of the European Academy of Design. Bremen, Germany.

Sanders, E., and C. William (2001). Harnessing people's creativity: Ideation and expression through visual communication. In J. Langford and D. McDonagh-Philp (eds.), *Focus Groups: Supporting Effective Product Development.* London: Taylor and Francis.

16 Using Storytelling to Introduce Girls to Computer Programming

Caitlin Kelleher

Although girls and boys use computers in similar numbers and report similar computer-related skills (Gallup 1997), women are underrepresented in computer science (Vegso 2005a). The Computing Research Association reported that in 2005 nearly 85 percent of computer science bachelor's degrees were awarded to male students (Zweben 2006). Further, the participation of female students in computer science is dropping; a recent survey by the Higher Education Research Institute found that among students entering college the percentage of women interested in studying computer science has dropped to its lowest levels since the early 1970s (Vegso 2005b).

Researchers have suggested that many boys develop interests in computing careers through video and computer game play (see Hayes this volume). However, little is known about how playing computer games contributes to boys' greater participation in computing careers. Based on a survey of more than twelve hundred school-aged children, Hayes found that boys are more likely to create in-game and game-related content than girls are and suggests that the process of creating in-game and game-related content may help boys to develop computing skills. Accordingly, one potential approach to increasing the participation of girls in computing is to develop software (both games and other activities) that appeals to girls and teaches skills that will help girls succeed. In this chapter, I describe a case study in designing a computer programming system targeted toward middle-school girls that presents computer programming as a means to the end of telling 3D animated stories, an activity that most girls find appealing. By presenting programming with a storytelling focus, girls are motivated to learn basic programming principles. Through storytelling we might find ways to encourage girls to engage with computers on a deeper level than simply as computer users. While getting girls to engage with computers is a first step, we need to consider and support paths by which girls (and boys) can progress from casual computer use toward careers in computer science.

For many students, learning to program a computer serves as a gateway into studying computer science. One potential strategy for increasing the number of women in computer science is to find an approach that will motivate more girls to learn to program computers. The activities girls find appealing vary considerably by age, so it is important to focus on a particular age group. Research has shown that girls tend to choose whether or not they are interested in pursuing mathematical or scientific disciplines, including computer science, before the end of middle school (AAUW 1996). Consequently, to have the greatest potential impact on the pipeline of people progressing toward careers in computer science, it is critical that we intercede with girls no later than middle school. Yet computer science does not appear in most schools until high school or college, years after many girls have already chosen not to pursue it. By providing girls with a positive computer programming experience during middle school, we hope that girls will be more interested and successful in taking computer science courses in high school and college.

Storytelling as a Motivating Context

In my experience, if you walk into a classroom full of middle-school girls and ask how many of them want to learn how to program a computer, very few girls raise their hand. However, if you walk into a classroom of middle-school girls and ask how many of them would like to create their own animated movie, you get a very different and very positive response. For that reason, I chose to focus on storytelling (via the creation of Pixar- or Dreamworks-style 3D-animated movies) because it is a context that is both motivating and approachable for middle-school girls. I define *storytelling* as the creation of an animated movie that communicates a sequence of events to a viewer. Given a little time, most girls can come up with a story they would like to tell. Further, creating animated stories provides girls with an opportunity to explore issues they encounter in their own lives and safely experiment with different roles, a central activity during adolescence. In addition to providing motivation, stories provide a gradual introduction to programming concepts and constructs; stories are naturally sequential and unlikely to require advanced programming concepts immediately. However, the stories that girls envision telling provide opportunities to introduce many of the programming concepts and constructs taught in introductory programming. Because girls' programs generate animated stories that can be readily understood and appreciated by nontechnical audiences, girls can get positive feedback from nonprogramming friends and family members.

In examining computer games that have been successful in attracting female players, it is interesting to note that two of the games that have been the most successful with girls, *Barbie Fashion Designer* (Subrahmanyan and Greenfield 1998) and *The Sims* (Jenkins 2003), have supported girls in the activity of storytelling. In fact, there is a strong community of people who capture game play from *The Sims* and use it to create movies.

Recently, there has been a broad interest in using students' desire to create video games as a hook to draw more students into computer science. At the college level, many schools are creating academic majors in video game development (Schiesel 2005). Several systems designed to introduce programming to younger students are similarly based around the activity of creating video games (Kahn 1996; Maloney et al. 2004; Morrison Schwartz 2005; Starlogo TNG 2006; Pelletier this volume). Based on informal user tests, middle-school-aged students are unlikely to design the simple games that are approachable by beginning programmers. Both simplifying students' designs to make them more approachable and presenting novice programmers with an inappropriate level of complexity have the potential to erode motivation to create the projects students' envision and their interest in learning to program. To allow students to freely design projects they want to work on, one has to select design space such that students can be successful. The domain of stories has the potential to gradually introduce students to a wide variety of programming concepts.

Even in the context of computer science curricula in which students create projects according to a well-defined specification rather than designing their own projects, I believe that using computer games as a primary end-goal to motivate students toward computer science is potentially dangerous. Currently, computer games do not appeal equally to girls and boys. Further, the curricula that we develop today will inevitably be based on these existing games. By focusing computer science curricula around computer games, we may help to increase the number of computer science majors while exacerbating existing diversity problems.

Researchers have done extensive work to design programming environments that support novices as they learn to program. Several programming systems for 2D animation such as Stagecast Creator (Smith, Cypher, and Spohrer 1997) and Squeak Etoys (Allen-Conn and Rose 2003) allow children to create animations that move or change the appearance of 2D sprites. In these systems, users create animations by rapidly cycling through a series of 2D images that are associated with a given sprite. Because the animations are composed of a series of images, the visual quality of an animation can be much more readily enhanced through artistic skills (by creating higher quality graphics for the sprites) than through programming skills. Systems for novice programmers use a variety of methods to allow users to create programs: specifying rules (Logo Computer Systems 1995; Logotron 2002 Smith, Cypher, and Spohrer 1997), assembling graphical tiles that represent commands in a programming language (Kay; Maloney et al. 2004), or assembling a sequence of icons (Tanimoto and Runyan 1986). ToonTalk (Kahn 1996) provides a 3D environment in which users can construct programs by demonstrating the actions of robot characters, but users' programs control 2D animations and games. Like other 2D animation systems, animations in ToonTalk are created by cycling through images. StarLogo TNG (StarLogo TNG 2006) is designed to allow users to create 3D games. Users can construct programs that control the position and orientation of 3D objects within a graphical environment. Another tool allows users to build 3D adventure and role-playing games by specifying rules (Pelletier this volume). However, users cannot create animations that change the body position of a character. It is possible to import body position animations created using third-party 3D modeling software. However, improving an animated story by importing animations does not require that students develop or refine their programming skills. An extensive survey and review of these environments and approaches has been completed by Kelleher and Pausch (2005a).

A system that presents programming as a means to the end of storytelling should encourage users to develop programming skills in order to realize their story ideas and provide supports that put the kinds of stories that users want to create within the reach of beginning programmers. I chose to base my system on Alice 2 (Alice 2005; Conway 1997; Conway et al. 2000); Alice 2 is the only programming environment designed for novice programmers and children that I am aware of in which programming skills rather than artistic skills are necessary to create good animations. In Alice 2, users create animations by combining basic motions like moving and turning either whole objects or parts of objects (e.g., a character's arm or leg). Further, Alice 2 provides two kinds of support to ease the process of learning to program a computer: (1) Alice uses a drag-and-drop method of program construction, which prevents users from making syntax errors, and (2) in Alice, programs are animated, which allows users to observe state changes as they occur. One of the key benefits of visible state changes is that users can see their mistakes and more readily fix them. By leveraging Alice, I was able to focus on finding the supports necessary to enable girls to create animated stories, rather than the mechanical difficulties associated with learning to program.

Evaluations of Storytelling Alice

While Alice 2 (hereafter called Generic Alice) provides support for learning to program (see figure 16.1), it was not designed to support storytelling. Although creating 3D animations using Generic Alice does require users to develop programming skills, it can take many hours to create stories by combining animations that control each joint of a character individually. I found that middle-school students using Generic Alice often gave up on stories they envisioned when they realized the difficulty of implementing those stories in Generic Alice.

Over the past three years, I have worked with more than three hundred middle-school girls to design and test a version of Alice that supports girls in learning to program through storytelling (hereafter called Storytelling Alice). In designing Storytelling Alice, I took an iterative approach based on user testing. In each user testing session, I identified the largest problems that girls had in creating their stories, modified Alice to better support common storytelling tasks, and then re-tested. My goal in supporting storytelling was to increase girls' engagement with the programming aspects of Alice. In designing for any user population, it is of critical importance to user test with a representative sample of that population. I drew most of my subjects from local Girl Scout troops. To ensure a broad participation, we donated ten dollars to the troop for each girl who participated in one of our user-testing sessions. In all, about two

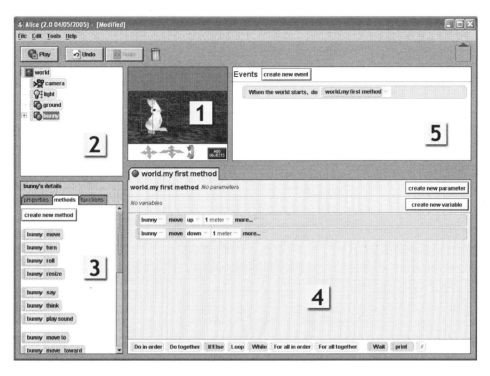

Figure 16.1   Alice interface.

hundred girls participated in the formative testing of the storytelling version of Alice. Most were Girl Scouts, but some of our early user testing included self-selected campers at science, technology, engineering, and math (STEM) camps and local home-schooled children—both are groups that tend not to be representative of the broader population of middle-school girls.

The design of Storytelling Alice was guided by several kinds of information including observations of girls using Storytelling Alice, automated logs of the actions girls took within Storytelling Alice, the animated movies that girls created, and their storyboards. The storyboards were particularly critical to our success because they enabled us to capture girls' visions for their stories before girls were exposed to the Alice program. Once girls began using Storytelling Alice, they tended to adapt their goals based on their impressions of Alice's capabilities, and without storyboards their original goals would have been lost. In each of the formative user testing sessions I asked girls to (1) create a storyboard of the animated movie that they wanted to create, (2) complete the Alice tutorial to gain familiarity with the system, and (3) create an animated movie using a version of Storytelling Alice.

The girls were instructed to create their storyboards using a three-step process that encouraged them to create detailed storyboards with some repeated information to ease the process of analyzing storyboards. In the first step, girls created a paragraph-length overview, what we called "the DVD box description" of their story. Then we asked each girl to break her story into scenes and describe the setting, action, and purpose of each scene. Finally, we had girls draw a traditional storyboard with six to nine frames per scene, each containing a textual description of the action occurring in that frame. Using this three-step storyboarding process, the storyboards tend to have sufficient detail and contain some rhetorical information, which makes them easier to interpret. Girls were encouraged to limit their stories to three or four scenes.

When I began the formative testing of Storytelling Alice, I had users work in pairs to create animated movies, a traditional user-testing technique designed to allow researchers to gain insight into users' goals and thoughts about the software system they are using (Nielson 1993). I found that traditional pair-based user testing is not well suited for creative tasks such as storytelling. Pairs spent most of their time negotiating the story plot and rarely discussed how to realize their storytelling within Alice. I found that it was more effective to have users work on their stories individually but organize their workspace such that they could easily see and discuss each others' work. Using this format, I found that girls often watched each other's work, exchanged tips, and discussed how they might solve problems they were encountering.

Design Insights

Through user testing, I found that it was necessary to make three major changes to Alice: provide high-level animations, create a gallery of 3D objects, and communicate the purpose.

1. *Provide high-level animations based on storytelling needs.* Generic Alice provides users with simple animations such as move, turn, and resize that were inspired by common 3D graphics transformations. While simple

Table 16.1 Design Insights

Storytelling Alice	Generic Alice
say, think	move
play sound	turn
walk to, walk off-screen, walk	roll
move	resize
sit on, lie on	play sound
kneel	move to
fall down	move toward
stand up	move away from
straighten	orient to
look at, look	point at
turn to face, turn away from	set point of view to
turn	set pose
touch, keep touching	move at speed, turn at speed, roll at speed

animations like move and turn are often useful for describing the motion of objects through space (e.g., move the chair forward one meter), they rarely show up in the stories that girls want to write. The vast majority of actions that girls wanted to include in their stories involved animating people and other characters (e.g., animals). Girls expected that the people in their stories would be able to perform peoplelike actions such as walking, sitting, and touching and were surprised that Generic Alice did not provide this functionality. Further, creating even basic actions such as walking in Generic Alice can be very complicated. In Storytelling Alice, I included a set of higher-level animations (see table 16.1) that more closely matches the kinds of actions that girls expect to be able to include in their stories.

2. *Make the gallery of 3D objects that comes with Alice a rich source of story ideas.* In observing users creating stories in Storytelling Alice, I found that the gallery of characters and scenery users can add to their stories can be a source of inspiration for girls. The storytelling gallery uses two techniques to help girls find story ideas: (1) highly caricatured characters and (2) character-specific animations that require explanation within the story. Caricatures like a secret agent, lunch lady, and chubby track coach have clear roles that

can suggest potential story lines. During user testing, we also found that animations requiring explanation could spark a startling variety of stories. The first example of this came through a robot character that had an animation titled "crazy go nuts" (see figure 16.2). Upon finding this animation, girls were often very motivated to create a story that culminated with the robot going crazy. Girls developed stories with the robot that touched on a wide variety of themes including struggling with parental authority, discovering that a girl's boyfriend is cheating on her, getting a bad grade, and coping with being unpopular.

3. *Make the system communicate that it can be used for storytelling.* Girls' introduction to Storytelling Alice must create the impression that Alice is a system for creating animated movies. I found that a mechanical tutorial that uses simple examples to demonstrate the usage of features without

Figure 16.2   "Crazy go nuts" robot (see color plate).

grounding them in the context of a story can easily disinterest girls. Instead, Storytelling Alice introduces users to basic programming while users create example stories.

Tutorial examples are often carefully selected for simplicity. Examples that are also stories can add complexity, creating more opportunities for girls to make mistakes not easily recovered from. To enable girls to successfully complete more complex tutorials, I created a new interaction technique for presenting tutorials called Stencils (Kelleher and Pausch 2005b) (see figure 16.3). The Stencils interaction technique places a virtual translucent blue screen on top of the Alice interface, which filters mouse and keyboard events. For each step (or Stencil) in the tutorial, holes are cut above user interface components with which the user needs to interact, accompanied by sticky-style notes containing appropriate instructions. Only user interface events occurring over a hole in the Stencil are passed through to the underlying interface, preventing most kinds of errors.

Impacts of Storytelling Focus on Girls' Programming Behavior

The evaluation of Storytelling Alice took place during a series of workshops, each four hours long. A total of eighty-eight Girl Scouts participated in the summative evaluation of Storytelling Alice, with between three and ten girls per workshop session. I compared the experience of girls using Storytelling Alice and Generic Alice to isolate the impact of the storytelling support from the impact of Alice's programming supports. Each girl was randomly assigned to use either Storytelling or Generic Alice. After working with their main version of Alice, girls had thirty minutes to try the version of Alice to which they were not originally assigned. Finally, girls were asked to select a world that they had built in either version of Alice to share with the other workshop participants. In analyzing my data, I found evidence that presenting programming as a means to the end of storytelling is a promising approach for motivating more girls to learn to program.

We found that the focus on storytelling makes the activity of learning to program more appealing to girls. Fundamentally, there are two activities within Storytelling Alice and Generic Alice: (1) scene layout, which includes adding and positioning 3D characters and objects within the virtual world, and (2) editing the program controlling the behavior of those 3D characters

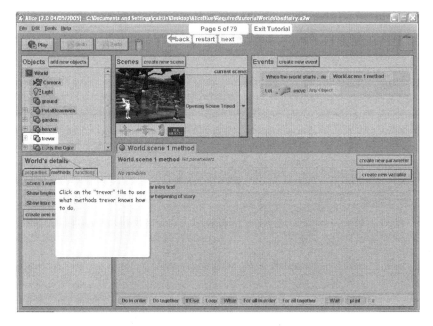

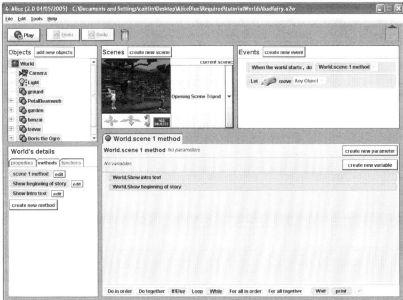

Figure 16.3   Storytelling Alice interface with stencils (top) and without stencils (bottom).

and objects. Girls who used Storytelling Alice spent a greater percentage of their time editing their programs than girls who used Generic Alice. Further, girls who used Storytelling Alice were nearly three times as likely to sneak extra time to continue working on their programs as girls who used Generic Alice.

Girls learned as much about programming using Storytelling Alice as they did using Generic Alice. With just under three hours of programming experience for girls in both the Storytelling Alice and Generic Alice condition, I did not expect to find a difference in programming achievement.

In addition to providing a motivating context, the kinds of stories that girls wanted to create using Storytelling Alice naturally motivated the usage of a variety of programming constructs. Girls often began their sessions with Storytelling Alice by creating simple sequences but most progressed to more complex programming. The need for multiple scenes within stories motivated the use of subroutines. The types of actions girls wanted their characters to perform motivated the use of loops, parallel execution, and parameterized methods: creating an animation in which a character bounces a basketball requires count loops; dance animations often require characters to move multiple body parts simultaneously; and actions like kissing, hugging, or slapping another character provide a natural lead-in to the concept of parameters (see figure 16.4).

Why Storytelling Works

One of the central activities of adolescence, for both boys and girls, is to determine who they are and how they fit in to the world (Stone and Church 1984). Many adolescents do this through experimenting with different roles (AAUW 1996). It is not uncommon to see girls try out vastly different personas from one year to the next in order to determine what kind of person they want to be. Storytelling Alice provides a safe space for girls to think through how they would handle a wide variety of situations. Many of the stories that girls created in our user-testing sessions addressed deep issues that adolescent girls face. Girls wrote about the difficulties of being unpopular and how they might behave if they suddenly became popular. They chronicled their relationships with boys, touching on issues ranging from asking a boy out to how to handle a cheating boyfriend. Girls created movies about their struggles with authority figures (see figure 16.5). Girls' stories gave them a way to think through

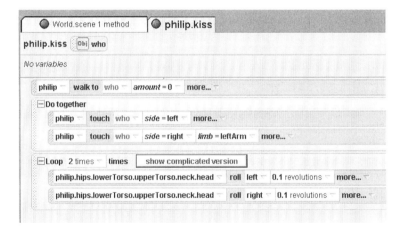

philip.kiss Obj who

No variables

philip — walk to who — amount = 0 — more... —

Do together

philip — touch who — side = left — more...

philip — touch who — side = right — limb = leftArm — more... —

Loop 2 times — times   show complicated version

philip.hips.lowerTorso.upperTorso.neck.head — roll left — 0.1 revolutions — more... —

philip.hips.lowerTorso.upperTorso.neck.head — roll right — 0.1 revolutions — more... —

Figure 16.4   Kiss action (top) and kiss code (bottom).

Figure 16.5   Storytelling Alice scene (see color plate).

courses of action that they would be unlikely to try in real life. Where some computer games have presented stories that touched on the issues I saw in girls' stories (Purple Moon 1997), a precreated story, even one with a wide variety of story-line options, may not relate directly to the issues that girls are puzzling through. As we continue to search for ways to engage girls with computers and computing, supporting girls in telling their own stories appears to have great promise.

In addition to providing a space that allows girls to create personally meaningful movies, Storytelling Alice allows girls to create an artifact that their friends can readily appreciate. In user-testing sessions, girls often shared their work with friends. The effect of seeing a friend watch one's movie and laugh at the appropriate moment is very powerful. At the end of the summative testing sessions, girls had an opportunity to share one of the two worlds they built. One would expect that the girls would nearly always choose to show the world they had two hours to build over the one they had thirty minutes to build. In fact, the appeal of sharing a story was so strong that fourteen of the forty-five girls using Generic Alice opted to show a world they created in their thirty

Figure 16.6   Alice characters (top) and Sims characters (bottom) (see color plate).

minutes with Storytelling Alice. All but one of the forty-three girls in the story condition showed a movie created in Storytelling Alice.

Next Steps: Making Alice More Expressive

The addition of storytelling support helped to make Storytelling Alice an expressive medium for middle-school girls. One potential way to improve girls' experiences is to increase Storytelling Alice's expressive power. Inspired by our initial success with motivating middle-school girls using storytelling, Electronic Arts has donated the characters and animations from *The Sims2*, the best-selling PC game in history (and one with more female than male players), for use in the next version of Alice (see figure 16.6). With state-of-the-art visual quality, the Sims characters perform a dizzying array of animations that we hope will enable us to create a more expressive storytelling-based programming environment.

References

AAUW (1996). *Girls in the Middle: Working to Succeed in School.* Washington, D.C.: American Association of University Women Educational Foundation.

Alice (2005). *Alice 2.* http://www.alice.org.

Allen-Conn, B. J., and K. Rose (2003). *Powerful Ideas in the Classroom: Using Squeak to Enhance Math and Science Learning.* Glendale, Calif.: Viewpoints Research Institute.

Conway, M. (1997). Alice: Easy-to-learn 3D scripting for novices. Unpublished doctoral thesis, University of Virginia, Charlottesville. http://www.alice.org/advancedtutorial/ConwayDissertation.PDF.

Conway, M., S. Audia, T. Burnette, D. Cosgrove, K. Christiansen, R. Deline, J. Durbin, R. Gossweiler, S. Koga, C. Long, B. Mallory, S. Miale, K. Monkaitis, J. Patten, J. Pierce, J. Shochet, D. Staack, B. Stearns, R. Stoakley, C. Sturgill, J. Viega, J. White, G. Williams, and R. Pausch (2000). Alice: Lessons learning from building a 3D system for novices. *Proceedings of Conference on Human Factors in Computing Systems,* pp. 486–493. ACM Press.

Gallup Organization in conjunction with CNN, *USA Today,* and the National Science Foundation (1997). *U.S. Teens and Technology.*

Jenkins, H. (2003). From Barbie to Mortal Kombat: Further reflections. In A. Everett and J. T. Caldwell (eds.). *New Media (AFI Reader).* New York: Routledge.

Kahn, K. (1996). ToonTalk: An animated programming environment for children. *Journal of Visual Languages and Computing.* 7(2). Boston: Academic Press.

Kay, A. Etoys and Simstories in Squeak. http://www.squeakland.org/whatis/tutorials.html.

Kelleher, C., and R. Pausch (2005a). Lowering the barriers to programming: A taxonomy of programming environments and languages for novice programmers. *ACM Computing Surveys* 37(2): 83–137. New York: ACM Press.

Kelleher, C., and R. Pausch (2005b). Stencils-based tutorials: Design and evaluation. In *Proceedings of Conference on Human Factors in Computing Systems,* 541–550. New York: ACM Press.

Logo Computer Systems, Inc. (1995). *My Make Believe Castle.*

Logotron (2002). *Magic Forest.*

Maloney, J., L. Burd, Y. Kafai, N. Rusk, B. Silverman, and M. Resnick (2004). Scratch: A sneak preview. In *Proceedings of Creating, Connecting, and Collaborating through Computing,* 104–109.

Morrison Schwartz, Inc. (2005). Kids programming language (KPL). http://www .kidsprogramminglanguage.com/.

Nielson, J. (1993). *Usability Engineering.* Boston, Mass.: Academic Press.

Purple Moon (1997). *Rockett's New School.*

RAPUNSEL. http://www.rapunsel.org.

Schiesel, S. (2005). Video games are their major, so don't call them slackers. *New York Times,* November 22. P. A21

Smith, D.C., A. Cypher, and J. Spohrer (1997). KidSim: Programming agents without a programming language. *Proceedings of the 6th European Conference on Software Engineering.*

StarLogo TNG. (2006). http://education.mit.edu/starlogo-tng/index.htm.

Stone, L. J., and J. Church (1984). *Childhood and Adolescence: A Psychology of the Growing Person,* 5th ed. New York: Random House.

Subrahmanyan, K., and P. Greenfield (1998). Computer games for girls: What makes them play? In J. Cassell and H. Jenkins (eds.), *From Barbie to Mortal Kombat: Gender and Computer Games.* Cambridge, Mass.: The MIT Press.

Tanimoto, S., and M. Runyan (1986). Play: An iconic programming system for children. In *Visual Languages. S. Chang, T. Ichikawa, P.A. Ligomenides (Eds). New York:* Plenum Publishing Corporation.

Vegso, J. (2005a) CRA Taulbee trends: Female students and faculty. http://www.cra.org/info/taulbee/women.html.

Vegso, J. (2005b) Interest in CS as a major drops among incoming freshmen. *Computing Research News* 17(3).

Zweben, S. (2006). Ph.D. production at an all-time high with more new graduates going abroad: Undergraduate enrollments again drop significantly. *Computing Research News* 18(3).

17   Design Heuristics for Activist Games

Mary Flanagan and Helen Nissenbaum

Computer games are more profitable and popular than ever and have become a major cultural medium across a wide range of social, economic, age, and gender categories. Indeed, from casual games played on the Internet to *The Sims, Metal Gear,* and *Grand Theft Auto* series, the popularity of computer games suggests a revolution measurable in terms of financial, social, and cultural impact. Annual retail sales of video games in the United States in 2007 exceeded $9 billion, not including hardware, peripherals, and related products.

Games are also a cultural medium, carrying embedded beliefs within their representation systems and structures, whether the designers intend them or not. In media effects research, this is referred to as "incidental learning" from media messages. For example, *The Sims* is said to teach consumer consumption, one of the values of capitalism: it encourages players to earn money so they can spend it and acquire goods. The *Grand Theft Auto* series was not created as an educational game, but nonetheless, it portrays its world as a violent place, rewards criminal behavior, and reinforces racial and sex stereotypes. Many scholars, makers, and consumers observe that games can embody antagonistic and antisocial themes—violence and gore, genocide, crime, cruelty, problematic representations of bodies in terms of sex and race, and even viciously competitive game interaction and game goals (see Anderson 2004; Johnston 1999; Media Education 2001; Melillo 1999). While of course this is not the case for all games, these issues arise in a notable number of popular games. Our goal is not to denigrate these games but offer alternatives. How can a game designer intentionally "break the mold," especially when designing for "new" or underserved players such as girls?

Building upon the significant insights of those engaged in the study of ethics, science and technology, and design disciplines (e.g., Akrich 1992; Brey 1997; Hughes 1987; Latour 1992; Lessig 1999; MacKenzie and Wajcman

1985; Mumford and Henshall 1978; Nissenbaum 2004; Winner 1980), we believe that it is not enough to stop at the point of recognizing that human principles (negative and positive) could be embodied in design—we must set forth particular principles as a design aspiration. As this book attests, there is a will, not only among concerned observers but also among those who play and create games, that existing games be changed, or rather, that games should at least be developed in a way, that they could include ethical ideals—or *human values.* Accordingly, our work urges designers and producers to include values in the criteria by which the quality of a given technology is judged, to strive actively for a world whose technologies not only are effective, efficient, safe, attractive, easy to use, and so forth but also promote the values to which the surrounding societies and cultures subscribe.

Research on sex differences in IT, game, and computer interests helped trigger the development of the framework presented here. Our team believes that the lack of values-oriented software environments or environments that embody the ideals of values such as creativity, security, and equity contributes to the large number of females who lose interest in IT fields overall (AAUW 2000; Bruner 1997; Flanagan 2006; Inkpen et. al. 1995; Varma 2003). We believe the Values at Play (V.A.P.) framework will be of use to educators and systems designers in the IT field considering game structures. This research will also be of significant value to scholars interested in the study of technology, society, and humanity (Lee 2003). Throughout this chapter, we draw examples from *RAPUNSEL,* a game that teaches girls basic programming skills with the underlying motivation to include girls' perspectives in software design. *RAPUNSEL* was designed to embody a suite of activist social values within the overarching goal of increasing girls' technological competence.

What is the best way to influence existing game paradigms? By now there is a tradition in technology studies that has stressed a relationship between design and values, and has made some progress in how to structure design practices (see Friedman, Kahn, and Borning 2002). We have developed a specialized version of this inquiry in relation to computer games, which we hope to promulgate in both industry settings as well as educational institutions. To develop a design approach (or best practices) for taking values systematically into account, we generated several key questions: How can values be consistently and systematically integrated into the design of software systems? How close can one get to making values investigations in the context of technical design scientifically rigorous? Is it possible to construct a viable set of general software design principles that could lead to the integration of values across a variety of design tasks, and in particular, games?

The Method

We have developed a methodological framework, Values at Play, to foster values integration into the science of design through the creation of a tool kit to go along with this framework. The V.A.P. framework has been further developed through work with *RAPUNSEL,* a dance game to teach girls programming. The V.A.P. framework is not intended to replace other well-established design approaches or methodologies such as participatory design (e.g., Cross 1971; Druin1999; Grudin, Ehn, and Schmidt 1988; Mumford and Henshall 1978), value sensitive design (e.g., Borning, Friedman, and Kahn 2004), reflective practice (e.g., Schön 1983), and critical technical practice (e.g., Agre 1997; Dourish et al. 2004; Mateas 2000). We rather intend to supplement them, to augment software design philosophies that currently only target, for example, reliability, usability, functional efficiency, good game play, et cetera. Although our core concern is how to design systems that meet the constraints suggested by important social values, we must also meet traditional software and game design criteria as well.

The V.A.P. methodology can be used to create games specifically intended to be activist games. But it can also be applied to the design of more mainstream commercial and educational games. When using V.A.P. to embed values into the mainstream game design process, values will be one of many competing game design requirements. Intentionally embedding values, however, stands a better chance of creating socially conscious games than ignoring the topic and thus leaving embedded values to chance. Why forego the opportunity to at least consider making a more socially conscious game?

Development of the Values at Play Approach

The preliminary approach [sketched out and applied to a case study in Flanagan, Howe, and Nissenbaum (2005)] comprises three constitutive and iterative activities: (1) *discovery* in which designers discover and identify values relevant to their project, (2) *translation* in which designers translate value considerations into architecture and features, and (3) *verification* in which designers verify that the values outcomes they sought have been realized in the system. Designers do not undertake these activities in serial order but in parallel, as outputs from each are expected to feed back into the other two, which, in turn build upon these outputs in iterative steps.

1. **Discovery**   The goal of this activity is to identify values that might be relevant to a given design project. Although the explicit output of discovery— a set of values—will vary radically from project to project, the steps we suggest designers follow remain stable across projects. The steps emerge from the overall need to answer the question "What values?" To start a values discussion, it is useful to start with a list—while the following list of values is far from exhaustive, it is offered to help designers start thinking broadly about social values in games: liberty, justice, inclusion, equality, privacy, security/safety, creativity, freedom of expression, trust, cooperation, sharing, diversity, fair representation, personal autonomy, improved IT participation for females, self-esteem, self-efficacy, and authorship. By adding to, deleting from, and ultimately creating their own lists, project designers can initiate an inquiry into the sources of values in a given project, and prioritize them in the design process.

Values may be expressed in the very definition of a project. For example, a company that wishes to make the next commercial-shooter-game smash hit might define the project within the first-person-shooter genre; this alone brings about embedded values in terms of competition, creativity, potential violence, and goals. The National Science Foundation has supported numerous game projects to increase girls' interest in science, technology, engineering, and math (STEM) topics (see Hughes this volume; Kelleher this volume). Designing games for girls is particularly challenging because doing so intersects with larger assumptions about what girls like and how to market to them as a group, running the risk of reinforcing antitechnology stereotypes in ways that might not match a designer's intention to empower girls. Even the general question "What do girls like?" is in itself rife with assumptions proffered through marketing, media, and cultural assumptions; the question itself must be reconsidered with more nuance to become useful. Designing to accommodate a variety of player styles rather than a generic "girl" player could, in this example, be far more useful.

Values may emerge in specification of game mechanics. Examples of game mechanics range from the reward structure to the point of view in the game. For example, a particular design enables cooperation—such as collective inventories, rewards for sharing, how much players are able to communicate and work together, or even the point of view in the game. The point here is not to say that competition is inherently bad, but there might be different forms of competitions girls express an interest in. Therefore, we designed several kinds of reward systems in *RAPUNSEL* to satisfy different competitive and cooperative urges. Players can seek rewards based on their creativity and know-how in designing clothes and dances; players can share and earn points, gaining status; and players can actively challenge each other to dance-based competitions. Players have the important option of turning down competitions if they are noncompetitive players. This approach accommodates diverse play styles. Another very different example lies in game-play perspective, and here too we can see how values are affected in the very game engine design. For example, a "god's-eye" controlling point of view and the ability to manipulate large scale events and characters in games implies different values from, say, collaborating with characters to produce a desired result—complete control over events, weather, or human or nonhuman characters in god's-eye mode may foster a player's sense of autonomy, authorship, security, and self-esteem, but the god's-eye control may not necessarily cultivate sharing, cooperation, equality, or diversity.

Stakeholders' values set up preliminary expectations that frame any given project. Stakeholders can be clients, nonprofit groups, publishers—anyone with investment in the success of the project. Many game designers, for example, design for clients who bring to the project concerns about markets and distribution as well as already successful titles that affect the design process and its outcomes. One issue in particular in designing "games for girls" are the goals of the stakeholders in relationship to assumptions about female and male play styles and interests—are these assumptions well researched and is intention deep? Is success defined in terms of market share, or in terms of principles such as self-esteem, self-efficacy, self-autonomy, creativity, et cetera? Can both commercial and social values be equally important?

Design team backgrounds mold the creative process. Designers themselves are shaped by their expectations, goals, education, culture, and economic and social contexts. Recognizing ones' own values is a first step. Assessing where the team is coming from is a difficult but necessary part of the reflection on the values held among those in the creative environment.

Presumptive social and political values, and sometimes legislation, generate background constraints. For example, how much privacy a log-in system offers, what is shared publicly, what is freely exchanged—these are all affected by larger cultural and social norms and have implications for the values embedded in a game.

The acts of discovery for a given activist design project are thus far-ranging and represent significant challenges to designers. This initial values discovery checklist can launch consideration of social values to embed in a game. For *RAPUNSEL,* the list of project values after the discovery phases included cooperation, sharing, diversity, and fair representation.

2. **Translation**   This is the activity of embodying or expressing values in systems design. It comprises three subactivities: operationalization, implementation, and resolving value conflicts.

Operationalization. This involves defining value concepts, which, like privacy, equity, social justice, access, autonomy, and sociality, are often understood only in abstract and general terms.

Particular game features are tied to values. The idea is to express values definitions in operationally accessible, concrete forms so they may be rendered as design features. Creating the design for a game, then, involves making meaningful play happen through the incorporation of these values. *Cooperation,* for example, is a value that the team must not only identify but also design for—as a guiding factor, principle, or constraint. studies show teenage girls are deeply engaged in instant messaging and chat as a means toward higher levels of computer use (Grinter and Palen 2002). *RAPUNSEL's* chat system was identified as a feature to facilitate cooperation and contribute to increasing female participation in IT and computer science.

Operationalizing values requires a leap from concept *to* feature. The process of designing project values into the fabric of the game interaction (the rules by which players interact inside a game, also known as the game mechanic) for any one world is not always straightforward. If the value is to be meaningful in the game, it must be integral to the game-play mechanic, but the leap between the ideal value and the feature could sometimes seem like a leap of faith. In order to implement the value of cooperation in a game, for example, one might create tasks that can be completed only by two or more players cooperating. Or, one might design a game that rewards large coordinated group efforts over those undertaken by an individual alone (figure 17.1). Whether this feature, after implementation, in fact leads to cooperation or unfriendly competition remains to be seen and must be verified (a later stage).

Implementation is, in some sense, the essense of design, wherein the central concern is transforming, or translating ideas, intentions, requirements, and concepts into concrete design specifications and then, even more concretely, to lines of code in a program. Similarly, this is true in the case of values, except that the concepts in question are operationalized values.

Implementation involves translating, testing, and iteration. Even if the design has incorporated the translated value into a cohesive design, a designer never actually knows if the design is successful unless players and testers are involved and feedback incorporated into a revised design.

Figure 17.1   Designing for cooperation: in *RAPUNSEL,* players can choose to chat or use chat interaction to swap bits of computer code for points and recognition (see color plate).

Continuous review of values during implementation safeguards important design features. Values must be reviewed and re-reviewed throughout the implementation process. Even if values are expressed and operationalized into the design document, the features or aspects that embody values are often the first to be cut due to constraints of time, energy, and funding. The problem is more severe with larger teams. In our work on *RAPUNSEL* we discovered that features omitted in a particular game build, such as a missing graphic or audio feedback for mouse movements, or more complex features, such as a map in a game, might irrevocably alienate girl players unaccustomed to playing games. Rather than increasing girls' interest in programming, a prototype missing a few small key features drove them away from technology.

Disagreements are natural. Great team arguments may ensue regarding values decisions. Explicit, common values goals for the project, and reviewing the values on a regular basis (in our case, weekly) provides opportunities to discuss disagreements and may keep features prioritized in implementation that supports values without going overboard. A disagreement on the *RAPUNSEL* team focused on how much to scaffold the options available to players to help them learn to program. One perspective advocated giving the players nothing to alter but a parameter, such as shoe color. Then the game would allow for more and more changes, introducing more aspects of code. This approach was favored by some team members and not others: many self-taught programmers favored allowing players to look at actual code and hack away at it to see what changing the code does.

Values must be reviewed and re-reviewed for "feature creep." Because game design is a highly iterative process, values must be cyclically reassessed. Inspiration and a particular round of player testing can lead to the adoption of new design decisions, some of which may actually improve embedded values but could also be detrimental or conflict with the values aspects of the project.

Resolution of value conflicts. This is an ever-present need in design. In many cases these conflicts may not even rise to the decision-making level because they appear obvious, such as when one of the values is clearly dominant, or a design option is overwhelmingly costly or simply trivial. But experience with software design has shown that certain conflicts are recurrent and difficult— for example, security versus ease of use, privacy versus accountability—because the science of assessing values is still developing, nuances in the definition of values may vary from team member to team member, or the team's relative commitment to the values in conflict is unclear. Our preliminary work has revealed two key strategies that we have called "dissolving conflict" and "values trade-off."

Dissolving values conflict means redesign. Here, in the case where two values conflict, designers find ways through creative redesign to satisfy both values simultaneously. Examples from real-life design in projects created for girls abound, especially given that the initial design questions are likely to hold conflicting values. Designers of "games for girls" tend to want to create fair representation of female characters—the characters in the *Team Up!* game, by Girls, Inc., for example, are simple, diverse-looking in terms of ethnicity, and cartoonishly plump. Players used to toys, cartoons, and fashion advertising, however, can tend to prefer overtly sexualized female characters. Various approaches can work to dissolve this conflict: character redesign to stay somewhere in the middle, or avoidance of human characters for animal or abstract characters, et cetera. Another example would be violent interaction. While the design team may wish to offer an alternative to violent games as a possible option, players may fervently wish for violence in games, or expect violence as part of any computer game. Here, the decisions are complex, but solutions can include providing several ways of competing or substituting intense body action (running, jumping, kicking) in favor of hand-to-hand combat.

Values trade-offs favor one design choice over another to support a particular value. Sometimes one value can take priority over another, and do so at the expense of a second. In this example, perhaps offering sexualized characters to attract the players to an educational game would be more preferable to their not playing the game at all. This would be opportunity for significant team discussion of the values in the project. In cases such as these, usually a middle ground is sought, but at times designers will reach a values impasse and will need to make difficult decisions. Resolving values in games is, in general, a fiercely difficult problem.

3. **Verification** This activity covers the appraisal of whether and to what extent designers have successfully embedded target values in a given system. Verifying attitudes and beliefs need not be an entire research project on its own, but rather this process can be embedded in the playtesting and user research that is already being conducted in the course of development.

Sociological methods for verifying attitudes and beliefs can be used to a project's benefit. Verification strategies for values are likely to resemble those used in the design of more conventional attributes such as functional efficiency and usability, which include critical reflection and analysis, comparison with historical precedent, playtesting within the design team as well as with third parties, user studies in controlled settings, formal and informal interviews, surveys, and so forth. Verifying the inclusion of values adds a layer to this process, but in practice, the values merely become another item on the observer's or researcher's list of what to look for and ask about. How to gauge whether a game promotes sharing and diversity and so forth can become a part of the process.

Pre- and post-attitudinal surveys, control groups, playtesting, and other methods may be used to get at the heart of a player's experiences in a game. Here, enlisting the aid of a trained social scientist is extremely beneficial to the project so that the questions are phrased correctly and data can be gathered reliably. Pairing with graduate students interested in researching games would be a step in the right direction for commercial developers on a budget. In *RAPUNSEL,* which was funded as both a design and research project, we collected data in-game from mouse clicks, code complexity generated by the player, kinds and amounts of items authored, interaction habits, and time on task. We also used online surveys to see how players felt before and after using the game. Preliminary survey results in a study involving more than one hundred middle-school-age players, for example, showed a significant change in general self-efficacy and confidence level about programming knowledge among female players, but not among male players (see Plass et al. 2007).

Embedding values within technological systems, and verifying that such systems actually reflect those values, has rarely been attempted with computer games outside the work of small developers (see Frasca 2004; Laurel 2001). Games provide tricky values cases, and the games developed with alternate values in mind are up against several factors, not the least of which are the expectations produced by existing games. In the recent assessment sessions for *RAPUNSEL,* players expressed a desire to kill the characters and enemies discovered in the game. One student asked in near agony, "Why won't she die??" In the best of all possible worlds, designers

Figure 17.2 Iterations of the *RAPUNSEL* interface (see color plate).

may rely on prior work and compare this work to verify consistent attitudes and beliefs generated from, or fostered with, the project.

Iterative review of values throughout the project may yield more consistent results. Values work is of utmost importance as computer technologies and games affect larger society. In earlier work, we suggest that verification by means of prototypes is promising, and hold forth that small, focused prototypes are key to measuring values in the designs embedded in games. In *RAPUNSEL* (figure 17.2) adding a backpack icon in which players could find their programmed clothes and dances, adding icons to the organizational and code-editing windows, and limiting the number of items hierarchically represented in the backpack not only made good design sense but also enhanced project values of self-efficacy and creativity among players in the design partner sessions. Long-term results of values integration will be more difficult to verify but are a next step in the evaluation process. What are the immediate and long-term impacts of the V.A.P. method on players' attitudes, knowledge, and behavior? Do sex, gender identity, prior knowledge, design experience, or other variables influence this impact?

Conclusions

In our work, increasing female participation in computer science and IT is the overall principle that takes a priority among others and informs and sustains our practical design endeavors. Many of the points made in this chapter about design to increase female participation in computer science and IT, however, also apply to social inclusion at large, and the V.A.P design process could be adopted for these concerns as well. Our goal in terms of game design is to create enjoyable games that support values—and to offer a well-crafted approach to embedding particular values in a given design. While we have lofty goals, we are tempered with a good dose of realism: we are not going to make sweeping changes in the nature of all computer games, but we are striving to put social and political values, where relevant, on the design agenda at a grassroots level. Initiatives such as Values-in-Design, the NSF-PORTIA project at Stanford ("Sensitive Information in a Wired World"), and others (e.g., the many "privacy-preserving" projects) already constitute a lively arena of bottom-up attempts to create better IT systems. Because of the popularity of computer games, universities throughout the United States and other parts of the world are creating games-focused course work and degrees (Fullerton et al. this volume). These programs have become a training site for IT professionals, not all of whom will go into game design as a profession. In 2005 there were more than fifteen degree programs (BS, MS, and PhD levels) established in the United States focusing on the development of computer games, and more in the works (e.g., Georgia Tech, University of Southern California, Carnegie Mellon, Univeristy of Pennsylvania, University of Denver, and Rochester Institute of Technology). The proliferation of computer game–focused course work translates to an opportunity to educate systems designers about values in design before they are employed in the industry. Ultimately, such educated designers will alter the industry from the inside.

Other chapters in this book discuss activist approaches to game design and play (see Taylor this volume; Hughes this volume; Kelleher this volume), demonstrating that the idea of activist game design and play is part of a larger, growing movement. The contribution our project makes to the next decade of game design is a rigorous, systematic means to meet the goal of taking values into consideration in design at many levels of generality. We do not mean to pit "concerned citizens" against "creators," because many creators themselves *are* conscientious. We see computer games as a compelling entry point and test-bed for integrating values into technology design from the beginning of the process. The arena is particularly challenging as we are still at the beginning of an effort to integrate values into the sphere of technology design, especially in the complex field of game design, where even conscientious designers who support the principle of integrating values into systems are likely to have trouble applying standard design methodologies to the unfamiliar terrain of values. Experienced designers will recall the not-too-distant past when user interface and usability were similarly neglected features of software design.

Acknowledgments

We would like to thank the *RAPUNSEL* team. *RAPUNSEL* was funded under grant HRD-0332898 from the Gender in Science and Engineering Program (GSE) of the National Science Foundation. The CREATE lab at NYU was instrumental in assessment of the game. The V.A.P. research was funded by the National Science Foundation Science of Design program in 2006, with co-PI Sophia Catsambis, of Queens College.

References

AAUW (2000). *Tech-Savvy: Educating Girls in the New Computer Age.* New York: American Association of University Women Education Foundation.

Agre, P. (1997). Toward a critical technical practice: Lessons learned in trying to reform AI. In G. C. Bowker, S. L. Star, W. Turner, and L. Gasser (eds.), *Social Science, Technical Systems and Cooperative Work: Beyond the Great Divide.* Hillsdale, N.J.: Erlbaum.

Akrich, M. (1992). The de-scription of technical objects. In W. Bijker and J. Law (eds.), *Shaping Technology/Building Society,* 205–224. Cambridge, Mass.: The MIT Press.

Anderson, C. A. (2004). An update on the effects of playing violent video games. *Journal of Adolescence,* 27, 113–122.

Borning, A., B. Friedman, and P. Kahn (2004). Designing for human values in an urban simulation system: Value sensitive design and participatory design. In *Proceedings From the Eighth Biennial Participatory Design Conference.* Toronto, Canada. July.

Brey, P. (1997). Philosophy of technology meets social constructivism. *Techne: Journal for the Society for Philosophy and Technology,* 2, 3–4.

Brunner, C. (1997). Opening technology to girls: The approach computer-using teachers take may make the difference. *Electronic Learning,* 16(4), 55.

Cross, N. (1971). *Design Participation: Proceedings of the Design Research Society's Conference.* Manchester, UK.

Dourish, P., J. Finlay, P. Sengers, and P. Wright (2004). Reflective HCI: Towards a critical technical practice. Extended abstract in *Proceedings of CHI 2004,* 1727–1728.

Druin, A. (1999). Cooperative inquiry: Developing new technologies for children with children. In *Proceedings of CHI 1999,* 592–599. ACM Press.

Flanagan, M. (2006). Making games for social change. *AI & Society: The Journal of Human-Centered Systems,* 20(1), 493–505.

Flanagan, M., D. C. Howe, and H. Nissenbaum (2005). Values at play: Design tradeoffs in socially oriented game design. In *Proceedings of CHI 2005: Portland Oregon.* New York: ACM Press, 751–760.

Frasca, E. (2004). Videogames of the oppressed. In *Electronic Book Review* 3, http://www.electronicbookreview.com/v3.

Frasca, G. (2004). Videogames of the oppressed: Critical thinking, education, tolerance, and other trivial issues. In P. Harrington and N. Wardrip-Fruin (eds.), *First Person: New Media as Story, Performance, and Game.* Cambridge, Mass.: The MIT Press.

Friedman, B., P. Kahn, and A. Borning (2002). *Value Sensitive Design: Theory and Methods.* Technical Report 02-12-01, Comp. Sci. & E., University of Washington, Seattle.

Grinter, R., and L. Palen (2002). Instant messaging in teen life. In *Proceedings of the 2002 Computer Supported Cooperative Work* (CSCW '02), New Orleans, La., 21–30.

Grudin, J., P. Ehn, and K. Schmidt (1988). Computer supported cooperative work. In *Proceedings of the 1988 ACM Conference on Computer-supported Cooperative Work,* 377–394. Portland, Ore.

Hughes, T. (1987). The evolution of large technological systems. In W. Bijker, T. Hughes, and T. Pinch (eds.), *The Social Construction of Technological Systems,* 51–82. Cambridge, Mass.: The MIT Press.

IGDA (2005). Game developer demographics report. International Game Developers Association. http://www.igda.org/diversity/report.php.

Inkpen, K., K. S. Booth, M. Klawe, and R. Upitis (1995). Playing together beats playing apart, especially for girls. In *Proceedings of Computer Support for Collaborative Learning,* 177–181 (CSCL '95). Bloomington, Ind.

Johnston, C. (1999). Doom made me do it. *Electronic Gaming Monthly,* July, 26.

Latour, B. (1992). Where are the missing masses? The sociology of a few mundane artifacts. In W. Bijker and J. Law (eds.), *Shaping Technology/Building Society,* 225–258. Cambridge, Mass.: The MIT Press.

Laurel, B. (2001). *The Utopian Entrepreneur.* Cambridge: The MIT Press.

Lee, S. S. (2003). "I lose, therefore I think": A search for contemplation amid wars of push-button glare. *Game Studies: The International Journal of Computer Game Research* 3(2).

Lessig, L. (1999). *Code and Other Laws of Cyberspace.* New York: Basic Books.

Mateas, M. (2000). Expressive AI. In *Proceedings of SIGGRAPH 2000: SIGGRAPH Art and Culture Papers.* CD-ROM, 23–28 July. New Orleans, La., New York: ACM Press.

MacKenzie, D., and J. Wajcman (eds.) (1985). *The Social Shaping of Technology.* Berkshire, UK: Open University Press.

Media Education Foundation (2001). *Game Over: Gender, Race & Violence in Video Games.* DVD.

Melillo, W. (1999). Video-game group creates ads to deflect criticism. *Adweek Eastern Edition,* November 15, 5.

Mumford, E., and D. Henshall (1978). *Participative Approach to Computer Systems Design: A Case Study of the Introduction of a New Computer System.* New York: Halstead Press.

Nissenbaum, H. (2004). Will security enhance trust online, or supplant it? In P. Kramer and K. Cook (eds.), *Trust and Distrust Within Organizations: Emerging Perspectives, Enduring Questions,* 155–188. New York: Russell Sage Publications.

Plass, J. L., R. Goldman, M. Flanagan, J. Diamond, C. Dong, S. Looui, H. Song, C. Rosalia, and K. Perlin (2007). RAPUNSEL: How a computer game designed based on educational theory can improve girls' self-efficacy and self-esteem. In *Proceedings of the American Educational Research Association.* Chicago. April.

Schön, D. (1983). *The Reflective Practitioner.* New York: Basic Books.

Varma, R. (ed.) (2003). Technology and society: Diversifying computing, special issue on women and minorities in information technology. *IEEE Technology and Society Magazine,* 22(3), 1–48.

Winner, L. (1980). Do artifacts have politics? *Daedalus* 109(1), 121–36.

18 Gender Identity, Play Style, and the Design of Games for Classroom Learning

Carrie Heeter and Brian Winn

There are compelling reasons for the enthusiasm scholars, teachers, and game designers feel regarding the potential of games for learning. The chapters in this volume portray games for entertainment as fun, appealing, and important yet complicated—an alluring colorful rose garden, complete with thorny gender issues. In this chapter we consider whether games for learning are experienced differently by girls and boys in the classroom, compare the impacts of different in-game reward structures on male and female players in *Life Preservers* (a game we designed to teach about adaptation and evolution), and offer considerations for learning game design and deployment.

Engaging games tend to embody great pedagogy (Gee 2003). Players solve problems through trial and error, think strategically, and build implicit knowledge about the game. A constant cycle of progressive challenges involving action, feedback, and reaction according to the constraints of the rules helps drive the learning and engagement that occurs during games. What happens to the intended pedagogical model, though, if a player in a learning game struggles to figure out how to play, doesn't want to shoot the sea monsters who keep interrupting her as she collects undersea specimens, feels incompetent rather than empowered, and is not so sure she wants to earn a higher score than her best friend?

Games in the Classroom Trigger Cultural Expectations about Gender

What we know about games and what we know about gender guides us to predict that playing electronic games for learning in kindergarten through twelfth-grade classrooms will trigger students' cultural and personal expectations about gender. David Shaffer's excellent *How Computer Games Help Children Learn* (2006) calls for consideration of different "kinds of players" in the design and deployment of games for learning, such as kids from differ- ent ethnic backgrounds, kids who do well in school and kids who don't, kids from wealthy families and poor families, and kids from urban and suburban neighborhoods. However, in the domain of video games, research shows that age and gender are much stronger predictors of video game use than socioeco- nomic status or ethnicity (Bickham et al. 2003). Shaffer and others who extol the benefits of learning from games (e.g., Van Eck 2006; Gee 2005; Prensky 2001) ignore what to authors of this volume is an obvious "different kind of player" to consider.

The nature of each learning game, the classroom context in which it is played, and the gender identity and gaming orientation of individual players contribute to making classroom learning games a gender-polarizing experi- ence. T. L. Taylor (2007) admonishes that adopting a gender-blind stance (in our context, making learning games for "kids" without thinking about gender) may feel appropriate and egalitarian but is in fact risky: "scripted denial" of gender differences discounts the power of cultural and individual expectations and performance of gender. She suggests that an "absence of explicit critical thinking can feed back into the stereotypes," (p. 110) thus propagating the dominant male paradigm of game design.

Playing Games Is Masculine

Commercial games today are still a predominantly male medium. Game genres, game content, and game mechanics have been defined and designed by and for young males (see Lazzaro this volume; Consalvo this volume; Ful- lerton et al. this volume). Although both sexes play electronic games, what they play, who they play with, how they play, and how much they play differs dramatically. Game play is such a pervasive group activity among boys that it may be risky for a boy not to play—it marks him out as not sharing popular peer interest (Durkin 2006). In a small pilot study, Jenson and de Castell (2005) found that boys say they play exclusively with other boys while girls play alone or with boys but only rarely with other girls. Girls and women who played extreme male-targeted games reported doing so with a male player. Hayes (this volume) points out that girls and boys choose different games, and boys are much more likely to engage in constructive activities related to the game beyond simply playing.

While there are girls who love games and boys who hate games, statistically the average differences between girl and boy gaming are vast. One result is a large, cumulative experience gap. This matters in the context of games for learning in part because experienced players often can learn and master a new game more quickly than nonexperienced players. Each year of school, the experience gap in game play by male and female students widens. Our research on electronic game play in middle school, high school, and college shows that boys play digital games for more hours per week than girls do at every age studied (Caywood and Heeter 2006). The magnitude of the gender gap in time spent playing games increases with age; boys play 2.8 times longer than girls in middle school, 4.4 times longer in high school, and 5.1 times longer in college. Extrapolating from this data, by the time a male graduates from college, he will on average have logged thousands more hours of digital game play than his average female classmate.

Girls Are Reluctant to Game or Compute in Mixed-Gender Public Settings

Educational video games are, of course, played using computer technology, another strongly masculine-identified pleasure (see Hayes this volume; Kelleher this volume; Flanagan and Nissenbaum this volume). The masculine culture of computing positions women and girls as less competent and/or confident in relation to computers (Jenson and de Castell 2005). Jenson and de Castell observed that when girls and women find themselves competing directly with their male counterparts they tend to "discount themselves as equal-opportunity competitors" and define themselves as less skilled and less competent.

When boys play games (or use computers) when there are fewer machines than people, girls step aside. It is difficult to determine whether it is the girls' "stepping aside" from their opportunity (Schott and Horrell 2000, p. 42) or the boys "crowding out" the girls (Ray 2004, p. 4). Nonetheless, this chemistry seems to exist between males and females pervasively when it comes to using gaming machines.

Playing a game is an ongoing, active performance as the player makes choices and takes actions to progress through the game, much more so than reading a book or listening to a lecture. In the public setting of a school computer laboratory, classmates can glance at each others' screens and compare progress and performance. Therefore, game play in the classroom is, in part, a public performance of gender. Learners' expectations about how people of their gender are supposed to play contribute to their own performance. Bryce and Rutter (2003) suggest that females experience psychological barriers when gaming in public, while private domains are more conducive to female gaming.

Females and Males Approach Competition Differently

Is competition different for males and females? Some argue that any distinction has disappeared now that a record number of girls participate in sports. Indeed, 73 percent of eighth-grade boys and 66 percent of eighth-grade girls competed in school athletics in 2004 (Child Trends Databank, 2007). However, the experience of competing in women's and men's sports is different, even within professional adult leagues. Kathleen DeBoer, a former professional women's basketball player, collegiate coach, and associate athletic director at University of Kentucky, writes about vast differences in coaching male and female athletes. Men battle for success, valuing individual achievement and hierarchical social structure, while women bond for success, valuing attachment, intimacy, and connectedness (DeBoer 2004). In the highly competitive arena of women's college basketball, a female athlete who excels risks becoming a social outcast on her team. A male athlete who excels is likely to become the team leader.

DeBoer notes that

> among males the importance of winning is largely unquestioned and unchallenged. . . . In females, winning is only one of several options. Women will evaluate the cost of winning in relation to other options. If the cost is too high, particularly in the area of interpersonal relationships, then winning will lose its significance. (p. 40)

She explains that scorekeeping is important to men because it tells them clearly where they stand in relation to others. Women are uncomfortable with scorekeeping because it segregates people into winners and losers, disrupting connectedness and producing anxiety.

Not surprisingly, gender differences in competition extend to video gaming. Jenson and de Castell (2005) note that girls tend to play games on their own. Under that circumstance, questions of competition and competitiveness do not arise. On the other hand, boys play games in the company of and in competition with other boys. Hartmann (2003) found that male players were more motivated to compete and chose more competitive games. Morlock and colleagues (1985) noted that "ultimate mastery over a game (and fellow players)" was often paramount for males, but that females seemed to be "willing to play without regard to the score." Raney, Smith, and Baker (2006) add that males report being upset by poor scores and conclude that "many video games do not engage a desire in females to master a game for its own sake (p. 169)." Hartmann and Klimmt (2006) conclude that "experiential and reward consequences" of game play appeal more to masculine than feminine social identities.

Gender and Play Style in Learning Games

Psychologists have used play style as a construct to characterize child play behavior, combining toy selection, rough-and-tumble play (or lack thereof), and activity level (for example, Maccoby and Jacklin 1987; Alexander and Hines 1994). During play, a child's style can be characterized as masculine or feminine. A feminine play style could include choosing feminine toys, a lack of rough and tumble play, and limited physical activity. But play style can be fluid. A child may move from one play style to another in a single period of play and may engage in different play styles on different days or in different contexts. Girls exhibit feminine play styles more often than boys do and vice versa, but both sexes engage in masculine and feminine play styles.

At home or on the playground, children are free to select toys, playmates, and activities. Play behavior is not always consistent with designer expectations. One can practice juggling using three Barbie dolls or play house using marbles that represent family members. Like toys, digital games can be designed to offer more or less gendered game experiences by using masculine, feminine, neutral, or mixed themes, game goals, and player interactions. Digital game design restricts or enables different play styles but it is the players who decide how they will play from moment to moment. For clarity in this chapter, *play style* will be used to describe the actions and choices a player makes while playing.

Current educational games offer more limited play variety than the massively multiplayer online (MMO) games for entertainment described by Yee (this volume). Yee grouped ten MMO player motivations into achievement, social, and immersion categories. Males, who comprise 85 percent of MMO players, were more motivated than females by two of three achievement factors and females were more motivated than males by one aspect in each of the social and immersion clusters, and females were more motivated than males by one aspect in each of the social and immersion clusters. However, like Lazzaro, Yee observed that the overwhelming majority of men and women like to do the same kinds of things in MMOs. He suggests that the achievement motivation difference may be better explained by age than sex differences: older players were attracted to motivations other than achievement, and female MMO players tended to be older. We are reminded to look at similarities and the influence of context, age, and other factors in addition to considering gender differences when observing play style.

Designing for Diverse Play Styles

Commercial games often provide hundreds of hours of game play and, in some cases, extensive player choice. Designers structure game mechanics such as navigation, advancement criteria, and levels to define (enable, guide, and restrict) player options. Progression through the game is motivated by game mechanics, including the reward structure.

Many learning games rely on speed to create the game experience. In some game scenarios, players are required to complete a task before time runs out. Other scenarios reward but may not require speed. As Hughes (this volume) and Klawe and colleagues (2002) note, boys often introduce an element of competition themselves by racing to finish, even if the game does not promote speedy play. Speed of play and points earned are consistent with Yee's Achievement motivations cluster and with Lazzaro's "hard fun" or "*fiero.*"

Public settings such as classrooms and museums may magnify differences in how males and females use technology, play video games, and compete. Klawe and colleagues (2002) observed ten thousand children playing various video and computer games at Science World's computer games museum exhibit hall. In this very public, voluntary setting, boys and girls approached (and did not approach) the games differently. The researchers concluded that while boys are more interested in completing or winning the game and trying to finish in the shortest amount of time possible, girls take a more exploratory approach. Laurel's design research (2001; this volume) for her Purple

Moon games, similarly concluded that boys are more likely to "rush to beat the game," and girls are more likely to take their time and explore.

Exploration of the game world, inhabitants, and aesthetic or content details beyond what is required to progress through the game is only possible if content to be explored is available, and if the game mechanics permit exploration. Exploration is consistent with the Discovery factor in Yee's Immersion motivations cluster and with Lazzaro's dimensions of "easy" and "serious" fun. Exploration is an internal, reflective player experience, harder to observe and measure than overt player actions and speed. Therefore, and perhaps unfortunately, learning game mechanics less often rewards this play style.

Games that require all players to play quickly force some players to adopt an unnatural or even aversive play style. Ideally from a player comfort and enjoyment perspective, learning games would be designed to accommodate speedy play, high score achievement, as well as play-style exploration. The relationship between play style and learning has received little attention. Does competitive or exploratory play style result in more learning from an educational game? Educational psychologist Anita Woolfolk (2005) refers to time spent actively involved in specific learning tasks as "engaged time" or "time on task." Time spent on content is usually correlated with student learning (Berliner 1998). On the other hand, Cordova and Lepper (1996) demonstrate the importance of intrinsic motivation to activate learning. Are speedy players more motivated than slower players? How strongly does a game design influence learners' play styles within the game?

The *Life Preservers* Game

We created *Life Preservers* (*LP*) as a vehicle to experimentally study play style, gender, and learning. Like most of the other chapters in this part, our audience was middle-school children. However, our target was the classroom, not after-school programs. Although games are considered a possible vehicle for eventually transforming education, for our experiment we needed the game to be easy for teachers to adopt and use in the context of teaching curricular requirements. The game needed to fit as easily as possible into existing school systems and be playable within a single class period (approximately fifty minutes). The game was designed to teach middle-school and high-school students national science standards about evolution (GEL Lab 2006), to accommodate

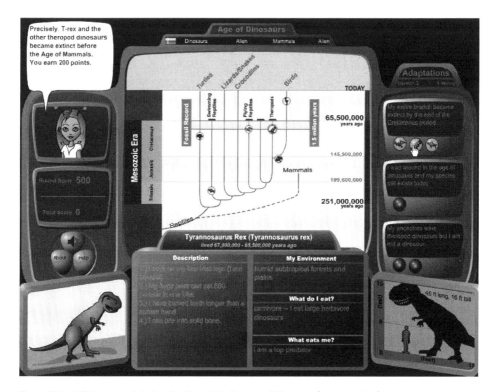

Figure 18.1   *Life Preservers* interface for Round 1 in the Age of Dinosaurs (see color plate).

diverse play styles, and to appeal to both girls and boys. These goals were achieved through a cycle of prototyping, playtesting, and revision.

In its final form, the game takes place within the Tree of Life, a diagram of the history of life on Earth. In the main interface, for each round, three adaptation challenges related to a national science standard appear along the right side. The Level 1 Tree of Life, for Mesozoic Era, appears in the middle of the screen (figure 18.1), with a time line along the right side. Six "critter dots" represent the animals in play for this round. Clicking on a critter dot reveals details in the multipanel display at the bottom, which includes a drawing of the animal, graphical size comparison to a six-foot-tall human; and an interesting, relevant description of the critter, its environment, what it eats, and what eats it. A customizable "Chief Scientist" character offers feedback and instructions. Players match critters with adaptation challenges to earn points and advance to the next round.

Design to Engage Both Sexes

The authors have written elsewhere about the iterative process of prototyping, playtesting, and revision used to create *LP*, including a design case study about the process (Heeter, Winn, and Greene 2005) and an analysis of how playtesting can be used not just to improve playability, as is done for commercial games, but also to resolve conflicts between pedagogy, game play, and content (Winn and Heeter 2006/2007). Lazzaro (this volume) adamantly advocates designing games around what players find fun, not around demographics. We agree with focusing on fun but believe attention to differences in what girl and boy players find fun can mitigate the danger of unconsciously adopting stereotypically male, mainstream game mechanics.

Our progression through three rounds of prototype, playtests, and revisions revealed that engaging girls was far more difficult than engaging boys. Our playtesting and revisions are consistent with the literature review: female playtesters were less experienced gamers, resisted learning complex rules, and needed a more compelling motivation than earning points to become engaged with the game. Playtesting facilitated refinement of the game mechanics and demonstrated the need to find additional ways to be clearer and more interesting in order to increase girls' engagement. We found that male playtesters would figure out how to play the game, and progress from beginning to end whether or not they were particularly interested in it. Female playtesters were slow to learn and unmotivated to progress until the game content and story aligned better with themes and topics they found interesting. Changes that improved the appeal for girls included streamlining the amount of information, restructuring the content to increase the likelihood players would attend to it, limiting the game's focus to more recent eras of evolution of interest to girls, simplifying game interactions, and integrating a story to provide coherence and motivate play.

Play Style and Bonus Points: Three Variations

LP was designed to accommodate speedy play and exploration. Exploration play is facilitated in *LP* by making more content available than is needed to play and win the game. For example, in Round 1 it is possible to correctly match critters for all three adaptation challenges without paying any attention to each critter's drawing, size diagram, or descriptive text. Players can be efficient and play quickly, or they can take their time and explore a wealth of interesting information. There is always more content available than is needed to advance in the game. An efficient player focused on winning quickly could ignore content that is not necessary to advance. Thus, the game allows not only for speedy but also explorative play.

LP served as the experimental stimulus for research on the relationship between play style, gender, and learning. It is reasonable to ask whether differences observed in gaming behavior might simply be caused by different amounts of gaming experience rather than gender identity. Our research examines the impact of gaming experience on play style and learning.

Rewards and punishments are typically built into a game to encourage or discourage certain behaviors, shaping future actions that players are likely to take (Salen and Zimmerman 2004). Three variations on the reward structure of *LP* were developed with the goal of encouraging particular play styles. The "plain" version offered no bonus points (NO BONUS). Players earned two hundred points for each correct match and they lost one hundred points for each incorrect match. This default point system was intended to discourage guessing and to encourage carefully chosen, correct matches. In the plain version, players could choose to play quickly, perhaps earning bragging rights in the classroom. But such rewards for speed, in the plain version, are entirely external to the game.

A second version explicitly rewarded speedy play (REWARD SPEED). In this version, a countdown clock appeared in each round. Completing the round before the clock ran out earned the player an extra five hundred bonus points. The presence of a countdown clock reminded players of the urgency of playing quickly. Bonus speed points served as both a reward to speedy players and a punishment (lack of points) for slower players. Between rounds they saw a tip: "Earn bonus points by completing the round before the countdown expires." Rewarding speed or setting time limits are techniques that game designers frequently use to increase the challenge or fun of a game.

The third version rewarded exploration (REWARD EXPLORE). Rewarding exploration is an unusual game mechanic that was accomplished by adding an onscreen "Critters Explored" counter. The counter kept track of and displayed the number of times the player looked at a different critter's details for at least seven seconds in that round. At the end of the round, players earned fifty bonus points for each critter explored. Between rounds they saw a tip: "Earn bonus points by spending time on each critter." Thus, this version encourages exploration and discourages speedy play.

Methods and Demographics

Seventh-graders from four cities in California played *Life Preservers* and completed an online pregame and postgame survey in early June 2006. Since evolution is taught in seventh grade in this state, all players had been exposed to some of the concepts in the game prior to playing. Students logged in to the pretest survey and were then randomly assigned to one of three versions of the game (plain, reward speedy play, or reward exploration). As they played, *LP* collected detailed play behavior data including time, score, and critter selection. At the end of the game, players were taken to the online postgame survey. The 292 study participants were equally split between girl and boy players. Random assignment of the bonus-point variations resulted in 91 plain, 91 reward speedy play, and 90 reward exploration players.

    LP successfully engages students' attention and motivates them to complete the game. Teachers who used the game with their middle-school classes reported their students were very engaged in the game. Postgame surveys found no significant differences in boys' and girls' enjoyment of *LP*. Girls and boys were equally neutral, rating *LP* at the midpoint between very fun to play and not fun at all. Girls' and boys' enjoyment of *LP* was identical in all three versions (plain, reward speedy play, and reward exploration). Although girls reported significantly less skill at playing games in general than boys, there was no difference in how well girls and boys thought they played *LP*.

    Girls in our sample spent significantly less time playing console and handheld games and computer games than boys did. On average girls played console and handheld games for a little less than forty-five minutes per week, compared to boys' two hours and forty minutes per week. On average girls played computer games for nearly the same amount of time as they played console and handheld games, forty-six minutes per week, compared to the three and one half hours per week spent by boys playing computer games.

    One-fourth of seventh-graders were classified as nongamers; students who played console, handheld, and computer games for a total of half an hour or less per week. Three-fourths of nongamers were girls. Sixty-two percent of girls were gamers compared to 88 percent of boys. The average time per week gamers spent playing electronic games was slightly more than four and one half hours.

We compared how much students liked console and computer games and the self-rated skill at playing between girls and boys and between gamers and nongamers. Boys said they like console, handheld, and computer games significantly more than girls did, and reported they were more skilled at playing than girls did. Nongamers were more extreme than girls overall in their disliking of games. Nongamers self-reported skill at playing games as much lower than gamers' perceived skill at gaming. Nongamer girls and nongamer boys did not like games and didn't feel they were good at playing games.

Learning was only measured in a posttest and therefore we cannot know how much knowledge seventh-graders had before playing *LP.* Players' postgame knowledge was quite high. After completing the game, seventh-graders correctly answered an average of 6.7 out of 10 standardized science test questions about evolution and adaptation. Female and male knowledge scores were not significantly different, although girls on average scored slightly higher (6.9) than boys did (6.5). Nongamers' and gamers' knowledge scores were also not significantly different.

Comparing Speed and Exploration Bonus Points

Table 18.1 reports results of a statistical comparison of girls' and boys' play styles measured by number of speedy rounds, number of critters explored, and number of mistakes overall and in each of the three reward conditions (NO BONUS, REWARD SPEED, and REWARD EXPLORE). Although only players in the REWARD SPEED condition were rewarded, we can compare how many rounds players in all conditions completed within the speedy play time frame, even though only players in the REWARD SPEED condition saw the countdown clock and received speed bonus points. Likewise, we can compare how many different critters the player looked at in blocks of at least seven seconds, even though only players in the REWARD EXPLORE condition saw the "critters explored" in-game tally and received corresponding bonus points for exploring critters. Mistakes count the number of incorrect matches, indicating whether a player did not look for, did not find, or did not understand the game content that would have permitted a correct match.

Table 18.1 Comparing Boys' and Girls' Play Styles by Reward Condition

	No. of speedy rounds		No. of critters explored		No. of mistakes	
	Girls	Boys	Girls	Boys	Girls	Boys
No bonus	0.7	1.6	23.1	19.1	9.9	9.1
Reward speed	1.4	1.7	20.7	18.9	13.6	11.1
Reward explore	0.7	1.0	23.7	22.4	10.0	7.5
Overall	1.0	1.4	22.4	20.2	11.3	9.1
	F = 9.075		F = 11.202		F = 3.914	
	df = 3,265		df = 3,265		df = 3,266	
	p = .000		p = .000		p = .009	
Gender	.001		.000		.051	
Reward condition	.000		.000		.020	
Interaction	.123		.144		.781	

There was a significant difference between boys and girls among reward conditions. The NO BONUS condition is likely to reflect each player's natural way of playing, uninfluenced by onscreen prompts rewarding a particular style of play. In the NO BONUS condition, on average boys played twice as quickly as girls did. Girls explored 21 percent more creatures. Girls made slightly more mistakes.

In the version of *LP* that rewarded speedy play, girls played faster than the girls who played the plain version, almost equaling boys' speed. However, girls also made many more mistakes in the speed condition. Furthermore, girls enticed to play quickly by speed bonus points explored fewer creatures, although they still explored more creatures than boys did. Boys' behavior did not change very much between the NO BONUS and the REWARD SPEED condition—their speed was the same and the number of creatures explored was the same. It is curious that even though boys' play was equally fast in NO BONUS and REWARD SPEED conditions, like girls, boys made more mistakes when speed was rewarded. Perhaps when a game is designed to instill a sense of urgency, a side effect is to encourage less thoughtful choices.

The findings are reversed in the REWARD EXPLORE condition. Here, girls' play style was identical to the NO BONUS condition. However, boys' play style changed a great deal. When exploration was rewarded with bonus points boys slowed down, explored more creatures, and made the fewest mistakes. Bonus points appear capable of reversing natural play style predilections but fail to make natural play style patterns more extreme. Rewarding speed was harmful to both boys and girls. Rewarding exploration (and not speed) was helpful to boys and not harmful to girls.

Table 18.2 reports results of a statistical comparison of gamers' and nongamers' play styles overall and in each of the three reward conditions. The overall average differences between nongamers and gamers parallel but are less extreme than the overall average differences between girls and boys. Nongamers played slower, explored more, and made more mistakes than gamers did. Rewarding speed resulted in faster play and more mistakes for both gamers and nongamers.

Multiple regression analysis was conducted to isolate the impact of gaming experience, player gender, and reward condition on play style. Being female was the most significant predictor of making more mistakes and of playing slower, above and beyond the impact of game experience and reward condition. Rewarding speed also contributed significantly to the number of mistakes and speed of play. Controlling for gender and reward condition, nongamers tended to make fewer mistakes. Being female and rewarding exploration were equally significant predictors of the number of creatures explored. Being a nongamer also contributed to exploration, in addition to gender and reward condition.

Nongamers did not appear to be hampered by their lesser gaming experience. Learning from and liking of *LP* was not different between gamers and

Table 18.2 Comparing Gamers' and Nongamers' Play Styles by Reward Condition

	No. of speedy rounds		No. of critters explored		No. of mistakes	
	Nongamer	Gamer	Nongamer	Gamer	Nongamer	Gamer
No bonus	.9	1.3	22.4	20.4	10.6	8.2
Reward speed	1.2	1.7	22.3	19.0	12.8	11.3
Reward explore	.5	.9	24.7	20.7	10.2	7.6
Overall	.9	1.3	23.0	20.7	11.3	8.9
	F = 7.33		F = 9.075		F = 3.50	
	df = 3,259		df = 3,259		df = 3,261	
	p = .01		p = .000		p = .016	
Nongamer	.018		.002		.038	
Reward condition	.000		.000		.047	
Interaction	.969		.714		.061	

Table 18.3 Multiple Regressions Comparing the Impact of Being Female, Being a Nongamer, Rewarding Speed, and Rewarding Exploration on Play Style

	No. wrong	Speedy rounds	Critters explored	Learning
Female	**.198**** (p = .002)	**−.189**** (p = .003)	**.189**** (p = .000)	ns
Nongamer	**−.150*** (p = .018)	−.093 (p = .133)	**.147*** (p = .017)	ns
Reward speed	**.163*** (p = .019)	**.153*** (p = .025)	−.114 (p = .089)	ns
Reward explore	−.013 (p = .852)	**−.138*** (p = .042)	**.189**** (p = .005)	ns
n	263	263	263	225
	F = 5.58	F = 8.02	F = 10.00	F = .649
	df = 4,260	df = 4,259	df = 4,259	df = 4,221
	p = .000	p = .000	p = .000	p = .628

nongamers. Above and beyond the effects of gender, nongamers made fewer mistakes in *LP* and they engaged in more exploration (see table 18.3).

There were no significant relationships between learning and player gender, gaming experience, or reward condition. Because learning was measured only by a posttest, we do not know whether *LP* was a great teacher or whether the students had good prior knowledge of the science. Also, the learning assessment uses actual national science standardized test questions. Most players either learned from LP or already knew most of what seventh-graders are supposed to know about evolution and adaptation. Players almost certainly learned creature-specific content and could have gained insights beyond the broad generalizations covered in national tests. A broader learning assessment could reveal player and play-style differences in this kind of incidental yet meaningful learning about the world.

Research Results

Rewarding speed is a common game mechanic. It is an easy way to transform a task into a game. In the context of a learning game, rewarding speedy play caused both boys and girls as well as gamers and nongamers to make more mistakes and it caused girls to play faster than they naturally would have. Overtly rewarding exploration in a learning game is less common but should be considered as a game mechanic. Rewarding exploration neither helped nor hindered girls' play, but it had a positive impact on boys. It slowed boys down and resulted in more focused play with fewer errors. This finding has powerful implications for the design of games for learning. For example, designers may decide to avoid rewarding speed and find ways to reinforce alternate play behaviors more closely tied to the desired learning behaviors in the game.

Discussion

Despite compelling arguments that today's games privilege and predominantly attract male players, games for learning offer great potential benefits in pedagogy and engagement. Certainly girls excel at and benefit more from some classroom activities and boys from others (Streitmatter 1994; Yates 1997; Daniels et al. 2001). If we were to ask middle-school kids whether they would prefer to listen to a lecture or play a game, quite likely most (boys and girls) would choose a game. However, because games are potentially such a gender-polarizing domain, designers of games for learning and teachers who teach with them could take intentional steps to improve the game experience for girls.

Interestingly, unlike most commercial games, *Click!,* Storytelling Alice, *RAPUNSEL,* and *Life Preservers,* had a woman as the project director. Authors of part II might ask, "How did a woman leading the project impact the design?" Often her expectations were different from those of the game design team. For *Life Preservers* and *RAPUNSEL,* conflicts arose between the project leader and game designers, sometimes explicitly concerning gender-related design values and other times more generally over the question "What is a game?" A common thread of all four games is their focus on goals other than winning. These "games for girls" emphasize meaningful accomplishment, self-expression, and personal mastery more than winning (using science and technology to solve a mystery, programming a cool animated story, programming great dance moves, or learning enough about evolution to protect Earth from invading aliens). These examples of "goals" are similar to those in the games created by girls in Denner and Campe (this volume), where winning often included getting an A on a test, staying out of trouble, or helping others. The *Click!* experience leads us to predict that if games were played by all-boy after-school groups, boys would invent ways to instill more competition.

The *LP* research found that learning games in the classroom can be used to engage girls and nongamers, despite their comparatively lesser experience and involvement with the medium. *LP* had been carefully designed to engage girls. Perhaps a different game, one that appealed less equally to girls and boys, would have different learning outcomes by gender or gaming experience. But there is no evidence for such an effect in this study.

Despite explanations of how differently boys and girls think about competition, bonus points influence both sexes. Based on the study results, boys and girls modify their play style in response to bonus points in the direction of play the bonus points intend (speed or exploration).

We can caution game designers against encouraging speedy play as a game mechanic in learning games. Rewarding speedy play appears to hurt the performance of both boys and girls, with a stronger adverse effect on girls. Thus, game designers might consider ways of rewarding exploration. Doing so improved the performance of boys, and did not harm girls. Perhaps by making exploration a competitive factor, boys are able to focus less on playing quickly while still satisfying a desire to compete. Gender identity was a stronger predictor of play style than gaming experience.

Our findings lend credence to the importance of considering gender identity differences when designing and deploying games for learning in the classroom. Assumptions about what games are "supposed to be" can be expanded as alternative genres and new game mechanics are contemplated. There is much more to discover about the relationship between play style and learning. Our quantitative *LP* study is a large-scale experiment. Qualitative research could more deeply examine how learning games are played in a classroom setting and derive a more richly detailed understanding of what is learned (beyond standardized test questions) and what exploration play actually means. For example, it is not clear how playing alone compares to playing with same-sex groups or mixed-sex groups. Competition and public performance of learning games are areas ripe for further study.

Acknowledgments

The design and study of *Life Preservers* was supported by a grant from the National Science Foundation (NSF-0217197). Any opinions, findings, and conclusions or recommendations expressed in this material are those of the author and do not necessarily reflect the views of the National Science Foundation. We wish to thank Ruta Sevo and Jolene Jesse from NSF and to acknowledge invaluable research, game design, and art support by graduate students Jillian

Winn, Patrick Shaw, and Amanda Flowers; Art Direction by Darcy Drew Greene; and great editorial feedback from Yasmin Kafai and Jill Denner.

References

Alexander, G., and M. Hines (1994). Gender labels and play styles: Their relative contribution to children's selection of playmates. *Child Development, 65*(3) 869–879.

Berliner, D. (1998). Simple views of effective teaching and a simple theory of classroom instruction. In D. Berliner and B. Rosenshine (eds.), *Talks to Teachers* (pp. 93–110). New York: Random House.

Bickham, D. S., E. A. Vandewater, A. C. Huston, J. H. Lee, A. G. Caplovitz, and J. C. Wright (2003). Predictors of Children's Electronic Media Use: An Examination of Three Ethnic Groups. Media Psychology, *5*(2), 107–137.

Bryce, J., and J. Rutter (2003). Gender dynamics and the social and spatial organization of computer gaming. *Leisure Studies, 22,* 1–15.

Butler, J. (1990, 1999). Gender trouble: Feminism and the subversion of identity. New York and London: Routledge Classics.

Caywood, J., and C. Heeter (2006). Leisure time and gender: Understanding why non-gamers don't play. *FuturePlay International Conference on the Future of Game Design and Technology,* London, Ontario, Canada.

Child Trends Databank. (2007). Child Trends Analysis of Monitoring the Future Survey Data 1991–2004. http://www.childtrendsdatabank.org/pdf/37_PDF.pdf.

Cordova, D. I., and M. R. Lepper (1996). Intrinsic motivation and the process of learning: Beneficial effects of contextualization, personalization, and choice. *Journal of Educational Psychology, 88,* 715–730.

Daniels, H., A. Creese, V. Hey, D. Leonard, and M. Smith (2001). Gender and learning: Equity, equality and pedagogy. *Support for Learning, 16*(3), 112–116.

DeBoer, K. J. (2004). *Gender and Competition: How Men and Women Approach Work and Play Differently.* Monterrey, Calif.: Coaches Choice.

Durkin, K. (2006). Game playing and adolescents' development. In P. Vorderer and J. Bryant (eds.), *Playing Video Games: Motives, Responses, and Consequences.* Mahwah, N.J.: Erlbaum.

Dye, M., and D. Bavelier (2004). Playing video games enhances visual attention in children. *Journal of Vision, 4*(11), 40a.

Gee, J. (2005). What would a state of the art instructional video game look like? *Innovate, 1*(6). http://www.innovateonline.info/index.php?view=article&id=80.

Gee, J. (2003). *What Video Games Have to Teach Us about Language and Literacy.* New York: Palgrave Macmillan.

GEL Lab (2006). Teacher web site for Lifer Preservers game including, national science standards, science backstory, and links to teaching evolution. http://gel.msu.edu/lifepreservers.

Green, C. S., and D. Bavelier (2003). Action video game modifies visual attention. *Nature, 42,* 534–537.

Hanor, J. H. (1998). Concepts and strategies learned from girls' interaction with computers. *Theory into Practice, 37*(1), 64–72.

Hartmann, T. (2003). Gender differences in the use of computer-games as competitive leisure activities. Digital Games Research Association (DiGRA) conference, Utrecht, Netherlands.

Hartmann, T., and C. Klimmt (2006). Personality factors and game choices. In P. Vorderer and J. Bryant (eds.), *In Playing Video Games,* Mahway, N.J.: Lawrence Erlbaum Associates.

Heeter, C., K. Chu, A. Maniar, P. Mishra, R. Egidio, and B. Winn (2003). Comparing 14 forms of fun in commercial versus educational space exploration digital games. Digital Games Research Association (DiGRA) conference, Utrecht, Netherlands. http://commtechlab.msu.edu/publications/files/forms_of_fun.pdf.

Heeter, C., B. Winn, and D. Greene (2005). Theories meet realities: Designing a learning game for girls. Proceedings of Designing the User eXperience (DUX), San Francisco, Calif. http://commtechlab.msu.edu/publications/files/dux2005.pdf.

Jenson, J., and S. de Castell (2005). Her own boss: Gender and the pursuit of incompetent play. DiGRA conference, Vancouver, Canada.

Joiner, R. (1998). The effect of gender on children's software preferences. *Journal of Computer Assisted Learning 14*(3), 195–198.

Joiner, R., D. Messer, K. Littleton, and P. Light (1996). Gender, computer experience and computer-based problem solving. *Computers and Education, 26*(1/2), 179–187.

Klawe, M., K. Inkpen, E. Phillips, R. Upitis, and A. Rubin (2002). E-GEMS: A project on computer games, mathematics and gender. In N. Yelland, A. Rubin, and E. McWilliam (eds.), *Ghosts in the Machine: Women's Voices in Research with Technology* (pp. 209–227, 248). New York: Peter Lang Publishing.

Laurel, B. (2001). *The Utopian Entrepreneur.* Cambridge, Mass.: The MIT Press.

Light, P., K. Littleton, S. Bale, R. Joiner, and D. Messer. (2000). Gender and social comparison effects in computer-based problem solving. In *Learning and Instruction, 10,* 483–496.

Littleton, K., P. Light, R. Joiner, D. Messer, and P. Barnes (1992). Pairing and gender effects in computer based learning. *European Journal of Psychology of Education, 7*(4), 1–14.

Maccoby, E., and C. Jacklin (1987). Child segregation in childhood. *Advances in Child Development, 20,* 239–287.

Morlock, H., T. Yando, and K. Nigolean (1985). Motivation of video game players. *Psychological Reports, 57,* 247–250.

Prensky, Marc. (2001). *Digital Game-Based Learning.* New York: McGraw Hill.

Raney A. A., J. Smith, and K. Baker (2006). Adolescents and the appeal of video games. In P. Vorderer and J. Bryant (eds.), *Playing Computer Games: Motives, Responses, and Consequences* (pp. 165–179), Mahwah, N.J.: Erlbaum.

Ray, S. G. (2004). *Gender Inclusive Game Design: Expanding the Market.* Hingham: Charles River Media.

Salen, K., and E. Zimmerman (2004). *The Rules of Play.* Cambridge, Mass.: The MIT Press.

Shaffer, D. W. (2006). *How Computer Games Help Children Learn.* New York: Palgrave Macmillan.

Schott, G. R., and K. R. Horrel (2000). Girl gamers and their relationship with the gaming culture. *Convergence, 6*(4) 36–53.

Streitmatter, J. (1994). *Toward Gender Equity in the Classroom: Everyday Teachers' Beliefs and Practices.* Albany, N.Y.: SUNY Press.

Taylor, T. L. (2007). *Play Between Worlds: Exploring Online Game Culture.* Cambridge, Mass.: The MIT Press.

Torre, R. (2005). MMOs and your teen Web site for parents. http://mmogsandyourteen.org/whatisammog.htm.

Van Eck, R. (2006). Digital game-based learning: It's not just the digital natives who are restless. *EDUCAUSE Review,* 41 (2) 16–30.

Winn, B., and C. Heeter (2006/2007). Resolving conflicts in educational game design through playtesting. *Innovate Journal of Online Education, 3*(2, December/January).

Woolfolk, A. (2005). *Educational Psychology.* Boston: Allyn & Bacon.

Yates, L. (1997). Gender equity and the boys debate: What sort of challenge is it?" *British Journal of Sociology of Education,* vol. 18, no. 3, 337–347.

Yee, N. (2006). The demographics, motivations and derived experiences of users of massively multiuser online graphical environments. *Presence: Teleoperators and Virtual Environments,* 15, 309–329.

Part V Industry Voices

Throughout this volume there are references to developments in the past and present gaming industry. Brenda Laurel's account of Purple Moon showcases many of the issues faced by a start-up company developing a product and brand that is different from the dominant Barbie line. Henry Jenkins and Justine Cassell refer to the 1990s as a unique time period for women's entrepreneurism driven by an unusual alliance between feminist theory and business development. Today the game industry has joined mainstream entertainment, and many companies are traded at the stock exchange. What does it mean for women to work, design, and play in such a climate? To answer these questions and more, we continue a tradition started in the *From Barbie to Mortal Kombat* and include a collection of interviews of women working in game design and business.

The interviewees of this part include game designers and developers, industry executives, and gamers. We invited Megan Gaiser, CEO of Her Interactive, to talk about her efforts to develop titles based on the popular Nancy Drew series. Morgan Romine works at Ubisoft and is the leader of a professional women gamers team, the Frag Dolls, that competes at game tournaments. Sheri Graner Ray is a longtime game designer and proponent of gender-inclusive design. Nichol Bradford, a vice president at Universal, leads international and new initiatives at the large media company. Finally, Brenda Braithwaite talks about her path in game design from *Ultima* to the Playboy Mansion to college professor.

Our questions focus on connections with the other chapters in this volume: gaming interests, career paths, experiences and challenges in this industry, and how they see the future for themselves and women in gaming. The interviews reveal consistencies with the other chapters, but from a personal perspective. Our interviewees report that the kinds of games that are interesting to girls and women are relative and not fixed. Megan Gaiser's many years of experience in designing for girls revealed to her that girls like a variety of games, and that her "job is to create a variety of compelling interactive entertainment solutions to satisfy all their needs." The interviewees' experiences also bear out that more women involved with the design of games leads to more female players: Sheri Graner Ray's *Serpent Isle* team had a 50 percent female design staff, and *Serpent Isle* was the game that was most accessible to women in the *Ultima* series. Megan Gaiser's successful *Nancy Drew* series also comes out of a staff that is 50 percent female.

Our interviewees concur that positive strides have been made in women's gaming in the recent years and they are optimistic of the future to come. In particular, MMOs and RPGs are seen as new arenas for women gamers because, as Sheri Graner Ray puts it, "they are more free-form, allowing alternate play patterns to emerge." Despite their optimism, we believe it is instructive to note that the Frag Dolls' existence nonetheless indicates that women gamers are still a "specialty item," and Brenda Brathwaite's decision to enter academia after becoming the mother of twins makes it clear that the game industry is far from being a women's world. These interviews provide an essential complement to the other chapters in this volume, which are written from academic, activist, and design perspectives.

19 Interview with Megan Gaiser, Her Interactive

As president and CEO of Her Interactive, a pioneering company in interactive entertainment targeted toward female play preferences, Megan Gaiser is responsible for short- and long-term corporate strategy as well as day-to-day operations of the company. Under her stewardship, Her Interactive has nearly quadrupled revenues and achieved combined worldwide sales of more than four million units for the company's *Nancy Drew* PC game series. The franchise has garnered fourteen consecutive Gold Medal awards for excellence from the respected Parents' Choice, and for the past three years it has been the number one PC adventure franchise in units. Prior to joining Her Interactive in 1997, Gaiser spent eleven years as editor and producer of several award-winning documentaries as well as corporate, educational, and public service announcements. She then went to Microsoft Corporation as producer of CarPoint, the company's first online-specific product. Gaiser also produced Microsoft's first online surround video segment, a virtual online chat environment, and several promotional ads, one of which received Microsoft's Consumer Division CD Sampler Award in 1995. She is the recipient of more than fifteen Cine Golden Eagle awards, three New York Festival awards, and the International Documentary Milano Award. Gaiser has also contributed works to the International Film and Video Congress in Zurich, and the International Eko Film in Czechoslovakia.

Tell us about how you got where you are.
My background is filmmaking. I produced and edited documentary and educational films/videos in D.C. for eleven years, and then moved to Seattle in 1994 to get into multimedia. I was interested in the creative potential of nonlinear versus linear medium. Seattle was the hub of start-ups at that time. Coincidentally, Microsoft was interested in creating content and looking for producers like me. I got several job offers from them, and figured

Microsoft wouldn't go under. I stayed there for about two and a half years; I learned a lot but wasn't creatively challenged. I started looking around, and someone said, "Oh you should meet the CEO of Her Interactive. They just got the Nancy Drew license." I got very excited about the potential of creating a game around Nancy Drew as she was one of my idols and inspirations growing up.

But you had no gaming background. What was it that clicked between you and Her Interactive?

I knew nothing about gaming, but I think film to games is a very natural transition. It's entertainment and an art form, and storytelling is part of every entertainment media, from films, to music, to books. I think that connection is what they saw, and for me, it's the passion around Nancy Drew and the idea of creating something targeted specifically for girls of all ages.

Have you always had a passion to do something for girls?

I've always been very interested in supporting the growth and opportunities of girls and women. One of the things I learned when I came onboard is that there was nothing out there for women, and nothing out there for girls except for Barbie. And that, to me, was ridiculous. Why just Barbie? Why not Nancy Drew? The prevailing wisdom at that time was: "make it pink and all the females will come," which is like saying "make games violent and all men will come." I believe there should be as many entertainment preferences in every medium for women as there are for men.

At the time when you joined the company, who were the visionaries in the company who saw that there was a market for games for girls even though everybody was saying no? In particular, who saw that there was a market for something that is brainy, like Nancy Drew versus Barbie?

Her Interactive was a division of American Laser Games, which was a video arcade company in Albuquerque back in the eighties, and created games like *Who Killed Johnny Rock* and *Mad Dog Macree*. When the arcade business went downhill in the early nineties, Her Interactive was born as the brainchild of the wife of the CEO at that time. Ultimately, American Laser Games went Chapter 11, and Her Interactive was the only division to survive because it seemed like it had a lot of promise. The game *McKenzie & Co.*, which the company created in 1995, sold thirty thousand units at a time when few believed in the market for girls. The only other game on the market for girls was a Barbie title. That success became the springboard for the next game, *Vampire Diaries*, which we used as R&D for the first *Nancy Drew* game.

How did you decide to do Nancy Drew? Did Nancy Drew represent something that resonated with the goals of the company?
It was an obvious choice. Nancy Drew represents all those characteristics we aspire to. As anyone familiar with the character knows, Nancy Drew is smart, she's gutsy, she's resourceful, and in the end she gets the job done. She's a positive role model, and there is such tremendous nostalgic power behind the Nancy Drew brand for women of all ages. It's also story driven, and our core expertise is storytelling.

It clearly resonated with you guys, but it's not so clear that it was going to be successful in the market, given that the only other example out there at that time was Barbie. Was that a leap of faith or did you do market research?
Well, I can't speak to anything before 1997, but the success of *McKinsey & Co.* selling thirty thousand units was a huge green light. Shortly after I joined Her Interactive, I learned that there was virtually nothing out there for girls with regard to interactive games. So we conducted formal focus groups to better understand their preferences. Additionally, as a way to learn directly from this underserved customer, I did usability testing at my apartment in Seattle. They played all sorts of games, most of them designed for boys and men, and I took notes. What was interesting is that because most of them had never played games before, they brought such fresh perspectives of what games could be. Their input actually helped us to improve on existing game play, rather than perpetuate gender stereotypes.

What were some of the things that you discovered from your usability testers that informed the design of your games and did not play into the stereotypes?
From a broad perspective, there were more similarities than there were differences between men and women in terms of what they want in entertainment. For example, the girls did not particularly like being portrayed as victims, or victims of violence, but hey, who would? And girls were bored by repetitive violence. But aside from that, they liked a variety of games. They had some comments, for example, where they thought it was silly that if they forgot to save the game, they'd have to start all over again after they'd invested ten hours.

So we put a second-chance button in our games, which takes you to the point before you make a fatal mistake.

Another interesting comment we heard was "We like shooters, but we prefer a reason before we shoot. So if somebody is stealing my baby or beating up my little sister, I'd be all over them." As a result, we put a mission statement of some sort in the beginning of a game to let them know their purpose.

We also keep the minimum configuration consistent with the customer because the girls were telling us that they get hand-me-downs from their brothers or dads. They don't have these super-duper computers, so we have to make sure that they could play it using older computers' technology.

We compiled this information, and created our first game in one and a half years. We took it to all the publishers to get it into retail, and every single publisher refused. They said, "We are not interested in taking it into retail, because females won't *play* games. The reason they won't play is because they are computer phobic." This was the last thing we expected as a response. We knew that it was not that girls and women were computer phobic. In fact, Grace Hopper was one of the first programmers in the fifties. It was just that they were critical of the current computer culture, which was largely male-dominated at the time. Also, all other entertainment industries target females with books, films, music. Why in the world would we stop at the next entertainment medium of gaming? Barbie had already proven the markets' existence; plus we're 50 percent of the population!

This was the pivotal point in the company, and we had to act quickly. Despite initial resistance from most major publishers in distributing our product, we decided to sell on Amazon.com. Sales began to take off. We started getting major consumer press and we started winning award after award. The *New York Times* dubbed us "The UnBarbie" of computer games. Not long after that, those same publishers came back to us to secure a distribution deal for retail. In 2002, we made the giant step of becoming retail publishers and we've been profitable ever since.

That was a tremendous learning experience! Can you tell me a little bit about your marketing strategies? Do you market with a particular type, or types, of girls or women in mind?

Guerrilla marketing is what we have done from the very beginning because we have had a very, very slim marketing budget. Over the years we have continued to learn what works and then hone our marketing efforts to increase consumer awareness and traffic to our Her Interactive site. Our core audience is still ten- to fifteen-year-old girls, but women have become a strong secondary audience.

It seems like it would be hard to design the marketing strategy for such a varied audience.

Our creative strategy has always been to preserve the integrity of the brand while bringing Nancy Drew into modern times. Currently, the target market is two-tiered, for ten[-] to fifteen-[year-old] girls and adult women. What happened is that moms bought the games for their daughters to inspire them as they were inspired as girls. Then, they got hooked and told their friends. Now, it's moms and grandmoms; it's girls ten to twenty-five to thirty. We have childless couples playing the game; we even have guys who like it—10 percent of our audience is male. So it's just quite a variety.

We also updated our Nancy Drew logo, making it more iconic to appeal to every girl and woman.

Many other endeavors to court the girl market have failed during the time that you guys succeeded. What do you think has made the difference?

Remember Purple Moon? Paul Allen put five million dollars in the company, and I remember being so envious because they got their character on the Got Milk? campaign, and we didn't have two pennies to rub together for our marketing budget. When they were sold to Mattel and went under, reporters called and said, "Well, why do you think you guys are going to make it?" The reason I knew we would succeed is because we had both a great brand and a great game. Purple Moon was trying to create a brand and a game at the same time.

We'd also assembled a talented and resourceful team committed to high-quality content. Everyone in product development contributes to the overall creation of the games. Our marketing and sales team takes the ball from there to make sure we maximize our customer experience. Our culture encourages creative license for all to contribute their ideas, which adds a lot of depth to the games. I also think our culture is part of our success; we have a collaborative culture, and I think that nurtures the creative process, which is critical not only in product development, but also in sales, marketing, customer support, and testing.

Creative problem solving is part of our daily jobs and being able to adapt quickly is another key element. One month after we got on the retail shelves with our first game, our price was dropped from $29.99 to $19. All of a sudden our business model didn't work. Within the month, we had to do a complete turnaround and learn how to make a game roughly every six months instead of ten. Incorporating what we've learned game after game has enabled us to consistently create high-quality games and do so on time. In a way, Nancy Drew is kind of the metaphor for who we are. She always gets the job done.

Your team is basically fifty-fifty, men–women. That's not typical in the game industry, as you know. Is that something you explicitly strive for or did it just happen?
We hire the best talent, and it turned out to be a fifty/fifty split.

I heard you say that you believe that everybody should enjoy her life. Does that imply that Her Interactive doesn't have the crunch time culture that many game companies do?
There are always crunch times; however, we have made it a goal to ensure that our workload is manageable as much as possible. Quality of home and work life is a value our team shares. The first few years were tough in this regard but over the years, our process-efficiency has assisted us in meeting this goal. Part of that efficiency resulted from our high employee-retention rate. Her Interactive has always sought to promote from within and we have many, many people who started at entry-level jobs and have now grown to head up departments. As a result, everyone from top to bottom is fluent in our process.

In the earlier days when we weren't profitable, we really didn't have a lot of benefits, so we really went out of our way to offer what we could and grow people as much as possible. That is a goal we continue to work to achieve. I believe a company is as good as the quality, expertise, and passion of the people you've assembled.

How do you think the industry should be reacting to the change in the market over these last six to eight years?
There is a lot of talk right now about finding out who are the women playing games today. The current buzz or noise is all about what types of women play casual games, how many hours they play, but the larger truth and historical context is that it is only quite recently that female player preferences have been taken seriously by the gaming industry. We know that women have been playing games since we first created ours in 1995. Many women don't shop in the

more male-targeted retail stores, so it makes perfect sense that they found the games online, since they spend so much time on the Internet. Now, I think the more important question we can ask is: "How can we better understand both the girl and adult female audience in general, and, in particular, how can we create even more genres and content offerings for this audience?" We need to satisfy all of their play preferences. Finally, the gaming industry has taken notice that women are a major customer group, and our job is to create a variety of compelling interactive entertainment solutions to satisfy all their needs.

So what is the next step for Her Interactive then? Get another title? Go for another age group?
With the success of *Nancy Drew,* we are in the process of diversifying our content offerings and our distribution channels.

What about ten years from now? Do you see yourself still at Her Interactive? Still doing games, or doing something else altogether?
I can honestly say that up until now, this has been the most rewarding job I've ever had, and contributing to the growth of Her Interactive has been a treasured experience. It's a really interesting time in general: the economy is changing, the way we interact, the way we do business, and the way we play. Gaming represents huge opportunities for us, and the games we create tell a cultural story, and this medium, like all mediums, will impact future generations. Traditional rules are also changing, and creativity has become the equalizer.

I am also proud to be a female CEO because it underscores the fact that females are making a difference in all aspects of the gaming industry—business development, management, art, game design, consumers, et cetera. We are currently at the tip of the iceberg when it comes to the potential for interactive entertainment and content for women, and the coming years promise to be an extremely exciting time for us. There are no limitations on how women can contribute and take a larger role in this industry, both from creating the games to being a customer to taking the lead [as] executives.

Morgan Romine, better known as "Rhoulette" in the video game online community, helped found and build Ubisoft's all-girl gaming team, the Frag Dolls. As captain of the team, she serves as spokesperson, gamer, road manager, and has participated in several panels discussing gender and games. Romine fell in love with video games when she was six years old and she's been playing ever since, with online games being her current passion. As an undergraduate at University of California, Berkeley, she coordinated and led a class about the "anthropology of online gaming communities." She used her personal experience with MMORPGs such as *EverQuest, Star Wars Galaxies, Lineage,* and *Dark Age of Camelot* to engage the class in discussions about this unique and growing social world. Her introduction to Ubisoft was through their MMORPG title *Shadowbane,* where she led a clan of more than two hundred players. She entered the game industry after graduating with her degree in anthropology and is now a community manager for Ubisoft, where she interacts directly with their core video game audience. In her personal gaming life, she is currently playing games like *World of Warcraft* and *Halo 2.* Romine is excited about the continued growth of the video game industry and how women will play an integral role as gamers and within the business itself.

What is your definition of a gamer?
I would say a gamer is somebody who loves video games and would declare that they love video games. A gamer is somebody who plays multiple games in a year or somebody who plays any one game a lot, all the time, probably every week or so. For many gamers, video games are a regular part of their life. So if it's something that they play every week, then they probably consider themselves a gamer.

Do you only consider digital games or do you also include paper games?
For me, I tend to associate the term *gamer* with video games in particular. But I usually think of board games or paper and pencil RPG as a different class. I don't know, though. I think it really depends on what they associate themselves with. I play paper and pencil RPGs, but I was also playing video games at the same time. So that's why I considered myself a gamer. I don't know if I would have considered myself a gamer if paper and pencil RPGs were all I did.

When did you start thinking about being a gamer?
I have always played video games, but I don't know that I actually self-identified as a gamer until I was playing *EverQuest* in high school. I had really, really spent a lot of time playing it. When so much of my life became about this game, calling myself a gamer came very naturally. Whenever I wasn't doing school or sports or stuck at home where I didn't have a computer that could run it, I played. I played at college as well, while I should have been studying. I probably averaged at least eight hours a day at my peak.

How did you play when you didn't have a computer to play it at home?
I played on my boyfriend's computer. He was the one who educated me. He primarily played *EverQuest,* though he played some racing games, too. While my boyfriend did introduce me to *EverQuest,* I was already familiar with video games because I had been playing them since I was little. I had all boy cousins and a little brother, and my best friends were usually boys, and so we all played video games together. When my parents got my brother and [me] a Sega Genesis for Christmas, that was a wonderful eye-opening experience for me. I fell in love with *Sonic the Hedgehog.* I love that game so much. That music actually is still so recognizable. I will frequently be like, "Oh my gosh, that sounds just like that level."

You becoming a gamer probably had something to do with having all boy cousins?
I am sure that if I had had girl cousins who were playing video games, I would have taken to it just as quickly. I don't remember playing video games with my girlfriends. I don't really remember having girlfriends who played.

What about now? Do your friends all tend to be gamers or not?
It's like my social life is kind of split down in the middle. I have my group of friends that don't understand exactly what I do. And then I have a bunch of friends who are all gamers. They are very separate. Gamers, especially online

gamers, have this kind of personality disorders inherent throughout our lives because we are constantly playing other people online, and then we interact with people in our everyday normal lives who don't have any clue whom we might have been spending 50 percent of our day with.

Do you find yourself typically playing women?

I have played male characters before, but I tend to play female characters because I like being a female in general. But the more I have played, the more I play female characters that are less and less like me. I have noticed it is a trend among girls who play: when they start out, they want to make a character that looks exactly like them. I have been asking some of my girlfriends why they do that when the game is fantasy and you are supposed to be branching out and trying something that's not normal. One of my friends pointed out that it makes gaming seem a little bit more immersive and realistic to put yourself in this fantasy environment.

What kind of characters do you tend to play and how are they not like you?

I tend to play shorty characters like Halflings, gnomes, or dwarfs. I don't know why I have gravitated toward those. I like them because they've got this kind of sassy personality. It's kind of interesting to create these characters that *seem* different but are really reflecting something about you. A lot of girls that I know play characters that not only look like themselves but like the most attractive possible version of themselves. I like to be a sexy Halfling because I like the concept of that. It's kind of funny.

So you generally prefer games that are more preferred by men versus women, or more neutral?

I think it's mixed. I like the games that I like, and I think some of them happen to be games that women really like, but others are games not a lot of women play. I just like games that are good. I like my shooter games, which mostly men tend to play, but I also like games like *Guitar Hero.* I think those games really cross all boundaries.

How much do you get to play now?

Not as much time as I would like to, because I work a lot in the game industry. When I come home, I kind of want to do stuff that's not game related. I don't usually play the games that my company makes because I work with those all the time. I probably get to play a couple hours every other day or so.

People have always said that video-game violence is one of the main things that turn women off games. But we do hear from you and from other female gamers who like shooter games. Why do you like the shooter games?

I like shooter games, though there are a couple of shooters out there that are too violent. While I associate them with violence, it is rare for me to feel like these games are violent in a realistic way and therefore relevant. I often don't really conceive of it as violence; it's more like a tag game. I really like those games because they are competitive and fast-paced. But it doesn't look realistic to me because *Halo* has this very fantastical side: all the physics are very unnatural because no person could really move like that. Everybody's wearing brightly colored suits, and seems very detached. Whereas games like *Call of Duty* have so much blood and gore and war. That game kind of bothers me, and I can't play it.

What about the other female gamers that you know? Do they feel the same way about this?

I think that my Frag Dolls do feel similarly. But I think we're somewhat unusual in that we were selected because we like shooter games. I wouldn't say that we're representative of all girl gamers. There might be some guys who really like shooters *because* of the violence, but I don't personally know any girl players that are drawn especially to that element. For us, it's mostly about the competition. It's pretty satisfying to beat them; it feels good to be able to break that stereotype and show them that I can play video games. Winning is just satisfying, no matter whom I am playing against. It feels really, really good.

How would you compare yourself with the other girl gamers that you know, Frag Dolls or otherwise, in terms of your style of play, motivations, and . . . ?

The biggest similarity between myself and other girl gamers is that I really like the social elements of all my games. Many girl gamers whom I play with are really into the social aspect of RPGs or MMOs. The fact that there is a community around a lot of these games is very appealing, as opposed to just playing them by yourself. It satisfies both the desire of having fun and having friends whom I can play with. This innovation has really opened gaming up to females and made it much more appealing to them. There is such a diversity of girl gamers at this point, but it's hard to generalize. I am pretty different from the ESA statistic of the 43 percent or more of gamers that are female. The majority of those women are playing casual games. I definitely like casual games, but they don't make up the bulk of what I play. For me and the other girls I know personally who play, we are motivated and driven by competition and conflict. I won't generalize and say that the majority of female gamers are offended by big-breasted female characters. I do know that there are some who find all that distasteful. But I am different from that group because I don't really care. I see video games more like a comic book, kind of fantasy. The representations of males in these games are not very realistic either.

What could or should the game industry be doing further to address the taste or styles of the female demographic?

Right now, most game companies don't put any sort of marketing budget behind marketing to women because it is not a proven demographic and it's not a guaranteed sale. Simply marketing games as something in which women might be interested is what the game industry could do, and is slowly starting to consider. But we have this overall cultural perception that games are a male-oriented thing. So most women think, "Why would I want that?" In my case, I like games that are all over the board, some marketed toward men, some toward women. Some of them are designed thinking that there's no woman who's going to be interested in playing these games, and some of them were probably designed specifically for women. It doesn't really matter to me. It just happens that I know about them. I am sure that the *Desperate Housewives* game is going to be pretty big because it is associated with a widely recognized brand which is seen as something women like.

How long have you been a Frag Doll?

I have been a Frag Doll for two years. There are seven of us. There are two of us who are full-time employees and two of us are going to school. One girl works for a Silicon Valley company, and another does Web development stuff. We also have a "housewife" who plays these video games all day, all the time.

I was working for Ubisoft at the time when a couple of people started talking about putting together a group of girl gamers to help promote games both online and in advertising events. They asked me to participate because I was the girl gamer that they knew and also because I had some experience with doing promotions online. So I was one of the original founders of the group; I helped hire the other girls and I have been the team captain since the beginning.

Tell me a little bit about your job as a Frag Doll.

As Frag Dolls, we do a couple of things. We are spokesgamers for Ubisoft. All of us played Ubisoft games before we were hired, but we all come from different backgrounds. Some of us have fairly extensive experience with MMOs and RPGs. I also like to play some shooters here and there, and then we have some girls who want to play shooters exclusively, and others who really like action adventure games.

They pulled us together to do competitions in a promotional format, but we also go online and play, and we talk to people about that stuff. We go to events, and we demo games at events, talk to people, and compete at these events. When we were at E3, we were demoing games and doing a lot of press interviews. The main goal in sponsoring the Frag Dolls was for the promotional elements, but it was also for exploring this girl gamer demographic. When it was started, we didn't really know it was going to be accepted or how many other girl gamers were out there. Now, so many women have come out and said, "Yeah I really like to play games too—that's awesome," or "I didn't ever think about playing games—I just watched my boyfriend or husband play, but now I am actually kind of interested." We wanted to help fix the perception that girls don't play games.

What kind of reception do you get as a Frag Doll when you go to these live events?

We usually come across very well; people really like us. At these events we are popular because as gamers we understand what gamers are interested in. For the most part it's hard to say because critics, if there are critics at these events, never come forward. We only have people support us coming forward, saying things like "We think you are awesome." I have countless stories of guy gamers who will literally say, "Yeah, you know, we really didn't take you seriously before but, damn, you fully really mean it."

There are also people who feel that we can't be legitimate gamers because we are promotional—they feel that if something is marketing, then it can't be legitimate. Or the perception that "Oh you guys are all good looking girls, so therefore you can't all be good gamers." I would say these stereotypes always end up being the source of this criticism.

What other girl gamer groups are there out there?

There are a bunch of other clans out there: GOD, which are Girls Of Destruction, is a well-known PC clan. Then there's a PMS clan, they play both console and PC games. There are also a lot of groups in Europe because they have such a well-established PC competitive community. Then there are a lot of girls who also play on coed teams or play with a bunch of guys.

Would you say that the girl gamer groups have been successful in changing the way guys think about gender in games?

I have noticed a significant difference since the inception of the Frag Dolls. I have seen a big decline in how frequently we run into the "Wait—girls like video games?" sentiment. There has been change, but not nearly as much change as I think there will eventually be. It's this cultural stereotype of gamers, that it's twenty-four- to thirty-four-year-old males who are still living in their mother's basement, that those are the type of people who play video games because video games are not, of course, played by people who have other things going on in their lives. That is the popular perception. But what surprises me is that there are still elements of that within [the] gamer community. There are hard-core gamer communities, who think that the Frag Dolls can't be good gamers because we are good-looking.

Now the events we participate in are becoming more spectator-oriented, and that will have an impact. When we are at these events, there are spectators who would not ordinarily know that we are women, but who can now see us competing. But as far as change in the mainstream, that's a matter of PRM [public relations measurement] press coverage more than it is about actually interacting with individuals on a personal level at these events.

When I was playing in elementary school, even in middle school, I didn't think of it as something that girls didn't do. But then when I was in high school, I developed more social awareness for what is accepted and what is not among certain social groups. That was when I started to have my girlfriends be like, "What are you doing all the time? What you do, like, it's crazy." But that was when I started to realize that gaming was something that I didn't see other girls doing.

I'm very much aware now of a lot of other girl gamers, but I don't know that there is [a] significantly larger number of them because I think we were just much more isolated before. We weren't aware of each other. As a Frag Doll, I have a lot of exposure to other gamers. I know that there are a lot of girls out there who play video games, and I get to meet them, which most people don't.

Have you seen the girl gamer groups change the way that the game industries work?

Not yet, but it's in the process. Microsoft just recently hired a girl team of seven girls who serve a promotional function for them. It's very flattering for us, of course, because they obviously thought Frag Dolls was a good idea. We certainly have made a big impact at Ubisoft as far as acknowledging that girls do play games, and that they should be considered as a demographic group with serious potential. They are starting to put more female characters or female skins in multiplayer games. I also noticed on tactical maps, opponents will show "his or her location." I had never seen that in games, there's always reference to he: he, he, his, him, everything was referred to in a masculine sense.

You expect to be a gamer all your life?

I expect to be a gamer all my life. I consider myself pretty diverse already, but I think it's possible that as my lifestyle changes, I'll probably be adopting games that fit it more easily. If I have more time then I will probably be playing some games and if I have less time, then I will probably be playing casual games.

What about the future—in five years? Do you expect to still be in the game industry?

I will probably always be doing something related to the game industry. In five years, I doubt that I will be doing Frag Dolls; I might be doing something related to the Frag Dolls. I am hoping to see that all-girl gamer groups won't be necessary to raise the awareness about girls playing video games. At that point, it will be a much more of a coed competitive environment.

An avid paper gamer, Sheri Graner Ray began as a writer and designer at Origin Systems, Inc., on the *Ultima* series of games. It was during the design phase of an unreleased game in which the player took on the role of one of the knights of the Round Table that she first stumbled across the "problem" of female gamers. Of course, there were no female knight characters in any of the tales of King Arthur. This caused Ray to ask the design team, "But . . . what if the player is female?" And thus began her quest to find out what girls liked in games and why. Ray worked her way up to become director of product development at Her Interactive, the first company dedicated exclusively to producing games for girls. While there, she produced the enormously popular *McKenzie & Co.,* as well as the licensed title *Vampire Diaries,* and designed the first title in the company's successful *Nancy Drew* series, *Secrets Can Kill.* While at Her Interactive, Ray concentrated on developing her theories of female entertainment criteria through research, focus groups, surveys, and studies. Since leaving Her Interactive, Ray has worked at her own studio, Sirenia Software; Metrowerks; Sony Online Entertainment; and in game design consulting and contracting, including serious games work. In 2003, her book *Gender Inclusive Game Design: Expanding the Market* was released. Ray is the founder of Women in Games International and a regular speaker on the topic of gender and games. She is a staunch advocate of diversity in the game industry.

Tell us a little bit about yourself, and how you got into the game design business.
I started in the game industry in 1990. I tell people that the reason I got into games is that it's the only industry where I can list twenty years of running Dungeons and Dragons™ on my résumé as legitimate experience. I am a gamer's gamer. I have been a gamer from way back. I still run a regular weekly paper game group, the same group that I've been running for almost ten years now. If I am not computer gaming, I am paper gaming.

What are the games that you have designed that you are the most proud of?
Oh, that's an interesting question. I really like *Vampire Diaries*™—I really think it is a pretty solid game. *Ultima Seven, Part Two: The Serpent Isle,* I think, is the best of the *Ultima* series. I was instrumental in that design. I am very proud of that. My first love is action adventure role-playing games.

How does it work in the industry? Do you get to choose the kind of games you work on?
No. In fact, when I talk to young designers, and I talk to people who want to be designers, I tell them, "Here is the truth: The truth is, you are never going to make your dream game, so get over it. Okay? You are going to work really, really hard, you are going to go to school, you are going to spend time learning, you are going to write papers, you are going to intern someplace where you work very hard, and when you finally get your first job, it's going to be designing levels for *Hello Kitty.*" And what I look for, when I am interviewing designers, I want a designer who can look at that and say, "Yeah, I don't play *Hello Kitty* myself personally, but I am going to make this the best darn *Hello Kitty* game those twelve-year-old girls have ever seen, and I am going to take pride in that design." That's a true designer, and that's what I look for. You have very little say over what you end up designing, and the mark of a really good designer is to be able to step up and design good games regardless of the genre, regardless of the audience.

Was there a particular title that you thought was a good example of a game that wasn't particularly marketed or directed at the female audience, but yet had no barriers for women? And what were the resulting demographics of this game?
I would probably refer back to the *Ultima* series. They were really pretty accessible, and consequently had higher than average levels of female players when compared with other games. Back in those days, nobody kept demographics. I had anecdotal evidence in the fact that I got to see the reg cards that came in from our games, and knew that 20 percent to 25 percent of the reg cards that came back were from women. In fact you can't even get those demographics today. The demographics of women that actually played games are just very tough to get. Nobody's done the research to find out really how many women are playing. We know the casual market is about 70 percent female, we know that the standard PC market is about 10 percent female, we know the standard

console market went to about 15 percent female, and we know that MMOs run about 20 percent female. We are just now starting to see the actual studies. Nobody really knows for sure how many women work in the industry. The demographics we have are all self-reported numbers, and getting somebody to actually do a study has been tough because, frankly, the companies aren't terribly excited about revealing those kinds of numbers.

What was it about the Ultima *series that made it more popular with women?*
Well, for instance, on the *Serpent Isle* team, we had a 50 percent female design staff, which is really unusual. I was very proud of that team. Because the graphics were much more primitive than we have today, we did not have the hypersexualization of the female. We made sure to provide female avatars in all classes, in all opportunities. We also provided racially diverse avatars. We used athletes for body models rather than any kind of crazy hypersexualized model. It also was very story-based, with a very emotional tie to your characters and what you were doing. There were a lot of things done right back then.

The press talks about Sims Online, *how the Sims game is the new dollhouse, the new game for girls. What's your reaction to that?*
The really scary thing is that this is terribly insidious. It's a way for the community or the game industry to say, "You want a girl's game? Well, pick up *The Sims*! All girls play Sims, therefore, we don't have to do anything different, because they don't play these other games." And to say, "Girls just don't play *Flight Simulators*," which makes it the girl's fault. "She doesn't play it because she is a girl, and I can't change that. So there is nothing I can do about the fact that she doesn't play my game."

I just was down in New Zealand organizing a workshop I call Guerrilla Game Design, which is aimed at game designers. We are working right now with what they can do to find the barriers in their titles and address those barriers, and how to make their title more acceptable to a wider market. I had twenty-five women in class, and what I usually do is lecture the first half of the day, and in the second half of the day, I bring in machines. I brought in five machines, and I put [in] one of each of these titles: *Half-Life, Max Payne, Diablo, Warcraft: Orcs and Humans,* and *Halo.* I put one of those titles on each machine. Then I broke the women up into groups of five, and sat them down in front of each machine. I gave them a check sheet that explained that they should look at the game, play the game, identify their barriers, identify what things [they] have done right, identify really good access points, things like that—analyze the games.

Now, not one of those women in that room had played any of those games. And so, the first question is why. And the second thing we have to know is they haven't even tried these games. So how can we say "Women don't like these games" if they are not even *trying* them? Something is stopping them at the door. I made them at least get through the tutorials. By the end of the evening, I had to threaten to unplug the machines because every single woman had decided *Warcraft,* the real-time strategy, was their new favorite game, and at the end of the seminar, they all got up together, and left together to go down to the computer shop to buy *Warcraft.*

So it wasn't the game playing that stopped them; something else stopped them. So we can't say women don't play these games, because we don't know. The women haven't tried them. But I will say that just as much as I would love to blame marketing, there are also issues in our design that stop games from selling. It's not about making pink fuzzy kitties or making guns that shoot marshmallows instead of bullets. It's about understanding what barriers we have in our games. Things like how we structure our tutorial, how we present our female characters, how we deal with conflict and conflict resolution, how we deal with punishment and reward. There are all these things that we do for a predominantly male perspective that is uncomfortable for our female players, and they are not going to play something that feels uncomfortable.

Tell me more about what you see as the gender differences in the way that men and women, girls and boys approach and resolve conflicts.
When I talk about this stuff, I talk about broad population generalities. Of course, there are people who cross the boundaries. We understand that the vast majority of women won't choose to revolve conflict in the head-to-head confrontational style. They will choose indirect competition. For example, gymnastics is indirect competition: Can I do this thing better than you, with someone else judging? There is no direct competition in gymnastics. When you are on the balance beam, I can't come and tackle you and take you off of it. Or racing is another example. I can't tackle the guy next to me to keep him from crossing the line. It's all about how fast I run—can I perform this thing better than you can perform this thing, even if we are performing it at the same

time. Consequently, a head-to-head style, such as a flight simulation game, is not going to be as comfortable to the majority of women.

Now, if we are in a team, and it's you and [me] versus somebody else, that's more comfortable for women if they are going to take on a more directly competitive model. If you and I are helping each other, working together, to defeat these other people, then it is more comfortable for the majority of females than a direct head-to-head, can-I-punch-you-in-the-nose-and-beat-you-down kind of game. This is something we need to know when we are designing our conflict models, if we can offer other forms of winning than head-to-head direct competition.

What about punishments and rewards?

This is from Yasmin Kafai's work. She had kids design games. One of the striking differences was the way the kids dealt with punishment and reward. The boys used punishment for error rather than forgiveness for error. In other words, when you [did] something wrong, they punished you for it; in one case they sent you flying to the moon and in another one they sent you flying in to hell. The player was stopped, and there was irretrievable loss of progress. The girls typically used a forgiveness-for-error model. Your progress was stopped or slowed, but nothing was irretrievably lost.

In the game industry, we have a very strong tradition of irretrievable loss of progress for error. You get surprised, you lose and have to start over. This is the classic model. Well, this is classic punishment for error, and anybody who is in any kind of education knows the punishment for error is the worst way to teach anybody. Subsequently, it's the worst way to get people to continue playing our games. You want to slow their progress or hold progress but no irretrievable loss. The female style is the forgiveness for error with no irretrievable loss, whereas the male model is punishment for error. And yet we know that for both genders, providing a forgiveness-for-error model is the best way for them to learn, the best way for them to want to continue to progress.

So you want the forgiveness model for all of your players, both male and female. This is less of a gender-differentiating thing; this is more a good design method.

That's right. This is what I try so hard to get people to understand. A lot of this is just about good game design. It also happens to encourage females to be more comfortable playing the game. They will play longer, and stick with it longer, if it is a forgiveness-for-error model.

Does playtesting help games be more female friendly?

If your playtesters include females, then yes. If the QA guys are all guys, then no. With Her Interactive, we playtested with a lot of girls. We worked very closely with the Albuquerque Independent School district. We brought in junior high–school girls and high-school girls all the time for every step of the games.

You mentioned that the Ultima design team was 50 percent female. In your experience then, does the gender of the design development team have an impact on how much the resulting game appeals to girls?

Yes, and it's not specific to gender. If you want your title to appeal to a broad audience, your workforce has to reflect that. If you bring in diversity into a workplace, you are going to get better products whether you are making widgets or you are making computer games. It's good design sense.

Have you entered into disagreement with other team members during the design process that were due to gender differences?

Absolutely! Usually when the art team brings in hypersexualized female characters. Also when marketing teams bring in advertising that very definitely has hypersexualized female characters and tell me that they cannot sell to males without using those characters, which I strongly disbelieve. I don't think men are quite that shallow or one-sided. Well, it goes beyond just the big breasts. There is a very definite difference in what we do with our female and male characters in the games. We do exaggerate both on male and female characters; in some ways we exaggerate them equally. We exaggerate those traits, which say they are young, they are strong, and they are fertile and virile, which says—the Western culture says—they are heroes. Our heroes are young, strong, and virile or fertile. That's what we think when we think of a hero character.

And so, we want our characters to be heroes. The things that say that for a male character are big shoulders, big arms, slim waist, slim hips, big legs, and long, thick hair. Those are the traits that the human eye perceives as being young and strong and virile. For the female, it is large breasts placed high on the chest, slim waist, round derriere, and long, thick hair. Again, these are traits that say, "I'm young, I'm strong, and I'm fertile"—traits we want in our hero characters. In fact, so much so that in *Star Wars Galaxies,* they introduced what they jokingly refer to as the "Boobs Slider," which allows the players to increase the bust size of their character, and they did so at the insistence of the female players. We want to be young and strong and virile or fertile, because that's how our heroes are.

Now, what happens with our female characters is we often add additional traits. We will exaggerate those traits that indicate sexual receptivity, or a body that is ready for sex right now. There is blood rush to the face and the head causing a reddening, enlarging of the lip tissue, and thickening of the eyelids. Any human sexuality course will tell you this. The thickening of the eyelids gives you that heavy bedroom-eye look. Also we will have erect nipples. These are things that we will put on our female characters, and we will exaggerate them, and then we will dress them to even draw more attention to these traits. So not only do our female characters say, "I'm young, I'm strong, I'm fertile"; they also say, "I'm ready for sex right now. Do me baby."

And, that's where the difference is. So it's not that she has big breasts. A female designing a character for herself is likely to give her an hour-glass figure because that says I'm young, I'm strong, and I'm fertile. We want to be heroes. What we don't want is to be hypersexualized, because that's not a comfortable feeling. We do not hypersexualize the male characters in any way, shape, or form. In fact we usually deemphasize any sexual receptivity in our male, because here is the interesting thing: All the traits that I just said are indicative of sexual receptivity—those are the same for males and females. Males react the same way with one additional piece.

But our male characters aren't designed that way. No! We would never do that for male characters. When I talk about this, I actually have these wonderful photographs of the Calvin Klein underwear models, the guys. I put them up on the screen and I say, "There you go, guys, ready? Give him a sword and send him into *Diablo*." Are you ready for that to be your avatar? Every guy in the room wants to crawl under his chair. Now you understand! Now you understand why I'm uncomfortable being given these hypersexualized females to play, to represent me. Because you wouldn't want these guys representing you.

It's not about painting boxes pink, or putting fuzzy pink kitties in the game. It's about understanding what barriers we have in our games and in our marketing today [that] is preventing women from playing our titles. We do not really know how many women like our games because they are being stopped at the door. This is the only industry I can think of that actively works to prevent a lucrative market from accessing their products.

What was the most important thing you've learned about designing for girls?
Girls can't be pigeonholed into any one game. Girls are not a genre; they are a market that's just as broad and diverse as any market anywhere. There is no silver bullet. There is no one game you can make for all girls or all women, and to think so is silly and naïve.

What are your thoughts about gender in the new gaming environments like the multiplayer online games?
I am very excited. I think the massively multiplayers are exciting. Because they are so free-form, they allow alternate play patterns to emerge, which I think is really exciting. What we have learned from our MMO work is that women are the glue that holds a social game together. They are typically the leaders of the guild, or if not leader, the second-in-command of the guild. They also are the ones to internalize their games, and take them outside of the game proper. They are the ones who do the Web sites, the fan art, the fan fiction. They really internalize the games. The MMOs really allow them to internalize the game and allow them to build the emotional connections. They are also absolutely the most loyal customers we have. When we turned out the lights on a game, we have a predominance of girls that are still there because they've built an emotional connection to the title.

As a woman in the industry yourself, what would you say is the biggest stumbling block or obstacle you had to overcome in order to succeed in this industry?
Overcoming the rumor that girls don't play games.

Do you think the market and interest is turning toward girls again?
I hope so. I think we still have a tendency right now to couch it in terms of casual games. People prefer saying casual games to saying girls' games. Maybe because it failed so badly last time. But the reason it failed so badly last time is because everybody tried to make Barbie. They decided that all girls' games are Barbie. And, they found out a very tough lesson, which is only Barbie can be Barbie. No one else can be Barbie. And, to try to shoehorn all women into the Barbie space was silly. When I had Serenia, I was pitching titles that were not Barbie, and was getting doors shut on my face again and again, and again. They say this is really great, but what can you bring us that is like Barbie?

Do you think that things are changing though?

I don't think there is any question that it's changing. When I first started talking and speaking on the subject, I literally had people who would stand up in the audience and call me names. What happens now is, after I speak, somebody will come up to me and say, "We put out an ad in the paper or in *Game Developer,* and we got 150 résumés, and we got two from women. How can we get more women in our company?" So there is an interest in industry right now in diversifying the workforce, and bringing in more women, and I find that to be really exciting.

What do you tell these people?

You've now touched on my latest biggest topic that I speak on. It's all about recruiting. You can't take out an ad in a game developer magazine, and expect that you are going to get female candidates. Females don't read game developer magazines in any kind of percentage at all. Women don't consider the game industry as a career. It's not that they look at it, and go "Ooh! I don't want to do that." It's not even on their radar. It's not something they consider.

And so we have to go to nontraditional places, and we have to recruit. We have to go to the radio/television/film programs, creative writing programs, architectural programs—places where there are women who have the skill sets we need—and we have to recruit them into our industry. Because the game industry is a glamour industry (meaning that we get more people who want jobs than we have jobs available), we are very, very spoiled. We just wait for the résumés to come in, and we pick from the best of them because it's easy. Recruiting is not easy.

Additionally, we have to support those organizations that support women in technology. We have to go to my organization, which is Women in Games International (WIGI), the IGDA's diversity committees, et cetera. We have to go to them, and we have to support them, and we have to help them to help raise awareness of the industry as a positive place for women to work.

Then the third thing we have to do is we have to farm today for tomorrow's employees. We have to get out there today and support organizations like Girl Scouts, Girls' Start, Tomorrow's Women in Science and Technology. All these places where girls are, we have to get out there, support them, and raise awareness for the game industry as the place to do it. It's up to the women in the industry to do this. Because women attract other women, we as women in this industry have to get out there and work with the girls, because that's how we are going to get them coming to us five years, six years, and ten years from now. That's the only way we are going to do it.

Where do you see your career path leading you?
Good question. I am doing some freelance contracting and consulting right now. Somewhere in the next twenty years I might end up running my own studio or teaching somewhere. Probably end up running my own studio. I would like to see that.

Nichol Bradford is the senior global director of strategic growth at Vivendi Games (VG), where she works on strategic planning and special projects. Before moving into this special role, Bradford spent two years in marketing at VG. As a senior global brand manager, she marketed video games tied to major film properties like *Van Helsing, Fight Club,* and *Scarface.* Prior to VG, Bradford spent two years at Disney Interactive/Buena Vista Games, a division of the Walt Disney Company, as a marketing and licensing manager on video games for *Finding Nemo, Pirates of the Caribbean, Haunted Mansion, Lilo & Stitch,* and *Spy Kids,* among others. She is committed to the growth and development of the video game industry as evidenced by her cofounding and three-year chairmanship of an annual art exhibit titled Into the Pixel: A Celebration of Video Game Art. She is also passionate about encouraging diversity in the video game industry. Bradford recently completed her first novel and in her spare time she studies the tango.

Tell me a little bit about your background and how you came to work at Vivendi Games.

I have been in the game industry for six years. Before working at Vivendi Games, I was a brand manager at Disney Interactive. Prior to that I was in graduate school. I received my MBA from the Wharton School of Business, and before that I was in the fashion industry. I was a business manager for Estée Lauder and subsequently I worked in fashion licensing at Ann Klein. Prior to that I was in college in Houston, Texas. I put myself through school as a professional fund-raiser targeting corporations and high-net-worth individuals. I raised money for nonprofits: I started out working for an intercity nonprofit arts organization, and then for a medical foundation, a women's economic development fund, and the University of Houston system.

When I was in graduate school, I was looking for something to be incredibly passionate about. The way I looked at it was: You can find a job simply to pay off the loan, or you can find the job that justifies having gotten the loan. If you are passionate and excited about what you do, then everything will eventually work out financially. Success is a function of passion.

You should know that I am a science fiction and fantasy fiction fan, and I have always been. I have always devoured sci-fi and fantasy fiction. Also I loved technology and I was looking for something that was always changing, always reinventing, so I wanted something with a really strong technology base, but I did not want to do deep infrastructure such as routers or switches.

The other thing about gaming that really intrigued me was that I am a storyteller myself. I also write novels. When you think about human expression and the various forms of human expression, there has been perfection in many areas prior to any sort of overlay with technology. You had extraordinary music prior to a mixing board. You had perfection in every form of human communication and expression. But while one could definitely say that *Pong* and a number of earlier minimalist games had their level of perfection, I think the full realization of what is possible for the video game industry is part and parcel with the tools and the processing power and the techniques that we develop. Technology is really integrated into it in a way that it is almost hybrid.

Also gaming is a fundamentally new thing under the sun compared to the other forms I mention, and that does not happen very often. Gaming is a hybrid between storytelling, communication, and technology. In storytelling there are lots of different ways to tell stories. But this particular form of human expression is integrated into its medium, and that medium is technology. In that sense, it is totally new. I think that this medium of interactive entertainment will lead to human beings finding new ways to see, which is completely fascinating to me. It matches my love of technology and my love of storytelling.

So, are you a gamer? Do you play a lot of games? Did you play a lot of games when you had time?
I did play prior to graduate school. I had *The Sims,* and I did a lot of PC games and classic arcade games. But like most people, I did not really know that this industry existed. In fact, when I first started telling people that I was targeting the game industry for a career, a number of very well-informed and

well-educated, sophisticated people asked me how I thought I would like living in Las Vegas. They thought I was talking about gaming in casinos! If I had a penny for each person to whom I had to explain the growth of the game industry, I would be rich.

When I got to graduate school, I became a console gamer because I read an article that said that when you are studying, you can only study for fifty-five minutes with maximum retention, and then you get diminishing returns. I guess this says something about who I am: I bought a PlayStation 2 and twitch games designed so that it didn't matter if you played for fifteen minutes, like *Crazy Taxi,* a couple of fighting games, and some other driving games. I would study for fifty-five minutes and then I played for twenty minutes, and then studied for fifty-five and then played for thirty minutes.

Let's talk about your work. What were some of the titles and games that you brand managed? When you work as a brand manager, do you manage one title at a time?
We typically have brand managers on more than one game at a time, but usually there will be some balance on workflow. You might have two really large brands, and then a couple of small ones, because usually brand managers have a couple of people working for them. Each game is a brand. Some people manage a franchise, so, if it's a game that we are going to be doing lots of repetitions on, then there might be someone who has become an expert on that game. The key is that consumers (for the most part, there are a couple of exceptions) do not go to see "a Warner Bros. movie"; they go to see *Batman.* The games industry is very much like that, with a few exceptions such as people who will catch any Blizzard product. Brand management in our business is about managing actual specific products.

When I was at Disney, I was a license manager and a brand manager. Disney published predominantly PC and handheld games and, for my products I did all the standard brand management. My products included *Kim Possible* and *Spy Kids.* In addition, I was a license manager for games on all of the major movies, working with licensees. I actually worked with pretty much every publisher in the game industry while I was at Disney in a licensor capacity, which meant approving creative, approving and reviewing marketing material, marketing plans, and also helping them get the value out of Disney. I worked with THQ, Activision, Take2, EA, and Bam—I have worked with everybody in that role. It was great.

With Disney, there is an overarching image that you brand manage for. Disney has style guides that are very specific about the characters, and a lot of the parameters flow from the property—especially for standard characters because they were created such a long time ago. Within Disney Consumer Products there are brand or franchise managers for Princess, for Power Rangers, and for Kim Possible. I did all of the games for the Kim Possible property. Kim Possible is your average girl by day and then she is also a superhero, or rather a super-sleuth. Kim Possible is a great girl-oriented brand because girls are watching it on the Disney Channel.

Spy Kids is one property that has male/female balance because you have the boy and the girl: a classic brother-and-sister pair. The marketing message is really about kids being heroes. He might run off without his weapons or without his gadgets, and she would run as well, but she would always grab her gadgets.

What are some of the titles that you've done with Vivendi Games?
I worked on *Scarface, Fight Club,* and *Van Helsing.* The demographics tend to be male, eighteen to thirty-four, and these titles are pretty male-oriented, though I find that more and more women are playing games of all kinds. I think that any publisher who isn't thinking about the potential market of women is probably missing half the population. If you are hungry, you've got to be looking at that group and trying to understand how to either convert them or find out what it is they are really interested in.

Compared to five years ago, what, if anything, have you seen change in the way that Vivendi Games or the industry as a whole does in terms of marketing to women?
I've seen a couple of things: One, there are quite a few women who work here at Vivendi Games. And women are in very senior positions. It's a great environment to be a woman. Also, I have seen a number of general changes since I went into the game industry. Before, in early conversations when I was trying to get into the game industry, people felt that there were certain genres that women just weren't interested in. Now, I hear more conversations about what would make women interested in those same genres. So I see less assumptions being made about what women want and more questions about what the industry can do.

Are women and girls right now part of the untapped potential?

I think there are lots of untapped marketplaces out there. We are a very large industry, but not every single American plays yet. It's incumbent upon all of us, if we want to tap those dollars and grow the industry, to bring those people in. That may mean exposing them to a current genre, which they might like without knowing it, or coming up with a different interface that's more accessible so that they don't give up before they feel the fun factor.

Have you seen any other changes?

I have also seen a growing interest in social responsibility. I have a couple of things that are near and dear to my heart. I am on the board of an organization called the Urban Video Game Academy.

Also, I talk to people in the game industry about being available for speakers bureaus because one other thing about our product is that most people don't know how games are made, and so they don't realize that there is a whole variety of careers in the game industry that are accessible to them. It's really just information, so it's also empowering parents to know that a game is really math, science, and literature, and that they can use their children's most loved extracurricular activity as a method to inspire them to take their mathematics, science, and English classes more seriously.

Another is Into the Pixel, an event dedicated to celebrating video game artists, which I personally feel very strongly about. When we first started, a lot of people didn't know exactly what we were doing, but now there is lot of enthusiasm about it.

We have a tremendous number of people in the industry who love what they do and can really be evangelists for the medium. I see a lot more interest in taking a social leadership role. I always take a look every year at the results from the Junior Achievement Career Survey, what kids say they want to do. And a few years ago, anything computer-related, which is where video games are, was way down [the] list and it was certainly below athlete and entertainer. And in the past year, or the year before last, it popped up past those careers. I think that's a tremendous opportunity for us, especially when you realize that the United States only graduated seventy thousand engineers last year. We have a whole generation who is not embracing the maths and the sciences. And then we have this tool, which is their number one thing that they want to do, which we could use to motivate them back into these needed careers.

In many other companies I have heard that there are a lot of barriers to entry, particularly for women. Did you experience that?

I don't feel that at all, not here, and I also didn't feel that coming into the industry. The biggest barrier for anyone is that being a player facilitates so many things in a game company. It allows you to participate in conversations. For example, a number of times I heard something described by citing four other games. If you haven't played these games, then you cannot participate in the conversation. Playing the games and loving the games are important.

So it's kind of a chicken-and-egg problem because many girls may not be playing games, because the games are not fun for them, because the people doing designing may have a team with very few women . . . this could be a self-perpetuating thing. Where do you think is the solution for something like that?

I think that solution for gender as well as ethnic diversity in the industry comes down to making the career path visible to people. I am African-American and I haven't felt any barriers in the industry for me. I have always been an advocate and very focused on my community. The career path isn't really illuminated. Most of the people that I knew of any background who were in the industry did not come to it directly. They did not pick the game industry and say, "I want to go there." For the most part, they were friends with a tester, or friend of a friend. People find out about game careers through relationship[s].

The truth of the matter is the lack of information. You have probably seen the salary survey. I think a good solid programmer makes like fifty-five to sixty thousand early, before they have a leadership role. The average American family makes $40,000 and has a kid who is playing video games. How motivating could this be for parents to say, when they hand over that game that they have paid $60 for, "Pay attention in algebra. You could make $60,000, and you could make more money than your mom and dad combined, doing this thing that you love." All we have to do is give parents the information, and they will do the rest.

What thoughts do you have for the future game designers, for improving the state of games to appeal to women and to African-Americans?

I think both of those audiences want quality. My advice, if someone chooses to be a game designer, is to become excellent: become an excellent experienced crafter of games, become an excellent storyteller. I also think that people of all backgrounds can make games for people of all backgrounds, but part of being a good storyteller is having some life experience under your belt, and a part of experience is diversity of experience. Have a wide circle of associations and be aware of what is going on in the world. There are lots of amazing games out there like *Katamari Damashi*. I know that lots of women love that game. I know lots of men that love that game. Everyone who plays that game loves that game regardless of gender, and I think that really speaks to its excellence.

23 Interview with Brenda Brathwaite, Savannah College of Art and Design

As a twenty-five-year veteran of the video game industry, Brenda Brathwaite is currently a game designer and professor of game design at the Savannah College of Art and Design. Her contributions to the field include leading game design teams, designing and writing several top-selling games such as *Playboy: The Mansion, Dungeons & Dragons: Heroes,* and *Wizardry 8,* which has received many accolades including multiple role-playing-game-of-the-year awards. She has worked on twenty-one published titles. Brathwaite is the founder and chair of the International Game Developers Association's Sex Special Interest Group and a passionate anticensorship advocate. She is a regular speaker at conferences and universities including the Game Developers Conference (GDC) 2007, 2006, and 2005, Future Play 2005, the Montreal Game Summit 2006, and the Massachusetts Institute of Technology, among others. Brathwaite is an expert on sexual content in video games and is the author of *Sex in Video Games.*

Tell us a little bit about how you got started in the game design business.
Let's see. It goes way back. I have been in the industry since '82, when I was fifteen years old. I started with the original *Wizardry* series. It was just an after-school job, and my job was to play the games until I knew everything there was to know about them so that when people called in and said, "How did you kill the wizard on the tenth level?" I had an answer for them. And then that morphed into doing whatever little tasks the designers didn't want to do or didn't have time to do, like assembling the item list, or coming up with monster suggestions, or names for places, or writing the text, or coming up with some of the puzzles, and eventually that evolved into doing design on *Wizardry 8.* I was a full-time lead designer by *Wizardry 8.* I think that was in '94.

So it sounds almost like an apprenticeship.

Yes. It's the only way really to learn game design. You learn by doing. I don't really think there is a book out there that could teach it well.

You got that first job obviously because you really enjoyed playing games.

Yes, yes, I did. Although back in 1982, even if I liked playing games, there weren't a heck of a lot of computer games to play. But I loved *Wizardry.* I was supposed to work from four o'clock until eight. Then I would show up at three and stay till nine, and then show at two and stay till ten. I just loved the game, and I got paid for playing. I don't know any fifteen-year-old who would have turned that down.

How was that job advertised? Did you apply for it? How did it happen?

They say it's who you know that matters, and in this case it's who you know and what you smoke. I wouldn't recommend it to anybody else, but I actually got this job because I was smoking. I was fifteen and smoking at high school, which of course I shouldn't have been, and this girl came in looking for a non-menthol cigarette. She asked all these people who all had Newports. Eventually I said, "Were you looking for a nonmenthol?" and she said, "Yes." To be polite, she struck up a conversation and asked if I had a job, which I didn't, and if I was interested in a job, which I was. Had I ever heard of *Dungeons & Dragons*? Well, of course. Had I ever heard of *Wizardry*? No. Had I ever heard of Sir-tech? No. Would I like a job? Yes. And that was my job interview, which I apparently passed with flying colors. The girl who interviewed me was Linda Currie. She had the job she was interviewing me for and didn't want it anymore because she wanted to move up and do other things. Linda is actually still in the industry. She's at Blue Fang, where they make *Zoo Tycoon.*

She was also a teenager in the game industry?

Yes, she was sixteen. She was the co-owner of the company, Sir-tech Software, Inc., which she started with her brothers.

What were some other titles that you worked on in these twenty-odd years?

I was with the whole *Wizardry* series, *Wizardry 1* to *Wizardry 8,* the whole *Jagged Alliance* series, the *Realms of Arkania* series, and *Dungeons & Dragons: Heroes,* and the *Playboy: The Mansion* game. I've worked on twenty-one different games altogether, in some capacity or another.

Were there any titles you worked on that were particularly accessible to girls or women?

Women tend to like role-playing games. All the *Wizardry* games were very popular with women. But I have never sat down to design a game and said to myself, "I want to make sure this is as accessible to women as possible." That said, since the last game I worked on, I have read a colleague's book that I recommend to everybody, *Gender Inclusive Game Design* by Sheri Graner Ray. I really like her book. The game that I am working on right now is a safe-sex game for at-risk urban youth. While working on this game, I am obviously taking into account people's genders, other people's sexualities, even their cultures.

Is there something that you think you did differently in your current game because you've read Sheri's book?

Yes, the design of the demo. Every demo I have ever done before takes the approach of throwing you in, and telling you what you do as you go through it. That's better for risk-takers. But using modeling behavior in a demo would be to say, "Here is how this works—now you try it." This type of demo takes into account the way women learn. All the demos that I am doing in my current game incorporate modeling behavior.

Do you have any anecdotes or examples of how your female sensibilities have influenced your game design?

Oh, sure. I can give you one that's incredibly shallow. After seeing so many quadruple-D women in games, I decided that I really wanted to see a guy who had a nice package. I felt it was only fair, and so in this game I worked on called *Druid,* the guy is obviously walking around with *something* solely because of that reason. I also don't have a problem putting women in positions of power in a game, or making the women more assertive and aggressive. I also think that the semi-soft-core sex scenes in *Wizardry 8* were probably more appealing than they may have otherwise been. A lot of [men] tell me that their girlfriends are playing *Playboy: The Mansion* and like it more than they do. So maybe I did something there too that I wasn't intending to do. But it's hard to tell how being a woman has affected my design. It's how I've always worked, and don't have a personal comparative reference. Since I can't show up as a man and design a game, I don't necessarily know how I would have done something differently.

What about examples of you designing something, and some male team member objected, or some male designer did something, and you thought, "Hey, that doesn't seem right to me."

There was one scene in *Playboy: The Mansion* where the two characters agreed to have sex. The [male] character in the game would head toward the couch, and the woman would follow. For some reason, that felt demeaning, and it felt demeaning to the other women in the office, too. None of the guys saw that, but every woman in the office agreed it felt icky.

How did you get involved in the Playboy: The Mansion *project?*

I was changing companies, looking around for a job, and I interviewed at Cyberlore Studios, Inc., and they were working on this *Playboy* game. It was fascinating for me, and I literally had worked on role-playing games for twenty years. I was really intrigued by the concept of doing something that was very different, this game of social simulation. Growing up as a straight girl in fairly conservative northern New York, *Playboy* wasn't high on my radar. It just seemed like a really exciting, cool project to work on.

What was the gender breakdown on the Playboy *design team?*

One female programmer, me as the lead designer, and the rest of the twenty-five-member team were men.

Was it strange at all to do adult content around a lot of guys?

There were moments that were awkward for them, but it was very short-lived. As development went on, I easily became one of the guys. But mostly, if you are sitting there having a discussion with other designers saying, "Okay so then he has sex with her, and they do this," and, "How do we get people to the position of having sex?" those are just bizarre conversations to be having with one another, whether you are a woman or a man, straight or gay. It's just weird, but then you get used to it. The funny part is, I bet the amount of press about me as "the sex lady" in gaming dwarfs the press stuff on me from the twenty years I worked in role-playing games.

Does that bother you?

No, not at all. First of all, it's an issue that somebody needs to address in a responsible way. Because games are still perceived as being just for kids, like comic books back in the 1950s, we are still largely a self-censoring industry, not really achieving the full range of expression that we otherwise could. Look at the game that was released in the UK as *Fahrenheit* and released here as *Indigo Prophecy*. There were story points censored out of that game, and all the stuff that was censored was sexual. Did they do it because they feared that it would get an AO [adults only] rating and wouldn't be carried by retailers? First of all, games aren't just for kids. Sexual content in games has a right to exist. Second, we need to talk about responsible distribution. If you do have a sex game, and you are selling it online, then you must have age verification. When you advertise the game, you must advertise responsibly, so you are not sending spam mails to some fifteen-year-old. The sites must be labeled so people know what's in there, and you can participate with services like Net Nanny so that parents can block access. There's also responsible content development. Some fairly hard-core games out there track every single thing a player types into the system to screen for incest, pedophilia, and bestiality, which are deemed as the ultimate gaming taboos, just as they are in real life. If you type in anything that leads the systems administrator to think that you are leaning in that direction, you're gone. I talk about responsible distribution, marketing, and development, all the way around, while simultaneously fighting for the rights of people to play sex games.

I read a quote of yours that says, "What hasn't changed are the fundamentals of design and the way one learns to do it." What are the fundamentals of design?
One fundamental element is your constraints. What's the IP [intellectual property]? What are the roles the license holder has? What console or platform are you designing for? What are the things that the game needs to do? Your constraints are key because you are always designing to some set of constraints. Another fundamental is the core of the game. What is the one thing your game is going to do phenomenally well? What's the *one* thing? I've broken that rule before and had five things that a game was supposed to do phenomenally, and those games never worked. When you play a game like *Ratchet and Clank 3,* which is one of my all-time favorite games, you blow stuff up in fun and creative ways, and that's what that game does well, and it does it again and again and again, but it's endlessly entertaining. Everything else in the game goes toward that. It makes your game so much easier to design because everything you do you ask yourself, "Does this make the core of my game stronger?"

I see. It creates a focal point for your design. How does that apply to MMOs, where you are talking about a whole virtual world? Isn't there room in MMOs for more than one focal point?

You would be surprised. In a game like *World of Warcraft,* the core of that MMO is probably building your character. It's all about character development. The process of developing your character forces you toward every other thing in the entire game. For every design element, you can ask, "How does this make the character better? What does this do for the character?" Every single thing in the game makes that experience stronger. Now you can add fluff on after, but having a core to your game really helps you know what the priorities are.

Has it been difficult reconciling family with career?

When I was thirty-seven-weeks' pregnant with twins, I was working seventy hours a week because I felt a need to be there as lead designer. My husband gave up his career as a CEO so that he could become a stay-at-home dad to our three kids. He is very respectful of my career and does everything in his power to support it. So we have been able to have the proverbial best of both worlds by doing the reverse of the 1960s family, with a stay-at-home dad and a working mom. It was a challenge, you know. When I had my twins, the company that I was at didn't even have in place a maternity-leave policy because it had never needed one. There was only one other woman there when I first started. I was sort of the great pioneer, and we had to do things like find a room where I could nurse my babies and all that. It was kind of awkward at first, but then the guys would make jokes about it, and it became something not quite so terrifying. As our industry is getting older, we are seeing more and more people with families, and so I don't feel like the only person who has family issues to attend to. Now, I have achieved a good family balance, but only through leaving full-time game development.

So what was it that finally made you leave? Was it the crunch-time tradition?

Well, it's not just crunch time. I literally didn't take a vacation for three years. That's a big reason that I decided to go into teaching. By going into teaching, I was able to get twenty-two weeks a year off. Sure, my pay is not what I would make in industry, but my time with my family more than makes up for that. I also feel completely creatively fulfilled by teaching and truly enjoy working with my students. I have time to spend with my family, I can choose what projects I work on, I can work really hard at the end of a quarter grading papers, meeting with students, but then I get the whole summer off. And, I can decide whether I want to accept a contract to work on a new game or not, and set my own schedule and give myself two months to do one week's worth of work.

If there were a game design company where you could design RPG games full-time, but also accommodate your family life through vacation days or flex hours, would you have gone into academia?
You know, I don't know. There were other reasons I went into academics. I really love teaching, and I really love working with people. And I am still doing game design. I have the best of both worlds. It seems like every time I open my e-mail there's "Brenda, listen, we have a senior design position and are you interested," but I really love what I do. And it also offers me stability. When was the last time you heard of a college closing down? And I can't keep yanking my five-year-old out of a school and saying, "Hey honey let's go. We are off to wherever."

What do you see yourself doing five years and ten years from now?
Teaching and having the opportunity to work on games so I still feel like a part of the industry. I am always at conferences so I still see all my peers. I still feel much more like a game developer than I do an academic. I just happen to get paid to talk to people about what I do, which is really fun. Kind of like being paid to play games when I got started.

What do you think is the path for getting more women designers into the industry?
Do you remember that old shampoo commercial, where it's like, "They tell two friends, and then they tell two friends, and then they tell two friends?" So if there is this opening at a company, and they say, "Hey don't forget to tell your friends about it," if you have two women employees and twenty-five guys, odds are, your candidate pool is going to be overwhelmingly male. As we get more women in, we are likely to continue to get more women in, and it will grow exponentially. I think efforts like Sheri's WIGI group are crucial, and I encourage colleges and sponsors to get behind them.

    Twenty years ago, I could count all the women who were doing this on my hands. Lori Cole, Roberta Williams, maybe Jane Jenson, Sheri, Linda

Currie, and that was about it. Now, there are many more women in the industry. I went to the Women's Roundtable at GDC last year, and it was really refreshing. There were all kinds of women in the room that I did not know. A lot more women are coming into the industry. It's also nice to see all the old guard really reaching out to the newcomers. Women reaching out to younger women who are interested in entering the games industry is vital.

Another thing that is really heartening to me is that I see a lot of women in my own classes that I teach here at Savannah College of Art and Design. And I see a lot of diversity, and that diversity could only make games stronger.

I would encourage women who are looking at coming into the industry to absolutely do it. I hear people saying, "Oh you don't want to consider going into games because of the hours." Well, I really think that's changing. Quality of life has now become a term in the industry, and it was never a term before. I can assure you of that. Our industry is maturing, and as it matures, it becomes a better and better place to work. In my mind, the games industry is still the best place in the world to work. I view my work as an academic studying games and apprenticing the next generation of designers as an extension of that. And I will always work directly on games, even if on a contract basis, because I have to. I love it. I consider myself so phenomenally fortunate for being here.

Contributors

Cornelia Brunner has been involved in the research, production, and teaching of educational technology in a variety of subjects for forty years. In addition to conducting research projects about the relationship between learning, teaching, and technology, she has designed and implemented educational materials incorporating technologies to support inquiry-based learning and teaching in science, social studies, media literacy, and the arts. She has worked extensively with staff and students in a variety of school environments on curriculum development projects, teacher support and training, and informal education. She works at the Education Development Center's Center for Children and Technology.

Shannon Campe is a research associate for ETR Associates (Education, Training, Research). She led the development and implementation of the Girls Creating Games program, where middle-school girls learned to program a computer game using Flash MX. She has also been involved in the research and implementation of health education programs in middle schools and high schools for nine years. She holds a California teaching credential with an emphasis in cross-cultural language and academic development.

Justine Cassell is the director of the Center for Technology and Social Behavior at Northwestern University, and a full professor in the departments of Communication Studies and Computer Sciences. Before coming to Northwestern, Cassell was a tenured associate professor at the MIT Media Laboratory. In 2001, Cassell was awarded the Edgerton Faculty Achievement Award at MIT. Cassell holds degrees in comparative literature from Dartmouth and in lettres modernes from the University de Besancon. She holds an MPhil in linguistics from the University of Edinburgh and a dual PhD from the University of Chicago in linguistics and psychology.

Mia Consalvo is an associate professor in the School of Telecommunications at Ohio University. She is the author of *Cheating: Gaining Advantage in Videogames* (2007, The MIT Press). She was the executive editor of the Association of Internet Researchers' Internet Annual series, and she edited the volume *Women and Everyday Uses of the Internet: Agency and Identity* with Susanna Paasonen. Her research focuses on women and games, the video game industry, and pedagogical uses of games. She has published related work in *The Video*

Game Theory Reader, and the journals *On the Horizon, Television & New Media,* and *The Journal of Communication Inquiry.*

Jill Denner is a senior research associate at ETR Associates (Education, Training, Research), a nonprofit agency in California. She has developed, implemented, and done research on multiple after-school and summer programs that put middle-school students in the role of game designers and programmers. She has published and presented her research to audiences in the fields of education, computer science education, digital media, and psychology. She has also edited a book of research on the positive development of Latina girls in the United States, published in 2006.

Mary Flanagan is an associate professor at Hunter College, in New York City, and director of the Tiltfactor Laboratory. The lab researches and develops socially inclusive software, including computer games using unique methods to teach science, math, and programming skills to young people, especially girls and minorities. She has fifteen years of experience in software design and has garnered more than twenty international awards for her work. She has published extensively about innovative design for social equity, as well as essays and books on computer games. She is also a computer and installation artist.

Janine Fron is a multimedia artist dedicated to constructing communities of shared knowledge to improve the way people play in the world together. As a key member of (art)n, she contributed to works that have been prominently featured in more than one hundred exhibitions in North America, South America, Europe, Asia, and Australia. Permanent collections include the Santa Barbara Museum of Art, the International Center of Photography, and the Musée Carnavalet. With the Ludica collective, she copresented game design workshops at DiGRA, SIGGRAPH, and ISEA, and presented Sustainable Play: Towards a New Games Movement for the Digital Age at the IT University in Copenhagen.

Tracy Fullerton, MFA, is a game designer, educator, and writer with fifteen years of experience. Currently, she is an assistant professor in the Interactive Media Division of the University of Southern California School of Cinema-Television and codirector of the Electronic Arts Game Innovation Lab. She is also the author of *Game Design Workshop: Designing, Prototyping and Playtesting Games,* a design textbook in use at game programs worldwide. Prior to joining USC, she was president of the interactive television game developer Spiderdance and served as a designer and creative director for R/GA Interactive, Interfilm Technologies, and Synapse Technologies.

Elisabeth Hayes is a professor in the College of Education at Arizona State University. Her current research interests focus on gender, digital technologies, and learning, particularly the development of IT fluency. She is a lead investigator on two MacArthur-funded projects: GameDesigner—a collaborative project with the New York City company gameLab to create innovative game design software that will help young people acquire technical, artistic, and cognitive skills—and the TechSavvy Girls project, which is investigating how gaming can be a starting point for the development of IT fluency, particularly for girls and women. She is the author or editor of numerous articles, chapters, and books including *Women as Learners* (2000), "Gendered Identities at Play: Case Studies of Two Women Playing Morrowind," (*Games and Culture,* January 2007) and "Women, Video Gaming, and Learning: Beyond Stereotypes" (*TechTrends,* December 2005). One of her current gaming obsessions is *The Sims.*

Carrie Heeter is Director of the Serious Games Online Graduate Certificate Program at Michigan State University and founder of Mindtoon Lab, a company that creates innovative, playful, yogic-meditative, technology-supported experiences to enhance daily life. Heeter lives in San Francisco and works as a virtual professor for Michigan State University. She teaches online graduate courses in serious game design, design research, and design for online learning. Current projects include National Science Foundation–funded research on the relationships among play style, gender, and learning; creation of an online repository for research about gender and gaming; and creation of games to improve and maintain cognitive performance.

Kristin Hughes is an assistant professor in Carnegie Mellon University's School of Design. Community and civic engagement are recurring themes in most of her research and professional practice. Currently she is looking at the design of products that allows participants agency over their own learning space. This question has led her to explore game design, learning, and ways play spaces provide powerful platforms for uninhibited learning. Game play is an invaluable way of developing new pedagogical methods for learning. Her most recent work is *Play-Ground,* a community-based game designed by and for players to educate and celebrate a healthy lifestyle.

Mizuko Ito is a cultural anthropologist of technology use, focusing on children's and youth's changing relationships with media and communications. She is part of a new research project supported by the MacArthur Foundation, Kids' Informal Learning with Digital Media, a three-year ethnographic study of kid-initiated and peer-based forms of engagement with new media. Her research on mobile-phone use in Japan appears in a book she has coedited, *Personal, Portable, Pedestrian: Mobile Phones in Japanese Life.* She is a research scientist at the School of Cinematic Arts at the University of Southern California, and a visiting associate professor at Keio University in Japan.

Henry Jenkins III, the John E. Burchard Professor of Humanities and director of MIT Comparative Media Studies, has spent his career studying media and the way people incorporate it into their lives. He testified in 1999 before the U.S. Senate during the hearings on media violence that followed the Littleton, Colorado, shootings; he testified before the

Federal Communications Commission about media literacy; and he spoke to the governor's board of the World Economic Forum about intellectual property law. Jenkins earned his doctorate in communication arts from the University of Wisconsin–Madison and a master's degree in communication studies from the University of Iowa.

Yasmin Kafai is a professor at the University of Pennsylvania Graduate School of Education. Before coming to Penn, she was on faculty at UCLA and worked at the MIT Media Laboratory. She received her doctorate from Harvard University. Her research has focused on children's learning as players and designers of educational software, video games, and virtual worlds. She has published *Minds in Play* (1995) and edited *Constructionism in Practice* (with Mitchel Resnick, 1996). She lives, plays, and works in Philadelphia.

Caitlin Kelleher is an assistant professor of computer science at Washington University in Saint Louis. She completed her doctorate in computer science at Carnegie Mellon University where she worked with Dr. Randy Pausch. Kelleher has been involved in the design and development of Alice (www.alice.org). Her research focuses on creating a version of Alice that will give middle-school girls a positive introduction to computer programming through creating short animated movies. Kelleher has interned with Alan Kay's research group developing and testing Squeak Etoys, and served on an advisory board for the Center for Children and Technology. She is the recipient of a National Science Foundation Graduate Fellowship.

Brenda Laurel is a designer, writer, researcher, and performer. She has been newly appointed as chair of Graduate Design at California College of Art in San Francisco. Since 1976, her work has focused on the intersection of culture and technology. She cofounded Purple Moon in 1996 to create interactive media for girls (acquired by Mattel in 1999). In 1990 she cofounded Telepresence Research, focusing on virtual reality and remote presence. Other employers include Atari, Activision, and Apple. A well-known speaker and writer, Laurel has written several books including *Computers as Theatre* (1991) and *Utopian Entrepreneur* (2001, MIT Press). She earned her PhD in theatre from Ohio State University in 1986.

Nicole Lazzaro is the founder and president of XEODesign, Inc. She has more than fifteen years of expertise in player experience research and design for mass-market entertainment and consumer creativity products. Clients include Sony, LeapFrog, Mattel, Sega, The Learning Company, Xfire, Broderbund, Roxio, Ubisoft, and Maxis. She has a degree in psychology from Stanford University.

Holin Lin is a professor of sociology at National Taiwan University whose specialty is social interaction in computer game communities. Her current research focuses are on the formation of in-game communities, game tip–writing behaviors, cash trades of in-game assets, MMORPG norm and deviance negotiation, and gendered gaming experiences in various play spaces.

Jacki Morie is a researcher and gamer at the University of Southern California. She has created specialized training for Disney, Blue Sky|VIFX, and Rhythm & Hues. She has also made games and affective virtual reality environments designed to evoke emotional responses at the University of Central Florida. Currently, Morie is developing, playing, and researching innovative gender-neutral games as a member of Ludica, a Los Angeles game collective. She speaks at many international venues about games for experiential learning. Her affiliations include ACM SIGGRAPH, the Visual Effects Society, the Digital Games Research Association (DiGRA), and the International Society of Presence Research (ISPR).

Helen Nissenbaum, an associate professor in the Department of Media, Culture, and Communication at New York University, conducts research in the social, ethical, and political dimensions of information and communications technology. Nissenbaum's books include *Emotion and Focus, Computers, Ethics and Social Values* (coedited with D. J. Johnson), and *Academy and the Internet* (coedited with Monroe Prince), and she is a cofounding editor of the journal *Ethics and Information Technology.* She holds a BA with honors from the University of Witwatersand, Johannesburg, an MA in education and a PhD in philosophy from Stanford University.

Celia Pearce is an award-winning game designer, researcher, artist, teacher, and author. Since 1983 she has worked as an attractions and interactive entertainment designer for such firms as Edwin Schlossberg Inc., Iwerks Entertainment, Walt Disney Imagineering, Universal Parks, LEGO Toys, the Jerde Partnership, and Turner Broadcasting. Since 1998, she has worked in academic institutions, conducting research, teaching, and helping to launch new initiatives for the University of Southern California and the University of California, Irvine. She is also a cofounder of the Ludica women's game collective. She is currently an assistant professor in the School of Literature, Communication, and Culture at Georgia Tech.

Caroline Pelletier is a researcher and project manager at the London Knowledge Lab, University of London. Her research focuses on the implications of new media for social theory, learning, and epistemology. Pelletier also coteaches a master's-level module called Gaming, Gaming Cultures and Education at the Institute of Education, London. Previously, she was an independent researcher and consultant advising publishing and technology companies on e-learning, and an editor in academic publishing.

Jennifer Y. Sun is president and one of the founders of Numedeon, Inc., the company that launched Whyville.net. *Whyville* is an educational virtual world targeted at children ages eight to fourteen with 3.3 million registrants and 25,000 unique visitors daily, two-thirds of which are girls. Prior to Numedeon, she cofounded Learning.net and was the director of educational development at Electric SchoolHouse. She holds a PhD in neuroscience from the California Institute of Technology and has published in *Nature and Nature Neuroscience* on visual perception.

T. L. Taylor is an associate professor at the IT University of Copenhagen and the Center for Computer Games Research. She has been working in the field of Internet and multiuser studies for more than a decade and has published on a variety of topics including values in design, avatars and online embodiment, play styles, pervasive games, and intellectual property in MMOs. Her book *Play Between Worlds: Exploring Online Game Culture* (2006, The MIT Press) uses her multiyear ethnography of *EverQuest* to explore issues related to play and game culture.

Brian Winn is an associate professor at Michigan State University and director of the Games for Entertainment and Learning (GEL) Lab. Winn designs, creates, and researches interactive media including game design, digital game-based learning, and interactive health communication. Winn's award-winning interactive media work has been presented, exhibited, and experienced internationally. Winn is also an accomplished teacher of serious game design who became an Apple Distinguished Educator in 2001 and a Lilly Teaching Fellow in 2005. Winn serves as faculty advisor of the MSU Spartasoft game developers student group and a coordinator of the Michigan Chapter of the International Game Developers Association.

Nick Yee is is a recent PhD graduate from Stanford University, where he worked at the Virtual Human Interaction Lab with Jeremy Bailenson in studying social interaction and self-representation in virtual environments. He is also well-known for his survey study of online gamers, the Daedalus Project. Over the past seven years, he has surveyed more than forty thousand online gamers on a wide variety of issues, such as demographic differences, motivations for play, and relationship formation. During his graduate career at Stanford, Yee also worked with a variety of companies, such as PARC and Sony Online Entertainment, where he analyzed server-side information from online games. His work has appeared in the *New York Times, Wall Street Journal,* and *Business Week,* among other places.

Index